Fodor's

VANCOUVER
AND VICTORIA

Welcome to Vancouver and Victoria

Set on Canada's west coast, Vancouver and Victoria blend urban sophistication and multicultural vitality with spectacular settings near mountains, ocean, and rain forest. Both cities are famously livable: Vancouver gleams with towering skyscrapers; the smaller Victoria charms with its historic waterfront. To see the appeal, stroll and bike in Vancouver's Stanley Park, eat fresh seafood, sip cocktails, browse boutiques, and visit renowned museums and gardens. Sure, it rains out here, but take a cue from the laid-back locals in their chic, all-weather clothes.

TOP REASONS TO GO

★ **First Nations Cultures:** Museums, art galleries, and cultural centers provide insight.

★ **Neighborhoods:** From Vancouver's buzzing Yaletown to Victoria's scenic Downtown.

★ **Outdoor Fun:** Terrific beaches, hiking, skiing, and whale-watching are all nearby.

★ **Food:** Granville Island's indoor market, top-notch seafood, superb Pacific Rim fare.

★ **Gardens and Parks:** Flowers in The Butchart Gardens, the seawall in Stanley Park.

★ **Excursions:** Winter sports in Whistler; storm-watching and scenery on Vancouver Island.

Contents

MAPS

EXPERIENCE VANCOUVER AND VICTORIA

20 ULTIMATE EXPERIENCES

Vancouver and Victoria offer terrific experiences that should be on every traveler's list. Here are Fodor's top picks for a memorable trip.

1 The Butchart Gardens

These world-renowned gardens have been drawing visitors to Vancouver Island since 1904. It employs 50 full-time gardeners to keep the millions of bedding plants and more than 900 varieties in top shape. *(Ch. 10)*

2 Stanley Park Seawall

Walk or bike the paved pathway around Stanley Park. The world's longest uninterrupted waterfront path stretches from Coal Harbour to Spanish Banks. *(Ch. 3)*

3 Whale-Watching

Thousands of whales migrate through these waters each year and watching them is a favorite pastime on the west coast. *(Ch. 3, 5, 10, 11)*

4 Seaplane Flight

Whether heading to Victoria, Tofino, or the Gulf Islands, this is an impressive way to enjoy the magnificent scenery of the Pacific Northwest. *(Ch. 10, 11)*

5 Storm-Watching in Tofino

Winter on the West Coast brings with it the lashings of violent coastal storms and fury of unpredictable weather. Storm season is from November to March. *(Ch. 11)*

6 Granville Island Public Market

This popular public market has local farm stalls and stands selling fish, meat, flowers, cheeses, pasta, bread and more, as well as local artists hawking artisanal wares. *(Ch. 5)*

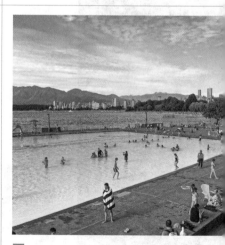

7 Kits Pool

Take a dip in Canada's longest pool. Kits Pool stretches 451 feet along the shore of the city's busiest beach, Kits Beach, home to sunbathers, beach volleyball players, picnickers and dog walkers alike. *(Ch. 6)*

8 Paddle a First Nations Canoe

For an authentic First Nations experience, paddle up scenic Indian Arm in a traditional 25-foot ocean-going canoe to learn the unique history of their ancestors. *(Ch. 8)*

9 Capilano Suspension Bridge

Set against the rain forest of Vancouver's North Shore mountains, the swaying cedar-plank bridge is suspended 70 meters above the Capilano River. *(Ch. 8)*

10 Tea at the Empress

Afternoon tea is served around the city, but nowhere is it more iconic than at the Fairmont Empress Hotel. The venerable grand dame is THE place to take afternoon tea in the capital city. *(Ch. 10)*

11 Sea to Sky Highway

Drive the Sea to Sky Highway along Howe Sound for a memorable experience. Stop in Squamish for a visit to the Stawamus Chief, one of the largest granite monoliths in the world. *(Ch. 12)*

12 Ferry Ride

The BC Ferries journey across Georgia Strait, through Active Pass to the Gulf Islands and beyond to Vancouver Island. If you're lucky, you'll see whales (the captain announces it when he spots them). *(Ch. 11)*

13 Polar Bear Swim

Every year, revelers take to the frigid waters of English Bay for the annual Polar Bear Swim. A New Year's Day tradition, the event is one of the largest in the world. *(Ch. 3)*

14 Ski and Golf the Same Day

Known as the Whistler Phenomenon by locals, it's possible to hit the slopes for a morning of skiing at Blackcomb, then stop for a round of golf in the afternoon. *(Ch. 12)*

15 Whistler

The PEAK 2 PEAK gondola ride between Whistler and Blackcomb Mountains is nothing short of breathtaking. The 11-minute trip is the highest of its kind, with an elevation of 436 meters. *(Ch. 12)*

16 Bard on the Beach

In summer, take a picnic to the billowing tents at Vanier Park to experience Western Canada's largest Shakespeare festival. Time it for a night when there are fireworks. *(Ch. 6)*

17 Yoga on the Beach

This city is known for its myriad outdoor activities including yoga on the beach. Often free or by donation, these classes let you unwind in the sunshine near the beaches at English Bay or Kits. *(Ch. 6)*

18 Olympic Experience at the Richmond Oval

Visit the Richmond Oval, site of the speed skating competition during the 2010 Winter Olympics. The glass-and-steel building houses the Olympic ice rinks and a huge fitness center. *(Ch. 9)*

19 Museum of Anthropology

This museum, located at the University of British Columbia campus on Point Grey, has one of the country's finest collections of Northwest Coast First Nations art. *(Ch. 6)*

20 Grouse Mountain Skyride Surf Adventure

To reach the top of Grouse Mountain, you can climb the Grouse Grind, or take the Skyride gondola, part of the largest aerial tramway system in North America. *(Ch. 8)*

WHAT'S WHERE

1 Vancouver. Many people argue that Vancouver is the most beautiful city in North America and situated as it is, between mountains and water, it's hard to disagree. The Vancouver area actually covers a lot of ground, but the central core—Downtown, the West End, Stanley Park, Gastown, Chinatown, and Yaletown—is fairly compact. An excellent public transportation system makes it easy to get around.

2 Victoria. At the southern tip of Vancouver Island, British Columbia's capital is a lovely, walkable city with waterfront paths, rambling gardens, and fascinating museums. In some senses remote, it's roughly midway between Vancouver and Seattle and about three hours by car and ferry from either city.

3 Vancouver Island. The largest island on North America's west coast, Vancouver Island has a diverse landscape, with striking coastal scenery, vineyards, farms, and dense rain forests. Just outside the city of Victoria, the island's southwest coast around the town of Sooke offers remote beaches and forested

hiking trails, while the Cowichan Valley to the north is the island's wine country. The Pacific Rim region, on the island's west coast, is known for its dramatically crashing waves and its fabulous wildlife-watching opportunities. Of the two west coast towns, Tofino is slightly north of Ucluelet and is a bit more established in terms of tourism, with upscale lodgings and fine-dining destinations.

4 Whistler. Just 120 km (75 miles) north of Vancouver—about a two-hour drive along the stunning Sea-to-Sky Highway—Whistler is an outdoor paradise in both winter and summer. The two mountains, Whistler and Blackcomb, are the focus of activities, and Whistler Village, at their base, is a compact mecca of lodgings, restaurants, shops, and cafés, where you can walk (or ski) to nearly all the town's attractions.

5 Okanagan Valley. About a five-hour drive east from Vancouver, the Okanagan Valley is the fruit-growing capital of Canada and a major wine-producing area—maybe you've heard it called the "Napa of the North." The sandy lakeside beaches and hot, dry climate help make it a wildly popular summer destination.

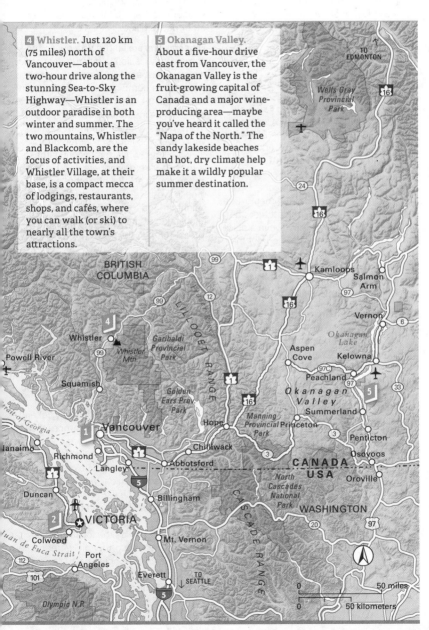

What's New in Vancouver and Victoria

Separated from the rest of Canada by the Canadian Rockies, Vancouver and Victoria have always marched to a west coast rhythm that is in many ways more similar to Seattle, Portland, and even parts of California than to their Canadian counterparts. Add to this their proximity to the sea and coastal mountains and you have winters that are mild, summers that are balmy, and landscapes that are lush with temperate forests and gardens. Nowhere else in Canada do daffodils bloom in February! And despite Victoria's old-English facades, these are young cities with active, outdoorsy, and health-conscious populations. Residents sometimes exude a slightly smug, laissez-faire attitude, but who can blame them? They live in a place that is consistently ranked as one of the most beautiful and livable in the world. It's little wonder Harry and Meghan of the British royal family opted to retreat here during a turbulent time.

The outdoors rule. Few cities have mountains, oceans, and pristine rain forests all on their doorstep. In both Vancouver and Victoria, locals take full advantage of these options themselves and have also realized the incredible opportunities in promoting ecotourism. Whatever your age or ability, the range of activities includes family whale-watching excursions, golf, hiking, fishing, rafting, and no-holds-barred extreme wilderness adventures. Victoria is a popular departure point for exploring the myriad culinary and eco-adventures on Vancouver Island, while Vancouver is the gateway to sophisticated Whistler and the more rugged interior regions of British Columbia. It's fair to say that all this fresh air makes for an extremely health-oriented population. Fitness clubs are part and parcel of many office and residential buildings, and smoking is prohibited in restaurants, bars, beaches, parks, and other public places.

Entrepreneurs are in. The Vancouver Economic Commission, a city-run economic development agency, likes to boast about the region's combination of natural beauty and brains. As an example, Meetup. com, the online network where people meet others with similar interests: in Vancouver, the largest Meetup group draws hikers, while the second largest is for software developers. Indeed, city coffee shops are full of laptop-tapping mobile workers, while in the Gastown neighborhood, developers continue their conversion of once-seedy structures into offices for high-tech firms and design studios.

Green is great. West coasters are more eco-conscious than the average North American. New construction out here usually involves eco-oriented practices from thermal heating to energy-saving fixtures; rooftop gardens add to the relatively pristine air; and recycling is a daily ritual in business and at home. The area's hotels were among the first to introduce green practices when they started installing dual-flush toilets (that's two levels of flushes, not flushing twice) and asking guests to use towels more than once. Car-sharing services are commonplace, and bicycle lanes rule; Vancouver has the highest percentage of two-wheel commuters in Canada; Victoria is also near the top of the list. Many companies provide free or subsidized transit passes to employees who give up commuting by car, too. To do as the locals do, be sure to carry an eco-friendly water bottle and a reusable shopping bag. Maximize your use of public transit with a Day Pass (C$10.50), which is good on the SeaBus,

SkyTrain, and local buses; or rent a bike to explore on two wheels.

Ethnic diversity is everywhere. The west coast's easy access to Pacific Rim destinations has generated a great influx of Asian immigrants, making Vancouver the most Asian metropolis outside of Asia. News is delivered in 22 different languages; shops and ATMs post signs in English, Mandarin, Cantonese, Punjabi, Farsi, and even Vietnamese. Ironically, French, Canada's other official language, is rarely seen or heard except on the two Radio Canada stations. This diversity creates a cultural mosaic that comes vibrantly to life in various festivals (such as the Celebration of Light), community activities (including the Richmond Night Market), and, above all, in a range of superb restaurants. While Victoria is less diverse, that's beginning to change; the city's population of visible minorities has been rising, and growing diversity remains on the upswing.

Eat local. Supporting local producers has always been part of the west coast lifestyle, so back in 2005 when two Vancouver writers originated the 100-mile diet, they didn't expect it to catch on across North America, let alone the world. Look for neighborhood farmers' markets, some open year-round. The renowned Granville Island Market, for example, sells handcrafted island cheeses, organic meats, freshly caught fish, salmon jerky "candy," homemade jams and honey, and seasonal fresh produce.

Be the change. Vancouver is a city of activists and change-makers. In addition to being at the forefront of living green (there's good reason the city has a reputation for being home to tree huggers always protesting pipelines), many folks here are fighting to address homelessness, the fentanyl crisis, and reconciliation with First Nations communities, too. Local nonprofit organizations are building affordable housing and safe injection sites. Most events start off with a land acknowledgment of the First Nations territory it's occupying. The city isn't perfect of course, but it's leading the way compared to many of its Canadian counterparts.

What to Eat in Vancouver and Victoria

NANAIMO BARS
Nanaimo bars, featuring a chocolate graham cracker coconut base, creamy custard in the middle, and chocolate ganache on top, are named for the Vancouver Island city. These yummy treats can be found at coffee shops and bakeries in Vancouver and on Vancouver Island.

ICE CREAM
With 238 flavors to choose from, you'll be spoiled for choice at La Casa Gelato on Venables, whose huge menu set a Guinness World Record in 2019. Local favorite Earnest Ice Cream, which was launched in 2012, has quickly reached cult status with its rotating small batches, including many vegan options.

DIM SUM
The Cantonese-style menu of bite-sized dumplings, steamed buns, rice noodle rolls, and pots of oolong tea is served midday at Asian restaurants around the city, in particular the nearby suburb of Richmond, which is also home of the "Dumpling Trail," a collection of restaurants serving the speciality.

SUSHI
If there's one thing Vancouverites are passionate about, it's their sushi. Whether you're at Miku for flame-seared aburi or Tojo's, the birthplace of the California roll, sushi is serious business. And with a bounty of fresh seafood on its doorstep, Vancouver's sushi scene is second only to Japan's.

OYSTERS
From Kusshi to Fanny Bay to Kumamotos, west coast oysters are mild, sweet, and smaller overall than other oysters and are said to be great for the beginner. So, if you've never tried one, now is the time and this is definitely the place to do it. Oyster bars around town include Fanny Bay Oyster Bar and Shellfish Market on Cambie Street in Downtown.

CHOCOLATE
There is no shortage of fabulous chocolates in Vancouver. A few must-visit shops include Rogers' Chocolates, started in 1885 in a Victoria grocery store across the street from their current location. Another can't-miss shop is Purdys, started in 1907 when former barber Richard Carmon Purdy started selling homemade chocolate in Downtown Vancouver. The chocolate hedgehogs are always a hit. At Chocolate Arts in Kits, small batches of their unique chocolates are crafted daily.

SPOT PRAWNS
Once mainly exported to Asia for use as a filler for fish stock and chowder,

Sushi at Miku's restaurant

this humble crustacean is now a prized local delicacy and the focus of an entire annual festival that takes place each spring. The harvest season, which starts in May in BC's coastal waters, typically lasts just six to eight weeks, so if you're visiting at that time you'll find the sweet shellfish on special menus around town.

SALMON
Wild Pacific salmon, either maple-cured, cedar-planked, candied, barbecued or smoked, is synonymous with the west coast. You can sample some at The Salmon House on the Hill in West Vancouver or in Steveston, once known as the "salmon capital of the world."

WHITE SPOT LEGENDARY BURGER
This local burger joint has been around since 1928 when founder Nat Bailey transformed his Model T into Canada's first food truck, serving hot dogs and peanuts at Lookout Point in Stanley Park. He opened his first location at the corner of Granville and 67th which then expanded to become Canada's longest running restaurant chain. The burgers are a legend among locals and feature secret Triple "O" sauce.

JAPADOG
A favorite of the late Anthony Bourdain, this street-food vendor offers hot dogs with a Japanese twist at stands and food trucks around Vancouver's Downtown core, including one small restaurant (there are now also two stands in LA). It's popular with the film industry and acclaimed by celebrities and locals alike, who line up for the Oroshi, a bratwurst topped with a special soya sauce glaze and freshly grated daikon radish. You can also try the best-selling Terimayo topped with nori seaweed, teriyaki sauce, and wasabi mayo–this is a fun fusion of Japanese flavors and tastes.

Best Things to Buy in Vancouver and Victoria

MAPLE SYRUP FUDGE

This must-try sweet treat is infused with real maple syrup not just maple flavoring. A great alternative to actual maple syrup, the boxes comprised of individually wrapped pieces are always a hit and make a great gift. You can buy some at Edible Canada on Granville Island.

CANDLES

Bring the scent of Vancouver home with one of the Vancouver Candle Co.'s beautiful artisanal designs. The clean-burning candles are made of premium soy wax and perfume-grade oils. You can purchase some candles to give as souvenirs at Chapters Indigo, Anthropologie, and other retailers around town.

FLUEVOGS

Step into the flagship store of venerable shoemaker John Fluevog in Gastown for some serious shoe business. Vancouver's native son is the footwear king of this town, and his funky exaggerated heels and bright designs have garnered a cult following around the globe, including Hollywood celebrities.

OKANAGAN ICE WINE

Canada is now the largest producer of ice wine in the world, and the vineyards of the scenic Okanagan Valley region in the interior of BC are blessed with ideal conditions for producing this unique sweet amber nectar. Traditionally a dessert wine primarily made from Riesling grapes, the rich, concentrated liquid gold is produced from the juice of grapes naturally frozen on the vine and harvested in winter. Okanagan ice wines are international recognized and highly sought after around the world.

SALMON

Smoked, candied, maple-cured, or ice wine–glazed— take your pick. Few places in the world are as renowned for salmon as Vancouver. You can purchase this quintessential west coast staple freeze-packed for travel or shipped worldwide from fish shops around the city, including those on Granville Island.

LOCAL ART

Exquisite coastal Native art, such as paintings, masks, and carvings by Northwest coast artists, can be purchased at galleries such as Hill's Native art in Gastown or the gift shop at the Museum of Anthropology. There's also Circle Craft Gallery, a co-op of local BC artists selling paintings, ceramics, clothing and jewelry, and the Inukshuk Gallery on Granville Island that sells Inuit sculptures.

Native art

FIRST NATIONS JEWELRY

Contemporary in design, while still encompassing the ancient west coast Native legends of the raven, eagle, frog, whale, hummingbird, and wolf, handmade First Nations jewelry makes a wonderful wearable souvenir of your time on the west coast. The gift shop at the Vancouver Art Gallery and Artina's Hand Crafted Canadian Jewellery in Victoria and Gastown, both offer a good selection of exquisite, one-of-a-kind pieces by local artists.

ATHLETIC APPAREL

Vancouver is a pioneer of "athleisure" apparel and Vancouverites preferred clothing is athletic and yoga wear. Stop by lululemon for a pair of their famous stretchy black yoga pants at the original location on West 4th Avenue in Kits or the flagship store on Robson. Or get cozy in technical cashmere from sister company Kit and Ace, started by lululemon founder Chip Wilson's wife and son.

CHOCOLATES

Chocolatiers have been perfecting their craft on the west coast for more than 100 years. Canada's first chocolate company, Rogers' Chocolates, has been making sweet treats in Victoria since 1885. The iconic Victoria creams now come in 19 different flavors. Purdy's Chocolates, another long-time local favorite, started in 1907 in Vancouver and now has shops all over Canada. Their distinctive purple-foiled boxes are a popular gift.

HUDSON'S BAY BLANKET

Pick up some beautiful multistriped blankets synonymous with the Hudson's Bay Company at the Downtown Vancouver location of this iconic department store. The blankets were first traded to First Nations in the 1700s and are still very much in demand today.

Under the Radar in Vancouver and Victoria

NEON VANCOUVER

The Neon Vancouver|Ugly Vancouver ongoing exhibit at the Museum of Vancouver explores the city's neon golden age in the 1950s, when the city was home to some 19,000 neon signs, second only to Las Vegas. That changed in the 1970s when a city law against neon "distractions" came into place.

THE 1931 GALLERY BISTRO CAFÉ

Don't miss this gem of an eatery during your visit to the Vancouver Art Gallery. The menu rotates seasonally and features locally sourced ingredients. The patio, cascading down the art gallery steps, is a great spot to sip a glass of wine.

THE GALLEY PATIO & GRILL

You don't have to sail to visit the Jericho Sailing Centre. Vancouver's ocean community club on Jericho Beach is also the setting of a low-key patio grill, with some of the best views of the city. Have a pub-style lunch of burgers, fish-and-chips or fish tacos, washed down with a local craft beer.

THE DIRTY APRON

This culinary academy, started by husband-and-wife team chef David and Sara Robertson, features a revolving menu of demo-and-dine or hands-on lessons for all skill levels. More than 10,000 students are taught each year, some as young as seven years old. At the on-site gourmet deli, sandwiches, cheeses, and charcuterie are served. A second location can also be found in YVR's domestic terminal.

SINS OF THE CITY TOUR

Learn all about Vancouver's dark past and history of drugs, prohibition, discrimination and scandal on this walking tour offered by the Vancouver Police Museum. Visit the narrow alleys, secret underground passageways, and abandoned opium dens of Chinatown and Gastown to learn about the criminals and deeds that once plagued the city. Tours are free with admission to the museum, which includes fascination exhibits, such as the former city morgue.

GHOSTLY WALKS

There's more to Victoria than beautiful gardens and lavish afternoon tea. From the tunnels running underneath the city's Chinatown to its reputation as BC's most haunted town, the capital has a dark history. Learn about it on a 90-minute haunted Victoria ghost tour developed by one of Victoria's foremost historians and storytellers, John Adams.

The Rennie Collection

THE RENNIE COLLECTION

Vancouver real estate marketing mogul Bob Rennie, known about town as the city's "condo king," is also a prolific collector of art. His impressive private collection of contemporary art is housed in Chinatown's oldest building, the Wing Sang at 51 East Pender in a converted heritage property with great views from the grass-topped deck on the roof. The museum is open free to the public, by appointment only.

GLASS SIDEWALKS

Keep an eye out while walking around Downtown Victoria for purple prisms underfoot. The historic glass blocks date back to the late 19th century when they were installed in the sidewalks to allow sunlight to filter into the basements below. You can find them on Johnson Street, in front of the Sayward building on Douglas Street, near the Ritz Hotel on Fort Street, and the Hamley building on Broughton Street.

THE WICKLOW

Located at Stamps Landing on the south side of False Creek, this cozy neighborhood pub with a patio has fantastic views overlooking False Creek and is a favorite of locals and boaters from the marina below. Grab a seat on the patio and tuck into the offerings, all made in-house daily, from the menu. Take the Aquabus to the dock from Yaletown, Science World, or Granville Island, for a uniquely Vancouver ride over.

PROHIBITION BAR

With a nod to the Roaring Twenties, this speakeasy in the Rosewood Hotel Georgia is a throwback to the age of decadence. Expect champagne cocktails, bespoke libations using house-made bitters, and oysters on the half shell.

Vancouver and Victoria with Kids

Vancouver and Victoria are great places to entertain children, especially ones who like the outdoors. Check the calendar for family-oriented special events, like the Vancouver International Children's Festival in May and the Vancouver Folk Music Festival in July.

IN DOWNTOWN VANCOUVER

Allow a day to enjoy the kid-friendly activities in Stanley Park: the miniature train, aquarium, pool, water park, and beaches are great for all ages. And getting around this huge park—on a horse-drawn wagon or the park shuttle—is half the fun. Make sure you also plan a trip on the mini Aquabus ferry to Granville Island, home of North America's largest free public water park and the Kids' Market, a two-story complex of toy stores and play areas. The Granville Island market is a great place for lunch or snacking, and even the pickiest kids should be able to find something they like. You can check out the interactive displays at Science World, or hop a foot-passenger ferry to see one of the kid-friendly museums at Vanier Park: the Maritime Museum or the H.R. MacMillan Space Centre.

BEYOND DOWNTOWN

Outside Downtown Vancouver, the North Shore is a wilderness playground. Older kids will no doubt enjoy terrifying their parents by trying to wobble the Capilano Suspension Bridge (or the Lynn Canyon Suspension Bridge). The Treetops Adventure at Capilano Suspension Bridge Park and the salmon-spawning displays at the nearby Capilano Salmon Hatchery tend to be big hits, too. Take a Skyride trip up Grouse Mountain, where you can skate or take a sleigh ride in winter, or hike and visit the bear refuge in summer. For a day at the beach, head west to Spanish Banks or Locarno for warm, shallow water and wide stretches of sand. Kits Beach is busier, but has a playground and a saltwater pool.

Don't underestimate the entertainment power of public transportation. For a few dollars, a SeaBus ride across Burrard Inlet (a larger ferry than the Granville Island Aquabus) provides a water-level view of the harbor; the same ticket gets you on an elevated SkyTrain ride across town.

IN VICTORIA

Like Vancouver, Victoria has small foot-passenger ferries zigzagging across the harbor, and Fisherman's Wharf, with its houseboats, seals, and fish-and-chips stands, is popular. Preschoolers are mesmerized by the tiny displays at Miniature World and charmed by the friendly critters at the Beacon Hill Park petting zoo, while older kids enjoy the Victoria Bug Zoo, the Royal British Columbia Museum, and shopping for allowance-priced souvenirs in Chinatown. Easy hikes, bike rides, and picnics are also popular. For serious "what I did on my summer vacation" material, you can't beat a whale-watching trip. For a night out, try a movie at the IMAX theaters or the spectacular fireworks displays on summer evenings at The Butchart Gardens.

AT THE BUTCHART GARDENS

If The Butchart Gardens is on your Victoria to-do list, you can make a full day of it by meandering through the peninsula—Sea Cider (about a 10-minute drive from the ferry and about 15 minutes from the gardens) is the place for craft cider (for moms and dads) and delicious local fare. Nearby, the Shaw Ocean Discovery Centre has amazing touchy-feely exhibits to entertain everyone from 8 to 80 years old.

Free and Almost Free

The best things in life are free and a surprising number of them are in and around Vancouver, Victoria, and Whistler. In fact, most of what's enjoyable in this part of the world—including beaches, parks, hiking trails, interesting architecture, great views, and fun-and-funky neighborhoods—is available without charge.

VANCOUVER

In Vancouver, you can visit Stanley Park, Granville Island, Downtown, Gastown, Chinatown, and Yaletown and rarely have to open your wallet to pay admission fees. Granville Island's markets and galleries are all free, as are Canada Place and Stanley Park.

If that's not enough, here are a few lesser-known ways to stretch those loonies and toonies:

On Tuesday evening between 5 and 9, the Vancouver Art Gallery charges admission by donation. In North Vancouver, most visitors head for the fun, if pricey, Capilano Suspension Bridge, but a few miles away, the equally thrilling Lynn Canyon Suspension Bridge, in Lynn Canyon Park, is absolutely free. It might be a bit of a trek, but also free on the North Shore is the Capilano Salmon Hatchery, where you can learn about the life cycle of salmon (and, in fall, watch them struggling upstream to spawn).

VICTORIA

In Victoria, Beacon Hill Park or any of the city's parks and beaches are free, as are most of the city's iconic buildings. A stroll through the public areas of the venerable Fairmont Empress Hotel or a guided tour of the Parliament Buildings won't cost a dime. The Inner Harbour Walk has views of Victoria's Edwardian architecture, boats, and seaplanes, and great people-watching. You can even watch the foot-passenger ferries perform a 12-minute water ballet (Sunday, 10:45 am, May through September; Saturday, 10:45 am, July and August).

BARGAINS IN WHISTLER?

Even in jet-set Whistler you can find a few bargains. In the village, you can make like the glitterati for the price of a latte: start with people-watching from a café patio, enjoy the street entertainers, then move on to a stroll through the village's half dozen or so art galleries. Even the village shuttle buses are free.

What to Read and Watch Before Your Trip

Vancouver's cultural scene is defined by ironies. Yes, it's nicknamed "Hollywood North," but a surprisingly slim number of major movies are, in fact, set here—Vancouver stars as foreign cities far more often than it stars as itself. And even as its writerly reputation grows, with underground publishing studios and book festivals aplenty, only a few B.C.-based authors are true household names. Indeed, Vancouver's independent filmmaking and literature communities demand closer inspection, with inventive and genre-blurring works that illuminate the plural identities of this west coast metro.

CITY OF GLASS BY DOUGLAS COUPLAND

One of Vancouver's most prolific writers, Douglas Coupland muses about the quirks and cultural touchstones of his home base in *City of Glass*, a love letter in the form of short essays on everything from sushi to ferries. First published in 2000 and updated in 2009, this playful title takes a cue from the design of Japanese zines and fills its pages with more than 100 photographs, archival images, illustrations, and maps.

DO NOT SAY WE HAVE NOTHING BY MADELEINE THIEN

Madeleine Thien's third book affirms the Vancouver native's place as one of Canada's greatest living writers. This sweeping historical novel opens with Thien's narrator ruminating on a chapter of her childhood in Vancouver when she and her mother opened up their home to a refugee, who was fleeing the Chinese government's crackdown after the Tiananmen Square massacre. Thien's musical prose dances gracefully through subplots that span three generations and two continents—a beautiful saga that's haunted by the ghosts of the Cultural Revolution and the suffering that spills across borders and ripples through time.

DOUBLE HAPPINESS

Generous tax credits have lured many U.S.-based studios north for a slew of big-dollar productions, but the heart of Vancouver's entertainment industry is its homegrown filmmaking community. No one embodies the city's creative spirit better than the director Mina Shum, whose semi-autobiographical first feature *Double Happiness* earned her international acclaim on the film-fest circuit in 1994. Sandra Oh plays an independent-minded 22-year-old trying to balance the traditional expectations of her Chinese-Canadian family with aspirations of an acting career. Such cross-cultural themes bubble up throughout Shum's filmography, most recently in her equally moving 2017 drama *Meditation Park*, which also stars Oh.

THE GREY FOX

The godfather of Vancouver cinema, director Phillip Borsos made his feature debut in 1982 with *The Grey Fox,* a revisionist western film portraying the infamous bandit Bill Miner as he plots Canada's first great train robbery in the early 1900s. True to life, the movie was filmed on location along the BC Railway. Regarded as one of the country's cinematic masterworks, Borsos manages to transcend period-piece clichés with his elegant depiction of this pivotal moment in British Columbian history.

JUNO

For the coming-of-age dramedy *Juno*, Canadian director Jason Reitman casts Vancouver's suburbs as Minnesota, where fellow Canadian-turned-Hollywood star Ellen Page plays a confident teen navigating her junior year of high school—four seasons defined by an unplanned pregnancy and her tangled relationship with a yuppie couple looking to adopt. This 2007 Academy Award winner is one of the best-regarded films in which Vancouver once again passes for its southern neighbor.

OBASAN BY JOY KOGAWA
Beneath the sheen of Vancouver's globally minded liberalism lingers the legacy of white supremacy and racial exclusion. Joy Kogawa, a BC-born author, grapples with one of the most unfortunate chapters in the region's history. This deeply personal work of autobiographical fiction chronicles the persecution and internment Japanese Canadians endured throughout the 1940s. Drawing on the experience of her own imprisonment, Kogawa weaves a sorrowful tale that ruminates on themes of justice, silence, and the trauma of remembering.

PAPER SHADOWS BY WAYSON CHOY
Propelled by his best-selling debut novel—*The Jade Peony,* now a staple in English classes throughout the country—author Wayson Choy looms large in the canon of contemporary Canadian literature. A series of surprising plot twists in his own life following the runaway success of his first book inspired 1999's *Paper Shadows,* the quintessential Vancouver memoir in which discoveries about Chow's own family history shed new life on memories of his childhood in the city's Chinatown. As one of the first openly gay writers of color to achieve widespread success, Choy's legacy remains an inspiration to a generation of writers, especially the LGBTQ and Asian Canadians to whom his work so intimately spoke.

THE BODY REMEMBERS WHEN THE WORLD BROKE OPEN
Technical ingenuity adds a sense of immediateness to Elle-Máijá Tailfeathers and Kathleen Hepburn's intimate and affecting feature, which momentarily brings two indigenous women together for a few fleeting hours. Captured in one unbroken long take on 16 mm film, the narrative unfolds in real-time with a documentary-like sense of urgency—a social realist portrayal of race, class, and family that's garnered widespread praise since its 2019 premiere. *The Body Remembers* is notable not only for its storyline and filmmaking technique but also as an indigenous film told from a First Nations' perspective.

THE 100-MILE DIET BY ALISA SMITH AND J.B. MACKINNON
Two environmentally minded journalists take Vancouver's locavore food culture to another level in this culinary memoir documenting their year of only eating food grown and produced within a 100-mile radius, a zone encompassing the Lower Mainland, half of Vancouver Island, and fringes of Washington. Exploring back-to-the-land themes of sustainability and regional food economies, Alisa Smith and J.B. MacKinnon's experiment doubles as an introduction to the fertile farmland found in close proximity to the city—a natural gift that's made BC's food scene one of the best on the continent.

VANCOUVER SPECIAL BY CHARLES DEMERS
If you want to dig into the distinctively Vancouverite psyche, look no further. Released during the buildup to the 2010 Winter Olympics, *Vancouver Special* finds its author, the comedian and activist Charles Demers, meditating on the state of a global city in flux. Witty and wide-ranging, Demers' essays double as an unconventional guide to Vancouver's present disposition—a guide that dishes insider references and personal anecdotes as it meanders from neighborhood to neighborhood in search of the city's soul.

How to Speak BC

In Canada we have enough to do keeping up with two spoken languages without trying to invent slang, so we just go right ahead and use English for literature, Scotch for sermons, and American for conversation. —Stephen Leacock (1869–1944)

Canadian humorist Stephen Leacock was right: Canadians don't like to confuse visitors with obscure regional dialects. For that, there is the metric system. Still, Canadians have their eccentricities, and a brief primer may help avoid some confusion.

Terms useful in BC include the words for money: loonies for the dollar coin (because of the loon that graces the coins) and toonies for the two-dollar version. British Columbians, like other Canadians, spell many things the British way (colour instead of color, for example), pronounce the letter "z" as "zed," and occasionally (okay, more than occasionally) tack an "eh?" to the end of a sentence—to turn it into a question, to invite a response, or just out of habit.

Canadianisms like toque (woolly cap) are used here, albeit less frequently given the temperate weather. What you will hear are many words for precipitation. A Vancouverite might observe that it's drizzling, spitting, pouring, or pissing down, but will avoid saying "Yup, it's raining again." That just shows a lack of imagination. Oh, and if someone does say, "It's raining again, eh?" he's not asking a question; he's just inviting you to discuss the situation.

A few words are uniquely west coast, including some derived from Coast Salish, a First Nations trading language. *Skookum*, for example, means big or powerful; *chuck* means water (as in a body of water); *salt chuck* is seawater. *Chinook*, which means a warm wind in Alberta, is a species of salmon in BC. Thus you might find: "He caught a skookum chinook then chucked it right back in the salt chuck."

Probably the best sources of confusion out in BC are geographical. The Okanagan, and anything else not on the coast, is called "the Interior" by Vancouverites—unless it's north of, say, Williams Lake, in which case it's "Up North." There are thousands of islands in BC, but "the Island" refers to Vancouver Island. (Many newcomers forget that Vancouver isn't on Vancouver Island; Victoria is.) The *Lower Mainland* is the term used to refer to Metro Vancouver, including the communities of Langley, Abbotsford, North Shore, Richmond, and even Maple Ridge and White Rock.

Food and drink offer more room for misunderstanding: order soda and you'll get soda water (Canadians drink pop). Homo milk? It's short for homogenized milk and it means whole milk. Bacon is bacon, but Canadian bacon is called back bacon in Canada. Fries are generally fries, but will be called chips if they come with fish, in which case they'll also come with vinegar.

And beer? You can just order "beer," but be prepared to discuss with the bartender your preference for lager, ale, porter, and so on. You'll probably also be told that Canadian beer is stronger than American. This is a widely held belief that simply doesn't hold water. The alcohol levels are the same—they're just measured differently.

Chapter 2

TRAVEL SMART

2

Updated by
Chris McBeath

★ **CAPITAL:**
Victoria

POPULATION:
Greater Vancouver: 2.5
million; Victoria: 368,000

LANGUAGE:
English

$ CURRENCY:
Canadian dollar

AREA CODES:
604 services Metro
Vancouver; 250, 236, 778, and
672 service the rest of the
province

⚠ **EMERGENCIES:**
911

🚗 **DRIVING:**
On the right

⚡ **ELECTRICITY:**
120–220 v/60 cycles;
plugs have two or three
rectangular prongs

🕐 **TIME:**
3 hours behind New York

🌐 **WEB RESOURCES:**
www.url.com, www.url.com,
www.url.com

✈ **AIRPORTS:**
YVR, YYJ

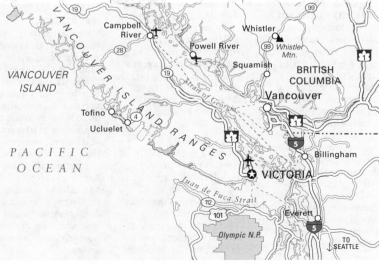

Know Before You Go

You can't blame Vancouverites for feeling smug about living here: its beauty is majestic and its culture eclectic. But issues of affordable housing, gentrification, and homelessness are straining the city's charm—dichotomies deserving of some inside advice.

THE VIBE

With the Canadian Rockies separating British Columbia from the rest of the country, west coasters thrive on that seeming independence, creating unpredictable politics, progressive social programs (like needle exchanges), and weather that allows for an enviable year-round outdoor lifestyle. Victoria counts its daffodils in February while other Canadian time zones are still under snow. But living here doesn't come cheap.

DIVERSITY DYNAMICS

Multicultural dynamics, particularly from Asia, are key influences in these "Gateway to the Pacific" cities; French may be Canada's second official language, but in Vancouver, it's more like Cantonese. Offshore investments are one reason for stratospheric house prices. First Nations (indigenous) are also flexing their influence, turning the wealth of their unceded land (upon which much of Vancouver lies) into controversial new developments. The multi-ethnities that make up Vancouver's fabric,

combined with the region's rich resources, have created some intriguing festivals and certainly, some of the finest farm-to-plate dining anywhere. Sushi is a staple. Craft beer is a food group.

LAYER UP

The temperate (and temperamental) climate means packing for a layered look. Check the long-term forecasts to give yourself a fighting chance of getting it right. It's usually *when*, rather than *if*, it rains, so get smart and put a disposable rainproof poncho in your bag. Great walking shoes are a must. Fleece and Gor-Tex are *de rigueur*; smart casual means no ties for guys and self-expression (i.e.,: anything goes) for gals, whether with stilettos or flats, or better yet, a style from John Fluevog.

HOLY SMOKE

Canada's legal cannabis culture is vibrantly prominent with specialty retailers promoting BC Bud as edibles, vapes, teas, or grams. Enjoy, but be aware than smoking and vaping, whether tobacco or marijuana, is prohibited

in all indoor public areas including public transit, shopping malls, and restaurants, or outdoors within six meters of a door or window of a public space. Parks, seawalls, and beaches are also taboo although the salt air often hints to something a little herbal. Get nabbed and risk a C$250 fine.

BE GREEN

Vancouverites are a health-conscious lot with a penchant for everything vegan, organic, and probiotic. Water bottles are a fashion accessory, as connected to them as their cell phones. Plastic bottles are frowned upon, turned into public sculptures of shame, and recycled so vigorously that their cashback deposits become a valued source of money for low-income earners. The back alleys of Downtown Vancouver are at their busiest (and noisiest) in the early hours before trash day.

NAVIGATION

Vancouver is laid out pretty much on the grid system—even the occasional squirrelly street leads back to dependable square routes. Use the mountains as your north compass; look for odd address numbers on the north and west sides of the street; and watch the numbers get higher the farther away from the harbor you are. Lost? Ask a friendly local or look out for the city's Downtown Ambassadors, dressed in blue, who roam the streets with brochures, advice, and smiles.

TO DRIVE OR NOT TO DRIVE?

Ditch the car if you're staying anywhere in or around Downtown Vancouver or Victoria. Limited and expensive parking, congested traffic, and one-way systems will drive you to distraction. And let's not forget the ever-growing number of bike lanes as part of the city's quest to become one of the greenest in the world. Transit is especially good in Vancouver, starting with a 25-minute automated-train transfer from the airport to Downtown, and extending to a network of trains, buses, and ferries to shuttle you around the city and across the harbor. Both cities are geared for easy walking.

PLAN TO EXTEND YOUR STAY

Vancouver is a great base for traveling farther afield: 2 hours north to Whistler; 4 hours east to the Okanagan wine country; 3 hours south to Seattle (you'll need a passport to cross the border), and 4 hours west to Victoria (including a ferry ride). In these instances, you're better off with a car because the vistas are stunning with a ton of selfie moments along the way. You must have a valid driving license on your person to drive; don't leave it in the hotel safe.

PET COMPANIONS

Vancouver and Victoria are super pet-friendly. Several hotels have dog concierges, pet day camps, and dog-walking services abound, and taking your pooch to one of the doggie beaches will be a real vacation for them as well. Owners must accompany all pets coming to Canada and each pet must have a certificate from a licensed U.S. or Canadian veterinarian verifying that the animal has had all the necessary and valid rabies shots. No shots, no papers, no entry.

TIPPING AND TAXES

Tipping or service charges are not usually included on a restaurant tab so tipping your drinks or meal server is standard practice. A tip of 15 to 20% on the pretax amount is the norm. A federal goods and services tax (GST) of 5% is applied to most purchases; a 7% provincial sales tax is applicable on most retail purchases. There's no tax rebate program for departing visitors so make that 11 percent a part of your budget.

ACCESSIBILITY

Vancouver has paid attention to making its streets and buildings part of one of the top most accessible cities in the world. Check out ⊕ www.tourismvancouver.com/plan-your-trip/accessible-vancouver to help plan your visit. The Sam Sullivan Disability Foundation (⊕ www.disabilityfoundation.org) is a resource for sailing and other recreational opportunities.

VANCOUVER'S UNDERBELLY

The downside for being one of the warmest cities in Canada is that Vancouver, and to a far lesser degree, Victoria, attract more than their fair share of homeless souls. Some panhandle along Granville Street, with many more gathering along Hastings Street toward Main Street. For the uninitiated, it can be a disturbing sight, but as a rule, this community keeps to itself. It's a gritty and historic part of town that appeals to plenty of locals and is not known to be particularly dangerous though at night you may prefer to grab a cab. Use common sense and don't be a flashy tourist—you're not far from the poorest postal code in Canada. Another anomaly of this beautiful city.

Getting Here and Around

Air

Flying time to Vancouver is 5½ hours from New York, 6½ hours from Montréal, 4 hours from Chicago, and 2½ hours from Los Angeles.

Security measures at Canadian airports are similar to those in the United States. Be sure you're not carrying anything that could be construed as a weapon: a letter opener, Swiss Army knife, a pair of scissors, or a toy weapon, for example.

Passengers departing from Vancouver must pay an airport-improvement fee before they can board their plane; however, this fee is now included directly in the cost of tickets, simplifying the process. The fee is C$5 for flights within British Columbia and the Yukon and C$25 for all other flights.

AIRPORTS

The major airport is Vancouver International Airport (YVR), in the suburb of Richmond about 16 km (10 miles) south of Downtown Vancouver.

Vancouver International Airport is Canada's second-busiest airport, but it's easy to get around this spacious facility. Getting through the immigration process, though, can add 45 minutes to your travel time, so plan on getting there early. Extensive duty-free shopping, dining, spa, children's play areas, and other services are available, plus free Wi-Fi. Regular courtesy shuttles run between the Main and South Terminals.

Vancouver Island is served by Victoria International Airport (YYJ). Otherwise, there are domestic airports in or near many towns on the island, including Campbell River, Comox, and Nanaimo. The tiny Tofino–Long Beach airport is 11 km (7 miles) outside the town of Tofino. Smaller communities without airports are served by floatplanes.

Vancouver International Airport is the closest airport to Whistler. The main airport for the Okanagan wine country is in Kelowna.

AIRPORT TRANSFERS

There are many options for getting Downtown from Vancouver International Airport, a drive of about 20 to 45 minutes, depending on traffic. If you're driving, go over the Arthur Laing Bridge and north on Granville Street (also sign-posted as Highway 99). Signs direct you to Vancouver city center.

The fastest and cheapest way to travel Downtown or to points en route is via the Canada Line, part of TransLink, Vancouver's rapid-transit system, which delivers you Downtown from the Vancouver International Airport in 25 minutes. The station is inside the airport, on level four, between the domestic and international terminals. The trains, which are fully wheelchair accessible and allow plenty of room for luggage, leave every six minutes from the airport and every three minutes from Downtown Vancouver. Fares are C$9 each way, which represents a regular bus fare and a C$5 "airport travel" add-on for out-of-Richmond destinations. If you're stopped by the transit authorities carrying a ticket that does not have the surcharge, they'll fine you C$173.

Taxi stands are in front of the terminal building on domestic- and international-arrivals levels. Taxis departing from the airport use a set fare zone system. To Downtown, the fee is approximately C$31–C$37 depending on the zone, which are listed at the entrance to the lineup. Metered rates apply on trips to the airport and to areas outside the zones. Area cab companies include Black Top & Checker Cabs and Yellow Cab.

LimoJet Gold Limousine Services and Pearl Limousine both have limo service between the airport and Downtown Vancouver for about C$75-C$95 one-way; both also offer service from the airport to Whistler for about C$300 to C$380 each way.

Transfers between Victoria International Airport and Downtown Victoria, include the YYJ Airport Shuttle, which costs about C$21, and taxi services at about C$60. The drive is about 40 minutes.

Ride shares as in Lyft and Uber are contentious issues in British Columbia. Both companies have offices in Vancouver and are navigating a locally imposed bureaucracy regarding safety, driver qualifications, and rates as compared to taxi and limo services. Ride shares are expected to hit the road sometime in 2020.

FLIGHTS

Several companies offer floatplane and small-plane service between Vancouver, Victoria, Whistler, and other destinations in British Columbia. Among these are Harbour Air Seaplanes (which also encompasses Whistler Air and Saltspring Air), Kenmore Air, KD Air, Northwest Seaplanes, Pacific Coastal Airlines, and Seair Seaplanes.

Additionally, the well-heeled may be interested in helicopter transfers. Among the companies operating in the Vancouver and Victoria area are Glacier Air and Helijet.

🚲 Bicycle

Despite British Columbia's demanding landscape, bicycle travel is extremely popular. Nicknamed Canada's Cycling Capital, Victoria is especially bike-friendly, and Vancouver is not far behind, with a growing number of bike-only lanes in the heart of Downtown and many designated bike thoroughfares via the most picturesque streets and beachfronts. The Ridgway Greenway runs 13 km (8 miles) east-west of the city, and the 8.5 km (5 miles) Arbutus Greenway, a former rail corridor runs north-south of the city. One of the most spectacular routes in the province follows the abandoned 600-km-long (370-mile-long) Kettle Valley Railway through the mountains of the BC Interior; Tourism Kelowna has details. Gentler options include the 55-km (34-mile) Galloping Goose Regional Trail near Victoria and the rolling hills of the Gulf Islands. Cycle Vancouver Island has information about bike touring on Vancouver Island and the Gulf Islands. Mountain-biking enthusiasts gravitate toward the trails on Vancouver's North Shore Mountains and at Whistler.

🚢 Boat and Ferry

Ferries play a central role in British Columbia's transportation network. In some areas, ferries provide the only access (besides floatplanes) to remote communities. For visitors, ferries are one of the best ways to get a sense of the region and its ties to the sea. BC Ferries operates one of the largest ferry fleets in the world, serving about 47 ports of call on BC's west coast. The ferries carry vehicles as well as bicycles and foot passengers.

Reservations are recommended between Vancouver and Vancouver Island and on most sailings between Vancouver and the Southern Gulf Islands, especially on weekends and holidays.

BC Ferries operates two ferry terminals outside Vancouver. From Tsawwassen (an hour south of Downtown Vancouver), ferries sail to Swartz Bay near Victoria, to

Getting Here and Around

Nanaimo on Vancouver Island, and to the Southern Gulf Islands. From Horseshoe Bay (45 minutes north of Downtown), ferries sail to the Sunshine Coast and to Nanaimo on Vancouver Island. Vehicle reservations on Vancouver to Victoria and Nanaimo and Vancouver to the Sunshine Coast routes are optional (but recommended especially for Vancouver to Victoria) and cost an additional C$17 to C$22. There is no charge for reservations on Gulf Island routes.

V2V Vacations operates a passenger ferry service from Vancouver harbor to Victoria's Inner Harbour, March through October. The once-a-day sailings leave Vancouver in the early morning and depart Victoria in the late afternoon. Day trip returns, one-way tickets, and overnight packages in Victoria are available. One-way tickets in high season are about C$200, depending on the class of travel you select; prices are discounted in the spring and fall.

There are several options for getting to Vancouver Island from Washington State: Black Ball Transport operates the MV *Coho,* a car ferry, daily year-round between Port Angeles, Washington, and Victoria's Inner Harbour. The car and passenger fare is US$67; bikes are US$6.50. The *Victoria Clipper* runs daily, year-round passenger-only service between Downtown Seattle and Downtown Victoria. Trips take about three hours, and the one-way fare from November to late February is US$115; bicycles and pets are an extra US$20, and reservations are recommended. Washington State Ferries runs a car ferry daily from April through December from Anacortes, Washington, to Sidney (some runs make stops at different San Juan Islands), about 30 km (18 miles) north of Victoria. Trips take about three hours. One-way high-season

fares are US$67 for a vehicle and driver, and bikes are US$6.

🚌 Bus

IslandLink Bus operates bus service to most towns on Vancouver Island, including Tofino, and connects with BC Ferries at Departure Bay in Nanaimo. They also offer year-round service to Whistler. Pacific Coach Lines and BC Ferries Connector (run by Wilson's Transportation) both operate frequent service between Victoria and Vancouver (both Downtown and the airport) on BC Ferries. The Tofino Bus provides daily service from Vancouver, Victoria, Nanaimo, and points en route to Port Alberni, Tofino, and Ucluelet. From May to September, the West Coast Trail Express shuttles hikers from Victoria and Nanaimo to the trailheads of the west coast and Juan de Fuca trails. All bus companies ban smoking, and most long-distance buses have restrooms on board. Some even play videos.

In British Columbia, Greyhound only provides a Seattle–Vancouver service. EBus offers transportation to Kelowna and Kamloops.

🚗 Car

Canada's highway system is excellent. It includes the Trans-Canada Highway, or Highway 1, the longest highway in the world—running about 8,000 km (5,000 miles) from Victoria, British Columbia, to St. John's, Newfoundland, using ferries to bridge coastal waters at each end. The second-longest Canadian highway, the Yellowhead Highway (Highway 16), follows a route from the Pacific coast and over the Rockies to the prairies. North of the population centers, roads become fewer and less developed.

The Sea-to-Sky Highway between Vancouver and Whistler is full of twists and turns, and although it was upgraded and widened prior to the 2010 Winter Olympics, drivers should still exercise caution. Landslides occasionally occur along this highway, also noted for its spectacular scenery along Howe Sound.

Within British Columbia, the Trans-Canada Highway (Highway 1), Highway 3, and the Coquihalla Highway (Highway 5) offer easy access to the Okanagan. Speed limits range from 50 kph (30 mph) in cities to a maximum of 100 kph (60 mph) on highways.

Border-crossing procedures from the U.S. are usually quick and simple. Most British Columbia land-border crossings are open 24 hours; exceptions are the crossing at Aldergrove and smaller border posts in eastern British Columbia, which are typically open 8 am to midnight. The Interstate 5 border crossing at Blaine, Washington, also known as the Douglas, or Peace Arch, border crossing, is one of the busiest border crossings between the United States and Canada. Weekend and holiday traffic tends to be heaviest; listen to local radio traffic reports for information about wait times, which can sometimes be as much as three hours.

CAR RENTALS

Renting a car is a good option if you're getting out of the cities, but if you plan to spend most or all your time in Downtown Vancouver, you won't need a car: parking can be difficult to secure and most attractions are within walking distance or a short cab or bus ride away. Downtown Victoria is even more compact.

GASOLINE

Gasoline prices vary significantly from neighborhood to neighborhood in British Columbia. Expect to pay at least C$1.40 per liter (1 gallon = 3.78 liters), with prices slightly higher in Vancouver. In BC, the price includes federal and provincial taxes, a gradually increasing carbon emissions tax, and in the Greater Vancouver region, 18.5 cents per liter of local transit tax. The combined taxes on every liter is more than 48 cents (not including the 5% GST).

PARKING

More than 300 parking lots (above- and belowground) are available in Vancouver. Underground parking prices Downtown typically run C$5 to C$9 per hour, depending on location. Parking meters are in effect 9 am to 10 pm daily and are strictly monitored. On-street parking can be hard to find Downtown, especially during workdays and on weekends. Read signs carefully to avoid being towed or fined; be aware that some spots must be vacated by the time rush hour begins at 3 pm. Fines run between C$35 and C$100, plus the cost of the tow truck.

ROAD CONDITIONS

Tire chains, studs, or snow tires are essential equipment for winter travel in the north and in mountain areas such as Whistler. If you're planning to drive into high elevations, be sure to check the weather forecast beforehand. Even the main-highway mountain passes can be forced to close because of snow conditions. The Ministry of Transportation website has up-to-date road reports.

ROADSIDE EMERGENCIES

In case of emergency anywhere in BC, call 911; if you are not connected immediately, dial "0" and ask for the operator. The British Columbia Automobile

Getting Here and Around

Association (BCAA) provides 24-hour roadside assistance to AAA and CAA members.

RULES OF THE ROAD

In Canada your own driver's license is acceptable. By law, you're required to wear seat belts and to use infant seats. In BC, babies under the age of one and under 20 pounds must travel in a rear-facing infant seat and not in a front seat with an active air bag; children over one year old and between 20 and 40 pounds need to be secured in child seats, while kids up to age nine or four-foot-nine inches tall (whichever comes first) must use booster seats. Motorcycle and bicycle helmets are mandatory. Unless otherwise specified, right turns are permitted on red signals. Speed limits, given in kilometers, are usually within the 50–100 kph (30–60 mph) range outside the cities.

Cruise

Many one-way (and some round-trip) Alaska cruises either embark or disembark in Vancouver because it's closer to Alaskan waters than Seattle. Sailing through Burrard Inlet, ships pass the forested shores of Stanley Park and sail beneath the graceful sweep of the Lions Gate Bridge. Ships calling at Vancouver dock at the Canada Place cruise-ship terminal on the Downtown waterfront, a few minutes' walk from the city center. Its rooftop of dramatic white sails makes it instantly recognizable.

Transfers between the airport and the piers are offered by the cruise lines, either as a fare add-on or, in the case of some luxury cruise lines or small-ship-cruise lines, included in the price of your cruise. Cruise-line representatives meet airport arrivals or are present at hotel transfer points to make the process stress-free. Expedition vessels offer itineraries to Alaska and along the coastal fjords.

From the south, Interstate 5 from Seattle becomes Highway 99 at the U.S.–Canada border. Vancouver is a three-hour drive (226 km [140 miles]) from Seattle. It's best to avoid border crossings during peak times such as holidays and weekends. Highway 1, the Trans-Canada Highway, enters Vancouver from the east. To avoid traffic, arrive after rush hour (8:30 am).

Vancouver's evening rush-hour traffic starts early—about 3 pm on weekdays. The worst bottlenecks outside the city center are the North Shore bridges, the George Massey Tunnel on Highway 99 south of Vancouver, and Highway 1 through Coquitlam and Surrey. The BC Ministry of Transportation (📞 800/550–4997 ⊕ www.drivebc.ca) has updates.

🚆 Train

Amtrak has service from Seattle to Vancouver, providing connections between Amtrak's U.S.–wide network and VIA Rail's Canadian routes. VIA Rail Canada provides transcontinental rail service. In BC, VIA Rail has two major routes: Vancouver to Jasper, and Jasper to Prince Rupert with an overnight stop in Prince George. A third route, Victoria to Courtenay on Vancouver Island, is not currently in service, although there is talk of bringing it back. Rocky Mountaineer Vacations operates a variety of spectacular all-daylight rail trips between the Canadian Rockies and the west coast. All trains are nonsmoking, and they do not run in winter.

Essentials

🍴 Dining

In Vancouver, where several thousand eateries represent almost every cuisine on the planet, deciding what to eat is as important as deciding what to see and do. Vancouverites are a health-conscious lot, so light, organic, and vegetarian meals are easy to find, and every restaurant and even most pubs ban smoking indoors and out. Good coffee is everywhere—Downtown you'll never have to walk more than half a block for a cup of high-test cappuccino.

In Victoria and on Vancouver Island, the farm-to-fork ethos is particularly strong, in part because the island's bounty is so accessible. Many chefs work directly with organic farmers when they are creating their distinctive regional dishes. You'll be pleased to find that in addition to top-draw destinations such as Whistler, you'll discover excellent food even in the most out-of-the-way places in the province.

Dining in British Columbia is affordable due to Canada's low dollar. To be sure, high-end entrées, especially where seafood is involved, can top C$45, but C$22 to C$27 is more the norm. Bargains abound: the densest cluster of cheap eats in Vancouver is along Denman Street in the West End. Another budget option is to check out the lunch specials at any of the small Asian restaurants lining the streets in both Vancouver and Victoria. They serve healthy hot meals for about the same cost as a take-out burger and fries. But beware: alcohol is pricey in BC. A bottle of wine can easily double your bill.

PAYING
Credit cards are widely accepted, but a few smaller restaurants accept only cash. Discover Cards are little known in Canada, and many restaurants outside Vancouver do not accept American Express.

RESERVATIONS AND DRESS
At the hottest restaurants in Vancouver, Victoria, and Whistler, you need to make reservations at least two weeks in advance, perhaps more if you want to dine between 7 and 9 pm, or on a Friday or Saturday night. On weeknights or outside the peak tourist season, you can usually secure a table by calling the same day.

What It Costs in Canadian Dollars			
$	$$	$$$	$$$$
AT DINNER			
under C$13	C$13–C$20	C$21–C$30	over C$30

🛏 Lodging

Vancouver has a wide range of accommodations, including bed and breakfasts and upscale hotels. Beyond Vancouver, particularly in places like Vancouver Island and Whistler, a varied array of lodging options are also available.

What It Costs in Canadian Dollars			
$	$$	$$$	$$$$
HOTELS			
under C$126	C$126–C$195	C$196–C$300	over C$300

💲 Money

The units of currency in Canada are the Canadian dollar (C$) and the cent, in almost the same denominations as U.S.

Essentials

currency ($5, $10, $20, 5¢, 10¢, 25¢, etc.). The C$1 and C$2 bill have been replaced by C$1 and C$2 coins—known as a "loonie," because of the loon that appears on the coin, and a "toonie," respectively. As of 2013, Canada phased out its one-cent coin.

U.S. dollars are accepted in much of Canada (especially in communities near the border), but you won't get the exchange rate offered at banks. ATMs are ubiquitous in Vancouver and Victoria, and credit cards are accepted virtually everywhere.

Item	Average Cost
Cup of Coffee	C$3.50
Glass of Wine	C$10
Glass of Beer	C$8
Sandwich	C$9
1-Mile Taxi Ride	C$7
Museum Admission	C$28

Packing

In Vancouver and the rest of British Columbia, attire tends to be casual but neat. T-shirts, polo shirts, and slacks are fine at tourist attractions and all but the most upscale restaurants. Waterproof, breathable fabrics are recommended for those planning outdoor excursions. Weather in British Columbia is changeable and varied; you can expect cool evenings and some chance of rain even in summer, so don't forget your umbrella. If you plan on camping or hiking in the deep woods in summer, particularly in northern British Columbia, definitely take insect repellent. In wilderness areas it's also a good idea to carry bear spray and/or wear bells to warn bears of your presence. Both are available in camping and hardware stores in BC.

Passport

Citizens of the United States need a passport to reenter the United States from Canada. Passport requirements apply to minors as well. Anyone under 18 traveling alone should carry a signed and dated letter from both parents or from all legal guardians authorizing the trip. It's also a good idea to include a copy of the child's birth certificate, custody documents if applicable, and death certificates of one or both parents, if applicable. Citizens of the United States, United Kingdom, Australia, and New Zealand do not need visas to enter Canada for a period of six months or less.

Tipping

Tips and service charges are not usually added to a bill in Canada. In general, tip 15% of the total bill. This goes for waiters, barbers and hairdressers, and taxi drivers.

Visitor Information

Regional visitor information services are available in British Columbia. In addition, Downtown Ambassadors, sponsored by the Downtown Vancouver Business Improvement Association, are easily spotted on Vancouver streets in their red uniforms. They can provide information, directions, and emergency assistance to anyone visiting Vancouver's central business district.

Tipping Guidelines

Bartender	C$1–C$5 per round of drinks, depending on the number of drinks
Bellhop	C$1–C$5 per bag, depending on the level of the hotel
Hotel Concierge	C$5 or more, if he or she performs a service for you
Hotel Doorman	C$1–C$2 if he helps you get a cab
Hotel Maid	C$1–C$3 a day (either daily or at the end of your stay, in cash)
Hotel Room-Service Waiter	C$1 to C$2 per delivery, even if a service charge has been added
Porter at Airport or Train Station	C$1 per bag
Skycap at Airport	C$1 to C$3 per bag checked
Taxi Driver	15%, but round up the fare to the next dollar amount
Tour Guide	10% of the cost of the tour
Valet Parking Attendant	C$2–C$3, but only when you get your car
Waiter	15%–20%, with 20% being the norm at high-end restaurants; nothing additional if a service charge is added to the bill

When to Go

Low Season: If you don't mind some rain and cooler temperatures, then in Vancouver, at least, it's mostly business as usual in terms of attractions, often at significantly discounted prices. In Victoria, however, the city seems to go into hibernation in the winter months. There's still plenty to see but many of the smaller attractions close November through March.

Shoulder Season: April–early May and late September–October attract the "older set" and kid-free travelers. Prices aren't at their zenith, crowds are less and even though you can expect the unexpected rain shower, both cities bask in spectacular spring blossoms and warm Indian summers.

High Season: Pricey, crowded but oh, so much fun from June through August, Vancouver and Victoria buzz with festivals and activities such as horse-drawn carriage rides, street entertainers, outdoor activities galore, beachside performing arts, great patios, and a walkability factor that makes exploring on foot a delight.

WEATHER

Vancouver has a mild climate. In winter snow falls on the surrounding mountains but rarely in the city. Summers are warm, averaging midtwenties Celsius (high 70s F) with cooler evenings. Protected by the mainland, Victoria (on Vancouver Island) sometimes boasts being one or two degrees warmer.

Great Itineraries

Food and Wine Tour

So many restaurants, so many wineries, so little time!

DAY 1: VANCOUVER

Your jumping-off point for a food-and-wine tour of British Columbia would start with a day browsing Vancouver's food markets. There's **Granville Island**, of course, (try the candied salmon!) and eight **farmers' markets** across the city. Most are open May through October, but one (**Hastings Park**) is open in the winter and one (**Riley Park**) is open year-round. Finish your day off with a dinner at one of the city's 5,000 or so restaurants.

Logistics: Farmers' markets are open on particular days throughout the week, check the website (eatlocal.org) for details.

DAY 2: VANCOUVER

Day two will consist of exploring Vancouver's busy craft brewery scene. Most breweries are clustered in two main neighborhoods: Main Street and East Van (affectionately known as "Yeast Van") which makes it convenient for an afternoon of hitting up two or three (or four) breweries. If there's not another restaurant on your go-to list, many of the breweries serve great grub.

Logistics: If you don't know which breweries to tackle, The Growler (bc.thegrowler.ca), BC's craft beer guide, is a good place to start.

DAY 3: VERNON

On day three, you'll want to head to the source of the bounty you've just sampled, traveling five hours east to the Okanagan Valley. There are more than 300 wineries that line Route 97, along a 200-km (120-mile) string of lakes. The northernmost tip of the region is Vernon, a small artsy city. Shop the downtown core for an incredible charcuterie board (**Olive Us**, **Sweet Hoopla**, **Hot Bread Shoppe**, and **Wedge Cheesery**) and then have a picnic by the lake.

Logistics: If you want to try something different before you get into the region's wine, Vernon's **BX Press Cidery** and **Okanagan Spirits** are good options.

DAY 4: VERNON TO KELOWNA

On day four, on your way south to Kelowna, rent an electric bicycle and tour Lake Country's wineries, if you please (you can also bike a portion of the **Okanagan Rail Trail**). Have lunch at **Pane Vino**, a charming little pizzeria. Once you arrive in Kelowna, the visitor center can help you make a list of what wineries you want to visit (based on what type of wines you like, whether the winery serves food, size of the winery, etc.). Popular options are **CedarCreek**, **Ex Nihilo**, and **Indigenous World Winery**.

Logistics: Pro tip: the northern Okanagan is known for their white wine; the southern Okanagan is known for their red wine.

DAY 5: SUMMERLAND, PEACHLAND, AND PENTICTON

On day five, as you continue to drive south, you'll pass through Summerland and Peachland. Make sure to stop off at any wineries you may have flagged, as well as the bounty of fruit stands. Eventually you'll get to Penticton. In the summertime, people love to float along the river channel here. But, if you're here for food and wine, spots like **Poplar Grove**, **Wayne & Freda**, and **Black Antler** won't disappoint.

Logistics: This itinerary suggests continuing to drive farther south, but there's also an option to drive back north, but up the eastern side of the lake to Naramata.

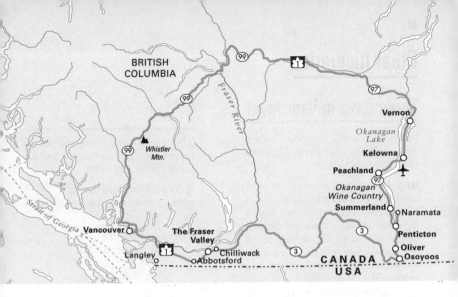

DAY 6: OLIVER AND OSOYOOS

Day six calls for a drive farther south to Oliver and Osoyoos, Canada's only desert. There's also a significant First Nations population here, so in between restaurant and winery stops, you may want to check out some of the area's history and culture at the **Nk'Mip Desert Cultural Centre**. Some food and wine highlights include **Oliver Eats**, **Moon Curser**, and **Nk'Mip Cellars**.

Logistics: Some wineries close their operations in the off-season (November to April), so do some research ahead of time if there are particular wineries you're keen to check out.

DAY 7: THE FRASER VALLEY

Day seven will have you driving back west towards Vancouver, another five-hour trip, so you may want to break it up with a stop or two along the way. The best route takes you through the Fraser Valley, which includes the cities of Abbotsford, Chilliwack, and Langley. The area is known for its agriculture (farms and dairies are aplenty), so be sure to stop in here for a meal, farm tour (depending on the season), or more sips at a winery or microbrewery.

Tips

If you happen to be in Vancouver in January/February, Dine Out is a festival where hundreds of restaurants offer special three-course menus at great prices.

Once you're in the Okanagan Valley, the most efficient way to get around is by car. If you plan on drinking at the plenty of wineries in the region, make sure you have a designated driver.

Many wineries have on-site restaurants and/or retail shops where you can buy lunch/picnic supplies.

Logistics: Circle Farm Tour (circlefarmtour.com) is a self-guided journey through many of the agriculture tourism destinations that are found in the Fraser Valley.

Great Itineraries

Three Days in Vancouver

It's possible to see Vancouver in three days, although you'll probably just have time to hit the highlights.

DAY 1

Start with **Stanley Park**: this rain forest has plenty of views, hikes, and activities, all within blocks of the city center. Highlights include the **Seawall**, a 10-km (6-mile) path that loops around the exterior edge of the park, the **totem poles** carved by First Nations artists, and **Prospect Point**, the highest point in the park, with incredible views of the ocean and Lion's Gate Bridge. In the afternoon, stroll through some Downtown neighborhoods like **Yaletown**, **Chinatown**, and **Gastown**. You'll also want to check out **Granville Island**; you can take the Aquabus across False Creek to this popular tourist destination, which is home to a giant food market, busker entertainment, galleries, shops, and more.

Logistics: There is parking in Stanley Park, but if you're going to spend the day exploring the park and some of the city's Downtown neighborhoods, a bicycle is your best bet. There are plenty of bike rental shops in Vancouver's West End neighborhood, right before you enter Stanley Park.

DAY 2

On day two, you'll want to explore the mountains and parks of the **North Shore** (**Capilano**, **Grouse**, or **Lynn Canyon**). There is a suspension bridge and treetop trekking at **Capilano**, and a free suspension bridge at **Lynn Canyon**. Popular hikes include the **Grouse Grind**, **Quarry Rock** in Deep Cove, **Dog Mountain**, and more.

Tips

If biking isn't your thing, you can also explore Stanley Park on foot (or horse-drawn carriage!).

Make sure you have the right workout gear (and plenty of water!) for those hikes.

Plan your trip to the beaches around sunrise or sunset.

Logistics: If you have a car, there's plenty of parking on the North Shore. In the summer, there's a free shuttle that runs from Downtown Vancouver to Capilano and Grouse. There are also public transit options from the city center or from Lonsdale Quay, which you get to from the SeaBus.

DAY 3

On day three, you'll want to spend your day on the city's west side. On the **University of British Columbia** campus, there's the **Museum of Anthropology**, which houses an outstanding collection of First Nations art and cultural artifacts. There are also several beaches with mountain views: **Kitsilano**, **Jericho**, and **Spanish Banks** are all popular choices.

Logistics: There is parking on UBC's campus, as well as at many of the city's beaches, but it might be difficult to come by on a hot summer day. The 99 bus is a solid choice, as is Mobi, Vancouver's bike share program, or any of the car sharing services, such as Evo or car2go.

On the Calendar

January

Dine Out Vancouver Festival. Restaurants all over the city offer special three-course menus at great prices at this festival that runs until early February.⊕ *www.dineoutvancouver.com*

Whistler Pride and Ski Festival. Held at the end of January into the beginning of February, the resort heats up for a week with naughty nightlife, fine dining, and fabulous après-ski. ⊕ *gaywhistler.com*

February

Talking Stick Festival. This multidisciplinary Aboriginal arts festival in Vancouver features musical acts, workshops, artist talks, and more.⊕ *www.talkingstickfest. ca*

March

Pacific Rim Whale Festival. This festival in Tofino and Ucluelet marks the spring migration of an estimated 20,000 Pacific gray whales between Mexico and the Arctic, with tours, talks, crafts, food, and cultural events for the whole family.⊕ *www.pacificrimwhalefestival.com*

Vancouver International Dance Festival. Three weeks of performances and workshops at various venues throughout Vancouver.⊕ *www.vidf.ca.com*

April

Vancouver Cherry Blossom Festival. Check out the 40,000 cherry trees lining the streets in Vancouver on community bike rides or viewing tours. There are also traditional Japanese festivities.⊕ *www. vcbf.ca*

World Ski & Snowboard Festival. This raucous end-of-season in Whistler bash fills 10 days with music, arts, fashion shows, and extreme sports. ⊕ *www.wssf.com*

May

DOXA Documentary Film Festival. Check out independent and critically acclaimed films at this 10-day documentary film festival in Vancouver.⊕ *www.doxafestival.ca*

Feast Tofino. Fishers, diners, and chefs gather to celebrate local fisheries and boat-to-table cuisine at this monthlong culinary event. ⊕ *www.feastoftofino.com*

Tofino Shorebird Festival. This festival celebrates the thousands of shorebirds that migrate north from Central and South America to tundra breeding grounds in the Arctic. ⊕ *www.tourismtofino.com*

June

Tough Mudder. This grueling military-style obstacle course in Whistler tests more than physical stamina. ⊕ *www. toughmudder.com*

Victoria International JazzFest. A 10-day music festival featuring jazz, blues, and world music.⊕ *www.jazzvictoria.ca*

July

Pacific Rim Summer Festival. Celebrate music, dance, and the arts during the first two weeks of July. ⊕ *www.pacificrimarts.ca*

Taste: Victoria's Festival of Food and Wine. Victoria's annual food and wine fest brings a wealth of local food and wine producers, tastings, and events to town every July. ⊕ *www.tourismvictoria.com/ eat-drink/dine-around*

On the Calendar

Vancouver Folk Music Festival. A week-end-long outdoor multistage music festival, located at Jericho Beach Park on the west side of Vancouver.⊕ *www.thefestival.bc.ca*

August

Crankworx. This Whistler mountain-bike festival showcases the sport's boldest athletes as they whip down double black-diamond runs. ⊕ *www.crankworx.com*

Pacific National Exhibition Fair. An annual 17-day summer fair in Vancouver that features games, rides, carnival food, concerts, and more.⊕ *www.pne.ca*

Tofino Lantern Festival. Hundreds of imaginatively crafted lanterns make this festival a sight to behold. ⊕ *www.tourismtofino.com*

Vancouver Island Feast of Fields. Celebrate and learn about local food during this festival that takes place on an area farm. ⊕ *feastsoffields.com*

September

Vancouver International Film Festival. This annual film festival sees more than 140,000 film fans enjoying 380 movies.⊕ *www.viff.org*

Whistler Village Beer Festival. Celebrate everything that makes the craft beer movement one of the world's fastest-growing drinking phenomenons. ⊕ *wvbf.ca*

October

Art of the Cocktail Festival. It's not only wine drinkers who can enjoy festival fun. Victoria's annual cocktail party includes tastings, workshops, and other sipping and supping events every October. ⊕ *www.artofthecocktail.ca*

Ghost Train in Stanley Park. Each year, you can take a spooky Halloween-themed train ride through Stanley Park. There's also a holiday train ride in December.⊕ *www.vancouver.ca/parks*

November

Clayoquot Oyster Festival The humble bivalve is celebrated during this three-day gastronomic adventure. ⊕ *facebook.com/Clayoquotoysterfestival*

Cornucopia. There's a little bit of everything at this Whistler festival for foodies and oenophiles. Spirits and craft beer also abound. ⊕ *www.whistlercornucopia.com*

East Side Culture Crawl. A four-day visual arts, design, and crafts festival extends an invitation to discover 500+ artist studios in 80 buildings throughout Vancouver's Eastside.⊕ *www.culturecrawl.ca.*

December

Canyon Lights at Capilano Suspension Bridge Park. Snap photos in front of thousands of magical lights twinkling across the suspension bridge and forest.⊕ *www.capbridge.com*

Contacts

🛪 Air

**AIRLINE SECURITY Trans-
portation Security Adminis-
tration.** ⊕ www.tsa.gov.

**CONTACTS Glacier
Air** . ☎ 604/898–9016,
800/265–0088 ⊕ www.
glacierair.com. **Harbour
Air Seaplanes.** ☎ 604/274–
1277, 800/665–0212
⊕ www.harbourair.com.
Helijet. ☎ 604/273–4688,
800/665–4354 ⊕ www.
helijet.com. **KD Air.**
☎ 800/665–4244 ⊕ www.
kdair.com. **Kenmore
Air.** ☎ 425/486–1257,
866/435–9524 ⊕ www.
kenmoreair.com.
Northwest Seaplanes.
☎ 425/277–1590,
800/690–0086 ⊕ www.
nwseaplanes.com.
Pacific Coastal Airlines.
☎ 604/273–8666,
800/663–2872 ⊕ www.
pacificcoastal.com. **Seair
Seaplanes.** ☎ 604/273–
8900, 800/447–3247
⊕ www.seairseaplanes.
com.

⛴ Boat and Ferry

CONTACTS BC Ferries.
☎ 888/223–3779 toll-free
in Canada and U.S.,
250/386–3431 from
outside Canada and
U.S. ⊕ www.bcferries.
com. **Canada Place Cruise
Terminal.** ✉ 999 Canada
Place Way, Vancouver

☎ 604/665–9000 ⊕ www.
portvancouver.com.
V2V Vacations. ✉ Downtown ☎ 855/554-4679
⊕ www.v2vvacations.
com. **Black Ball Ferry
Line.** ☎ 250/386–2202,
360/457–4491 ⊕ www.
cohoferry.com. **Clipper
Navigation Inc.** ☎ 250/382–
8100, 800/888–2535
⊕ www.clippervacations.
com. **Washington State
Ferries.** ☎ 206/464–6400,
888/808–7977 ⊕ www.
wsdot.wa.gov/ferries.

🚌 Bus

CONTACTS Greyhound.
☎ 800/661–8747 in Cana-
da, 800/231–2222 in U.S.
⊕ www.greyhound.ca.
BC Connector. ☎ 800/788-
8840, 604/428-9494
⊕ www.bcfconnector.
com. **EBus.** ☎ 877/769-
3287 ⊕ www.myebus.
ca. **IslandLinkBus.** ⊕ www.
islandlinkbus.com. **Pacific
Coach.** ☎ 604/662–7575,
800/661–1725 ⊕ www.
pacificcoach.com.
Tofino Bus Island Express.
☎ 250/725–2871,
866/986–3466 ⊕ www.
tofinobus.com. **West Coast
Trail Express.** ☎ 250/477–
8700, 888/999–2288
⊕ www.trailbus.com.

🚗 Car

**EMERGENCY SERVICES
British Columbia Automobile
Association.** ☎ 888/268–
2222 roadside assistance
⊕ www.bcaa.com.

**LOCAL AGENCIES Lo-Cost
Rent-A-Car.** ☎ 888/556–
2678 ⊕ www.locostrenta-
car.com.

🚢 Cruise

**CRUISE LINES Bluewater
Adventures.** ☎ 604/980–
3800, 888/877–1770
⊕ www.bluewateradven-
tures.ca. **Lindblad-National
Geographic Expeditions.**
☎ 800/397–3348
⊕ www.expeditions.
com. **Marine Link Tours.**
☎ 250/286–3347 ⊕ www.
marinelinktours.com.
Mothership Adventures.
☎ 888/833–8887 ⊕ www.
mothershipadventures.
com. **UnCruise Adventures.**
☎ 888/862–8881 ⊕ www.
uncruise.com.

⚠ Emergencies

**U.S. EMBASSY CONTACT
U.S. Consulate General Vancouver** . ✉ 1075 W. Pender
St., Vancouver ☎ 604/685–
4311 ⊕ ca.usembassy.
gov/embassy-consulates/
vancouver.

Contacts

Train

CONTACTS Amtrak.
☎ *800/872–7245*⊕ *www.amtrak.com.* **Rocky Mountaineer Vacations.**
☎ *604/606–7245, 877/460–3200*⊕ *www.rockymountaineer.com.* **VIA Rail Canada.**
☎ *888/842–7245*⊕ *www.viarail.ca.*

◉ Visitor Information

CONTACTS Aboriginal Tourism Association of British Columbia. ☎ *604/921–1070,* ⊕ *www.aboriginal-bc.com.* **Granville Island.**
☎ *604/666–6655*⊕ *www.granvilleisland.com.* **Hello BC.** ☎ ⊕ *www.hellobc.com.* **Tourism Victoria Visitor Centre.** ☎ *250/953–2033, 800/663–3883*
⊕ *www.tourismvictoria.com.* **Tourism Vancouver Visitor Centre.** ☎ *604/683–2000*⊕ *www.tourismvancouver.com.*

Chapter 3

DOWNTOWN, WEST END, AND STANLEY PARK

Updated by
Chris McBeath

3

👁 Sights   🍴 Restaurants   🏨 Hotels   🛍 Shopping   🍸 Nightlife
★★★★☆   ★★★★★   ★★★★★   ★★★★☆   ★★★☆☆

NEIGHBORHOOD SNAPSHOT

TOP EXPERIENCES

■ **Stanley Park:** 1,000 acres of rain forest is beloved for its trails, gardens, beaches, First Nations heritage, and family attractions. Cycle the seawall or take a tour. Just don't miss it.

■ **Denman Street:** Foodie nooks sit cheek-by-jowl along this perennially busy West End thoroughfare. It's diverse, chaotic, and very local.

■ **Canada Place:** Extending into Canada's busiest harbor with cruise ships docked alongside, the views are eye-popping and Fly Over Canada an adventure.

■ **Take to the Air:** A seaplane tour above rain forest, skyscrapers, and mountains is hard to beat. Take off and landing is half the fun.

■ **Robson Square:** In summer the ice-rink floor gives way to salsa and *So You Think You Can Dance* enthusiasts, for free.

GETTING HERE

Driving to Stanley Park, head northwest on Georgia Street from Downtown. There's parking at or near all the major attractions; costs are C$3.60 per hour/C$13 per day April–September (less in winter). For public transit, catch Bus 19 "Stanley Park" along West Pender Street Downtown; it runs to the park bus loop, which is within walking distance of the aquarium. The ticket allows you to park all day.

PLANNING YOUR TIME

The intersection of Georgia and Granville streets is Downtown's epicenter. You'll find many key attractions within a five-minute walk, including the Vancouver Art Gallery, Robson Square, and Pacific Mall. The West End and Stanley Park are about a 30-minute walk, as are Yaletown, Gastown and Chinatown.

For the West End and Stanley Park, head east on Robson or any parallel street and you'll find beautiful period homes. Or head east along the seawall from Canada Place—simply one of the finest urban seashore walks anywhere.

QUICK BITES

■ **Bella Gelataria.** Tucked into the corner at Fairmont Pacific Rim, this tiny shop has handcrafted gelato that Italian connoisseurs have begrudgingly judged to be better than their own. If wait lines test your patience, head to Uno Gelato at the Vancouver Convention Centre West for even more inspired choices. ✉ *1001 W. Cordova St., Downtown* ⊕ *www.bellagelateria.com* Ⓜ *Westbound W. Penter St.*

■ **Breka Bakery & Cafe.** Fresh-baked bread, strudels, and treats are offered alongside oven-baked comfort food like shepherd's pie at these inviting hangouts at 821 Denman St. *(West End)*, and others in Yaletown (855 Davie St.) and Kitsilano. ✉ *812 Bute Street, Downtown* ⊕ *www.breka.ca* Ⓜ *Eastbound Robson St.*

■ **Peaked Pies.** Amazing Aussie pies in the form of sweet delights topped with peaks of whipped cream and savory pies topped with mashed potatoes and gravy. ✉ *975 Denman St., West End* ⊕ *www.peakedpies.com.*

■ **Prospect Point Cafe.** At Stanley Park's highest point, this café has a deck overlooking the Lions Gate Bridge—a perfect place for a caffé mocha and a summer to-die-for ice-cream. ✉ *5601 Stanley Park Drive.*

Vancouver's Downtown compact juxtaposes historic architecture with gleaming new buildings. There are museums and galleries to visit, and shopping along Robson Street which runs into the city's West End. To get a feel for what Vancouver is all about, walk the seawall, all the way to Stanley Park.

Robson Street, Vancouver's prime shopping boulevard, runs from Downtown into the West End, a partly residential and partly commercial district. The West End has Vancouver's prettiest streetscapes and harks back to the early 1930s when it housed the affluent middle class: trees are plentiful, gardens are lushly planted, and homes and apartment buildings exude the character of that era. Vancouver's large gay community has a major presence here, too. There are lots of restaurants and cafés along the main arteries: Robson, Denman, and Davie streets.

At 1,000 acres and only blocks from a major city's Downtown, Stanley Park is a rare treasure and Vancouverites make use of it to bike, walk, jog, in-line skate, play cricket and tennis, go to the beach, and enjoy outdoor art shows and theater performances alongside attractions such as the renowned aquarium. The fact that Stanley Park is so close to the city is actually sort of thanks to the Americans. In the 1860s, because of a threat of American invasion, this oceanfront peninsula was designated a military reserve, though it was never needed. When the City of Vancouver was incorporated in 1886, the council's first act was to request the land be set aside as a park. Permission was granted two years later and the grounds were named Stanley Park after Lord Stanley, then governor general of Canada and the same gentleman who gave his name to ice-hockey's Stanley Cup.

Downtown

At the top of a gentle rise up from the water, the intersection of Georgia and Granville streets is considered Downtown's epicenter, and it's always bustling with activity. Georgia Street runs east–west, past Library Square and Rogers Arena (home of the NHL's Vancouver Canucks), straight through to Stanley Park and the Lions Gate Bridge (which leads to the North Shore and on to Whistler, a two-hour drive away). North–south Granville Street is a pedestrian-friendly strip of funky shops, nightclubs, and street-side cafés, with a few pockets of grunge to keep things feeling real. From this corner of Georgia and Granville, there are many key attractions within a five-minute walk, including the Vancouver Art Gallery, Robson Square, and Pacific Centre Mall.

Sights ▼

1 Bill Reid Gallery **E4**
2 Canada Place **H2**
3 Cathedral Place.......... **E4**
4 Christ Church
Cathedral **D4**
5 HSBC Bank Building..... **E5**
6 Marine Building.......... **F3**
7 Olympic Cauldron........ **E2**
8 Robson Square.......... **D6**
9 Robson Street............ **F7**
10 Sinclair Centre **G3**
11 Vancouver
Art Gallery **D5**
12 Vancouver
Lookout Tower **H4**
13 Waterfront Station **H3**

Restaurants ▼

1 Bel Café.................. **E5**
2 Boulevard Kitchen &
Oyster Bar **C5**
3 Café Medina **F6**
4 Caffè Artigiano **D2**
5 Chambar **I6**
6 Cibo Trattoria **E7**
7 CinCin **B4**
8 Coast Restaurant **C4**
9 Glowbal **F6**
10 Hawksworth
Restaurant............... **E5**
11 Hydra Restaurant........ **F3**
12 Japadog **E7**
13 Joe Fortes Seafood
and Chop House **C4**
14 Kirin Restaurant
Downtown.............. **B3**
15 Le Crocodile **C6**
16 Miku Waterfront **G3**
17 Nightingale
Restaurant............... **F3**
18 Royal Dinette **E4**
19 Sciué **F4**

Hotels ▼

1 The Burrard **B7**
2 Century Plaza
Hotel & Spa.............. **B6**
3 Delta Vancouver Suites
by Marriott............... **H4**
4 EXchange Hotel.......... **F3**
5 Executive Hotel
Le Soleil.................. **E4**
6 Fairmont Hotel
Vancouver **D5**
7 Fairmont Pacific Rim **F2**
8 Fairmont Waterfront
Hotel..................... **G3**
9 Kingston Hotel **F6**
10 L'Hermitage Hotel........ **F7**
11 Loden Hotel.............. **C3**
12 Metropolitan Hotel
Vancouver............... **E4**
13 Pan Pacific
Vancouver **G2**
14 Pinnacle Hotel
Harbourfront **D2**
15 Rosewood Hotel
Georgia **E5**
16 St. Regis Hotel **F5**
17 Shangri-La Hotel,
Vancouver............... **C4**
18 Sheraton Vancouver
Wall Centre............. **B7**
19 Sutton Place Hotel
Vancouver............... **C5**
20 Trump International
Hotel & Tower
Vancouver............... **C3**
21 Vancouver Marriott
Pinnacle Downtown
Hotel..................... **D2**
22 Victorian Hotel **H5**
23 Wedgewood
Hotel & Spa............. **D5**
24 Westin Grand,
Vancouver............... **F7**
25 YWCA Hotel **H7**

3

Downtown, West End, and Stanley Park DOWNTOWN

◉ Sights

★ Bill Reid Gallery

MUSEUM | Named after one of British Columbia's preeminent artists, Bill Reid (1920–98), this small aboriginal gallery is as much a legacy of Reid's works as it is a showcase of current First Nations artists. Displays include wood carvings, jewelry, print, and sculpture, and programs often feature artist talks and themed exhibitions such as basket weaving. Reid is best known for his bronze statue *The Spirit of Haida Gwaii, The Jade Canoe*—measuring 12 feet by 20 feet; it is displayed at the Vancouver International Airport, and its image was on the back of Canadian $20 bills issued between 2004 and 2012. More Bill Reid pieces are at the Museum of Anthropology. ⊠ *639 Hornby St., Downtown* ☎ *604/682–3455* ⊕ *www.billreidgallery.ca* ⊠ *C$13* ⊗ *Closed Mon. and Tues., Oct.–May.*

Canada Place

BUILDING | Extending four city blocks (about a mile and a half) north into Burrard Inlet, this complex mimics the style and size of a luxury ocean liner, complete with exterior esplanades and a landmark roofline that resembles five sails (it was made with NASA-invented material: a Teflon-coated fiberglass once used in astronaut space suits). Home to Vancouver's cruise-ship terminal, Canada Place can accommodate up to four liners at once. Altogether, the giant building is definitely worth a look and the very cool **Flyover Canada** *(604/620–8455, www. flyovercanada.com)* attraction, a simulated flight that takes you on a soaring and swooping virtual voyage across the country, is an excellent reason to go inside. If this dramatic journey above Niagara Falls, the Rocky Mountains, and the vast Arctic sparks your curiosity about other parts of Canada, follow the **Canadian Trail** on the west side of the building, which has displays about the country's provinces and territories. Use your smartphone or tablet to access multimedia content along the way: there's free Wi-Fi. Canada Place is also home to the posh **Pan Pacific Hotel** and the east wing of the **Vancouver Convention Centre**. On its western side stands the newer and much larger convention center—its plaza stages the 2010 Olympic cauldron and the Digital Orca sculpture by Canadian artist Douglas Coupland. A waterfront promenade from Canada Place winds all the way to (and around) Stanley Park, with spectacular vantage points from which to view Burrard Inlet and the North Shore Mountains; plaques posted at intervals have historical information about the city and its waterfront. At the **Port of Vancouver Discovery Centre** at Canada Place, at the north end of the Canada Place complex, you can take in a history wall with artifacts, imagery, and interactive displays. ⊠ *999 Canada Pl. Way, Downtown* ☎ *604/665–9000* ⊕ *www. canadaplace.ca* ⊠ *Flyover Canada C$29, Discovery Centre Free.*

Cathedral Place

BUILDING | One of Vancouver's most handsome postmodern buildings, the 23-story Shaw Tower at Cathedral Place has a faux-copper roof that mimics that of the Fairmont Hotel Vancouver nearby. The three large sculptures of nurses at the building's corners are replicas of the statues that adorned the Georgia Medical–Dental Building, the art deco structure that previously occupied this site. Step into the lobby to see another interesting sculpture: Robert Studer's *Navigational Device,* suspended high up on the north wall. The small garden courtyard, which also leads to the entrance of the Bill Reid Gallery, is an unexpected respite from Downtown's bustle. ⊠ *925 W. Georgia St., Downtown* ☎ *604/669–3312* ⊕ *www.925westgeorgia.com.*

Christ Church Cathedral

RELIGIOUS SITE | Built between 1889 and 1895, this is the oldest church in Vancouver. Constructed in the Gothic style, the Anglican church looks like the parish church of an English village from the outside, though underneath the sandstone-clad exterior it's made of Douglas fir from what is now south Vancouver. The 32 stained-glass windows depict Old and New Testament scenes, often set against Vancouver landmarks (St. Nicholas presiding over the Lions Gate Bridge, for example). The building's excellent acoustics enhance the choral evensong and it hosts many concerts. Gregorian chants are performed every Sunday evening at 8 pm. The cathedral's Labyrinth makes for a meditative walk that's hard to find elsewhere in the city's core. ⊠ *690 Burrard St., Downtown* ☎ *604/682–3848* ⊕ *www.thecathedral.ca.*

HSBC Bank Building

BUILDING | Kitty-corner to the Fairmont Hotel Vancouver, this building has a five-story-high public atrium with a branch of the Sciué Italian café minichain (⇨ *see Where to Eat*), regularly changing art exhibitions, and one of the city's more intriguing public-art installations: *Pendulum,* by BC artist Alan Storey, is a 90-foot-long hollow aluminum sculpture that arcs hypnotically overhead. ⊠ *885 W. Georgia St., Downtown* ☎ *604/525–4722.*

Marine Building

BUILDING | Inspired by New York's Chrysler Building, the Marine Building is worth stopping for a look. The terra-cotta bas-reliefs on this 21-story, 1930s art deco structure depict the history of transportation—airships, steamships, locomotives, and submarines—as well as Mayan and Egyptian motifs and images of marine life. Step inside for a look at the beautifully restored interior, then walk to the corner of Hastings and Hornby streets for the best view of the building. ⊠ *355 Burrard St., Downtown.*

Olympic Cauldron

PUBLIC ART | A four-pronged sculpture towering more than 30 feet, the Olympic Cauldron is next to the Vancouver

Wasserman's Beat ◉

At the northwest corner of Georgia and Hornby streets, an area once filled with nightclubs, is a yellow street sign that says "Wasserman's Beat." Most passersby have no idea what it means, but we'll fill you in: the sign recalls Jack Wasserman, a high-society reporter of the '50s and '60s whose most famous celebrity scoop was the death of 50-year-old Errol Flynn, who had a heart attack in a West End apartment in 1959 while traveling with his 15-year-old girlfriend.

Convention Centre's West Building. In 2010, when Vancouver hosted the Winter Olympic and Paralympic Games, it burned with the Olympic flame and it's relit occasionally, for Canada Day and other special events. The Cauldron overlooks the Burrard Inlet on Jack Poole Plaza, which is named for the Canadian businessman who led the bid to bring the Olympics to Vancouver. Sadly, Poole died of cancer just one day after the flame for the Olympic torch relay was lit in Olympia, Greece, at the start of its journey to Vancouver. ⊠ *Foot of Thurlow St., at Canada Pl., Downtown.*

Robson Street

NEIGHBORHOOD | Running from the Terry Fox Plaza outside BC Place Stadium down to the West End, Robson is Vancouver's busiest shopping street, where fashionistas hang out at see-and-be-seen sidewalk cafés, high-end boutiques, and chain stores. Most of the designer action takes place between Jervis and Burrard streets, and that's also where you can find buskers and other entertainers in the evenings. ⊠ *Downtown* ⊕ *www.robsonstreet.ca.*

3

Downtown, West End, and Stanley Park **DOWNTOWN**

Robson Square

PLAZA | Architect Arthur Erickson designed this plaza to be *the* gathering place for Downtown Vancouver, although it's not accessible at street level, which makes it a bit of a secret. Landscaped walkways connect the Vancouver Art Gallery, government offices, and law courts at street level while the lower level houses a University of British Columbia satellite campus and bookstore. In winter, there's also a covered, outdoor, public ice skating rink; in summer the rink becomes a dance floor for weekly (free) salsa sessions, usually Friday nights and Sunday afternoons. Political protests and impromptu demonstrations take place on the grandiose gallery stairs facing Georgia Street, a tradition that dates from the days when the building was a courthouse. ⊠ *Bordered by Howe, Hornby, Robson, and Smithe Sts., Downtown.*

Sinclair Centre

BUILDING | Vancouver architect Richard Henriquez knitted four buildings together into Sinclair Centre, an office–retail complex that takes up an entire city block between Cordova and Hastings, and Howe and Granville streets. Inside are high-end designer-clothing shops, federal government offices, and services including UPS and a multilingual travel agency. The two Hastings Street buildings—the 1910 **Post Office**, which has an elegant clock tower, and the 1911 **Winch Building**—are linked with the 1937 **Post Office Extension** and the 1913 **Customs Examining Warehouse** to the north. As part of a meticulous restoration in the mid-1980s, the post-office facade was moved to the Granville Street side of the complex. The original clockwork from the old clock tower is on display inside, on the upper level of the arcade. ⊠ *757 W. Hastings St., Downtown* ☎ *604/488–0672* ⊕ *www.sinclaircentre.com.*

Vancouver Art Gallery

MUSEUM | Canadian painter Emily Carr's haunting evocations of the British Columbian hinterland are among the attractions at western Canada's largest art gallery. Carr (1871–1945), a grocer's daughter from Victoria, BC, fell in love with the wilderness around her and shocked middle-class Victorian society by running off to paint it. Her work accentuates the mysticism and danger of BC's wilderness, and records the diminishing presence of native cultures during that era (there's something of a renaissance now). The gallery, which also hosts touring historical and contemporary exhibitions, is housed in a 1911 courthouse that Canadian architect Arthur Erickson redesigned in the early 1980s as part of the Robson Square redevelopment. Stone lions guard the steps to the Georgia Street side (the plaza is often the site of festivals and other events); the main entrance is accessed from Robson Square or Hornby Street. ⊠ *750 Hornby St., Downtown* ☎ *604/662–4719* ⊕ *www.vanartgallery.bc.ca* ◪ *C$24; higher for some exhibits; by donation Tues. 5–9.*

Vancouver Lookout Tower

VIEWPOINT | **FAMILY** | Resembling a flying saucer stuck atop a high-rise, the 553-foot-high Vancouver Lookout Tower has fabulous views of Vancouver and its surrounding landscapes—on a clear day, as far as Mt. Baker in Washington State. A glass elevator whizzes you up 50 stories to the circular observation deck, where knowledgeable guides point out the sights and give a (free) tour every hour on the hour. The top-floor restaurant (*604/669–2220* ⊕ *www.topofvancouver.com*) makes one complete revolution per hour; the elevator ride up is free for diners. Tickets are good all day, so you can visit in daytime and return for another look after dark. ⊠ *555 W. Hastings St., Downtown* ☎ *604/689–0421* ⊕ *www.vancouverlookout.com* ◪ *C$18.25.*

Canada Place, located along the waterfront, is a popular tourist destination.

Waterfront Station

BUILDING | This former Canadian Pacific Railway passenger terminal was built between 1912 and 1914 as the western terminus for Canada's transcontinental railway. After Canada's two major railways shifted their focus away from passenger service, the station became obsolete, but a 1978 renovation turned it into an office–retail complex and depot for SkyTrain, SeaBus, and the West Coast Express (a suburban commuter rail). In the main concourse, murals up near the ceiling depict the scenery travelers once saw on journeys across Canada. This is where you catch the SeaBus for the 13-minute trip across the harbor to the waterfront public market at Lonsdale Quay in North Vancouver. ✉ *601 W. Cordova St., Downtown.*

🍴 Restaurants

Downtown dining is a little bit of everything, from food trucks, cafés, and old-style diners to lively local bistros, upscale contemporary restaurants, and luxe hotel dining rooms.

Bel Café

$$ | CAFÉ | Run by the same team that oversees the adjacent Hawksworth Restaurant, this upscale little café at the Rosewood Hotel Georgia serves fine coffee, a few salads and sandwiches, and exquisite pastries, from colorful macarons to beautifully crafted fruit tarts. Downtown business types like to meet up here, and both shoppers and sightseers stop in to recharge; it's opposite the Vancouver Art Gallery and just a short stroll from Robson Street's boutiques. **Known for:** great coffee; beautiful pastries; busy meet-up venue. $ *Average main: C$13* ✉ *Rosewood Hotel Georgia, 801 W. Georgia St., Downtown* ☎ *604/673–7000* 🌐 *www.belcafe.com* 🕐 *No dinner.*

Boulevard Kitchen & Oyster Bar

$$$$ | SEAFOOD | Settle into a deep cream-toned banquette or nab a sidewalk table for a seafood-centric meal at this stylish spot in the Sutton Place Hotel that manages to feel both trendy and warm. Start with fresh local oysters or indulge in Canadian caviar from the nearby Sunshine Coast. **Known for:** strong BC wine list; local seafood; award-winning chefs. [$] *Average main: C$42* ✉ *Sutton Place Hotel, 845 Burrard St., Downtown* ☎ *604/642–2900* ⊕ *www.boulevardvancouver.ca.*

Café Medina

$$ | MEDITERRANEAN | For Mediterranean-inspired breakfast and lunch fare, from skillets piled high with eggs, roasted potatoes, and caramelized onions to Moroccan *tagine* stews, try this casually chic (and always busy) Downtown café just off Robson Street. Don't leave without sampling their specialty: Belgian waffles, with toppings like dark chocolate or salted caramel. **Known for:** Belgian waffles; breakfast skillets; friendly service. [$] *Average main: C$18* ✉ *L'Hermitage Hotel, 780 Richards St., Downtown* ☎ *604/879–3114* ⊕ *www.medinacafe. com* ☾ *No dinner.*

Caffè Artigiano

$ | CAFÉ | Some of Vancouver's best coffee is served at the several locations of Caffè Artigiano, where the baristas have won prizes for their latte art—making patterns in the froth. Come for the java, although you can assuage your hunger with a pastry or sandwich, too. **Known for:** excellent coffee; latte art; award-winning baristas. [$] *Average main: C$6* ✉ *1101 W. Pender, Downtown* ☎ *604/685–5333* ⊕ *www. caffeartigiano.com* ☾ *No dinner.*

Chambar

$$$$ | BELGIAN | In this hip, brick-walled eatery, classic Belgian dishes are reinvented with flavors from North Africa and beyond. The *moules* (mussels) are justifiably popular, either steamed in white wine or sauced with exotic smoked chilis, cilantro, and coconut cream. **Known for:** moules frites; Belgian beer; specialty meats. [$] *Average main: C$32* ✉ *568 Beatty St., Downtown* ☎ *604/879–7119* ⊕ *www.chambar.com.*

Cibo Trattoria

$$$ | ITALIAN | The space is fun and funky—a mix of early-1900s architectural details, modern furnishings, and oversize pop art—and the seasonally changing menu of updated Italian fare is creative and delicious. The lengthy wine list emphasizes Italian labels, but BC is ably represented. **Known for:** seasonal Italian dishes; three-course prix fixe; funky decor. [$] *Average main: C$30* ✉ *Moda Hotel, 900 Seymour St., Downtown* ☎ *604/602–9570* ⊕ *www.cibotrattoria. com.*

CinCin

$$$$ | ITALIAN | Gold walls, terra-cotta tiles, and a crowd-pleasing modern Italian menu make this Tuscan-inspired restaurant appropriate for a business meal, a romantic tête-à-tête, or a relaxing dinner after a long day. The heated terrace, shielded with greenery, feels a long way from busy Robson Street below. **Known for:** wood-fired grill; lively marble bar; seasonal menus. [$] *Average main: C$35* ✉ *1154 Robson St., Downtown* ☎ *604/688–7338* ⊕ *www.cincin.net* ☾ *No lunch.*

Coast Restaurant

$$$$ | SEAFOOD | If a fish house makes you think of lobster traps and buoys, you'll be pleasantly surprised when you come by this see-and-be-seen two-floor seafood palace. There's plenty of bling to be found here, from the shimmering lights to the sparkle-sporting patrons. **Known for:** lively atmosphere; fresh seafood; excellent steak. [$] *Average main: C$40* ✉ *1054 Alberni St., Downtown* ☎ *604/685–5010* ⊕ *www.coastrestaurant.ca.*

Glowbal

$$$ | CANADIAN | The two-level, bustling eatery never seems to lose its energetic vibe in the seasonal fare it presents or in the patron it attracts. Whether it's a seat at the bar beside the open kitchen, a gathering by the fire, a tête-â-tête in a cozy booth or joining the throng on the heated outdoor patio, this place rocks. **Known for:** happening vibe; a please-everyone menu; 2:30 happy hour. [$] *Average main: C$28* ✉ *Telus Garden, 590 West Georgia St., Downtown* ☎ *604/602-0835* 🌐 *www.glowbalgroup.com.*

Hawksworth Restaurant

$$$$ | MODERN CANADIAN | With sleek white tables and sparkling chandeliers, chef David Hawksworth's modish restaurant welcomes locals toasting new clients or celebrating a romantic anniversary. The food (and the crowd) is suave and swanky, too. **Known for:** upscale dining; seasonal menus; flavor combinations and presentation. [$] *Average main: C$45* ✉ *Rosewood Hotel Georgia, 801 W. Georgia St., Downtown* ☎ *604/673–7000* 🌐 *www.hawksworthrestaurant.com.*

Hydra Restaurant

$$$$ | MEDITERRANEAN | Located in the same former Stock Exchange building as the luxe EXchange Hotel, Hydra Estiatoria transports you to the Greek islands. Check in at the long bar for mezzes and cocktails, including items from the raw bar such as ceviche, or linger over specialties that include forno-roasted leg of lamb, pan-roasted salmon, and the catch of the day either grilled or baked. **Known for:** platters and sharing plates; friendly service; great atmosphere. [$] *Average main: C$32* ✉ *EXchange Hotel, 825 West Pender St., Downtown* ☎ *604/416-0880* 🌐 *www.hydravancouver.com* ⏲ *No dinner Mon.*

Japadog

$ | ECLECTIC | There might be other places in the world that sell Japanese-style hot dogs but the phenomenon is so very multiculti Vancouver and this storefront is the sit-down spin-off of a wildly successful food cart with a loyal following. Bratwurst and wieners are topped with teriyaki sauce, nori, and other Asian condiments. **Known for:** Japanese hot dogs; Asian condiments; a Vancouver icon. [$] *Average main: C$7* ✉ *530 Robson St., Downtown* ☎ *604/569–1158* 🌐 *www.japadog.com* 💳 *No credit cards.*

Joe Fortes Seafood and Chop House

$$$$ | SEAFOOD | Named for a much-loved English Bay bartender and lifeguard from the city's early days (he arrived in Vancouver in 1885), this lively brasserie has a piano bar, bistro, oyster bar, and a delightful covered rooftop patio. The menu is wide-ranging, but steaks, chops, and generous portions of fresh seafood are the main draw. **Known for:** fresh oysters; seafood tower; exceptional service. [$] *Average main: C$38* ✉ *777 Thurlow St., at Robson St., Downtown* ☎ *604/669–1940* 🌐 *www.joefortes.ca.*

Kirin Restaurant Downtown

$$$$ | CHINESE | A striking silver mural of a *kirin* (a mythical dragonlike creature) presides over this elegant two-tier restaurant, one of the best choices for Chinese food Downtown. Specialties here are northern Chinese and Szechuan dishes, which tend to be richer and spicier than the Cantonese cuisine served at Kirin's other locations. **Known for:** spicy jellyfish; Peking duck; dim sum. [$] *Average main: C$32* ✉ *1172 Alberni St., Downtown* ☎ *604/682–8833* 🌐 *www.kirinrestaurants.com.*

★ **Le Crocodile**

$$$$ | FRENCH | Chefs prepare classic Alsatian-inspired food—including the signature onion tart—at this long-established Downtown restaurant which sets the standard for French cuisine in Vancouver. Despite the white-tablecloth sophistication, the breezy curtains, golden yellow walls, and burgundy banquettes keep things cozy. **Known for:** lobster with beurre blanc; veal medallions; truffle omelet. $ *Average main: C$38 ⊠ 100–909 Burrard St., Downtown* ☎ *604/669–4298* ⊕ *www.lecrocodilerestaurant.com* ⊗ *Closed Sun. No lunch Sat.*

★ Miku Waterfront

$$$ | SUSHI | This is fusion sushi so purists be warned. The restaurant introduced Vancouver to flame-seared *aburi* and also pressed *oshi* sushi to Canada, and its imaginative combinations since have certainly made their mark. **Known for:** extraordinary sushi; stunning views; sake pairings. $ *Average main: C$22 ⊠ 200 Granville Square, Suite 70, Downtown* ⊹ *Beside Canada Place* ☎ *604/568-3900* ⊕ *www.mikurestaurant.com.*

★ Nightingale Restaurant

$$ | SUSHI | A former gentlemen's club turned upscale tapas-style bistro turns shared dining, as in generous small plates, into a deliciously classy experience. Roasted cauliflower, orange braised fennel, and buttermilk fried chicken with spiced maple syrup come alongside oven-fired pizzas with toppings such as roasted mushroom and Fontina, bison cheek, and braised meatballs with San Marzano tomatoes and pine nuts. **Known for:** great sharing plates; historic location; renowned chef. $ *Average main: C$18 ⊠ 1017 West Hastings St., Downtown* ☎ *604/695-9500* ⊕ *www.hawknightingale.com.*

Royal Dinette

$$$ | MODERN CANADIAN | FAMILY | House-made pickles and preserves line the walls of this bright and modern "farm to Downtown" hot spot, extending the availability of BC produce throughout the drizzly Vancouver winter. Don't let the old-fashioned diner-style counter fool you—the food here is seasonal and local with menus changing quarterly to showcase what's fresh. **Known for:** house-made pasta; gluten-free dining; local ingredients. $ *Average main: C$25 ⊠ 905 Dunsmuir St., Downtown* ☎ *604/974–8077* ⊕ *www.royaldinette.ca* ⊗ *Closed Sun. No lunch Sat.*

Sciué

$ | CAFÉ | Inspired by the street foods of Rome, this cafeteria-style Italian bakery–café (Sciué is pronounced "Shoe-eh") starts the day serving espresso and pastries, then moves to panini, soups, and pastas. One specialty is the *pane romano*, essentially a thick-crust pizza, sold by weight. **Known for:** thick-crust pizza; lunchtime crowds; fast service. $ *Average main: C$12 ⊠ 110–800 W. Pender St., Downtown* ☎ *604/602–7263* ⊕ *www.sciue.ca* ⊗ *No dinner.*

🛏 Hotels

Broadly speaking, to stay Downtown is to pay a premium. Most of the top-star hotels are in the Downtown core where great dining, shopping, and many attractions are nearby. Several have spas, complimentary bicycles, and top-notch restaurants. A word to the wise: to offset the competitive nature of online booking engines, some properties are experimenting with '"facilities fees"' to include Wi-Fi and the use of a gym, for example, and even charging for daily towel service in the name of the environment. Be forewarned and check inclusions upon booking.

The Burrard

$$$ | HOTEL | Freebies abound at the fun and funky Burrard, including water in recyclable bottles, biodegradable bath products, calls to anywhere in North America, Wi-Fi, and movie channels on the huge flat-screen TVs. **Pros:** doesn't take itself too seriously; short walk to the heart of Downtown; complimentary bicycles and umbrellas. **Cons:** a/c units

are quite noisy; opposite a hospital, so ambulance sirens might be disturbing; rooms on the small side. [$] *Rooms from: C$255* ✉ *1100 Burrard St., Downtown* ☎ *604/681–2331* 🌐 *www.theburrard.com* 🛏 *72 rooms* 🍴 *No meals.*

Century Plaza Hotel & Spa

$$$ | **HOTEL** | **FAMILY** | Full kitchens and an indoor pool make this 30-story Downtown high-rise a good family choice. **Pros:** pampering spa; on-site laundry; large rooms. **Cons:** staff not always helpful; next to hospital with the occasional noisy ambulance siren; overnight parking C$17. [$] *Rooms from: C$300* ✉ *1015 Burrard St., Downtown* ☎ *604/687–0575, 800/663–1818* 🌐 *www.century-plaza.com* 🛏 *240 rooms* 🍴 *No meals.*

Delta Vancouver Suites by Marriott

$$$$ | **HOTEL** | Exuding a contemporary 5th Avenue swank throughout, this upscale, all-suites business hotel is centrally located in Downtown Vancouver. **Pros:** fitness center open 24 hours; friendly service; windows that actually open. **Cons:** one-way roads make getting here a bit of a headache; overnight parking C$37; 3 blocks from less salubrious part of town. [$] *Rooms from: C$625* ✉ *550 W. Hastings St., Downtown* ☎ *604/689–8188* 🌐 *www.deltavancouversuites.ca* 🛏 *225 rooms* 🍴 *No meals.*

EXchange Hotel

$$$$ | **HOTEL** | Opened December 2018, the EXchange is a chic and contemporary conversion of the 1929 former stock exchange building, the largest heritage conversion in the city. **Pros:** central location; modern retro atmosphere; enthusiastic staff. **Cons:** room climate control slow to react; no stair access to rooms without staff enabling access; gym shared with building residents. [$] *Rooms from: C$675* ✉ *475 Howe St., Downtown* ☎ *604/563-4693, 833/381-7623* 🌐 *www.exchangehotelvan.com* 🛏 *202* 🍴 *No meals.*

Executive Hotel Le Soleil

$$$$ | **HOTEL** | The staff prides itself on attentive service at this classy, old-world-style boutique hotel with luxurious touches. **Pros:** chic and romantic; central location; Aveda bath products. **Cons:** no on-site spa; room views of surrounding buildings; expensive to park. [$] *Rooms from: C$630* ✉ *567 Hornby St., Downtown* ☎ *604/632–3000, 877/632–3030* 🌐 *www.lesoleilhotels.com* 🛏 *113 rooms* 🍴 *No meals.*

Fairmont Hotel Vancouver

$$$$ | **HOTEL** | The copper roof of this 1939 château-style hotel dominates Vancouver's skyline, and the elegantly restored property is considered the city's gracious grande dame—aptly referred to as the Castle in the City. **Pros:** full-service spa; great location for shopping; stunning architecture. **Cons:** standard room sizes vary greatly; pricey parking; a busy convention hotel. [$] *Rooms from: C$549* ✉ *900 W. Georgia St., Downtown* ☎ *604/684–3131, 866/540–4452* 🌐 *www.fairmont.com/hotelvancouver* 🛏 *557 rooms* 🍴 *No meals.*

Fairmont Pacific Rim

$$$$ | **HOTEL** | Overlooking the Downtown waterfront, and across from the impressive convention center, this ultraluxurious 47-story tower represents the Fairmont's first foray into the condominium-hotel format. **Pros:** prime location; Fairmont high quality throughout; hip and happening vibe. **Cons:** pricey all round; attracts a lot of business- and convention-goers; a bit pretentious. [$] *Rooms from: C$720* ✉ *1038 Canada Pl., Downtown* ☎ *877/900–5350* 🌐 *www.fairmont.com/pacific-rim-vancouver* 🛏 *367 rooms* 🍴 *No meals.*

Fairmont Waterfront Hotel

$$$$ | **HOTEL** | Stunning views of the harbor, mountains, and Stanley Park from the floor-to-ceiling windows of the guest rooms are one of the highlights of this luxuriously modern 23-story hotel across the street from Vancouver's cruise-ship terminal. **Pros:** harbor views; proximity to the waterfront; inviting pool terrace. **Cons:** long elevator queues; busy lobby lounge; lots of cruise passengers and tours groups. [$] *Rooms from: C$620* ✉ *900 Canada Pl. Way, Downtown* ☎ *866/540–4509* 🌐 *www.fairmont.com/waterfront-vancouver* 🛏 *513 rooms* 🍴 *No meals.*

Kingston Hotel
$$ | B&B/INN | Convenient to shopping and nightlife, the budget-friendly, family-run Kingston occupies a four-story elevator building dating back to 1910—this is the type of lodging you'd expect to find in Europe. **Pros:** great location; breakfast included; single rooms available. **Cons:** some shared bathrooms; limited amenities; no in-room safe. [$] *Rooms from: C$204* ✉ *757 Richards St., Downtown* ☎ *604/684–9024* 🌐 *www.kingstonhotelvancouver.com* 🛏 *51 rooms, 13 with bath* 🍴 *Free breakfast.*

L'Hermitage Hotel
$$$$ | HOTEL | Get beyond the marble floors, silk and velvet walls, and gold-cushion benches in the lobby and you'll discover a warm residential character at this boutique hotel. **Pros:** uptown hotel with a refreshingly residential quality; excellent concierge; complimentary shuttle service. **Cons:** one-way streets can make driving to the hotel frustrating; awkwardly placed/inadequate outlets; limited counter space in bathroom. [$] *Rooms from: C$495* ✉ *788 Richards St., Downtown* ☎ *778/327–4100, 888/855–1050* 🌐 *www.lhermitagevancouver.com* 🛏 *60 rooms* 🍴 *No meals.*

Loden Hotel
$$$$ | HOTEL | This chic, designer boutique hotel has all manner of perks to enhance your stay, including rooms equipped with Wi-Fi, TVs with oversize LCD screens, a Nespresso machine, and a yoga mat for a stretch and sun salutation. **Pros:** quiet, central location; free Downtown car service for shopping and theater pickups; 1,400-square-foot BeFit Studio. **Cons:** locals tend to snag best lounge and restaurant seats; no pool; a 15-minute walk to the city center. [$] *Rooms from: C$612* ✉ *1177 Melville St., Downtown* ☎ *877/225–6336* 🌐 *www.theloden.com* 🛏 *77 rooms* 🍴 *No meals.*

Metropolitan Hotel Vancouver
$$$$ | HOTEL | "The Met," as the locals call it, is one of the city's top business-district hotels, with design elements that follow the principles of feng shui, from the two lions guarding the entrance to the spacious, luxurious rooms. **Pros:** luxurious rooms; excellent restaurant; pet-friendly. **Cons:** somewhat pretentious; very business oriented; dated decor. [$] *Rooms from: C$525* ✉ *645 Howe St., Downtown* ☎ *604/687–1122, 800/667–2300* 🌐 *www.metropolitan.com/vanc* 🛏 *197 rooms* 🍴 *No meals.*

Pan Pacific Vancouver
$$$$ | HOTEL | Located in the waterfront Canada Place complex, the sophisticated Pan Pacific has easy access to the city's convention center and the cruise-ship terminal. **Pros:** lovely harbor views; staff has a "go the extra mile" attitude; fabulous spa. **Cons:** atrium is open to the convention center, so it's often full of executives talking shop; parking is expensive; Wi-Fi is not free. [$] *Rooms from: C$529* ✉ *999 Canada Pl., Downtown* ☎ *604/662–8111, 800/663–1515 in Canada, 800/937–1515 in U.S.* 🌐 *www.panpacific.com/en/hotels-resorts/canada/vancouver.html* 🛏 *504 rooms* 🍴 *No meals.*

Pinnacle Hotel Harbourfront
$$$$ | HOTEL | FAMILY | A quality hotel with large rooms, the Pinnacle Hotel Harbourfront is a good base for exploring Downtown by foot, bicycle, or car. **Pros:** surrounding financial district is quiet at night; near the waterfront; great views. **Cons:** a five-block walk to shopping and

theaters; a five-block walk to Stanley Park; reception at the top of stairs. [$] *Rooms from: C$399* ⊠ *1133 W. Hastings St., Downtown* ☎ *604/689–9211, 844/337–3118* ⊕ *www.pinnacleharbourfronthotel.com* ⤳ *442 rooms* ¶○¶ *No meals.*

★ **Rosewood Hotel Georgia**

$$$$ | **HOTEL** | The classy Rosewood is one of the city's most historic properties: the 1927 Georgian Revival building once welcomed prestigious guests such as Elvis Presley and Katharine Hepburn. **Pros:** at the center of the city's action; top-rated spa; destination restaurant. **Cons:** expensive valet parking; restaurant can get very busy; on Vancouver's busiest thoroughfare. [$] *Rooms from: C$566* ⊠ *801 W. Georgia St., Downtown* ☎ *604/682–5566, 888/767–3966* ⊕ *www.rosewoodhotels.com/en/hotel-georgia-vancouver/* ⤳ *156 rooms* ¶○¶ *No meals.*

★ **Shangri-La Hotel, Vancouver**

$$$$ | **HOTEL** | On the first 15 floors of the tallest building in Vancouver—a 62-story tower of angled glass studded with gold squares that glint in the sunshine—is this upscale Asian chain's first hotel in North America (the second is in Toronto). **Pros:** first-rate concierge service; not as expensive as you might think; central location. **Cons:** on the city's busiest thoroughfare; hotel's driveway is hard to find (at back of property); restaurant and lounge feel hidden away. [$] *Rooms from: C$428* ⊠ *1128 W. Georgia St., Downtown* ☎ *604/689–1120* ⊕ *www.shangri-la.com/vancouver* ⤳ *119 rooms* ¶○¶ *No meals.*

Sheraton Vancouver Wall Centre

$$$$ | **HOTEL** | This stunning pair of ultra-modern glass high-rises is on Downtown's highest ground, which means that the top floors of both towers have unrivaled views of the water, mountains, and city skyline. **Pros:** amazing views from higher floors; dog-friendly; pool and fitness center. **Cons:** no on-site spa; although Downtown, a bit of a walk from

the action; hotel layout is confusing. [$] *Rooms from: C$380* ⊠ *1088 Burrard St., Downtown* ☎ *604/331–1000, 866/716–8134* ⊕ *www.sheratonvancouver.com* ⤳ *745 rooms* ¶○¶ *No meals.*

St. Regis Hotel

$$$$ | **HOTEL** | It's the oldest continuously operating hotel in the city, but edgy, modern decor livens up the 1913 boutique property, and Canadian artwork (including in the stairwells) and heritage furnishings gives it a unique sense of place. **Pros:** hot location; complimentary global long-distance calling; à la carte breakfast for two. **Cons:** no views; slow elevator; front rooms can be noisy. [$] *Rooms from: C$419* ⊠ *602 Dunsmuir St., Downtown* ☎ *604/681–1135, 800/770–7929* ⊕ *www.stregishotel.com* ⤳ *65 rooms* ¶○¶ *Free breakfast.*

Sutton Place Hotel Vancouver

$$$$ | **HOTEL** | This refined, European-style hotel has gracious service, elegantly furnished rooms, and a location close to Downtown. **Pros:** terrific seafood restaurant; wonderful spa; great concierge. **Cons:** spa gets booked quickly; expensive parking; occasional sirens from adjacent fire station. [$] *Rooms from: C$491* ⊠ *845 Burrard St., Downtown* ☎ *604/682–5511, 866/378–8866* ⊕ *www.vancouver.suttonplace.com* ⤳ *396 rooms, 164 apartments* ¶○¶ *No meals.*

Trump International Hotel and Tower Vancouver

$$$$ | **HOTEL** | Rising over 606-foot high, the twisting tower ensures that every room is unique with curved windows showing off superb views. **Pros:** great location; lavish spa and indoor pool; excellent service. **Cons:** entrance is actually at the back of the hotel; lobby is small and plain; standard rooms on the modest side. [$] *Rooms from: C$575* ⊠ *1160 West Georgia St., Downtown* ☎ *604/979-8888, 866/660-9243* ⊕ *www.trumphotels.com/vancouver* ⤳ *147 rooms* ¶○¶ *No meals.*

Vancouver Marriott Pinnacle Downtown Hotel

$$$$ | HOTEL | Close to the cruise ship terminal and midway between the central business district and Stanley Park, the Marriott Pinnacle is a sleek, large-scale hotel with stunning views—once you get past the rather jumbled welcome of the atrium lobby trying to be all things from lounge to bar to restaurant to registration area. **Pros:** accessible to waterfront; walking distance to Stanley Park; great happy hour prices. **Cons:** check-in time is 4 pm; generic decor; overnight parking C$38. Ⓢ *Rooms from: C$408* ✉ *1128 W. Hastings St., Downtown* ☎ *604/684–1128, 800/207–4150* ⊕ *www.vancouvermarriottpinnacle.com* ⤴ *438 rooms* ⦿ *No meals.*

★ Victorian Hotel

$$$ | B&B/INN | This handsome boutique hotel, on the edge of Downtown and historic Gastown, is one of Vancouver's best values—note that some rooms have shared bathrooms. **Pros:** nice small-hotel feel; complimentary continental breakfast; historic atmosphere. **Cons:** take a cab after midnight in this area; some shared bathrooms; no in-room safes. Ⓢ *Rooms from: C$282* ✉ *514 Homer St., Downtown* ☎ *604/681–6369, 877/681–6369* ⊕ *www.victorianhotel.ca* ⤴ *47 rooms, 28 with private baths* ⦿ *Free breakfast.*

★ Wedgewood Hotel & Spa

$$$$ | HOTEL | A member of the exclusive Relais & Châteaux group, the luxurious, family-owned Wedgewood is all about pampering. **Pros:** personalized service; great location close to shops; Bacchus Lounge is a destination in its own right. **Cons:** hotel fills up quickly, book well ahead; Bacchus Lounge can get very busy; no pool. Ⓢ *Rooms from: C$435* ✉ *845 Hornby St., Downtown* ☎ *604/689–7777, 800/663–0666* ⊕ *www.wedgewoodhotel.com* ⤴ *83 rooms* ⦿ *No meals.*

Westin Grand, Vancouver

$$$$ | HOTEL | With its dramatic modern design and all-suites layout, the Westin Grand is one of Vancouver's most stylish hotels, although not as '"grand"' as its name suggests. **Pros:** walking distance to major theater and stadium events; within three blocks of designer shopping district; great staff. **Cons:** escalator access to reception; small lobby; slow elevators. Ⓢ *Rooms from: C$460* ✉ *433 Robson St., Downtown* ☎ *604/602–1999, 888/680–9393* ⊕ *www.westingrandvancouver.com* ⤴ *206 suites* ⦿ *No meals.*

YWCA Hotel

$$ | HOTEL | FAMILY | A secure, modern high-rise in the heart of the entertainment district, the YWCA Hotel has bright, comfortable rooms—a few big enough to sleep five. **Pros:** clean and friendly; access to fitness center; a terrific alternative to hostels. **Cons:** some shared bathrooms; no on-site restaurant; basic amenities. Ⓢ *Rooms from: C$136* ✉ *733 Beatty St., Downtown* ☎ *604/895–5830, 800/663–1424* ⊕ *www.ywcavan.org/hotel* ⤴ *155 rooms, 52 with bath* ⦿ *No meals.*

🅨 Nightlife

Granville Street is the flashy entertainment drag at the center of Downtown and, in general, the area bars fill up after work. There are usually crowds of young clubbers to be found when the clock passes midnight. Meanwhile, music venues and chic hotel lounges get busy around the business district, and a posh crowd of glitterati flocks to small wine bars or patios on the Coal Harbour waterfront.

BARS
Bacchus

PIANO BARS/LOUNGES | Always an elegant choice, the lounge at Bacchus, in the Wedgewood Hotel, is a gathering place for Vancouver's movers and shakers. There's music every evening, as well as classic cocktails. ✉ *Wedgewood Hotel,*

845 Hornby St., Downtown ☎ *604/608–5319* ⊕ *www.wedgewoodhotel.com.*

Hawksworth Bar and Lounge

BARS/PUBS | You'll find quality cocktails blended with house-made bitters, fresh herbs, and other local ingredients at this Vancouver hot spot, which, although it's leather-paneled and clubby, is surprisingly unstuffy. Also in the Rosewood Hotel Georgia are the narrow, mahogany-paneled 1927 Lobby Lounge, the open-air rooftop oasis of Reflections, and posh basement speakeasy Prohibition. ⊠ *Rosewood Hotel Georgia, 801 W. Georgia St., Downtown* ☎ *604/673–7000* ⊕ *www.hawksworthrestaurant.com.*

Johnnie Fox's Irish Snug

BARS/PUBS | This wee sliver of a pub pulls pints of Guinness and other Emerald Isle beers. It's a cozy nook, where expats find a home-away-from-home and locals come for a casual drink amid the Granville Street neon lights. ⊠ *1033 Granville St., Downtown* ☎ *604/685–4946* ⊕ *www. johnniefox.ca.*

★ Long Table Distillery

WINE BARS—NIGHTLIFE | A 14-foot communal table crafted from a redwood plank is the heart of this tasting room and distillery, which produces small-batch gins, vodka, and special liqueurs. The house-made spirits are the basis of excellent cocktails, and though the tasting room has fairly limited hours (Friday for gin and tonics, Thursday and Saturday for cocktails), the family charm makes the experience a worthwhile treat. Plan ahead, as it's closed Sunday to Wednesday. ⊠ *1451 Hornby St., Downtown* ☎ *604/266–0177* ⊕ *www.longtabledistillery.com.*

The Morrissey

BARS/PUBS | There's a melancholy, lost-in-time feel to this quintessential Granville Street bar; the decor features aged chandeliers, a fireplace, and old-world kitsch. It's the kind of place where rock 'n rollers (old and new) hang their shingle into the early hours. There's a wide selection of beer, comfy seating, and dark corners in which to disappear. ⊠ *1227 Granville St., Downtown* ☎ *604/682–0909* ⊕ *www. themorrisseypub.ca.*

★ Tap & Barrel

BARS/PUBS | The 360-degree views from this convention center patio take in Stanley Park, the seaplane terminal, and the North Shore Mountains. You can sit inside, amid the wooden casks of wine, but waiting for a seat on the deck is worth it if the weather even hints at sunshine. There's another location—and similarly large patio—on False Creek (*75 Athlete's Way*), and yet another at North Vancouver's Shipyards district with equally stunning harbor views on a giant patio. ⊠ *1055 Canada Pl., Downtown* ☎ *604/235–9827* ⊕ *www.tapandbarrel. com.*

Uva Wine & Cocktail Bar

WINE BARS—NIGHTLIFE | At street level in the century-old Moda Hotel, Uva puts a modern spin on the Italian wine bar concept, with bold decor and sleek furnishings. The well-dressed crowd comes for the not-too-wild atmosphere, often for a drink before heading to one of nearby Granville Street's performance venues, particularly The Orpheum across the road. ⊠ *Moda Hotel, 900 Seymour St., Downtown* ☎ *604/632–9560* ⊕ *www. uvavancouver.com.*

Wine Room

WINE BARS—NIGHTLIFE | The Wine Room is devoted to nurturing the inner oenophile in all of us by offering wines usually only available by the bottle—this is one of a growing number of bars offering by-the-glass service, thanks to cutting-edge, wine-dispensing technology. It's part of the Joey Bentall One restaurant but has its own dedicated entrance off Pender Street. ⊠ *507 Burrard St., Downtown* ☎ *604/915–5639* ⊕ *www.joeyrestaurants. com.*

The Yale Saloon

BARS/PUBS | Home to all things country, The Yale attracts a friendly crowd. There's Southern-style family eats from a huge in-house smoker, rockabilly music, and even a mechanical bull. Line dancing lessons and live music gets raucous on some nights. ✉ *1300 Granville St., Downtown* ☎ *604/428–9253* ⊕ *www.yalesaloon.com.*

DANCE CLUBS

Cabana Lounge

DANCE CLUBS | Bask in the aura of South Beach with fluorescent colors, chic cabanas, and a dance floor beneath the boughs of an acai tree. Local and international DJs keep the energy high and happening. You'll want to dress to impress! ✉ *1163 Granville St., Downtown* ☎ *778/251-3335* ⊕ *www.cabanavancouver.com.*

Commodore Ballroom

MUSIC CLUBS | This 1929 dance hall has been restored to its art deco glory, complete with massive dance floor and state-of-the-art sound system. Indie rock bands and renowned DJs play here most nights. ✉ *868 Granville St., Downtown* ☎ *604/739–4550, 855/985–5000 tickets* ⊕ *www.commodoreballroom.com.*

The Red Room

DANCE CLUBS | A club for the crowds featuring a sunken dance floor and a mix of styles including reggae, salsa, hip-hop, merengue, and top-40 faves. ✉ *398 Richards St., Downtown* ☎ *604/687-5007* ⊕ *www.redroomvancouver.com.*

MUSIC: ROCK AND BLUES

Vogue Theatre

MUSIC CLUBS | A former art deco movie palace, the Vogue hosts a variety of concerts by local and visiting performers. ✉ *918 Granville St., Downtown* ☎ *888/732–1682* ⊕ *www.voguetheatre.com.*

Craft Brews Ⓨ

In the past few years, dozens of craft breweries have popped up around Vancouver, most of which can be found in East Vancouver. Make an afternoon out of it, as their close proximity to one another make it easy to walk or bike to a few. Favorites include Red Truck Beer Company (✉ *295 E. 1st Ave.*) for their outdoor patio, yummy food, and country feel, and Storm Brewing (✉ *310 Commercial Dr.*) for their experimental beers and grungy, authentic vibe. Check out ⊕ *www.craftbeervancouver.ca* for a complete city craft brewery map and let the tasting begin!

🎭 Performing Arts

CLASSICAL MUSIC

Vancouver Opera

OPERA | Stepping away from a season of performances, the city's opera company stages occasional works plus a three-week festival in May at the Queen Elizabeth Theatre and plaza. ✉ *Queen Elizabeth Theatre, 650 Hamilton St., Downtown* ☎ *604/683–0222* ⊕ *www.vancouveropera.ca.*

Vancouver Symphony Orchestra

MUSIC | The resident company at the Orpheum Theatre presents classical and popular music. Some of their performances are at other city venues such as the Chan Centre *(6265 Crescent Rd., Point Grey)*. ✉ *601 Smithe St., at Seymour St., Downtown* ☎ *604/876–3434* ⊕ *www.vancouversymphony.ca.*

DANCE

Ballet British Columbia

DANCE | Innovative dances and timeless classics by internationally acclaimed choreographers are presented by

Ballet BC. Most performances are at the Queen Elizabeth Theatre (*650 Hamilton St.*). ✉ *601 Smithe St., Downtown* ☏ *604/732–5003, 855/985–2787 tickets* ⊕ *www.balletbc.com.*

The Dance Centre

DANCE | The hub for dance in British Columbia, this striking former bank building with an art deco facade hosts full-scale performances by national and international artists, informal showcases, and also classes and workshops. There are often informal noon performances as part of the Discover Dance! series. ✉ *677 Davie St., Scotiabank Dance Centre, Downtown* ☏ *604/606–6400* ⊕ *www.thedancecentre.ca.*

FILM

Locals sometimes refer to Vancouver as Hollywood North, mostly because of the frequent film and television shoots around town. Movie theaters featuring first- and second-run, underground, experimental, alternative, and classic films make up the urban fabric. Here's a tip from the locals: tickets are reduced-price on Tuesday at most chain-owned movie theaters.

Fans of Vancouver

FILM | FAMILY | Movie buffs will love these behind-the-scenes, 45- to 75-minute tours of how Vancouver morphs into incarnations featured in films including *50 Shades of Grey, Supernatural, Dead Pool, Flash, Ghost Protocol,*and many others. Tours start at different Downtown points; all bookings are online. ✉ *Downtown* ⊕ *www.fansofvancouver.com* 🎟 *C$40.*

Pacific Cinémathèque

FILM | FAMILY | This not-for-profit society is dedicated to all things celluloid, from exhibitions and lectures to independent and international features. Cinema Sundays can be good for families (depending on the screening), with discussions, games, or activities following the film. ✉ *1131 Howe St., Downtown* ☏ *604/688–3456* ⊕ *www.thecinematheque.ca.*

THEATER

Queen Elizabeth Theatre

DANCE | Ballet, opera, touring Broadway musicals, and other large-scale events take place at the Queen Elizabeth. It seats more than 2,700 people, making it one of the largest proscenium theaters in Canada. ✉ *650 Hamilton St., Downtown* ☏ *604/665–3050* ⊕ *www.queenelizabeththeatre.org.*

🛍 Shopping

The main Downtown shopping streets radiate from the intersection of Granville and West Georgia streets. In this Downtown area, shoppers will find major department stores, including the Bay, Nordstrom, and Holt Renfrew, as well as lots of North American chains.

ART AND ANTIQUES

DoDa Antiques

ANTIQUES/COLLECTIBLES | Concentrating on mid-20th-century jewelry, ceramics, glass, paintings, and prints, this old-timey treasure box is crammed with intriguing finds. It also stocks First Nations art. ✉ *434 Richards St., Downtown* ☏ *604/602–0559* ⊕ *www.dodaantiques.com.*

BOOKS

MacLeod's Books

BOOKS/STATIONERY | One of the city's best antiquarian and used-book stores, this jam-packed shop is a treasure trove of titles from mainstream to wildly eclectic. ✉ *455 W. Pender St., Downtown* ☏ *604/681–7654.*

CLOTHING

Leone

CLOTHING | Marble alcoves in an elegantly palatial store set the scene for men's and women's fashions by Versace, Alexander McQueen, Moschino, Dior, Miu Miu, Pinko, and others. On the lower level is L-2 Leone, where you'll find edgier fashions and an Italian café. ✉ *Sinclair Centre, 757 W. Hastings St., Downtown* ☏ *604/683–1133* ⊕ *www.leone.ca.*

Did You Know?

The view from Stanley Park out over the marina and the harbor shows just how close this fabulous 1,000-plus-acre park is to Downtown.

★ lululemon athletica

CLOTHING | Power-yoga devotees, soccer moms, and anyone who likes casual, comfy clothes covets the fashionable, well-constructed workout wear with the stylized "A" insignia from this Vancouver-based company. In addition to this flagship location at 2123 West 4th Avenue in Kitsilano, there are several branches around town, including a lululemon lab at 50 Powell Street in Gastown that showcases the latest athleisure lines. ✉ *970 Robson St., Downtown* ☎ *604/681–3118* ⊕ *www.lululemon.com.*

DEPARTMENT STORES

★ Holt Renfrew

CLOTHING | This is Canada's ritziest department store, a swanky showcase for international high fashion and accessories for men and women. Think Prada, Dolce & Gabbana, and other designer labels. ✉ *Pacific Centre, 737 Dunsmuir St., Downtown* ☎ *604/681–3121* ⊕ *www. holtrenfrew.com.*

Hudson's Bay

DEPARTMENT STORES | A Canadian institution (though it's now American-owned), the Bay was founded as part of the fur trade in the 17th century. There's a whole department selling the signature tricolor blankets and other Canadiana. On the lower level, the Topshop and Topman boutiques carry imports from the trendy British retailer. ✉ *674 Granville St., at Georgia St., Downtown* ☎ *604/681–6211* ⊕ *www.thebay.com.*

★ Nordstrom

DEPARTMENT STORES | Nordstrom Vancouver, the chain's flagship store in Canada, sizzles with fashion buzz alongside the well-known Nordstrom-style service. Three elegantly designed floors showcase label boutiques (think Saint Laurent, Valentino, and Stella McCartney), lots of Canadian designers, and themed pop-up shops, and include a restaurant, a lounge, and a wealth of concierge services, from personal stylists to free

Downtown delivery. ✉ *799 Robson St., Downtown* ☎ *604/699–2100* ⊕ *shop. nordstrom.com.*

Winners

DEPARTMENT STORES | This discount department store chain is heaven for bargain hunters. Among the regularly changing stock, you might unearth great deals on designer fashions, shoes, and housewares. ✉ *798 Granville St., at Robson St., Downtown* ☎ *604/683–1058* ⊕ *www. winners.ca.*

FOOD

Purdy's Chocolates

FOOD/CANDY | A chocolatier since 1907, Purdy's once made a liqueur-filled line, which was hawked to Americans during Prohibition. These days, Purdy's purple-foiled boxes of chocolate temptations are a popular gift. Outlets are scattered throughout the city. ✉ *Pacific Centre, 700 W. Georgia St., Downtown* ☎ *604/683–3467* ⊕ *www.purdys.com.*

Urban Fare

FOOD/CANDY | Vancouver's most stylish supermarket brims to the rafters with mouthwatering food displays that come from all corners of the globe, plus upmarket everyday items and lots of foodie gift ideas. The eat-in deli is a great spot for a budget lunch. In addition to this Downtown store, there are also branches at 305 Bute Street (Downtown), 177 Davie Street in Yaletown, and at 1688 Salt Street in the Olympic Village, just west of Main Street. ✉ *1133 Alberni St., Downtown* ☎ *604/648–2053* ⊕ *www. urbanfare.com.*

Viti Wine and Lager Store

WINE/SPIRITS | What this diminutive shop lacks in size it makes up in quality. The shelves are stocked with a strong selection of wines, beers, and liquors, with an emphasis on regional products. Beer and spirits tastings are regularly held on Friday from 5 to 8; wine tastings are held Saturday at the same time. ✉ *Moda*

Hotel, 900 Seymour St., Downtown
☎ 604/683–3806 ⊕ www.vitiwinelagers.
com.

JEWELRY

Birks

JEWELRY/ACCESSORIES | Vancouver's link in this Canada-wide chain of high-end jewelers—a national institution since 1879—is in a neoclassical former bank building. ✉ 698 W. Hastings St., Downtown ☎ 604/669–3333 ⊕ www.maisonbirks. com.

Palladio

JEWELRY/ACCESSORIES | This is one of Vancouver's most stylish jewelers. Expect high-fashion pieces in gold and platinum, top-name timepieces, and distinguished accessories. ✉ 900 W. Hastings St., Downtown ☎ 604/685–3885 ⊕ www. palladiocanada.com ☉ Closed Sun.

SHOPPING CENTERS

Pacific Centre

SHOPPING CENTERS/MALLS | Filling three city blocks in the heart of Downtown, this mall is filled with mostly mainstream clothing shops, with some more sophisticated and pricier boutiques scattered throughout. There are several street-level entrances as well as access via Holt Renfrew, Nordstrom, and Hudson's Bay and both the Granville Street and Vancouver City Centre Stations—worth knowing about on rainy days. ✉ 701 W. Georgia St., Downtown ☎ 604/688–7235 ⊕ www. cfshops.com/pacific-centre.html.

⚙ Activities

Exceptional for North American cities, the Downtown peninsula of Vancouver is entirely encircled by a seawall along which you can walk, in-line skate (which is still quite popular in Vancouver), cycle, or otherwise propel yourself for more than 22 km (13½ miles), with plenty of picturesque jumping-on and -off points. It's so popular that it qualifies as an, albeit unofficial, national treasure. There

are places along the route where you can windsurf, kayak, or simply go for a swim. Top-rated skiing, snowboarding, mountain biking, fishing, diving, and golf are just minutes away by car or transit.

BIKING

For biking on city streets, Downtown Vancouver's "separated bike lanes" have made biking even safer—most bike lanes have a barrier between them and the traffic. Especially useful ones are along Hornby and Dunsmuir streets. These lanes are in addition to the city's many bikeways, identified by green bicycle signs.

There are detailed maps and other information on the website operated by the City of Vancouver (⊕ www.vancouver.ca/ streets-transportation/biking-and-cyclists. aspx). Cycling maps are also available from most bike shops and bike-rental outlets. Helmets are required by law, and a sturdy lock is essential.

★ Seawall

BICYCLING | The paved bike paths of Vancouver's 28-km (17-mile) seawall start Downtown at Canada Place, go around Stanley Park (for 9km/5.5-miles), and follow False Creek to Kitsilano and the University of British Columbia. It is one of the longest seashore paths of its kind in the world. ✉ Downtown ⊕ www. vancouver.ca/parks-recreation-culture/ seawall.aspx.

HOCKEY

Vancouver Canucks

HOCKEY | The city's most beloved sports team, the Vancouver Canucks, plays at Rogers Arena. ✉ 800 Griffiths Way, Downtown ☎ 604/899–4625 ⊕ www.nhl. com/canucks/.

ICE SKATING

Robson Square Ice Rink

ICE SKATING | FAMILY | Rent skates and lace them up tight to enjoy this free ice-skating rink in the city center. It's the best of indoor and outdoor skating combined—with a glass dome covering the open-air rink. The season runs December through February. ✉ *800 Robson St., Downtown* ☎ *604/646–3554* ⊕ *www.robsonsquare.com* ☜ *Free.*

SPAS

Absolute Spa at the Century-Plaza Hotel

FITNESS/HEALTH CLUBS | This expansive spa has an A-list of celebrity clients—Jennifer Lopez, Ethan Hawke, Gwyneth Paltrow, and Ben Affleck, to name a few. What makes this 15,000-square-foot spa really stand out, though, are all the extras, which turn even a simple manicure into an experience: every treatment comes with a complimentary eucalyptus steam, a swim in the ozonated pool, and a healthful snack (champagne and chocolate-coated strawberries are optional extras). Jet-lagged? The spa's several branches at Vancouver International Airport give antifatigue treatments and quick chair massages. Prefer to stay put? Absolute Mobile will come to you. There's also an Absolute Spa in the Fairmont Hotel Vancouver. ✉ *Century-Plaza Hotel, 1015 Burrard St., Downtown* ☎ *604/684–2772* ⊕ *www.absolutespa. com/century-plaza-hotel.*

Absolute Spa at the Fairmont Hotel Vancouver

FITNESS/HEALTH CLUBS | Originally a spa with high masculine-appeal, the decor is now more gender neutral. The black-leather pedicure thrones and widescreen TVs are still there, but men and women enjoy its unisex appeal and services. Couples' treatments such as side-by-side massages are particularly popular, as are mother-daughter pedicures included on the teen menu of services. Guys will still find thoughtful touches like extra-large robes and slippers as well as man-specific treatments like the "Gentlemen's Facial." ✉ *Fairmont Hotel Vancouver, 900 W. Georgia St., Downtown* ☎ *604/684–2772* ⊕ *www.absolutespa. com/fairmont-hotel-vancouver.*

BLO

FITNESS/HEALTH CLUBS | Canada's first blow-dry bar specializes in catwalk-quality blowout styles, at only C$45 for 30 minutes. A visit to these funky pink-and-plastic-outfitted lounges is a must-do for your 'do before a fancy dinner, or just because. Guys can get in on the act with the C$35 "Blo Bro" service. There is also a BLO at 1529 West 14th Avenue in South Granville. ✉ *1150 Hamilton St., Yaletown* ☎ *604/909-9495* ⊕ *www. blomedry.com.*

Spa Utopia

FITNESS/HEALTH CLUBS | If you're looking for supreme pampering, it's hard to beat this lavish spa at the Pan Pacific Hotel. Freestanding fountains, floor-to-ceiling windows, and waterfront views add a luxurious touch. There's a wide range of services but the massages are especially enjoyable. For the ultimate treat, book one of the hotel's spa suites and let the treatments come to you. ✉ *Pan Pacific Hotel, 999 Canada Pl., Downtown* ☎ *604/689–7700* ⊕ *www.spautopia.ca.*

Wedgewood Hotel Spa

FITNESS/HEALTH CLUBS | What it lacks in size, the Wedgewood Hotel Spa makes up for in intimacy. With only three treatment rooms (one is large enough for couples), this second-story spa has understated elegance and graceful attention to detail. Many services include extras like foot, hand, or scalp massages, and the complimentary steam room gets hot enough to soak out any tension. The spa carries Epicuren, a live-enzyme skin-care line favored by many dermatologists. The hotel also has an in-room spa program for guests. ✉ *Wedgewood Hotel, 845 Hornby St., Downtown* ☎ *604/608–5340* ⊕ *www.wedgewoodhotel.com.*

West End

Robson Street, Vancouver's prime shopping boulevard, runs from Downtown into the West End, a partly residential and partly commercial district. The West End has Vancouver's prettiest streetscapes and harks back to the early 1930s when it housed the affluent middle class: trees are plentiful, gardens are lushly planted, and homes and apartment buildings exude the character of that era. Vancouver's large gay community has a major presence here, too, so expect to see rainbow flags, rainbow crosswalks, and hot-pink garbage cans. There are lots of restaurants and cafés along the main arteries: Robson, Denman, and Davie Streets. As you're walking around, take note of the laneways: many are named after noted West End residents and help tell the more recent history of this vibrant neighborhood.

◉ Sights

Roedde House Museum
HISTORIC SITE | On a pretty residential street, the Roedde (pronounced *roh*-dee) House Museum is an 1893 home in the Queen Anne Revival style, set among Victoriana gardens. Tours of the restored, antiques-furnished interior take about an hour. On Sunday, tours are followed by tea and cookies. Museum hours are usually 1–4 pm, but can vary, so it's a good idea to phone before visiting. The gardens (free) can be visited anytime. The museum also hosts a concert series (classical music on the second Sunday of the month at 3 pm, jazz on the second Thursday at 7 pm). ⊠ *1415 Barclay St., between Broughton and Nicola Sts., West End* ☎ *604/684–7040* ⊕ *www.roeddehouse.org* 🎫 *C$10; Sun. C$10 includes tea and cookies* ⊙ *Closed Mon. and Sat.*

◉ Beaches

Greater Vancouver is well endowed with beaches—from the pebbly coves of West Vancouver to a vast tableau of sand at Spanish Banks, in Point Grey—but the waters are decidedly cool, with summer water temperatures ranging from 12°C to 18°C (54°F to 64°F). Aside from kids and the intrepid, most stick to quick dips, sunbathing, or wearing a wet suit for water activities.

If you're staying in the Downtown core and looking for convenient beaches, English Bay is most accessible, followed by Kits, the Stanley Park beaches, then Jericho and Spanish Banks. Jericho and English Bay are good options if you want to rent kayaks.

English Bay Beach
BEACH—SIGHT | The city's best-known beach, English Bay, lies just to the east of Stanley Park's southern entrance. A long stretch of golden sand, a waterslide, volleyball courts, kayak rentals, and food trucks keep things interesting all summer. Known locally for being gay-friendly, it draws a diverse crowd. Special events include summer Celebration of Light fireworks and a New Year's Day swim. The oversized *A-maze-ing Laughter* sculptures will make you smile. **Amenities:** food and drink; lifeguards; parking (fee); toilets; water sports. **Best for:** atmosphere; partiers; sunset; swimming; walking. ⊠ *1700 Beach Ave., between Gilford and Bidwell Sts., West End* ☎ *604/665–3424* ⊕ *www.vancouver.ca/parks-recreation-culture/english-bay-beach.aspx.*

Sunset Beach
BEACH—SIGHT | Farther along Beach Avenue toward Burrard Bridge, Sunset Beach, between Thurlow and Broughton streets, is too close to the Downtown core for clean, safe swimming, but is a great spot for an evening stroll. It's also a "quiet" beach, which means no amplified music. You can catch a ferry to

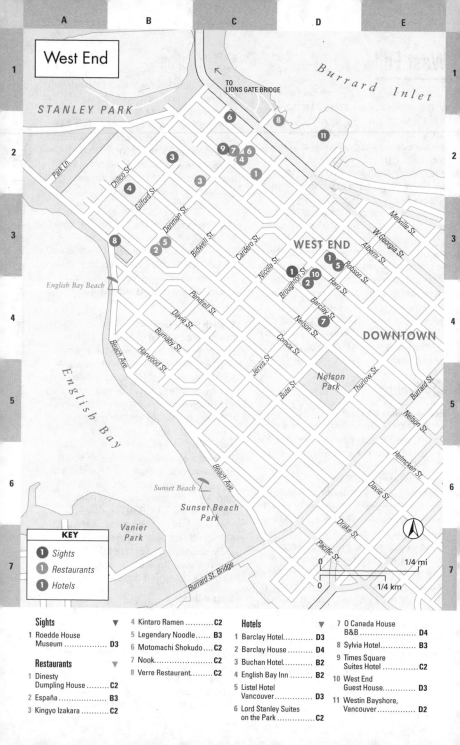

West End

A   B   C   D   E

Burrard Inlet

TO LIONS GATE BRIDGE

STANLEY PARK

Park Ln.

Chilco St.

Gilford St.

Denman St.

Bidwell St.

Cardero St.

Nicola St.

Broughton St.

Haro St.

Robson St.

Melville St.

W. Georgia St.

Alberni St.

WEST END

English Bay Beach

Pendrell St.

Davie St.

Burnaby St.

Harwood St.

Beach Ave.

Comox St.

Jervis St.

Bute St.

Barclay St.

Nelson St.

DOWNTOWN

Nelson Park

Thurlow St.

Burrard St.

Nelson St.

Helmcken St.

English Bay

Sunset Beach

Beach Ave.

Sunset Beach Park

Vanier Park

Davie St.

Drake St.

Pacific St.

Burrard St. Bridge

0   1/4 mi
0   1/4 km

KEY

- ❶ *Sights*
- ❶ *Restaurants*
- ❶ *Hotels*

Sights ▼

1 Roedde House
Museum **D3**

Restaurants ▼

1 Dinesty
Dumpling House **C2**
2 España **B3**
3 Kingyo Izakara **C2**

4 Kintaro Ramen **C2**
5 Legendary Noodle **B3**
6 Motomachi Shokudo **C2**
7 Nook. **C2**
8 Verre Restaurant........ **C2**

Hotels ▼

1 Barclay Hotel............ **D3**
2 Barclay House **D4**
3 Buchan Hotel............ **B2**
4 English Bay Inn **B2**
5 Listel Hotel
Vancouver............... **D3**
6 Lord Stanley Suites
on the Park **C2**

7 O Canada House
B&B **D4**
8 Sylvia Hotel............. **B3**
9 Times Square
Suites Hotel **C2**
10 West End
Guest House............. **D3**
11 Westin Bayshore,
Vancouver................ **D2**

Granville Island here. **Amenities:** food and drink; lifeguards; parking (fee); toilets. **Best for:** sunset; walking. ⊠ *1204 Beach Ave., between Broughton and Thurlow Sts., West End* ⊕ *www.vancouver.ca/ parks-recreation-culture/sunset-beach. aspx.*

 Restaurants

Storefronts full of savories line Robson, Denman, and Davie streets, making the West End a multicultural stew of Asian, European, and other cuisines. Particularly notable are the Japanese choices, from lively *izakayas* (Japanese tapas bars) to comfort-in-a-bowl ramen noodle shops. Many of these tiny restaurants are neighborhood institutions with a loyal following: lineups and people-watching are part of this 'hood's lifestyle.

Dinesty Dumpling House
$$ | CHINESE | FAMILY | Watch the dumpling makers at work in the open kitchen and you'll know what to order at this bustling Chinese eatery specializing in traditional Shanghainese and Taiwanese-style food. From *xiao long bao* (delicate pork-and-crab-filled soup dumplings) to freshly steamed vegetable buns, you'll find plenty of doughy deliciousness here. **Known for:** handmade dumplings; Shanghai-style noodles; stir-fries. $ *Average main: C$17* ⊠ *1719 Robson St., West End* ☎ *604/669–7769* ⊕ *www.dinesty.ca.*

España
$$ | SPANISH | Relax, you're in Spain—or at least you'll feel like it when you enter this narrow West End nook, a traditional Spanish tapas bar that serves classic (and not so classic) small bites and daily variations of paella. Order a sherry or a glass of Spanish bubbly, then graze on anchovies on toast, crispy squid with mint yogurt and jam, or fried zucchini flowers stuffed with potato and salt cod. **Known for:** Spanish tapas; intimate atmosphere; fabulous paellas. $ *Average main: C$18* ⊠ *1118 Denman St., West*

End ☎ *604/558–4040* ⊕ *www.espanares-taurant.ca* ☉ *No lunch.*

Kingyo Izakaya
$$ | JAPANESE | Behind its ornate wooden door, this *izakaya* occupies the stylish end of the spectrum, with a carved wood bar, lots of greenery, and sexy mood lighting. The intriguing Japanese small plates, from salmon carpaccio to grilled miso-marinated pork cheeks to the spicy *tako-wasabi* (octopus), are delicious, and the vibe is bustling and fun. **Known for:** Japanese small plates; shochu and sake; stylish room. $ *Average main: C$16* ⊠ *871 Denman St., West End* ☎ *604/608–1677* ⊕ *www.kingyo-izakaya. ca* ⊟ *No credit cards.*

Kintaro Ramen
$ | JAPANESE | With thin, fresh egg noodles and homemade broth (it's a meat stock, so vegetarians won't find much on the menu), a bowl of noodle soup here is cheap, filling, and ever so tasty. Expect long lines, but you can use the wait to decide between lean or fatty pork and rich, medium, or light stock. **Known for:** top-notch ramen; fast-paced dining; value for money. $ *Average main: C$11* ⊠ *788 Denman St., West End* ☎ *604/682–7568* ⊟ *No credit cards* ☉ *Closed Mon.*

Legendary Noodle
$ | CHINESE | As you'd expect from the name, this compact storefront specializes in noodles, and they're made by hand in the open kitchen, so you can watch. The choices are simple—noodles in soup or in straight-up stir-fries—but you can also order a plate of garlicky pea shoots or a steamer of dumplings to accompany your meal. **Known for:** handmade noodles; open kitchen; local fave. $ *Average main: C$12* ⊠ *1074 Denman St., West End* ☎ *604/669–8551* ⊕ *www.legendarynoo-dle.ca.*

Motomachi Shokudo
$ | JAPANESE | The Japanese-style wooden furnishings here reveal some flair, and the menu offers noodle soup choices for

patrons who don't eat pork. A popular specialty is smoky charcoal ramen (trust us, it tastes better than it sounds); the *gyoza* (dumplings) are a good choice for appetizer. **Known for:** charcoal ramen; vegetarian options; fast service. [$] *Average main: C$12* ✉ *740 Denman St., West End* ☎ *604/609–0310* 💳 *No credit cards* ⏲ *Closed Wed.*

Nook

$$ | **ITALIAN** | House-made pasta, antipasto, and out-of-the-ordinary wood-fired pizzas with out-of-the-ordinary toppings such as burrata with prosciutto apple. Reservations aren't available; rather the queuing system is chalking your name on a blackboard and knowing that the food is worth the wait. **Known for:** flavorful small plates; fun atmosphere; enthusiastic service. [$] *Average main: C$20* ✉ *781 Denman St., West End* ☎ *604/568-4554* 🌐 *www.nookrestaurant.com* ⏲ *No lunch.*

Verre Restaurant

$$$ | **EUROPEAN** | This glass-clad brasserie on Coal Harbour's seawall sparkles with inventive Mediterranean flavors. Highlights include whole fillet arctic char with green bean almondine, seared Humboldt squid puttanesca, and 48-hour short rib on the bone with herb polenta. **Known for:** harbor views; food combos; great service. [$] *Average main: C$25* ✉ *550 Denman St., West End* ☎ *604/334-4348* 🌐 *www.verreyvr.com* ⏲ *Closed Mon. No lunch weekdays.*

Hotels

Many West End accommodations take on the ambiance of this picturesque, residential neighborhood, so whether it's an historic B&B or an apartment-style building, stay here and you're quite likely to feel like a local.

Barclay Hotel

$ | **HOTEL** | The location just steps from great shopping and affordable rates make this three-story building one of the city's best-value *pensione*-style 2-star hotels. **Pros:** great location; spacious rooms; no-frills value. **Cons:** can be noisy; books up quickly; a lot of group tours. [$] *Rooms from: C$125* ✉ *1348 Robson St., West End* ☎ *604/688–8850* 🌐 *www.barclay-hotel-vancouver.at-hotels.com* 🛏 *85 rooms* 🍴 *No meals.*

Barclay House

$$$ | **B&B/INN** | If you want to get a feel for living in one of the West End's upscale homes, just a few blocks from Stanley Park, book a room at this comfortable B&B. **Pros:** lovely historic building; residential neighborhood; helpful staff. **Cons:** there are a number of steps to climb; not wheelchair accessible; street parking hard to find. [$] *Rooms from: C$230* ✉ *1351 Barclay St., West End* ☎ *604/605–1351, 800/971–1351* 🌐 *www.barclayhouse.com* 🛏 *6 rooms* 🍴 *Free breakfast.*

Buchan Hotel

$$ | **HOTEL** | On a tree-lined residential street a block from Stanley Park, this rather plain looking, 1926 *pensione*-style hotel is one of Vancouver's best values. **Pros:** quiet neighborhood; close to the beach; airport shuttle a five-minute walk away. **Cons:** parking is limited; some rooms share a bath; no elevator. [$] *Rooms from: C$161* ✉ *1906 Haro St., West End* ☎ *604/685–5354, 800/668–6654* 🌐 *www.buchanhotel.com* 🛏 *58 rooms, 27 with bath* 🍴 *No meals.*

English Bay Inn

$$$$ | **B&B/INN** | Close to Downtown and Stanley Park, this elegantly furnished B&B serves excellent four-course breakfasts around a communal table. **Pros:** elegant atmosphere; knowledgeable concierge; central location. **Cons:** leaded-glass windows make rooms a bit dark; street parking difficult to find; staff not on-site for afternoon arrivals. [$] *Rooms from: C$325* ✉ *1968 Comox St., West End* ☎ *604/683–8002, 866/683–8002* 🌐 *www.englishbayinn.com* 🛏 *6 rooms* 🍴 *Free breakfast.*

Vancouver's Best Food Trucks 🍴

The food truck phenomenon has taken up wheels in Vancouver and a growing number of mobile kitchens has taken to the streets, selling fresh juices, spicy tacos, down-home barbecue, freshly caught seafood, and more. Needless to say, the assortment is as eclectic as the region's multicultural mix. Most trucks operate Downtown and the surrounding neighborhoods during the lunch hours, generally from 11 or 11:30 until 2:30 or 3, although when they sell out, they close up for the day. Some trucks roll into town only on weekdays. With over 100 food trucks roaming the streets, schedules of which is where changes weekly. The best way to find what truck is where is to check the local street food app (🌐 *www.streetfoodapp.com/vancouver*). These are some top hits.

The Juice Truck. Freshly squeezed juices and fruit smoothies are often available at the corner of Abbott Street and Water Street in Gastown (🌐 *www.thejuicetruck.ca*).

Japadog. Terimayo, Oroshi, Misomayo, and Okonanu hot dogs are so famous that Japadog introduced its trucks to New York City where their dogs are now among that city's (and Vancouver's) top street eats. Look for Japadog throughout the Downtown core including on Howe Street at Dunsmuir Street and outside Waterfront Station. (🌐 *www.eatmogu.com*).

Mom's Grilled Cheese Truck. Triple-decker grilled cheese sandwiches (made with love, of course) can usually be had at Howe Street at Robson Street Downtown (🌐 *www.momsgrilledcheesetruck.com*).

Oh My Gado. *Gado gado* (an Indonesian warm-salad dish), literally translates as mix-mix, so you can expect a fusion of Canadian-Indonesian flavors such as poutine with chunks of grilled chicken, and topped with peanuts. Finding the truck somewhere along Robson Street is a good bet. (🌐 *www.facebook.com/EatSohoRoad*).

Tacofino. Chicken *karaage* in a taco? Why not. You can also find more classic options like pork *al pastor* or a huge vegetarian burrito at this truck, found most weekdays Downtown outside the Burrard SkyTrain station, at Burrard Street and Dunsmuir (🌐 *www.yolks.ca*).

Listel Hotel Vancouver
$$$$ | **HOTEL** | Art gallery and accommodations come together in this eco-friendly hotel on one of Vancouver's most vibrant streets. **Pros:** eclectic decor; green attitude; great on-site restaurants. **Cons:** on a busy thoroughfare; C$40+ overnight parking; cramped bathrooms. [$] *Rooms from: C$416* ✉ *1300 Robson St., West End* ☎ *604/684–8461, 800/663–5491* 🌐 *www.thelistelhotel.com* 🛏 *129 rooms* 🍽 *No meals.*

Lord Stanley Suites on the Park
$$ | **HOTEL** | **FAMILY** | For longer stays, these compact but fully equipped suites, in a high-rise building at the edge of Stanley Park, are good value. **Pros:** residential neighborhood; good views; 24-hr concierge. **Cons:** small (but bright) fitness room; furnishings bright but a bit plain; 30-day minimum stay in high season. [$] *Rooms from: C$130* ✉ *1889 Alberni St., Stanley Park* ☎ *604/688–9299, 888/767–7829* 🌐 *www.lordstanley.com* 🛏 *50 rooms* 🍽 *Free breakfast.*

O Canada House B&B

$$$$ | **B&B/INN** | This beautifully restored 1897 Victorian is home to an elegant but comfortable B&B with fun historical significance: it's where the first version of "O Canada," the country's national anthem, was penned in 1909. **Pros:** limited off-street parking; fantastic breakfast; within walking distance of Downtown. **Cons:** many rooms on the small side; no elevator to the upper rooms; some heritage aspects feel a bit shabby. [$] *Rooms from: C$329* ✉ *1114 Barclay St., West End* ☎ *604/688–0555, 877/688–1114* 🌐 *www.ocanadahouse.com* 🛏 *7 rooms* 🍴 *Free breakfast.*

Sylvia Hotel

$$$ | **HOTEL** | **FAMILY** | This Virginia-creeper-covered 1912 heritage building is continually popular because of its affordable rates and near-perfect location: a stone's throw from the beach on scenic English Bay, two blocks from Stanley Park, and a 20-minute walk from Robson Street. **Pros:** beachfront location; close to restaurants; a good place to mingle with the locals. **Cons:** older building; parking can be difficult; walk to Downtown is slightly uphill. [$] *Rooms from: C$209* ✉ *1154 Gilford St., West End* ☎ *604/681–9321, 877/681–9321* 🌐 *www.sylviahotel.com* 🛏 *120 rooms* 🍴 *No meals.*

★ **Times Square Suites Hotel**

$$$ | **HOTEL** | **FAMILY** | You can't get much closer to Stanley Park than this chic but understated all-suites hotel near plenty of restaurants. **Pros:** next to Stanley Park; good location for restaurants; roof deck for guest use. **Cons:** on a very busy intersection; back rooms overlook noisy-at-night alley; lack of storage for large suitcases. [$] *Rooms from: C$266* ✉ *1821 Robson St., West End* ☎ *604/684–2223* 🌐 *www.timessquaresuites.com* 🛏 *42 rooms* 🍴 *No meals.*

West End Guest House

$$$$ | **B&B/INN** | Built in 1906, this antique-filled Victorian B&B is ideally located a two-minute walk from Robson Street and five minutes from Stanley Park. **Pros:** heritage-registered; quiet residential location; free parking. **Cons:** furnishings a bit precious; 8 am breakfast time is non-negotiable; no air-conditioning. [$] *Rooms from: C$360* ✉ *1362 Haro St., West End* ☎ *604/681–2889* 🌐 *www.westendguesthouse.com* 🛏 *8 rooms* 🍴 *Free breakfast.*

Westin Bayshore, Vancouver

$$$$ | **RESORT** | **FAMILY** | Next to Stanley Park and with the marina on its doorstep, the Westin Bayshore, Vancouver has impressive harbor and mountain views. **Pros:** resort amenities; fabulous water views; great waterside walkways. **Cons:** conference center draws many business travelers; tower rooms are a long walk from registration; a 20-minute walk to Downtown; expensive overnight parking (C$42). [$] *Rooms from: C$527* ✉ *1601 Bayshore Dr., off Cardero St., West End* ☎ *604/682–3377, 800/627–8634* 🌐 *www.westinbayshore.com* 🛏 *499 rooms* 🍴 *No meals.*

Nightlife

The gay-friendly West End—that's Denman, Davie, and Robson streets—tends to be all about bumping and grinding in retro bars and clubs, though there are a few casual pubs and chill lounges in between.

BARS

Fountainhead Pub

BARS/PUBS | An icon in the gay community and with one of the largest street-side patios on Davie Street, absolutely everyone is welcome. So do as the locals do here: sit back, down a few beers, enjoy the lively atmosphere, and watch the beautiful people pass by. ✉ *1025 Davie St., West End* ☎ *604/687–2222* 🌐 *www.thefountainheadpub.com.*

LGBTQ
Celebrities
DANCE CLUBS | True to its name, this gay hot spot has had celeb cred since the 1980s. Expect to find a young, scantily clad crowd bumping and grinding to club hits, house, electronic, and Top 40 on a huge dance floor equipped with the latest in sound, lighting, and visuals. Men and women are welcome. ☒ *1022 Davie St., West End* ☎ *604/681–6180* ⊕ *www. celebritiesnightclub.com.*

Numbers
DANCE CLUBS | This veteran of the Davie Street strip features three levels of furious fun, from nightly DJs to karaoke, darts, and pool. There's dancing, too. ☒ *1042 Davie St., West End* ☎ *604/685– 4077* ⊕ *www.numbers.ca.*

🛍 Shopping

Robson Street, particularly the blocks between Burrard and Bute streets, is the city's main fashion-shopping and people-watching artery. The Gap and Banana Republic have their flagship stores here, as do Canadian fashion outlets Club Monaco and Roots. Souvenir shops, shoe stores, and cafés fill the gaps. Shops offering big-name European brands, including Prada, De Beers, Burberry, and Saint Laurent, form a luxury shopping enclave around Thurlow and Alberni streets. West of Bute, the shops cater to the thousands of Asian students in town to study English: Japanese, Korean, and Chinese food shops, video outlets, and noodle bars abound, particularly near the intersection of Robson and Denman.

CLOTHING
★ Roots
CLOTHING | For outdoorsy clothes that double as souvenirs (many sport maple-leaf logos), check out these Canadian-made sweatshirts, leather jackets, and other comfy casuals for men, women and kids. In addition to this Downtown flagship store, there's a smaller branch down the street at 1153 Robson Street, branches on South Granville Street and on West 4th Avenue in Kitsilano, and a number of outlet stores, called Roots 73, in the suburbs. ☒ *1001 Robson St., West End* ☎ *604/683–4305* ⊕ *www.roots.com.*

FOOD
Ayoub's Dried Fruits and Nuts
FOOD/CANDY | The freshly roasted almonds, pistachios, and cashews from this pretty Persian-style shop make excellent snacks; try them with the signature lime-saffron seasoning. Boxes of nuts and sweets make excellent gifts, too. There are other locations at 2048 West 4th Avenue in Kitsilano and 1332 Lonsdale Avenue in North Vancouver. ☒ *986 Denman St., West End* ☎ *604/732–6887* ⊕ *www.ayoubs.ca.*

🏃 Activities

BIKING
Vancouver E-Bike Adventures
BICYCLING | **FAMILY** | E-bikes are an effortless way of cycling, so if jet lag is pulling its weight, check out these self-guided (with GPS) and guided tours around the city, including the West End and Stanley Park. The sunset picnic trip to Sunset Beach is especially romantic. ☒ *Downtown* ☎ *778/241-6151* ⊕ *www. vancouverebikeadventures.com* ☞ *C$89 self guided; C$124 guided.*

Spokes Bicycle Rentals
BICYCLING | Near Stanley Park, Spokes has a wide selection of mountain bikes, tandem bikes, e-bikes, and children's bikes. Everything from hourly to weekly rentals are available. Helmets, locks, and route maps are complimentary. ☒ *1798 W. Georgia St., West End* ☎ *604/688–5141* ⊕ *www.spokesbicyclerentals.com.*

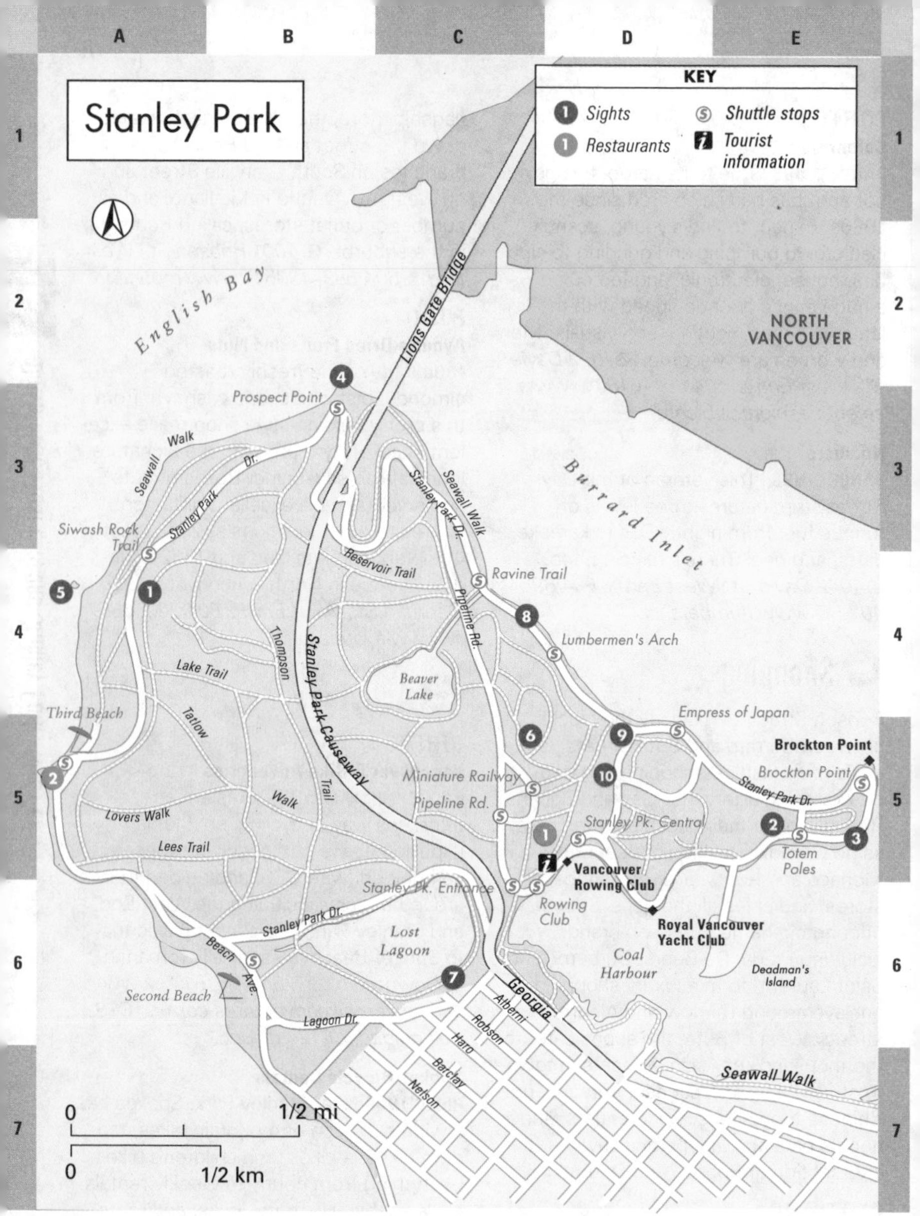
A
B
C
D
E
1
2
3
4
5
6
7
Stanley Park
KEY
Sights
Restaurants
Shuttle stops
Tourist information
English Bay
Lions Gate Bridge
NORTH VANCOUVER
Burrard Inlet
Prospect Point
Seawall Walk
Stanley Park Dr.
Siwash Rock Trail
Reservoir Trail
Ravine Trail
Pipeline Rd.
Lumbermen's Arch
Beaver Lake
Thompson Trail
Stanley Park Causeway
Lake Trail
Tatlow Walk
Third Beach
Empress of Japan
Brockton Point
Miniature Railway
Stanley Pk. Central
Totem Poles
Lovers Walk
Lees Trail
Vancouver Rowing Club
Rowing Club
Stanley Pk. Entrance
Royal Vancouver Yacht Club
Lost Lagoon
Coal Harbour
Deadman's Island
Beach Ave.
Second Beach
Lagoon Dr.
Georgia
Alberni
Robson
Haro
Barclay
Nelson
Seawall Walk
0
1/2 mi
0
1/2 km

Sights

1 Hollow Tree............. A4

2 Lumbermen's Arch E5

3 Nine O'Clock Gun........ E5

4 Prospect Point B3

5 Siwash Rock A4

6 Stanley Park Miniature Train........... C5

7 Stanley Park Nature House C6

8 Stanley Park Seawall ... C4

9 Totem poles.............. D5

10 Vancouver Aquarium D5

Restaurants

1 Stanley's Bar and Grill............ D5

2 The Teahouse in Stanley Park............ A5

RUNNING
Running Room
RUNNING | This Canada-based business is a good source for gear, advice, training, and downloadable route maps. There are many branches around the city and throughout British Columbia and the rest of Canada. A free running club leaves from this location at 6 pm on Wednesday, 9:30 am on Saturday, and 8:30 am on Sunday. ✉ *679 Denman St., Suite 103, West End* ☎ *604/684–9771* ⊕ *www.runningroom.com.*

WHALE-WATCHING
Between April and October pods of orca whales migrate through the Strait of Georgia, near Vancouver. The area is also home to year-round pods of harbor seals, elephant seals, minke whales, porpoises, and a wealth of birdlife, including bald eagles. Other migrating whales include humpbacks and grays.

Stanley Park

A 1,000-acre wilderness park, only blocks from the Downtown section of a major city, is a rare treasure and Vancouverites make use of it to bike, walk, jog, in-line skate, play cricket and tennis, go the beach, and enjoy outdoor art shows and theater performances alongside attractions such as the renowned aquarium. It also has one of North America's largest colonies of Pacific great blue herons—their brackish nests are near the tennis courts.

The fact that Stanley Park is so close to the city is actually sort of thanks to the Americans. In the 1860s, because of a threat of American invasion, this oceanfront peninsula was designated a military reserve, though it was never needed. When the City of Vancouver was incorporated in 1886, the council's first act was to request the land be set aside as a park. Permission was granted two years later and the grounds were named

Stanley Park after Lord Stanley, then governor general of Canada.

When a storm swept across the park's shores in 2006, it destroyed close to 10,000 trees as well as parts of the perimeter seawall. Locals contributed thousands of dollars to the cleanup and replanting effort in addition to the monies set aside by local authorities. The storm's silver lining was that it cleared some dead-wood areas, making room for the reintroduction of many of the park's original species of trees.

 ## Sights

Hollow Tree
LOCAL INTEREST | Near Siwash Rock, this centuries-old 56-foot-wide burnt cedar stump has shrunk over the years but still gives an idea of how large some of the old-growth trees can grow. (You can also view an exact, to scale, replica of the 43-foot high Hollow Tree, coated in gold finish at the corner of Marine and Cambie streets, designed by Canadian artist Douglas Coupland.) ✉ *Stanley Park.*

Lumbermen's Arch
BUILDING | FAMILY | Made of one massive log, this archway, erected in 1952, is dedicated to the workers in Vancouver's first industry. Beside the arch is an asphalt path that leads back to Lost Lagoon and the Vancouver Aquarium. There's a picnic area, a snack bar, and small beach here, too. The Variety Kids Water Park is across the road. ✉ *Stanley Park.*

Nine O'Clock Gun
CLOCK | This cannonlike apparatus by the water was installed in 1890 to alert fishermen to a curfew ending weekend fishing. Now it signals 9 o'clock every night. ✉ *Stanley Park.*

Prospect Point
VIEWPOINT | At 211 feet, Prospect Point is the highest point in the park and provides striking views of the Lions Gate Bridge (watch for cruise ships passing below),

The Stanley Park Seawall is one of Vancouver's most scenic spots for walking or cycling.

the North Shore, and Burrard Inlet. There's also a year-round souvenir shop, a snack bar with terrific ice cream (summer only), and a restaurant. From the seawall, you can see where cormorants build their seaweed nests along the cliff ledges. ⊠ *Stanley Park*.

Siwash Rock

LOCAL INTEREST | According to a local First Nations legend, this 50-foot-high offshore promontory is a monument to a man who was turned into stone as a reward for his unselfishness. The rock is visible from the seawall; if you're driving, you need to park and take a short path through the woods. ⊠ *Stanley Park*.

Stanley Park Miniature Train

TOUR—SIGHT | FAMILY | This child-size steam train takes kids and adults on a ride through the woods. In summer, the railway travels a 2-km (1.2-mile) winding journey through Stanley Park. Halloween displays draw crowds throughout October for the annual "Ghost Train," and at Christmastime, an elaborate light display

illuminates the route during "Bright Nights." The train periodically runs outside of these special events, too; call or check the website for details. ⊠ *Off Pipeline Rd., Stanley Park* ☎ *604/257–8531* ⊕ *vancouver.ca/parks-recreation-culture/ stanley-park-miniature-train.aspx* ✉ *C$7, special events (Ghost Train, Bright Nights) C$12* ☺ *Hrs vary, check website for details.*

Stanley Park Nature House

COLLEGE | Vancouver's only ecology center is a treasure trove of information and showcases Stanley Park's true natural beauty with a host of programs and guided walks. The Nature House is on the south shore of Lost Lagoon, at the foot of Alberni Street. ⊠ *Stanley Park, Alberni St., north end, under viewing platform, Stanley Park* ☎ *604/257–8544* ⊕ *www. stanleyparkecology.ca* ✉ *Programs and guided walks vary in price* ☺ *Closed Mon. in July and Aug.; closed weekdays rest of year.*

A Tour of Stanley Park

Stanley Park Drive circles the park, often parallel to the **Seawall walking/cycling path**. If you're walking or cycling, start at the foot of Alberni Street, beside Lost Lagoon. Go through the underpass and veer right, following the cycle-path markings, until you reach the seawall.

Whichever mode you travel, the old wooden structure that you pass on your right is the Vancouver Rowing Club, a private athletic club established in 1903. Ahead and to your left is a parking lot, an information booth, and a turnoff to the aquarium. A Salmon Demonstration Stream near the information booth has facts about the life cycle of the fish.

Continue along past the Royal Vancouver Yacht Club until you reach the causeway to Deadman's Island. The **totem poles,** a bit farther down Stanley Park Drive and on your left, are a popular photo stop. The **Nine O'Clock Gun** is ahead at the water's edge, just past the sign for Hallelujah Point. Brockton Point and its small lighthouse and foghorn are to the north. Brockton Oval, where you can often catch a rugby game in winter or cricket in summer, is on your left. On the water side, watch for the *Girl in a Wetsuit*, a sculpture that mimics Copenhagen's *Little Mermaid.* A little farther along the seashore stands a replica of the dragon-shaped

figurehead from the SS *Empress of Japan*, which plied these waters between 1891 and 1922.

Lumbermen's Arch, a log archway, is at km 3 (mile 2) of the drive. There's a picnic area, a snack bar, and a small beach. The Variety Kids Water Park, across the road, is a big draw in summer. Cyclists and walkers can turn off here for a shortcut back to the **Vancouver Aquarium,** the **Miniature Railway,** and the park entrance.

At the Lions Gate Bridge: cyclists go under the bridge, past **Prospect Point**; drivers go over the bridge to a viewpoint–café at the top of Prospect Point. Both routes continue to the English Bay side of the park and its beaches. Keep an eye open for the **Hollow Tree**. The imposing monolith offshore (not visible from the road) is **Siwash Rock**, the focus of a Native legend. Continue to the swimming area and snack bar at Third Beach, then the heated pool at Second Beach. If you're walking or cycling, you can shortcut from here back to Lost Lagoon by taking the perpendicular path behind the pool that cuts into the park. Either footbridge ahead leads to a path along the south side of the lagoon that will take you to Alberni and Georgia streets. If you continue along the seawall from Second Beach, you'll emerge into a residential part of the West End.

★ **Stanley Park Seawall**

TRAIL | Vancouver's seawall path includes a 9-km (5½-mile) paved shoreline section within Stanley Park. It's one of several car-free zones in the park and it's popular with walkers and cyclists. If you have the time (about a half day) and the energy, strolling the entire seawall is an exhilarating experience. It extends an additional mile east past the marinas, cafés, and waterfront condominiums of Coal Harbour to Canada Place in Downtown, so you could start your walk or ride from there. From the south side of the park, the seawall continues for another 28 km

Catch dolphins and other marine animals in action at the Vancouver Aquarium.

(17 miles) along Vancouver's waterfront to the University of British Columbia, making it the longest shoreside path in the world, and allowing for a pleasant, if ambitious, day's bike ride. Along the seawall, cyclists must wear helmets and stay on their side of the path. Within Stanley Park, cyclists must ride in a counterclockwise direction. The seawall can get crowded on summer weekends, but inside the park is a 27-km (16-mile) network of peaceful walking and cycling paths through old- and second-growth forest. The wheelchair-accessible Beaver Lake Interpretive Trail is a good choice if you're interested in park ecology. Take a map—they're available at the park-information booth and many of the concession stands—and don't go into the woods alone or after dusk. ✉ *Stanley Park.*

Totem Poles

NATIVE SITE | Totem poles are an important art form among Native peoples along British Columbia's coast. These nine poles—eight carved in the latter half of the 20th century, and one created in 2009—include replicas of poles originally brought to the park from the north coast in the 1920s, as well as poles carved specifically for the park by First Nations artists. The several styles of poles represent a cross section of BC Native groups, including the Kwakwaka'wakw, Haida, and Nisga'a. The combination of carved animals, fish, birds, and mythological creatures represents clan history. An information center near the site has a snack bar, a gift shop, and information about BC's First Nations. ✉ *Brockton Point, Stanley Park.*

★ Vancouver Aquarium

ZOO | FAMILY | Massive floor-to-ceiling windows let you get face-to-face with sea otters, sea lions, dolphins, and harbor seals at this award-winning research and educational facility. In the Amazon Gallery you walk through a rain-forest jungle populated with piranhas, caimans, and tropical birds; in summer, hundreds of free-flying butterflies add to the mix. The Tropic Zone is home to exotic freshwater and saltwater life, including clown fish, moray eels, and black-tip reef sharks. Other displays, many with hands-on features for kids, show the underwater life of coastal British Columbia and the Canadian Arctic. Sea lion and dolphin shows, as well as dive shows (where divers swim with aquatic life, including sharks) are held daily. Be sure to check out the stingray touch pool, as well as the "4-D" film experience (it's a multisensory show that puts mist, smell, and wind into the 3-D equation). For an extra fee, you can help the trainers feed and train otters, belugas, and sea lions. There's also a café and a gift shop. Be prepared for lines on weekends and school holidays. In summer, the quietest time to visit is before 11 am or after 4 pm; in other seasons, the crowds are smaller before noon or after 2 pm. ✉ *845 Avison Way, Stanley Park* ☎ *604/659–3474 information line* 🌐 *www.vanaqua.org* 🎟 *C$40.*

Beaches

★ Stanley Park Beaches

BEACH—SIGHT | There are two fine beaches accessed from Stanley Park, with other unnamed sandy spots dotted along the seawall. The most popular with families is **Second Beach,** which has a playground and large heated pool with slides. **Third Beach** is a little more removed than the other central beaches. It has a larger stretch of sand, fairly warm water, and unbeatable sunset views. It's a popular evening picnic spot. **Amenities:** food and drink; lifeguards; parking (fee); toilets. **Best for:** sunset; swimming; walking. ✉ *7495 Stanley Park Dr., Stanley Park* 🌐 *www.vancouver.ca/parks-recreation-culture/third-beach.aspx.*

Restaurants

Stanley's Bar and Grill

$$ | **CANADIAN** | **FAMILY** | In a 1911 manor house, this bar and grill with a large patio is very family-friendly, with a menu of burgers, fish, soups, and salads as well as sharing plates and vegetarian options. The location right in Stanley Park is great, especially mid–bike ride; it overlooks the Rose Garden and is steps from Malkin Bowl, where outdoor theater and concerts are held in summer. **Known for:** location; patio; famil- friendly. [$] *Average main: C$20* ✉ *610 Pipeline Rd., Stanley Park* ☎ *604/602-3088* 🌐 *www.stanleyparkpavilion.com/stanleys-bar-and-grill/* 🕒 *no dinner Oct-Apr.*

The Teahouse in Stanley Park

$$$$ | **CANADIAN** | The former officers' mess at Ferguson Point in Stanley Park is a prime location for water views by day, and for watching sunsets at dusk. The Pacific Northwest menu is not especially innovative, but its broad appeal will please those looking for local fish, rack of lamb, steaks, and a host of other options, including gluten-free pasta. **Known for:** tasting boards; lovely patio; Pacific Northwest cuisine. [$] *Average main: C$33* ✉ *7501 Stanley Park Dr., Stanley Park* ✣ *At Ferguson Point* ☎ *604/669–3281* 🌐 *www.vancouverdine.com/teahouse.*

Performing Arts

Stanley Park's outdoor theater has been a local tradition since the 1940's and although staged by a largely amateur cast and crew, productions are consistently professional in tone and many participants go on to professional careers. During the Fringe Festival, park trails and gardens often become pop-up stages for fringe performers.

Theatre Under the Stars

THEATER | FAMILY | In summer, family-friendly musicals like *Shrek, Beauty and the Beast,* and *Oliver !* are the main draw at Malkin Bowl, an outdoor amphitheater in Stanley Park. You can watch the show from the lawn and bring a picnic to make it dinner theater. Ask about the exchange insurance when buying tickets as plein-air shows happen rain or shine. If there's a downpour mid-show, audience members are provided with ponchos. ✉ *Stanley Park, Malkin Bowl, 610 Pipeline Rd., Stanley Park* ☎ *877/840–0457* ⊕ *www.tuts.ca.*

 Activities

WALKING

Stanley Park Ecology Centre

WILDLIFE-WATCHING | FAMILY | A calendar of guided nature walks and discovery sessions is filled with fun, kid-friendly options. Despite its urban access, Stanley Park offers incredible wildlife diversity—from the namesake rodents in Beaver Lake to a rookery of great blue herons near the tennis courts. The organization also operates the Stanley Park Nature House on the shores of Lost Lagoon. A park ranger station also operates daily beside the concession stand at Second Beach. ✉ *Alberni St. at Chilco St., Stanley Park* ✛ *Southeast corner of Lost Lagoon* ☎ *604/257–8544, 604/718–6522* ⊕ *www.stanleyparkecology.ca* 🎫 *Free.*

Chapter 4

GASTOWN, CHINATOWN, AND YALETOWN

4

Updated by
Lesley Mirza

● Sights   🍽 Restaurants   🛏 Hotels   🛍 Shopping   🍸 Nightlife
★★★☆☆   ★★★★★   ★★★★☆   ★★★★★   ★★★★★

NEIGHBORHOOD SNAPSHOT

TOP EXPERIENCES

■ **Dr. Sun Yat-Sen Classical Chinese Garden:** A reflective retreat that is known to be one of the best small city-gardens in the world.

■ **John Fluevog Shoes:** Red-carpet celebrities and shoe-fetish enthusiasts can't get enough of this Vancouver designer's extraordinary creations.

■ **Alibi Room:** With 50 craft beers on tap, Alibi is a fave late-night haunt for film crews, actors, musicians, and like-minded souls.

■ **Gastown Steam Clock:** This gaseous, melodic clock deserves a been-there, seen-it selfie.

■ **The Irish Heather:** An Irish pub actually owned by Irish! Guinness aside, the 100+ whiskey brands round the back is a sight to behold.

GETTING HERE

Getting to Gastown is easy: just head for the waterfront. It's a 5-minute walk from Waterfront Station, east along Cordova Street and into Water Street. Chinatown is two blocks south; turn up either Carrall or Columbia streets.

Walking to Yaletown is also easy from anywhere Downtown as well as from Gastown, and there's a Yaletown stop on the SkyTrain's Canada Line. Catching a False Creek or Aquabus ferry is fun; they run frequently between Granville Island, Science World, Yaletown, and the south shore of False Creek. Note that parking is tight in Yaletown; if you must drive, your best bet is the lot at Library Square nearby.

PLANNING YOUR TIME

Allow about an hour to explore Gastown—that's without shopping too much. Chinatown could easily consume another hour wandering around, checking out the architecture and exotic wares; add yet another 60-minutes if you want to visit the Dr. Sun Yat-Sen Classical Chinese Garden. Be aware that you might come across one or two seedy corners in Chinatown; it's all pretty safe by day, but you might prefer to cab it at night.

QUICK BITES

■ **Revolver.** Its raison-d'etre revolves around java beans from all over the world, often available in coffee-tasting flights (very cool) alongside freshly baked goods. ⊠ 325 Cambie St., Gastown ⊕ www.revolvercoffee.ca Ⓜ W. Cordova St., at Home St., Bus 50.

■ **Nelson the Seagull.** One of Gastown's older buildings has been restyled into a casual, open bakery-cum-kitchen eatery for dash-and-go, or stay-awhile daytime dining. ⊠ 311 Carrall St., Gastown ⊕ www.nelsontheseagull.com Ⓜ E. Hastings at Carrall St., Bus 20.

■ **Urban Fare.** Gastronomes salivate at the international and local food products this happening grocery provides, including meals in the café or as takeout snacks. ⊠ 177 Davie St., Yaletown ⊕ www.urbanfare.com Ⓜ Canada Line, Yaletown Roundhouse.

■ **O-Cha Tea Bar.** It's a tiny venue but the multitude of tea blends will soothe, warm, and refresh; the "Cold Blaster" (a blend of tea, orange juice, honey, ginger, and cayenne pepper) might even blast away any sniffles or jet lag. ⊠ 1116 Homer St., Yaletown Ⓜ Canada Line, Yaletown Roundhouse.

Gastown is known for its cobblestone streets and Victorian era–style streetlamps; it's also joined Yaletown as one of Vancouver's trendiest neighborhoods, as überhip stores, ad agencies, high-tech companies, and restaurants take over refurbished brick warehouses.

It's a relatively small area, bordered by Hastings, Richards, and Main streets and it was nicknamed for the garrulous ("Gassy") Jack Deighton who opened his saloon where his statue now stands on Maple Tree Square. This is essentially where Vancouver originated and it's the zero point from which all Vancouver street addresses start. By the time the first transcontinental train arrived in 1887, the waterfront area was crowded with hotels, warehouses, brothels, and dozens of saloons—you can still see place names such as Gaoler's Mews and Blood Alley, which hint at those early rough-and-tumble days.

Back in about 1985 the BC provincial government decided they were going to take a derelict industrial site on the north shore of False Creek, clean it up, and build a world's fair. Twenty million people showed up for Expo '86, and Yaletown, on the site of the fair, was born. The brick warehouses were turned into apartment buildings and offices, and the old loading docks are now terraces for cappuccino bars and trendy restaurants. There are brewpubs, day spas, retail and wholesale fashion outlets, and shops selling upscale home decor. There's also a seaside walk and cycle path that completely encircles

False Creek. It's hard to imagine that back in the 1880s and '90s this was probably the most lawless place in Canada: it was so far into the woods that the Royal Canadian Mounted Police complained they couldn't patrol it.

Gastown

This neighborhood celebrates the city's orgins and has unique architecture and trendy restaurants.

⊙ Sights

Coastal Peoples Fine Arts Gallery
CRAFTS | The collection of First Nations jewelry, ceremonial masks, prints, and carvings at this gallery is impressive. Check out the gorgeous books and postcards if you're looking for more affordable souvenirs. ⊠ *332 Water St., Unit 200, Gastown* ☎ *604/684–9222* ⊕ *www.coast-alpeoples.com.*

Byrnes Block
BUILDING | After the 1886 Great Fire, which wiped out most of the fledgling settlement of Vancouver, George Byrnes built what is now Vancouver's oldest brick building. It now houses shops and

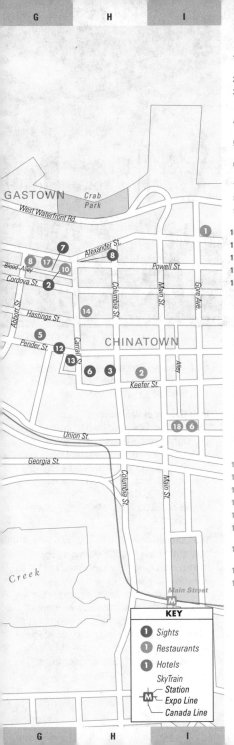

Sights ▼

1 BC Sports Hall of Fame and Museum **F6**
2 Byrnes Block............ **G4**
3 Chinese Cultural Centre Museum & Archives **H5**
4 Coastal Peoples Fine Arts Gallery.............. **F3**
5 Contemporary Art Gallery **C6**
6 Dr. Sun Yat-Sen Classical Chinese Garden......... **H5**
7 Gaoler's Mews.......... **G4**
8 Hotel Europe **H3**
9 Inuit Gallery of Vancouver **F3**
10 The Landing **F3**
11 Library Square **E5**
12 Millennium Gate **G5**
13 Sam Kee Building....... **G5**
14 Steam Clock.............. **F3**

Restaurants ▼

1 Ask For Luigi.............. **I3**
2 Bao Bei **H5**
3 Blue Water Cafe **C7**
4 Cioppino's Mediterranean Grill & Enoteca **C7**
5 Hapa Izakaya............ **B7**
6 Harvest Community Foods........................ **I6**
7 Homer St. Cafe and Bar **D6**
8 Jules **G4**
9 La Pentola **C7**
10 L'Abattoir................. **G4**
11 Meat & Bread............ **F4**
12 Nuba **F4**
13 O-Cha Tea Bar **C7**
14 Pidgin **H4**
15 Provence Marinaside **C8**
16 Rodney's Oyster House............ **B8**
17 Salt Tasting Room....... **G4**
18 The Union.................. **I6**

Hotels ▼

1 Douglas Hotel **E7**
2 Hotel BLU Vancouver ... **E6**
3 JW Marriott Parq Vancouver **E7**
4 OPUS Vancouver Hotel....................... **C8**
5 Skwachàys Lodge **G4**

4

Gastown, Chinatown, and Yaletown GASTOWN

Works of art on display at the Coastal Peoples Fine Arts Gallery.

offices, but for a while this two-story building was Vancouver's top luxury hotel, the Alhambra Hotel, charging a dollar a night. The site of Deighton's original saloon, east of the Byrnes Block where his statue now stands, is the starting point from which all Vancouver street addresses begin. ⊠ *2 Water St., Gastown.*

Gaoler's Mews

NEIGHBORHOOD | Once the site of the city's first civic buildings—the constable's cabin and customs house, and a two-cell log jail—this atmospheric brick-paved courtyard is now home to cafés and offices. ⊠ *Behind 12 Water St., Gastown.*

Hotel Europe

BUILDING | Once billed as the best hotel in the city, this 1908 flatiron building is one of the world's finest examples of triangular architecture. Now used for government-subsidized housing and not open to the public, the building still has its original Italian tile work and lead-glass windows. The glass tiles in the sidewalk

on Alexander Street were the former "skylight" for an underground saloon. ⊠ *43 Powell St., Gastown.*

Inuit Gallery of Vancouver

CRAFTS | In addition to quality Inuit art like the signature carvings in soapstone and antler, there's also an excellent collection of Northwest Coast Native art such as baskets, totems, bentwood boxes, and masks. ⊠ *206 Cambie St., Gastown* ☎ *888/615–8399, 604/688–7323* ⊕ *www. inuit.com.*

The Landing

BUILDING | Built in 1905 with gold-rush money, this elegantly renovated brick warehouse is now home to offices, shops, and Steamworks, a popular brew-pub. From the oversized bay window at the rear of the lobby you can appreciate where the shoreline was 100 years ago, as well as enjoy terrific views of Burrard Inlet and the North Shore Mountains. ⊠ *375 Water St., Gastown.*

Steam Clock

CLOCK | An underground steam system, which also heats many local buildings, supplies the world's first steam clock—possibly Vancouver's most photographed attraction. On the quarter hour, a steam whistle rings out the Westminster chimes, and on the hour a huge cloud of steam spews from the apparatus. The ingenious design, based on an 1875 mechanism, was built in 1977 by Ray Saunders of Landmark Clocks to commemorate the community effort that saved Gastown from demolition. Fun fact: yes, the clock does use steam power, but three electric motors help it run, too. ⊠ *Water St. at Cambie St., Gastown.*

🍴 Restaurants

Gastown has become a hub for dining and drinking, with lively bars (many with good food) and innovative restaurants.

★ Ask For Luigi

$$$ | **ITALIAN** | Neighborhood residents queue before opening to secure one of the 30 seats in this cozy Italian bistro serving up house-made pasta and prosecco on tap. Antipasti like smoked mackerel, crispy polenta, and—of course—meatballs, are served family-style, so bring some friends for the best experience. **Known for:** family-style dining; Italian antipasti; house-bottled Spritz. $ *Average main: C$25* ⊠ *305 Alexander St., Gastown* ☎ *604/428–2544* ⊕ *www.askforluigi.com* ⊗ *Closed Mon.*

★ Jules

$$$ | **FRENCH** | From garlicky escargots and steak frites to duck confit and crème caramel, traditional French bistro fare is alive and well at this intimate Gastown spot. You won't find many funky fusion creations or East-meets-West innovations—just the classic dishes you might find at a neighborhood bistro in Paris. **Known for:** classic French dishes; light afternoon fare; cozy room. $ *Average main: C$25* ⊠ *216 Abbott St., Gastown* ☎ *604/669–0033* ⊕ *www.julesbistro.ca* ⊗ *Closed Mon.*

L'Abattoir

$$$$ | **MODERN CANADIAN** | On the site of Vancouver's first jail, this two-level restaurant with exposed brick walls and classic black-and-white floor tiles has a bold collection of cocktails and an intriguing modern menu. From the restaurant's name—French for "slaughterhouse" (the surrounding neighborhood was once a meatpacking district)—you'd expect a meat-focused menu, and although you'll find veal sweetbreads on toast, seafood shines as well, in dishes like the grilled lobster tail or baked Pacific oysters with Burgundy truffle. **Known for:** creative cocktails; modern meat dishes; tempting desserts. $ *Average main: C$40* ⊠ *217 Carrall St., Gastown* ☎ *604/568–1701* ⊕ *www.labattoir.ca* ⊗ *No lunch weekdays.*

Meat & Bread

$ | **DELI** | At this trendy sandwich shop, you simply wait in line (there's nearly always a queue) and choose from the short daily menu of five sandwiches. The rich and crispy house-made porcetta (Italian-style roast pork) with salsa verde on a freshly baked ciabatta bun is a must-try. **Known for:** house-made porchetta; communal table; hearty soups. $ *Average main: C$10* ⊠ *370 Cambie St., Gastown* ☎ *604/566–9003* ⊗ *Closed Sun. No dinner.*

Nuba

$$$ | **MIDDLE EASTERN** | You can make a meal of *meze*—appetizers like falafel, tabbouleh, or crispy cauliflower served with tahini—at this subterranean Lebanese restaurant. If you're looking for something heartier, the kitchen serves roast chicken glazed with honey and red pepper, lamb kebabs, and other meat dishes but much of the menu is vegetarian-friendly. **Known for:** vegetarian dining; Lebanese cuisine; small

Did You Know?

The most famous Gastown attraction is the Steam Clock built in 1977. On the quarter hour a whistle rings out, and on the hour a larger steam cloud fills the air.

plates. [$] *Average main: C$28* ✉ *207 W. Hastings St., Gastown* ☎ *604/668–1655* 🌐 *www.nuba.ca.*

★ Pidgin

$$$ | ASIAN FUSION | The menu in this glossy white space draws inspiration from Asia for inventive sharing plates that are some of Vancouver's most exciting eating options. From the ever-changing menu, you might choose chicken *karaage* with spicy yuzu kosho mayo and tosazu pickle daikon, a foie-gras rice bowl with chestnuts, daikon, and a unagi glaze, or the Korean rice cake with gochujang bolognese and spiced hazelnut. **Known for:** inventive sharing plates; creative cocktails; bold flavors. [$] *Average main: C$26* ✉ *350 Carrall St., Gastown* ☎ *604/620–9400* 🌐 *www.pidginvancouver.com* ⏲ *No lunch.*

Salt Tasting Room

$$ | ECLECTIC | If your idea of a perfect light meal revolves around fine cured meats, artisanal cheeses, and a glass of wine from a wide-ranging list, find your way to this sleek space in a decidedly unsleek Gastown location. The restaurant has no kitchen and simply assembles the selection of top-quality provisions—perhaps smoked beef tenderloin or British Columbian–made Camembert, with accompanying condiments—into artfully composed delights. **Known for:** local charcuterie; extensive wine list; three-course set menu. [$] *Average main: C$16* ✉ *45 Blood Alley, off Abbott St., Gastown* ☎ *604/633–1912* 🌐 *www.salttastingroom.com* ⏲ *No lunch.*

Hotels

Skwachàys Lodge

$$ | HOTEL | FAMILY | Everything about Skwàchays Lodge (pronounced skwatch-eyes), Canada's first Aboriginal arts hotel, celebrates First Nations heritage. **Pros:** unique property; gracious service; original artwork. **Cons:** showers but no tubs; the neighborhood sometimes attracts transients; pastries at breakfast go fast. [$] *Rooms from: C$160* ✉ *31 Pender St., Gastown* ☎ *604/687–3589* 🌐 *www.skwachays.com* 🛏 *18 rooms* 🍴 *No meals.*

Nightlife

Hipster Gastown is famed for its clusters of late-night establishments and is now the place to go for crowded nightspots, relaxed pubs, and trendy cocktail bars.

BARS

Alibi Room

BARS/PUBS | If beer is your thing, head to Alibi, which specializes in pairing beer with your meal. Kegs of microbrews from around BC and beyond are the pride and joy here and it's known for having one of the best selections of craft beers in Vancouver. There are also organic wines and a few fun cocktails if you're not feeling beer-inclined. ✉ *157 Alexander St., Gastown* ☎ *604/623–3383* 🌐 *www.alibi.ca.*

The Diamond

TAPAS BARS | At the top of a narrow staircase above Maple Tree Square, the Diamond occupies the second floor of one of the city's oldest buildings. A cool hangout and cocktail lounge, the venue serves a mix of historic tipples and inventive house concoctions. There's a daily, and very welcoming, after-work happy hour. ✉ *6 Powell St., at Carrall St., Gastown* 🌐 *www.di6mond.com.*

The Irish Heather

BARS/PUBS | Expect a mixed crowd of local hipsters and out-of-towners enjoying properly poured pints of Guinness, mixed beer drinks (try a shandy, which is lager and lemonade), wine, and live Irish music some nights. The food menu focuses on pub favorites. Out back in an atmospheric coach house is Shebeen Whisk(e)y House, where you can try any of 200-plus whiskeys. ✉ *210 Carrall St., Gastown* ☎ *604/688–9779* 🌐 *www.irishheather.com.*

The Portside Pub

BARS/PUBS | Nautical kitsch and a friendly maritime bent woo many a landlubber to the Portside Pub. Live bands, weekend DJs, and whiskey on tap handily turn the two-level bar into a packed venue. Pub eats are above par, but lineups start early and get long. ⊠ *7 Alexander St., Gastown* ☎ *604/559–6333* ⊕ *www.theportsidepub. com.*

★ Pourhouse Vancouver

BARS/PUBS | The brick-and-beam 1910 architecture, antiques, and a 38-foot bar are in keeping with the menu of classic cocktails. Most are inspired by the 1862 bartending bible *How to Mix Drinks* by Jerry Thomas, the first bartending manual ever to put oral traditions to print, with recipes such as a Tom Collins. Book ahead for one of the family-style dinners that serve four to six people: everything is set in the center of the kitchen table, and it's a help-yourself affair, just like at home. There's also live music Sunday through Thursday nights. ⊠ *162 Water St., Gastown* ☎ *604/568–7022* ⊕ *www. pourhousevancouver.com.*

Revel Room

BARS/PUBS | A slightly older Gastown crowd comes to indulge at this two-story bar and eatery with a late-night kitchen. The Southern style means bourbon-focused cocktails and an overall welcoming charm. There's live music most nights. ⊠ *238 Abbott St., Gastown* ☎ *604/687– 4088* ⊕ *www.revelroom.ca.*

Salt Tasting Room

WINE BARS—NIGHTLIFE | The allure here is the selection of local and international wines, beers, and sherries that can be paired with a rotating selection of cured meats and artisanal cheeses. You can choose your own tasting menu or leave it to the professionals. Legend has it that the address, Blood Alley, is so called because this used to be the city's meat-packing district and the name comes from the buckets of blood butchers threw down the cobblestone street. ⊠ *45*

Blood Alley, Gastown ☎ *604/633–1912* ⊕ *www.salttastingroom.com.*

Steamworks

BREWPUBS/BEER GARDENS | This multilevel brewpub welcomes urban professionals with a selection of traditional ales and lagers brewed in-house, in small batches, using the neighborhood's steam heat— the same stuff that powers Gastown's Steam Clock. There is patio seating with harbor views, as well, when the weather permits. ⊠ *375 Water St., Gastown* ☎ *604/689–2739* ⊕ *www.steamworks. com.*

DANCE CLUBS

Guilt & Co.

MUSIC CLUBS | The menu at this Gastown favorite features lagers, pale ales, pilsners, stouts, and ciders, and then there's what's on tap, a wine list, and a cocktail menu—in short, the thirsty have many ways to imbibe. The food menu offers lots of sharing options. Rock bands (plus jazz, folk, and blues artists) aren't all the basement music club hosts—there are also burlesque and cabaret nights. ⊠ *1 Alexander St., Gastown* ☎ *604/288–1704* ⊕ *www.guiltandcompany.com.*

🎭 Performing Arts

Firehall Arts Centre

DANCE | Innovative theater and modern dance are showcased at this intimate Downtown space, set in a 1907 firehouse on the border of trendy Gastown and the struggling Downtown East Side. ⊠ *280 E. Cordova St., Downtown East Side* ☎ *604/689–0926* ⊕ *www.firehallartscentre.ca.*

🛍 Shopping

A hip crowd—restaurateurs, advertising gurus, photographers, and other creative types—have settled into Gastown, which has made the boutiques here correspondingly cool. Look for locally designed and one-of-a-kind clothing and accessories, First Nations art, and souvenirs—both kitschy and expensive. The best blocks for browsing are Water Street between Richards and Carrall, and West Cordova between Richards and Cambie. Also check out the ever-changing shops on Abbott and Carrall streets, between Water and Cordova.

CLOTHING
Kit and Ace
CLOTHING | More evidence of Vancouver style making its mark on the world hangs at the Gastown flagship of this homegrown international chain. Billed as "technical apparel for real life," Kit and Ace's stylish, washable, packable silk and cashmere blends take Vancouverites (and anyone else) from cycling to work to dancing till dawn. ✉ 165 Water St., Gastown ☎ 604/559-8363 ⊕ kitandace.com.

lululemon lab
CLOTHING | One of only two lululemon labs (the other is in New York), this test site for Vancouver's iconic yoga wear brand is the place to pick up the company's latest athleisure and streetwear looks before they hit the malls. You can even see the designers at work in the open-plan shop. ✉ 50 Powell St., Gastown ☎ 604/708–1126 ⊕ www.lululemonlab.com.

Oak + Fort
CLOTHING | Based in Vancouver, with locations elsewhere in Canada, Oak + Fort sells simple but stylish locally designed women's clothing and accessories plus a small selection of menswear and home decor items at its spacious storefront. ✉ 355 Water St., Gastown ☎ 604/566–9199 ⊕ www.oakandfort.ca.

One of a Few
CLOTHING | The clothing and accessories here, from local and international makers, may not be one of a kind, but as the name of this funky little shop attests, you won't see the designs at mass-market retailers either. ✉ 354 Water St., Gastown ☎ 604/605–0685 ⊕ www.oneofafew.com.

Secret Location
CLOTHING | Design students and celebrities alike flock to this airy, white gallery of highly curated clothing, accessories, jewelry, and art books. The constantly evolving collection favors cutting-edge European designers over household names. ✉ 1 Water St., Gastown ☎ 604/685–0090 ⊕ www.secretlocation.ca.

SHOES AND ACCESSORIES
★ John Fluevog
SHOES/LUGGAGE/LEATHER GOODS | You might have seen John Fluevog shops in New York and Los Angeles, but did you know that these funky shoes were created by a Vancouverite? The Gastown location is worth a look for the store itself, with its striking glass facade and soaring ceilings. There's another branch Downtown at 837 Granville Street. ✉ 65 Water St., Gastown ☎ 604/688–6228 ⊕ www.fluevog.com.

Chinatown

Although a large percentage of Vancouver's Chinese community has shifted to suburban Richmond, there's still a wonderful buzz of authenticity in the open-front markets, bakeries, and herbalist and import shops of the city's historic Chinatown. Street signs are in Chinese lettering, streetlights look like lanterns topped with decorative dragons, and much of the architecture is patterned on that of Guangzhou (Canton). Chinatown's early residents, immigrants who arrived from China in the late 1800s, came primarily to seek work in BC's emerging railroad and mining industries. More recently, hip young newcomers have been settling in the neighborhood, bringing funky shops, eclectic eateries, and even a few condominium buildings. You can still linger over a traditional dim sum lunch, but you can also settle in for a creative cocktail, a currywurst, or a slice of pie before scoping out the indie fashions.

Gastown, Chinatown, and Yaletown CHINATOWN

4

You could easily spend an hour wandering around Chinatown, checking out the architecture and exotic wares; add at least an hour if you also want to visit the Dr. Sun Yat-Sen Classical Chinese Garden. Be aware that you might come across one or two seedy corners in Chinatown; it's all pretty safe by day, but you might prefer to cab it at night.

⊙ Sights

Chinese Cultural Centre Museum & Archives

LOCAL INTEREST | The Chinese have a rich, grueling, and enduring history in British Columbia, and it's well represented in this Ming Dynasty–style facility. The art gallery upstairs hosts traveling exhibits by Chinese and Canadian artists, and an on-site military museum recalls the role of Chinese Canadians in the two world wars. Across the street is the Chinatown Memorial Monument, commemorating the Chinese-Canadian community's contribution to the city, province, and country. The monument, shaped in the Chinese character "zhong," symbolizing moderation and harmony, is flanked by bronze statues of a railroad worker and a World War II soldier. ⊠ *555 Columbia St., Chinatown* ☎ *604/658–8880* ⊕ *www. cccvan.com* ✉ *Donations welcome* ⊙ *Closed Mon.* Ⓜ *Stadium-Chinatown.*

★ Dr. Sun Yat-Sen Classical Chinese Garden

GARDEN | The first authentic Ming Dynasty–style garden outside China, this small garden was built in 1986 by 52 Chinese artisans from Suzhou. No power tools, screws, or nails were used in the construction. It incorporates design elements and traditional materials from several of Suzhou's centuries-old private gardens. Guided tours (45 minutes long), included in the ticket price, are conducted on the hour between mid-June and the end of August (call ahead or check the website for off-season tour times); these are valuable for understanding the philosophy and symbolism that are central to the garden's design. Covered walkways make this a good rainy-day choice. A concert series, including classical, Asian, world, jazz, and sacred music, plays on Thursday evenings in July and August. The free public park next door is a pleasant place to sit, but lacks the context that you get with a tour of the Sun Yat-Sen garden. ⊠ *578 Carrall St., Chinatown* ☎ *604/662–3207* ⊕ *www.vancouverchinesegarden.com* ✉ *C$13.33* ⊙ *Closed Mon., Oct.–Apr.* Ⓜ *Stadium-Chinatown.*

Millennium Gate

MEMORIAL | This four-pillar, three-story-high, brightly painted arch spanning Pender Street was erected in 2002 to mark the millennium and commemorate the Chinese community's role in Vancouver's history. The gate incorporates both Eastern and Western symbols, and both traditional and modern Chinese themes. Just east of the Millennium Gate, a right turn will take you into Shanghai Alley. Also known as Chinatown Heritage Alley, this was the site of the first Chinese settlement in the Vancouver area. By 1890 Shanghai Alley and neighboring Canton Alley were home to about 1,000 Chinese residents. At the end of the alley is a replica of the West Han Dynasty Bell, a gift to Vancouver from the city of Guangzhou, China. Surrounding the bell is a series of panels relaying some of the area's early history. ⊠ *Pender St. at Taylor St., Chinatown* Ⓜ *Stadium-Chinatown.*

Sam Kee Building

BUILDING | *Guinness World Records* recognizes this 6-foot-wide structure as the narrowest office building in the world. In 1913, after the city confiscated most of the then-owner's land to widen Pender Street, he built a store on what was left, in protest. Customers had to be served through the windows. The glass panes in the sidewalk on Pender Street once provided light for Chinatown's public baths, which, in the early 20th century, were in the basement here. The presence of this and other underground sites has fueled rumors that Chinatown and Gastown were connected by tunnels, enabling residents of the latter to anonymously enjoy the vices of the former. No such tunnels have been found, however. ✉ *8 W. Pender St., Chinatown* [M] *Stadium-Chinatown.*

🍴 Restaurants

A growing number of hip eateries have moved into Chinatown, alongside the more traditional Chinese restaurants.

Bao Bei

$$ | **CHINESE** | Start with an eclectic Chinatown storefront, stir in funky Asian-flavored cocktails, then add a creative take on traditional Chinese dishes, and the result is this hip and happening hangout. Load up your table with nibbles like Chinese pickles and steamed prawn, scallop, and chive dumplings or tapas-size dishes like *shao bing* (sesame flatbread with cumin-scented lamb, pickled red onion, cilantro, and chilis), *mantou* (steamed buns stuffed with pork belly and preserved turnip), or steelhead trout with kabocha cumin gnocchi, rapini, and shiso butter clam sauce. **Known for:** Asian-inspired cocktails; creative Chinese tapas; you tiao (donuts). [$] *Average main: C$18* ✉ *163 Keefer St., Chinatown* ☎ *604/688–0876* 🌐 *www.bao-bei.ca* 💳 *No credit cards* 🕗 *No lunch.*

★ Harvest Community Foods

$$ | **ASIAN FUSION** | This hip yet neighborhood-cozy Chinatown eatery is the sister restaurant of Burdock & Co. Enjoy health-conscious dishes that are delicious and hearty, like rice noodles with charred chili and almond-hazelnut sauce, ramen with squash and miso broth, and udon with sake kazu chicken, all of which utilize the very best of seasonally available produce. **Known for:** signature noodle soups; vegan dishes; community-supported agriculture. [$] *Average main: C$14* ✉ *243 Union St., Chinatown* ☎ *604/682-8851* 🌐 *www.harvestunion.ca.*

The Union

$$ | **ECLECTIC** | At this casually cool restaurant and lounge whose tagline could be "Asia's greatest hits," the sharing plates and fun cocktails have elements from Japan to India and everywhere in between. Start with a Banga, a cocktail in a jar, then choose Thai papaya salad, a Vietnamese *banh mi* (sandwich), or Indonesian *nasi goreng* (fried rice). **Known for:** pan-Asian menu; refreshing cocktails; steamed bao buns. [$] *Average main: C$15* ✉ *219 Union St., Chinatown* ☎ *604/568–3230* 🌐 *www.theunionvancouver.ca* 🕗 *No lunch weekdays.*

🍸 Nightlife

Development is rapidly expanding east in the city, and venues in the newly cool Chinatown are emerging as strong competition for those in adjacent Gastown.

BARS

The Emerald

PIANO BARS/LOUNGES | This second-floor venue on the eastern fringes of Vancouver's changing Chinatown includes a lounge, supper-club dining, and private rooms, all with a clubby, 1960s Las Vegas feel. There are excellent cocktails, and the occasional jazz, karaoke, or comedy show. ✉ *555 Gore St., Chinatown* ☎ *604/559–8477* 🌐 *www.emeraldsupperclub.com.*

★ The Keefer Bar

BARS/PUBS | The Keefer Bar has fully capitalized on its Chinatown connection, using ingredients sourced from local herbalists (magnolia bark anyone?)—ginseng, tea-based tinctures, or astragalus root, for example. Small plates of Asian dishes make good nibbling. The decor is dark and red, with hanging cylindrical neon lights that layer a sultry, hidden vibe over nights of live music and DJs. ✉ *135 Keefer St., Chinatown* ☎ *604/688–1961* 🌐 *www.thekeeferbar.com.*

A Bit About Buying Aboriginal Art

With 198 First Nations groups in British Columbia alone, it's easy to be mesmerized, even confused, by the range and diversity of the indigenous art you'll see. Different bands have traded materials, skills, and resources for centuries, so today it's often difficult to attribute any particular style to any one group. It's this blending, though, that has created such a rich cultural mosaic. That said, there are still some groups, such as the Haida and Coast Salish, who have strong identifiable traits.

Broadly speaking, First Nations art is a language of symbols, which come together to describe the legends and stories that link one community with another. Contrary to popular belief, although these symbols may share a similar meaning, they are by no means a common language: the Coast Salish, for example, view the hummingbird differently from how the Tsimshian Tribe do.

According to Rikki Kooy, whose Shuswap name is Spirit Elk Woman, there are two heartfelt ways many people purchase First Nations art. "The first is to fall in love with a region of British Columbia, and find the First Nations group that represents that area," she says. "The second is to fall in love with a piece for its calling." Kooy has been involved with retailing aboriginal art for more than 35 years and is a former adviser to Aboriginal Tourism BC.

Once you've found yourself drawn to a particular piece, whether it's jewelry, a mask, or a print, there are three essential questions to consider in judging its integrity and authenticity.

Does the work or design have a title? Because First Nations art is highly symbolic, authentic pieces will be titled. The title will usually allude to mythical lore, real-life stories, and/or the artist's ancestry.

Is the cultural group identified? Every piece holds a story, against which there is often a broader background of heritage, hierarchy, and geographic origin. For example, a Haida piece will likely have come from Haida Gwaii, or have been made by a descendant from that region. By knowing the region, the nuances of the piece's symbolic language are more easily identifiable.

Is the artist named, or better still, is there a background sheet available? First Nations peoples hold relationships in high esteem, so dealers with integrity will have a relationship with the artists they represent and should have a background sheet on the artist and his or her heritage. This adds to the authenticity of the work and gives background about the artist and his or her other works.

DANCE CLUBS
Fortune Sound Club
DANCE CLUBS | This sound-system-centric dance club and performance venue keeps the audience guessing with a mix of shows (often with hip-hop leanings). The second-floor space has red oak flooring and manages to incorporate local and eco-friendly elements into the design—so Vancouver! ⊠ *147 E. Pender St., Chinatown* ☎ *604/569–1758* ⊕ *www.fortunesoundclub.com.*

🛍 Shopping

Bustling Chinatown—centered on Pender and Main streets—is full of Chinese bakeries, restaurants, herbalists, tea merchants, and import shops, as well as a new crop of funky boutiques, cocktail lounges, and casual eateries.

FOOD

T&T Supermarket

FOOD/CANDY | Check out this chain of Asian supermarkets for exotic produce, baked goods, and prepared foods. You can assemble an inexpensive lunch-to-go from the extensive hot food counter. In addition to this Chinatown location, there are nine other branches around Metro Vancouver. ✉ *179 Keefer Pl., Chinatown* 🕿 *604/899–8836* ⊕ *www.tnt-supermarket.com.*

Yaletown

Yaletown is one of Vancouver's most fashionable areas and one of the most impressive urban-redevelopment projects in North America.

Back in about 1985 the BC provincial government decided they were going to take a derelict industrial site on the north shore of False Creek, clean it up, and build a world's fair. Twenty million people showed up for Expo '86, and Yaletown, on the site of the fair, was born. The brick warehouses were turned into apartment buildings and offices, and the old loading docks are now terraces for cappuccino bars and trendy restaurants. There are brewpubs, day spas, retail and wholesale fashion outlets, and shops selling upscale home decor.

There's also a seaside walk and cycle path that completely encircles False Creek. It's hard to imagine that back in the 1880s and '90s this was probably the most lawless place in Canada: it was so far into the woods that the Royal Canadian Mounted Police complained they couldn't patrol it.

👁 Sights

BC Sports Hall of Fame and Museum

MUSEUM | FAMILY | Inside the BC Place Stadium complex, this museum celebrates the province's sports achievers in a series of historical displays. One gallery commemorates the 2010 Winter Olympics that were held in Vancouver; another honors the province's aboriginal artists. You can test your sprinting, climbing, and throwing prowess in the high-tech participation gallery. The Scavenger History Hunt quiz is equally engaging though not as energetic. An hour-long audio tour is included with admission. As you leave the museum, the **Terry Fox Memorial** is to your left. Created by artist Douglas Coupland, this series of four statues, each larger than the next, was built in honor of Terry Fox (1958–81), a local student whose cross-Canada run—after he lost his leg to cancer—raised millions of dollars for cancer research. Although Fox succumbed to the disease before he could complete his "Marathon of Hope," a memorial fund-raising run is now held annually in cities across Canada and around the world. ✉ *BC Place, 777 Pacific Blvd. S, Gate A, at Beatty and Robson Sts., Yaletown* 🕿 *604/687–5520* ⊕ *www.bcsportshalloffame.com* 💵 *C$18* Ⓜ *Stadium-Chinatown.*

Contemporary Art Gallery

MUSEUM | On the lobby level of a modern apartment tower, this small nonprofit public gallery has regularly changing exhibits of contemporary local and international visual art. Events include artists' talks, lectures, and tours. ✉ *555 Nelson St., Yaletown* 🕿 *604/681–2700* ⊕ *www.contemporaryartgallery.ca* 💵 *Free* 🕙 *Closed Mon.* Ⓜ *Yaletown-Roundhouse.*

Top Places to Stroll

Vancouver is a city for getting outdoors and walking around. These are some of our favorite streets for a stroll.

Robson Street: A shopaholic's dream come true, Robson has everything from finger-licking-good fudge to fashionista shopping.

Granville Island: It's always a voyage of discovery for fabulous local art, foodstuffs, boutique shops, street entertainment, and more.

West 4th Avenue: This Kitsilano strip is a prime shopping and eating destination, with funky fashions, fun gifts, and fine food.

Main Street: On the city's East Side, this is where many of Vancouver's independent fashion designers have set up shop: you'll find creative clothing and jewelry, plus several vintage and consignment boutiques.

Chinatown: Take your pick of exotic teas, sea cucumbers, dried seahorses, and nifty gifts along Keefer and East Pender streets; look for a growing number of eclectic boutiques around the neighborhood, too.

Commercial Drive: From coffeehouses to the cantinas, "The Drive" has a healthy serving of cultural cool with an eclectic array of people and shops.

The West End: This lovely, tree-lined neighborhood is a refreshing change of pace from the urban commotion steps away.

Harborfront shoreline: With the water's edge on one side and glassy, million-dollar condo developments and commercial high-rises on the other, a walk along the harborfront epitomizes the future of this city.

Marinaside Crescent: Residents of Yaletown's intense-density condos flock to this walking and cycling path around False Creek. Combine your walk with a ride on an Aquabus ferry if time is short or your feet get weary.

Library Square

LIBRARY | The spiraling library building, open plazas, and lofty atrium of Library Square, completed in the mid-1990s, were built to evoke images of the Colosseum in Rome. A high-tech public library is the core of the structure; the outer edge of the spiral houses cafés and fast-food outlets. ✉ *350 W. Georgia St., Yaletown* ☎ *604/331–3603* 🌐 *www.vpl.ca* [M] *Stadium-Chinatown.*

🍴 Restaurants

Stylish restaurants have taken up space in the old warehouse buildings and nearby spaces in this now-trendy neighborhood.

★ **Blue Water Cafe**

$$$$ | **SEAFOOD** | Executive chef Frank Pabst focuses his menu on both popular and lesser-known local seafood (including frequently overlooked varieties like mackerel or herring) at his widely heralded, fashionable fish restaurant. You can dine in the warmly lighted interior or outside on the former loading dock that's now a lovely terrace. **Known for:** seafood-centric menu; top-notch sushi; great local wine list. [$] *Average main: C$38* ✉ *1095 Hamilton St., Yaletown* ☎ *604/688–8078* 🌐 *www.bluewatercafe.net* ⏲ *No lunch.*

Cioppino's Mediterranean Grill & Enoteca

$$$$ | **ITALIAN** | Cioppino, the eponymous seafood stew, is the signature dish at this lofty candlelit room. Chef Pino

BC Place in Yaletown, where professional soccer matches and other events take place, has one of the largest retractable roofs in the world.

Posteraro impresses with homemade pastas and such Italian-Mediterranean dishes as Haida Gwaii hailbut with confit garlic and Sicilian capers, and roasted rack of lamb with a candied garlic-lemon reduction. **Known for:** rustic Italian fare; street-side patio; impressive wine list. $ *Average main: C$45* ⊠ *1133 Hamilton St., Yaletown* ☎ *604/688–7466* ⊕ *www. cioppinosyaletown.com* ⊗ *Closed Sun. and Mon. No lunch.*

Hapa Izakaya
$$ | JAPANESE | Serving small plates designed for sharing, this spirited Japanese tapas bar is known for the mackerel dish, seared table-side with a blowtorch. Also worth trying are the *ebi mayo* (tempura shrimp with spicy mayonnaise), the *ishi-yaki* (a Korean-style stone bowl filled with rice, pork, and vegetables), and anything on the daily fresh sheet. **Known for:** table-seared mackerel; daily fresh sheet menu; Japanese tapas. $ *Average main: C$14* ⊠ *1193 Hamilton St., Yaletown* ☎ *604/681–4272* ⊕ *www.hapaizakaya. com* ⊗ *No lunch.*

Homer St. Cafe and Bar
$$$ | MODERN CANADIAN | Chicken is the specialty at this classy bistro where the juicy rotisserie-roasted birds are served with peewee potatoes and (optionally) an extra portion of crispy skin. Other creative comfort foods include crispy fish balls with lemon-chili aioli; salmon with couscous, olives, yogurt, and lemon; and grilled steak served with sweet corn, peppers, and red chimichurri. **Known for:** rotisserie chicken; daily fresh menu; notable brunch. $ *Average main: C$26* ⊠ *898 Homer St., Yaletown* ☎ *604/428–4299* ⊕ *www.homerstreetcafebar.com.*

La Pentola
$$$ | ITALIAN | This chic dining room at the Opus, Yaletown's most stylish hotel, serves innovative interpretations of Italian classics. The pastas are homemade, the fish is freshly grilled, and dishes like Gorgonzola risotto or the 16-ounce veal chop would do any *nonna* proud. **Known for:** family-style tasting menu; Italian classics; great breakfast. $ *Average main: C$25* ⊠ *Opus Hotel Vancouver, 350 Davie*

St., Yaletown ☎ 604/642–0557 🌐 www.lapentola.ca.

O-Cha Tea Bar

$ | **CAFÉ** | Because Vancouverites don't live by coffee alone—they're also tea drinkers—look for this tiny Yaletown tea bar that serves 60 of its own blends, including rich, milky "Lat-Teas." If you're feeling under the weather, order the "Cold Blaster," a rejuvenating blend of tea, orange juice, honey, ginger, and cayenne pepper. **Known for:** unique tea blends; tea lattes. [$] *Average main: C$6 ✉ 1116 Homer St., Yaletown ☎ 604/633–3929 💳 No credit cards ⏲ Closed Sun.*

Provence Marinaside

$$$$ | **MEDITERRANEAN** | You can imagine yourself on the Provençal seaside at this airy, modern, Mediterranean-style bistro on Yaletown's waterfront, where the focus is on French and Italian takes on seafood. Among the specialties are a delicious bouillabaisse, grilled halibut, and lush, garlicky wild prawns. **Known for:** marina-view patio; Mediterranean antipasti; breakfast pastries. [$] *Average main: C$36 ✉ 1177 Marinaside Crescent, at Davie St., Yaletown ☎ 604/681–4144 🌐 www.provencemarinaside.ca.*

Rodney's Oyster House

$$ | **SEAFOOD** | This faux fishing shack in Yaletown has one of the city's widest selections of oysters (up to 18 varieties), from locally harvested bivalves to exotic Japanese Kumamotos—they're all laid out on ice behind the bar—or try the clams, scallops, mussels, and other mollusks from the steamer kettles. If you're fishing for an afternoon snack, swim in between 3 and 6 pm when a light menu of raw oysters, steamed clams, garlic prawns, and a few additional seafood nibbles are served. **Known for:** extensive oyster selection; happy hour specials; delicious clam chowder. [$] *Average main: C$20 ✉ 1228 Hamilton St., Yaletown ☎ 604/609–0080 🌐 www.rohvan.com.*

Hotels

★ Douglas Hotel

$$$$ | **RESORT** | The Douglas, an Autograph Collection Hotel, is a stunning one-of-a-kind property created by Marriott and situated within the city's newest entertainment destination, Parq Vancouver. **Pros:** steps from False Creek and the seawall; multiple dining options; dog-friendly. **Cons:** strong signature fragrance in lobby; several minutes' walk to the heart of Downtown; hotel parking is expensive. [$] *Rooms from: C$320 ✉ Parq Vancouver, 39 Smithe St., Yaletown ☎ 604/676-0889 🌐 thedouglasvancouver.com 🛏 288 rooms 🍴 No meals.*

Hotel BLU Vancouver

$$$ | **HOTEL** | A designer blend of comfort, high-tech, and, especially, eco-friendly features, Hotel BLU Vancouver could almost be called "Hotel Green" because of the focus on sustainability. **Pros:** close to theaters and sports arenas; free guest laundry; indoor pool and sauna. **Cons:** only suites and lofts have bathtubs; sports crowds swarm the neighborhood on event days; pricey parking fees. [$] *Rooms from: C$225 ✉ 177 Robson St., Yaletown ☎ 604/620–6200, 855/284–2091 🌐 www.hotelbluvancouver.com 🛏 75 rooms 🍴 No meals.*

★ JW Marriott Parq Vancouver

$$$$ | **RESORT** | Within the Parq Vancouver complex, the JW Marriott Parq Vancouver occupies two towers. **Pros:** amazing spa; 60,000 square feet of meeting and event space; multiple dining options. **Cons:** several minute walk to the heart of Downtown; rooms have the hotel's signature scent; hotel parking is expensive. [$] *Rooms from: C$320 ✉ Parq Vancouver, 39 Smithe St., Yaletown ☎ 604/676-0888 🌐 www.JWMarriottParqVancouver.com 🛏 329 rooms 🍴 No meals.*

OPUS Vancouver Hotel

$$$ | HOTEL | Groundbreakingly trendy when it opened in 2002, the OPUS continues to reinvent itself and live up to the motto of being a "place to be, not just a place to stay." The design team created a set of online fictitious characters, then decorated the rooms to suit each "persona." Guests are matched with room styles using the Lifestyle Concierge. **Pros:** great Yaletown location, right by rapid transit; funky and hip vibe; the lobby bar is a fashionable meeting spot. **Cons:** trendy nightspots nearby can be noisy at night; expensive and limited parking; fitness center could be larger. $ *Rooms from: C$300* ✉ *322 Davie St., Yaletown* ☎ *604/642–6787, 866/642–6787* ⊕ *www. vancouver.opushotel.com* ➔ *96 rooms* ⦿ *No meals.*

ⓨ Nightlife

Restaurants become cocktail lounges after dark in Yaletown. Once warehouse loading docks, the brick-lined patios are prime for people-watching (and fancy-car-spotting: luxury vehicles are a common sight on Mainland and Hamilton streets). This area gets busy early and continues to late night.

BARS

Opus Bar

PIANO BARS/LOUNGES | Traveling executives in suits and film industry creatives sip martinis (or perhaps a cocktail made with bourbon and blood oranges) while scoping out the room, on the ground floor of the Opus Hotel. During the day, it's a sleek café. ✉ *Opus Hotel, 350 Davie St., Yaletown* ☎ *604/642–0557* ⊕ *www. opusbar.ca.*

Yaletown Brewing Company

BREWPUBS/BEER GARDENS | In a renovated warehouse with a glassed-in brewery turning out several tasty beers, this always-crowded gastropub and patio has a lively singles scene and reliable happy hour. Even though it's super

popular it still feels like a neighborhood place. ✉ *1111 Mainland St., Yaletown* ☎ *604/681–2739* ⊕ *www.mjg.ca/ yaletown.*

CASINOS

Parq Casino

CASINOS | Opened in 2017, this entertainment mecca encompasses a casino, two high-end hotels, several excellent dining options, and a spa. The 72,000-square-foot gaming space features 600 machines and Fortune high-limit slots, as well as table games that span two floors. Access to the casino is 24/7. ✉ *Parq Vancouver, 39 Smithe St., Yaletown* ☎ *604/683-7277* ⊕ *www.parqvancouver. com/casino.*

DANCE CLUBS

Bar None

DANCE CLUBS | Once you hit Bar None you never really have to leave Yaletown. This longtime favorite is the place to get your groove on after dinner and drinks. Wide wood beams, exposed brick, and trendy lighting give it that Yaletown warehouse history-meets-hip feel. Celebrated Vancouver DJs spin house and electronica on weekend nights, and international stars sometimes take over as well. ✉ *1222 Hamilton St., Yaletown* ☎ *604/689–7000* ⊕ *www.barnoneclub.com.*

🛍 Shopping

Frequently described as Vancouver's SoHo, Yaletown, on the north bank of False Creek, is where you'll find boutiques, home furnishings stores, and restaurants—many in converted warehouses—that cater to a trendy, moneyed crowd.

FOOD AND WINE

Fine Finds Boutique

CLOTHING | It's hard to predict what you'll find in this pretty little shop—it's a fun spot to browse for cute women's clothing, jewelry, and accessories. ✉ *1014 Mainland St., Yaletown* ☎ *604/669–8325* ⊕ *www.finefindsboutique.com.*

Ganache Patisserie

FOOD/CANDY | In true Parisian style, every delicious and decadent item here is a work of art. You can buy whole cakes—perhaps a chocolate-banana cake or a coconut mango cheesecake—but just a slice will perk up your shopping day. ✉ *1262 Homer St., Yaletown* ☎ *604/899–1098* ⊕ *www.ganacheyaletown.com.*

Swirl

WINE/SPIRITS | To learn more about British Columbia wines, or to pick up a bottle (or a few), visit the knowledgeable staff at this Yaletown store that stocks more than 750 varieties produced in the province. There are complimentary tastings offered weekend afternoons. ✉ *1185 Mainland St., Yaletown* ☎ *604/408–9463* ⊕ *www. swirlwinestore.ca.*

 # Activities

BIKING

Reckless Bike Stores

BICYCLING | This outfit rents bikes on the Yaletown section of Vancouver's Seawall route. To explore Granville Island, check out the branch at 1810 Fir St. in Kitsilano and 1357 Hornby St. by the Burrard St. Bridge. ✉ *110 Davie St., Yaletown* ☎ *604/648–2600* ⊕ *www.reckless.ca.*

SPAS

Skoah

SPA/BEAUTY | By specializing in facials, Skoah has created a niche for itself. There's no froufrou here, just top-quality skin care for men and women that raises the facial to a level all its own. The contemporary design has a New York sassiness and the staff even does foot and hand "facials." There are several branches throughout Vancouver and the lower mainland. ✉ *1007 Hamilton St., Yaletown* ☎ *604/642–0200* ⊕ *www. skoah.com.*

Chapter 5

GRANVILLE ISLAND

Updated by
Lesley Mirza

👁 Sights	🍴 Restaurants	🛏 Hotels	🛍 Shopping	🍸 Nightlife
★★☆☆☆	★★★☆☆	★★☆☆☆	★★★☆☆	★★☆☆☆

NEIGHBORHOOD SNAPSHOT

TOP EXPERIENCES

■ **Get Lost:** Explore and lose yourself, secure in the knowledge that the island's layout doesn't allow you actually to get lost.

■ **Kayak False Creek:** A guided paddle promises a very different perspective about living by and on the water; watch for seal encounters of the close-up kind.

■ **Take a Foodie Tour:** A feast awaits when you take a guided graze through the fun and flavors of the market.

■ **Enjoy the Buskers:** The curb-side entertainers audition to earn a coveted island spot so applaud their performance: put a dollar or two into their hat.

■ **Eagle Spirit Gallery:** Displaying its impressive collection in a museum-like setting, this is Vancouver's largest First Nations gallery.

GETTING HERE

The mini Aquabus ferries are a favorite way to get to Granville Island. They depart from the south end of Hornby Street and take passengers across False Creek to the Granville Island Public Market (it's about a two-minute ride). The larger False Creek ferries depart for Granville Island from a dock behind the Vancouver Aquatic Centre, on Beach Avenue. Still another option is to take a 10-minute ride on a Trans-Link bus: from Waterfront Station or stops on Granville Street, take Bus 50 to the edge of the island. Several other Granville Street buses, including the 4, the 7, the 10, the 14, and 16, stop at West 5th Avenue and Granville Street, a 10-minute walk from the island. Come by public transit if you can, because the island's narrow roadways get clogged with traffic. If you do drive, parking is free for up to three hours (free spots can be hard to find); paid parking is available in several island garages.

PLANNING YOUR TIME

If your schedule is tight, you can tour Granville Island in two to three hours. If you like to shop, you could spend a full day.

QUICK BITES

■ **Off the Tracks Espresso Bar & Bistro.** *Organic*, *sustainable*, and *local* describe the ethos of this café—everything you eat and/or drink has been sourced with those words at heart. ✉ *1363 Railspur Alley, Granville Island* ⊕ *www.tracksbistro.ca* Ⓜ *Granville Island, Bus 50.*

■ **Blue Hat Bakery.** This is where the culinary students of the adjoining school strut their stuff; standards are high and the artisanal breads, soups, wraps, and gourmet desserts are outstanding. ✉ *101-1505 West 2nd Ave., Granville Island* ⊕ *www.picachef.com* Ⓜ *Granville Island, Bus 50.*

■ **Go Fish.** Located beside the seawall leading to the island, don't let the shabbiness of the shack be your guide: it dishes up some of the best fish-and-chips in Vancouver. ✉ *1505 West 1st Ave., Granville Island Granville Island, Bus 50.*

An indoor food market and a thriving diversity of artist studios as well as performing arts spaces, specialty shops (there's not a chain store or designer label in sight), and a busy marina make Granville Island one of Vancouver's top attractions.

Explore at your leisure but try to plan your expedition over a meal, because the market is an excellent place for breakfast, lunch, snacks, and shopping. The buildings behind the market are as diverse as the island's main attractions and house all sorts of crafts shops. The waterside boardwalk behind the Arts Club and around the Creekhouse building will bring you to Ocean Art Works, an open-sided longhouse-style structure where you can watch First Nations artists at work. Make time to visit the free contemporary galleries beside the covered walkway, and Sea Village, one of the few houseboat communities in Vancouver. Other nooks and alleys to note are Ron Basford Park, a natural amphitheater for outdoor performances, and Railspur Alley, home to about a dozen studios and galleries that produce everything from jewelry to leather work and sake.

In the early 20th century, False Creek was dredged for better access to the sawmills that lined the shore, and the sludge was heaped onto a sandbar that grew large enough to house much-needed industrial and logging-equipment plants. Although businesses thrived in the 1920s, most fell into derelict status by the '60s. In the early '70s, though, the federal government came up with a creative plan to redevelop the island with a public market, marine activities, and

artisans' studios. The refurbished Granville Island opened to the public in 1979 and was an immediate hit with locals and visitors alike.

◉ Sights

Granville Island Brewing
WINERY/DISTILLERY | Daily tours of Canada's first modern microbrewery last about 50 minutes and include a 5-ounce taste of three brews. Tours are booked on a first-come, first-served basis and run at 11:30, 1:00, 2:30, 4:00, and 5:30. Note: You must be 19 years old and wearing closed-toed shoes to take a tour. ✉ *1441 Cartwright St., Granville Island* ☎ *604/687–2739* ⊕ *www.gib.ca* 💲 *Adults C$12; Seniors/Students C$10.*

★ Granville Island Public Market
MARKET | FAMILY | The dozens of stalls in this world-renowned market sell locally grown fruits and vegetables direct from the farm and farther afield; other stalls stock crafts, chocolates, artisanal cheeses and pastas, fish, meat, flowers, and exotic foods. On Thursdays in the summer (July to October), farmers sell fruit and vegetables from trucks outside. At the north end of the market, you can pick up a snack, lunch, or coffee from one of the many prepared-food vendors. The Public Market Courtyard, on the waterside, has great views of the city and is

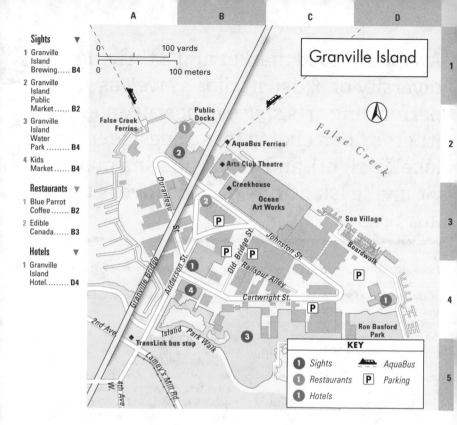

Granville Island

KEY

- ● Sights
- ● Restaurants
- ● Hotels
- 🚢 AquaBus
- **P** Parking

---

also a good place to catch street entertainers—be prepared to get roped into the action, if only to check the padlocks of an escape artist's gear. Weekends can get madly busy. ✉ *1689 Johnston St., Granville Island* ☎ *604/666–6655* ⊕ *www. granvilleisland.com.*

Granville Island Water Park

AMUSEMENT PARK/WATER PARK | FAMILY | North America's largest free public water park has multiple sprays and fountains for children to run through and a great slide to zoom down. There's a grassy patch for picnics, and clean washrooms are at the adjacent community center. ✉ *1318 Cartwright St., Granville Island* ☎ *604/257–8194* ⊕ *www.falsecreekcc. ca/waterpark* 🎫 *Free* ⊗ *Closed Labor Day–mid-May; closed weekdays from mid-May to end of June.*

Kids Market

MARKET | FAMILY | A converted factory warehouse sets the stage for a slice of kids' heaven on Granville Island. The Kids Market has an indoor play area and two floors of small shops that sell all kinds of toys, magic gear, books, and other fun stuff. ✉ *1496 Cartwright St., Granville Island* ☎ *604/689–8447* ⊕ *www. kidsmarket.ca.*

🍴 Restaurants

Most visitors to Granville Island assemble a picnic or a light meal from the public market but the island has a few sit-down bistros, too.

Blue Parrot Coffee

$ | CAFÉ | Granville Island has several coffee places, but only the Blue Parrot provides sweeping views of False Creek.

If you haven't eaten your fill elsewhere in the market, accompany your espresso with a sticky cinnamon bun. **Known for:** unbeatable views; good coffee; hearty sandwiches. $ *Average main: C$8* ⊠ *Granville Island Public Market, 1689 Johnston St., Granville Island* ☎ *604/688–5127* ⊕ *www.blueparrotcoffee.com.*

Edible Canada

$$$ | **MODERN CANADIAN** | At this contemporary bistro with a patio for people-watching, you can sample foods from BC and across Canada. Smaller appetites might gravitate toward the bison tartare, while hungrier travelers can sup on wild Pacific salmon with sunchokes, fennel, beets, and a butter sauce. **Known for:** Canadian cuisine; duck-fat fries; seasonal menus. $ *Average main: C$25* ⊠ *1596 Johnston St., Granville Island* ☎ *604/682–6681* ⊕ *www.ediblecanada.com.*

🛏 Hotels

Granville Island Hotel

$$$ | **HOTEL** | **FAMILY** | Granville Island is one of Vancouver's most popular destinations, for locals and visitors, but unless you've moored up in a houseboat, the only overnight option is the Granville Island Hotel. **Pros:** unique island location; within steps of great dining and theater; free Wi-Fi. **Cons:** island gets busy on weekends; walk or use ferry transit to get here; some rooms are small. $ *Rooms from: C$300* ⊠ *1253 Johnston St., Granville Island* ☎ *604/683–7373, 800/663–1840* ⊕ *www.granvilleislandhotel.com* ⤴ *82 rooms* ⊚ *No meals.*

☮ Nightlife

Dockside patios are the thing here, especially before or after a performance at one of the area's many theaters.

BARS

Bridges

BARS/PUBS | This bright yellow landmark near the Granville Public Market has a cozy nautical-theme pub and the city's biggest marina-side deck. In warm weather the outdoor seating has breathtaking views of the harbor, mountains, and city. ⊠ *1696 Duranleau St., Granville Island* ☎ *604/687–4400* ⊕ *www.bridges-restaurant.com.*

Dockside Restaurant

WINE BARS—NIGHTLIFE | Overlooking False Creek and Yaletown, the Dockside's patio is the big draw, especially for owners of chic yachts moored alongside. Because it faces east, sunsets are behind the building and cool shadows come early, so grab a table beneath a heater. Floor-to-ceiling windows make the inside feel like the outside with decor that exudes a modern vibe and includes a 50-foot aquarium. House-brewed ales and lagers are served from the adjoining casual brewpub. ⊠ *Granville Island Hotel, 1253 Johnston St., Granville Island* ☎ *604/685–7070* ⊕ *www.docksidevancouver.com.*

Granville Island Brewery

BREWPUBS/BEER GARDENS | This small-brewery-gone-big is where the craft beer revolution began. Back in 1984, it was Canada's first microbrewery. It has grown incredibly since, and the bustling Granville Island atmosphere is perfect for a tour and tasting of beer history. ⊠ *1441 Cartwright St., Granville Island* ☎ *604/687–2739* ⊕ *www.gib.ca.*

The Sandbar

PIANO BARS/LOUNGES | With a seafood restaurant, a sushi bar, and live music nightly (piano Sunday to Thursday; rotating acts Friday and Saturday) in the wine bar, this venue has something for everyone. For dramatic views over False Creek, reserve a table on the rooftop patio, which is open year-round. Make sure to try their to-die-for crab cake! ⊠ *1535 Johnson St., Granville Island* ☎ *604/669–9030* ⊕ *www.vancouverdine.com/sandbar.*

Did You Know?

The rainbow-colored Aquabus ferries, one of the most popular ways to get to Granville Island, have been serving False Creek and the surrounding area since 1985.

COMEDY CLUBS

★ Vancouver TheatreSports League

COMEDY CLUBS | Since 1980, this award-winning theater troupe has been performing hilarious improv. Catch a show before an enthusiastic crowd Wednesday to Saturday evenings (January–June), and during the second half of the year (July–December, including the holiday season), VTS performs Tuesdays through Sunday evenings, plus some weekend matinees in the holiday season. The rookie showcase on Sunday can be entertaining. ⊠ 1502 Duranleau St., Granville Island ☎ 604/738-7013 ⊕ www.vtsl.com.

MUSIC: ROCK AND BLUES

Backstage Lounge

MUSIC CLUBS | Local bands and solo artists of varying genres—from jazz to tribute bands—perform most nights. Even though the music is hit or miss, the drink specials are cheap and reliable. ⊠ 1585 Johnston St., Granville Island ☎ 604/687-1354 ⊕ www.thebackstagelounge.com.

🎫 Performing Arts

THEATER

★ Arts Club Theatre Company

THEATER | The Arts Club Theatre Company stages productions (a few by local playwrights) on three principal stages: the Stanley Industrial Alliance Stage on South Granville, the Granville Island Stage, and a third in False Creek's Olympic Village. ⊠ 1585 Johnston St., Granville Island ☎ 604/687-1644 ⊕ www.artsclub.com.

Carousel Theatre for Young People

THEATER | FAMILY | Children's theater is the focus here, with most performances across the street at the Waterfront Theatre, though some are elsewhere in the city. ⊠ 1411 Cartwright St., Granville Island ☎ 604/685-6217 ⊕ www.carouseltheatre.ca.

Waterfront Theatre

THEATER | Next door to Granville Island's Kids Market, this theater often hosts children and youth-oriented performances. Its intimate size is also lovely for writers' readings, dance shows, and plays. ⊠ 1412 Cartwright St., Granville Island ☎ 604/685-1731 ⊕ www.waterfronttheatre.ca.

🛍 Shopping

On the south side of False Creek, Granville Island has a lively food market and a wealth of galleries, crafts shops, and artisans' studios, many of which you'll find in the Net Loft building in the center of the island.

Granville Island gets so busy, especially on summer weekends, that the crowds can detract from the pleasure of the place; you're best off getting there before 11 am or going during the week. The **Kids Market,** in a converted warehouse, has kids' shops as well as an indoor play area.

ART AND ANTIQUES

Circle Craft

CRAFTS | This artist co-op sells finely crafted textiles, wood pieces, jewelry, ceramics, and glass works. Chosen by juried selection, the artists are all local to British Columbia and all their work must be made by hand. ⊠ Net Loft, 1–1666 Johnston St., Granville Island ☎ 604/669-8021 ⊕ www.circlecraft.net.

Craft Council of BC Shop & Gallery

CRAFTS | Run by the Craft Council of British Columbia, this tiny structure contains a veritable smorgasbord of works by local artisans. The artworks range from jewelry and other small gift items to large investment pieces. For last-minute shopping, visit their location at the Vancouver International Airport, on the Domestic Departures level. ⊠ 1386 Cartwright St., Granville Island ☎ 604/687-7270 ⊕ www.craftcouncilbc.ca.

The Granville Island Public Market is a can't-miss attraction on Granville Island.

Eagle Spirit Gallery

ART GALLERIES | The museum-style gallery showcases some of the finest and refreshingly contemporary First Nations and Inuit art in Vancouver. The collection is constantly changing and although several pieces are geared for the serious investor, others are more affordable. If First Nations art is of interest, then a look-see here is a must. ✉ *1803 Maritime Mews, Granville Island* ☎ *604/801-5277* ⊕ *www.eaglespiritgallery.com.*

Lattimer Gallery

CRAFTS | Stocking native arts and crafts in all price ranges, this shop, which is designed to resemble a Pacific Northwest longhouse, is a short stroll from Granville Island. Look for masks, jewelry, bentwood boxes, carvings, and other works that reflect First Nations and Inuit designs. ✉ *1590 W. 2nd Ave., Granville Island* ☎ *604/732-4556* ⊕ *www.lattimergallery.com.*

CLOTHING

Dream Apparel and Articles for People

CLOTHING | This tiny shop showcases a variety of wares by up-and-coming local designers. The creative selections target the hip twentysomething crowd. ✉ *Net Loft, 130–1666 Johnston St., Granville Island* ☎ *604/683-7326* ⊕ *www.dream-vancouver.com.*

FOOD AND WINE

Artisan Sake Maker

WINE/SPIRITS | You can learn all about sake (Japanese rice wine), and sample the locally made product, at Vancouver's own sake brewery. ✉ *1339 Railspur Alley, Granville Island* ☎ *604/685-7253* ⊕ *www.artisansakemaker.com.*

★ Edible Canada

FOOD/CANDY | Tucked behind the Edible Canada bistro, this little shop sells jams, sauces, chocolates, and dozens of other edible items from around the country. It's a great place to find gifts for foodie friends. ✉ *1596 Johnston St., Granville Island* ☎ *604/682-6675* ⊕ *www.edible-canada.com.*

Liberty Distillery

WINE/SPIRITS | Crafting organic, artisanal vodka, gin, and whiskey from 100% BC grain, this distillery offers tastings in its stylish Granville Island shop. You can take a guided distillery tour (C$10) on weekends at 11:30 am or 1:30 pm. ⊠ *1494 Old Bridge Rd., Granville Island* ☎ *604/558–1998* ⊕ *thelibertydistillery.com.*

Liberty Wine Merchants

WINE/SPIRITS | The helpful employees at this local chain can assist you in selecting wines from BC or around the world. ⊠ *1660 Johnston St., Granville Island* ☎ *604/602–1120* ⊕ *www.libertywinemerchants.com.*

SPAS

Semperviva Yoga Studios

AEROBICS/YOGA | The Granville Island location of Semperviva, one of Vancouver's most popular yoga studios, is called the Sea Studio, and it overlooks False Creek. The drop-in fee is C$25+ tax, including a mat. ⊠ *1333 Johnston St., Suite 200, Granville Island* ☎ *604/739–2009* ⊕ *www.semperviva.com.*

SPECIALTY STORES

Granville Island Hat Shop

CLOTHING | You name the hat and somewhere on the walls, rafters, or shelves you'll find it. There are fedoras, cloches, toques, sun hats, rain hats, straw hats, and pretty much any other hat you might want. ⊠ *Net Loft, 4–1666 Johnston St., Granville Island* ☎ *604/683–4280* ⊕ *www.thehatshop.ca.*

⊛ Activities

FISHING

Bonnie Lee Fishing Charters

FISHING | From moorings by the Granville Island Maritime Market, this company runs five-hour fishing trips into Burrard Inlet and the Strait of Georgia, year-round. Guided outings start at C$550 for the boat. ⊠ *104–1676 Duranleau St., Granville Island* ☎ *604/290–7447* ⊕ *www.bonnielee.com.*

KAYAKING

Vancouver Water Adventures

SAILING | Established in 2009, the company offers rentals of Sea-Doos, kayaks, and paddleboards, kayak and paddleboard lessons, and a variety of tours. They also have locations at Kitsilano Beach and English Bay. ⊠ *1812 Boatlift Ln., Granville Island* ☎ *604/736-5155* ⊕ *www.vancouverwateradventures.com.*

WHALE-WATCHING

Wild Whales Vancouver

WHALE-WATCHING | Boats leave Granville Island in search of orca pods in the Strait of Georgia, often traveling as far as Victoria. Rates are C$145 for a three- to six-hour trip in either an open or glass-domed boat (trip lengths depend on where the whales are hanging out on a particular day). Each boat leaves once daily, April through October, conditions permitting. ⊠ *1806 Mast Tower Rd., Granville Island* ☎ *604/699–2011* ⊕ *www.whalesvancouver.com.*

WEST SIDE

KITSILANO, POINT GREY, SOUTH GRANVILLE, CAMBIE CORRIDOR

6

Updated by
Vanessa Pinniger

◉ Sights
★★★★★

🍴 Restaurants
★★★★★

🛏 Hotels
★★☆☆☆

🛍 Shopping
★★★★★

🍸 Nightlife
★★★★★

NEIGHBORHOOD SNAPSHOT

TOP EXPERIENCES

■ **Kits Beach:** The city's busiest beach is home to Kits Pool, the longest pool in Canada and one of the few heated outdoor saltwater pools in the world.

■ **Bard on the Beach:** Pack a picnic and head to the beach for some classic theater. The Shakespeare festival takes place every summer under billowing tents right on the water at Vanier Park.

■ **VanDusen Botanical Garden:** An Elizabethan maze, formal rose garden, meditation garden, and a collection of Canadian heritage plants are among the many displays at this tranquil 22-hectare (55-acre) site.

■ **Shopping on West 4th Avenue:** Shop like a local along West 4th Avenue in Kitsilano, where boutiques, houseware emporiums, and gift shops are dotted between coffee shops and first-rate restaurants.

GETTING HERE

Individual attractions on the West Side are easily reached by the Canada Line and TransLink buses, but a car makes things easier, especially if you want to see more than one of these sites in a day. From Downtown, take the Burrard, Granville, or Cambie Street bridges to get to the West Side.

For Point Grey, take Bus 4, traveling south on Granville Street from Downtown, toward UBC or from Kits, take Bus 84 traveling west on West 4th Ave. If you cross the Granville Bridge from Downtown, you'll be in South Granville. Several TransLink buses can take you here; Bus 10 runs the length of Granville Street, Bus 4 or 7 will drop you at West 5th and Granville, and Bus 14 or 16 stop at the corner of Broadway and Granville.

PLANNING YOUR TIME

With beaches and museums to enjoy during the day, and restaurants and nightlife hopping after dark, the West Side is enjoyable anytime of the day or night.

QUICK BITES

■ **49th Parallel Cafe & Lucky's Doughnuts.** Stop for an espresso on the airy enclosed patio at the West 4th location of this local coffee roaster, where delicious doughnuts are made on-site. ✉ *2198 West 4th Ave., Kits* ⊕ *www.49thcoffee.com* Ⓜ *UBC Bus 4, West 4th at Arbutus stop.*

■ **Caffe Barney.** A favorite with locals for their hearty pub fare and craft beers, it is also one of South Granville's best places for brunch. ✉ *2975 Granville St. South Granville* ⊕ *www. caffebarney.com* Ⓜ *Bus 10 and N10, Granville St. at West 13th Ave. stop.*

■ **Purebread.** This Whistler-based bakery offers its yummy handmade goodies and freshly baked bread at three locations in town, including a bright storefront café in Kits. ✉ *2887 West Broadway, Kits* ⊕ *www.purebread.ca* Ⓜ *Bus 99, West Broadway and MacDonald stop.*

The West Side, the set of diverse neighborhoods just south of Downtown, has some of Vancouver's best gardens and natural sights as well as some chic shopping. "Kits," as the locals refer to Kitsilano, though, is really where all the action is.

Most references to "the West Side" have moneyed connotations: there are South Granville's chic galleries and upscale shopping, the old-family mansions of Shaughnessy, the tony university district around Point Grey, and the revitalized area along the Cambie Street corridor. Even the once-hippie Kitsilano neighborhood has evolved into an upscale district of shops, restaurants, museums, and one of the city's best people-watching beaches. Basically, the West Side is the antithesis of the city's funkier, eclectic East Side.

Kitsilano

The beachfront district of Kitsilano (popularly known as Kits) is one of Vancouver's trendiest neighborhoods. Originally inhabited by the Squamish people, whose Chief Khatsahlano gave the area its name, Kitsilano has fashionable shops, popular clubs and cafés, and three museums (the Museum of Vancouver, the Vancouver Maritime Museum, and the H.R. MacMillan Space Centre), all in beachside Vanier Park. Kits has hidden treasures, too: rare boats moored at Heritage Harbour, stately mansions on forested lots, and, all along the waterfront, quiet coves and shady paths within a stone's throw of lively **Kits Beach** (⇨ *see the Beaches section of Sports and the Outdoors*), one of the city's most popular spots for sun and sand.

◉ Sights

Gordon Southam Observatory
OBSERVATORY | When the sky is clear, the ½-meter telescope at the Gordon Southam Observatory is focused on whatever stars or planets are worth watching that night. Admission to the observatory is by donation and it's open year-round Saturday evenings, from 7 to 11, weather permitting. ✉ *100 Chestnut St., Kitsilano* ☎ *604/738–7827* ⊕ *www. spacecentre.ca* ✑ *By donation.*

H.R. MacMillan Space Centre
OBSERVATORY | **FAMILY** | The interactive exhibits and high-tech learning systems at this center include a Virtual Voyages ride, where visitors can take a simulated space journey (definitely not for those afraid of flying); GroundStation Canada, showcasing Canada's achievements in space; and the Cosmic Courtyard, full of hands-on space-oriented exhibits including a moon rock and a computer program that shows what you would look like as an alien. You can catch daytime astronomy shows or evening music-and-laser shows at the **H.R. MacMillan Planetarium.** ✉ *Vanier Park, 1100 Chestnut St., Kitsilano* ☎ *604/738–7827* ⊕ *www.spacecentre.ca* ✑ *C$21.*

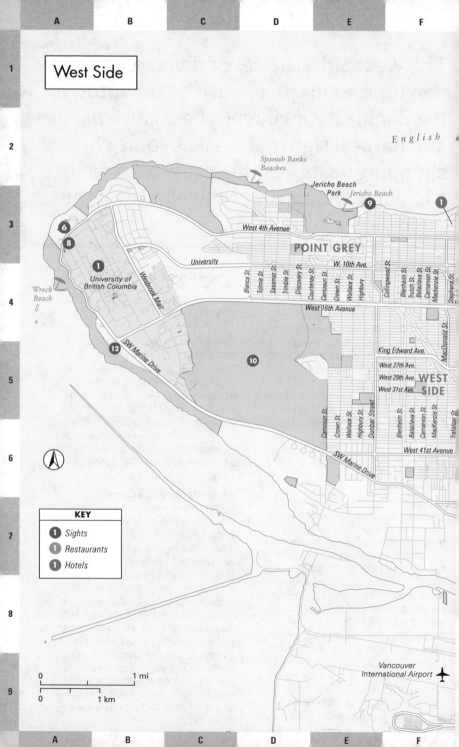

West Side

English

Spanish Banks Beaches

Jericho Beach Park *Jericho Beach*

(9)

(1)

West 4th Avenue

POINT GREY

University

W. 10th Ave.

Blanca St.
Tolmie St.
Sasamat St.
Trimble St.
Discovery St.
Courtenay St.
Camosun St.
Crown St.
Wallace St.
Highbury

Collingwood St.
Blenheim St.
Trutch St.
Balaclava St.
Carnarvon St.
Mackenzie St.

Stephens St.

(6)

(8)

(1)

University of British Columbia

Westbrook Mall

West 16th Avenue

Wreck Beach

King Edward Ave.

West 27th Ave.

West 29th Ave.

West 31st Ave.

WEST SIDE

(12)

SW Marine Drive

(10)

Camosun St.
Crown St.
Wallace St.
Highbury St.
Dunbar Street

Blenheim St.
Balaclava St.
Carnarvon St.
MacKenzie St.

Trafalgar St.

MacDonald St.

West 41st Avenue

SW Marine Drive

KEY

(1) *Sights*

(1) *Restaurants*

(1) *Hotels*

Vancouver International Airport ✈

0 _____ 1 mi

0 _____ 1 km

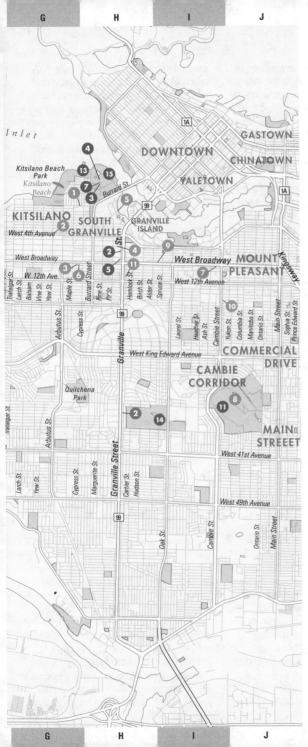

Museum of Vancouver

MUSEUM | FAMILY | Vancouver's short-but-funky history comes to life at this seaside museum. The 1930s gallery remembers some poignant episodes involving the Japanese internment during WWII, as well as local stories of the war effort. The 1950s Gallery has a 1955 Ford Fairlane Victoria and a Seeburg Select-o-Matic jukebox. The 1960s-theme Revolution Gallery revisits the city's days as the hippie capital of Canada: visitors can hear local bands from the '60s and poke around a re-created communal house. The museum regularly mounts intriguing temporary exhibits and hosts lectures and other public events. ✉ *Vanier Park, 1100 Chestnut St., Kitsilano* 🕾 *604/736–4431* ⊕ *www.museumofvancouver.com* 🖃 *C$20.50.*

Vancouver Maritime Museum

MUSEUM | FAMILY | Sharing the seafaring history of the Pacific Northwest and Arctic regions, this family-friendly museum houses the *RCMP Arctic St. Roch,* the first ship to sail in both directions through the treacherous Northwest Passage and the first to circumnavigate North America. You can scramble around the decks and into the St. Roch's cabins, imagining yourself as a sea captain attempting to navigate the Arctic. About a third of this museum has been turned over to kids, with touchable displays offering a chance to drive a tug, maneuver an underwater robot, or dress up as a seafarer. Toddlers and school-age children can work the hands-on displays in Pirates' Cove and the Children's Maritime Discovery Centre. The museum also has an extensive collection of model ships. While you're here, take a moment to look at the 100-foot-tall replica Kwakiutl totem pole in front of the museum. The massive white-and-yellow contraption behind the Vancouver Maritime Museum is the *Ben Franklin* submersible. It looks like something a Jules Verne character would put to sea but was actually built in 1968

as a marine research tool to, among other things, chart the Gulf Stream. A more fascinating claim to fame is that it was once the largest of its kind in America and was instructional for NASA: the information about how people lived in such close quarters for extended periods of time provided preliminary research data on the dynamics of living aboard a space station. ✉ *Vanier Park, 1905 Ogden Ave., north end of Cypress St., Kitsilano* 🕾 *604/257–8300* ⊕ *www.vancouvermaritimemuseum.com* 🖃 *C$13.50.*

Vanier Park

CITY PARK | Home to the **Museum of Vancouver**, the **Vancouver Maritime Museum**, and the **H.R. MacMillan Space Centre**, Vanier Park is also known as the best kite-flying venue in the city. Every summer, this is also where you'll find the Children's Festival and Bard on the Beach theater—both presented under billowing tents. ✉ *Vanier Park, 1100 Chestnut St., Kitsilano* 🖃 *Free.*

🌀 Beaches

★ Kitsilano Beach

BEACH—SIGHT | West of the southern end of the Burrard Bridge, Kits Beach is the city's busiest beach—Frisbee tossers, beach volleyball players, and sleek young people are ever present. Facilities include a playground, restaurant, concession stand, and tennis courts. **Kitsilano Pool** is here: at 137.5 meters (451 feet), it's the longest pool in Canada and one of the few heated saltwater pools in the world (open May to September). Just steps from the sand, the Boathouse on Kits Beach serves lunch, dinner, and weekend brunch inside and on its big ocean-view deck. There's also a take-out concession at the same site. Inland from the pool, the Kitsilano Showboat, an outdoor amphitheater hosts music and dance performances during the summer. **Amenities:** food and drink; lifeguards; parking (fee); toilets; water sports. **Best**

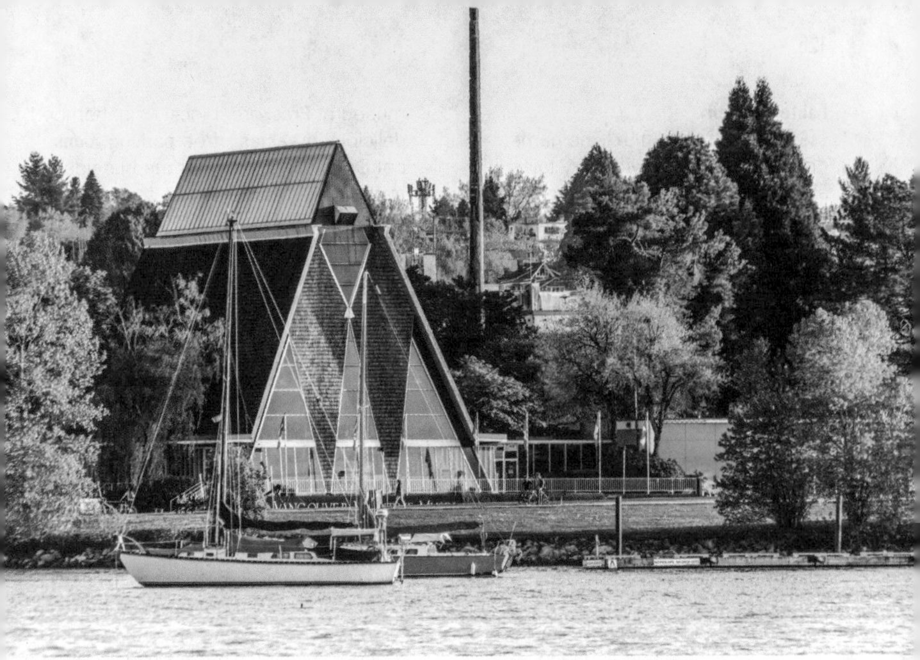

The Vancouver Maritime Museum explores the seafaring history of the Pacific Northwest.

for: atmosphere; sunrise; sunset; swimming; walking. ✉ *Kits Beach, Kitsilano* ☎ *604/731–0011* 🌐 *www.vancouver.ca/parks-recreation-culture/kitsilano-beach.aspx.*

🍴 Restaurants

Kits has it all, from easygoing neighborhood bistros to grab-a-bite sandwich shops to higher-end dining rooms.

Bean Around the World

$ | CAFÉ | This local minichain, of the "Fuelled by Caffeine" slogan, runs a number of comfortable coffeehouses around town. If you like your cappuccino with no pretension (and perhaps with a muffin or slice of banana bread), head for "The Bean." In addition to this branch near Kitsilano Beach, their many Vancouver locations include 175 West Hastings Street (at Cambie) in Gastown, 1002 Mainland Street in Yaletown, 2977 Granville Street in South Granville, and on Main Street at No. 2528 and No. 3598. **Known for:** great coffee; laid-back atmosphere; fresh baked goods. [$] *Average main: C$5* ✉ *1945 Cornwall Ave., Kitsilano* ☎ *604/739–1069* 🌐 *www.batw.ca* 💳 *No credit cards.*

★ **Bishop's**

$$$$ | MODERN CANADIAN | Before "local" and "seasonal" were all the rage, this highly regarded restaurant was serving West Coast cuisine with an emphasis on organic regional produce. Menu highlights include starters like tuna tartare with pickled garlic scapes and arugula seed pods, while Haida Gwaii halibut with broccoli puree, roasted cauliflower, and crispy potato, and heritage pork with clams are among the tasty main dishes. **Known for:** impeccable service; extensive local wine list; West Coast cuisine. [$] *Average main: C$42* ✉ *2183 W. 4th Ave., Kitsilano* ☎ *604/738–2025* 🌐 *www.bishopsonline.com* 🕒 *Closed Sun. and Mon. No lunch.*

Fable Kitchen

$$$ | **MODERN CANADIAN** | The name doesn't have to do with fairy tales: it's about "farm to table," which encapsulates the philosophy of this bustling Kitsilano bistro. The idea is creative comfort food, and while the menu looks straightforward—wild BC salmon, smoked duck breast—it's full of surprising plot twists. **Known for:** inventive menu; local ingredients; creative comfort food. $ *Average main: C$28* ⊠ *1944 W. 4th St., Kitsilano* ☎ *604/732–1322* ⊕ *www.fablekitchen.ca* ⊘ *Closed Tues.*

★ Go Fish

$$ | **SEAFOOD** | If the weather's fine, head for this seafood stand on the seawall overlooking the docks beside Granville Island. The menu is short—highlights include fish-and-chips, grilled salmon or tuna sandwiches, and fish tacos—but the quality is first-rate. **Known for:** seaside location; fish-and-chips; long queues. $ *Average main: C$12* ⊠ *Fisherman's Wharf, 1505 W. 1st Ave., Kitsilano* ☎ *604/730–5040* ⊘ *Closed Mon. No dinner.*

★ Maenam

$$$ | **THAI** | Chef Angus An's modern Thai menu brings this Asian cuisine to a new level. Although some of his dishes may sound familiar—green papaya salad, pad Thai, curries—they're amped up with local ingredients, fresh herbs, and vibrant seasonings. **Known for:** modern Thai food; sleek dining room; exotic cocktails. $ *Average main: C$25* ⊠ *1938 W. 4th Ave., Kitsilano* ☎ *604/730–5579* ⊕ *www.maenam.ca* ⊘ *No lunch Sun. and Mon.*

🛏 Hotels

★ Corkscrew Inn

$$$ | **B&B/INN** | This restored 1912 Craftsman-style house near the beach in Kitsilano combines the comforts of a B&B with a quirky tribute to the humble corkscrew: guests are encouraged to explore the small wine paraphernalia museum. **Pros:** great local neighborhood; delicious breakfast; free parking. **Cons:** not Downtown; a 15-minute bus ride to the Canada Line airport connection; no pets. $ *Rooms from: C$295* ⊠ *2735 W. 2nd Ave., Kitsilano* ☎ *604/733–7276, 877/737–7276* ⊕ *www.corkscrewinn.com* ➪ *5 rooms* ⦿| *Free breakfast.*

🍸 Nightlife

Known as the Venice Beach of Vancouver, Kitsilano attracts a laid-back crowd that enjoys sipping beer and cocktails on outdoor patios, especially in the summer.

BARS

Kits Beach Boathouse

BARS/PUBS | A summer visit to Vancouver isn't complete without an afternoon enjoying cocktails on this rooftop patio overlooking sand-court volleyball matches at Kits Beach. At other times of the year, the views of the vivid sunsets and dramatic winter storms are exceptional, though you may want to retreat behind the floor-to-ceiling windows to sip in comfort. ⊠ *1305 Arbutus St., Kitsilano* ☎ *604/738–5487* ⊕ *www.boathouserestaurants.ca.*

Local Public Eatery

BARS/PUBS | It won't win awards for service, but this large, sports-inclined bar has its gimmick: an enviable proximity to Kits Beach. The spacious but usually packed patio is across from a grassy park and Kitsilano Pool. Inside, multiple televisions show whatever sports game is happening while the kitchen serves inexpensive pub grub. ⊠ *2210 Cornwall Ave., Kitsilano* ☎ *604/734–3589* ⊕ *www.localpubliceatery.com.*

🛍 Shopping

West 4th Avenue, between Burrard and Balsam, is the main shopping strip in funky Kitsilano. There are clothing and shoe boutiques, as well as housewares and gift shops. Just east of Burrard, several stores on West 4th sell ski and snowboard gear. Look for food boutiques on West 2nd and 3rd.

BOOKS

★ Kidsbooks

BOOKS/STATIONERY | FAMILY | The helpful staff at this cheery shop is happy to make recommendations about books appropriate for young people ranging from toddlers to teens. Choose from the many titles by Canadian authors—excellent for take-home gifts or on-the-road reading. ⊠ *2557 W. Broadway, Kitsilano* ☎ *604/738–5335* ⊕ *www.kidsbooks.ca.*

Wanderlust Travel Store

BOOKS/STATIONERY | Travelers and armchair travelers love this shop, which feeds everyone's wanderlust. There are thousands of travel books and maps, as well as luggage, gear, and accessories. ⊠ *1929 W. 4th Ave., Kitsilano* ☎ *604/739–2182, 844/234-6762* ⊕ *www.wanderlustore.com.*

CLOTHING

lululemon athletica

CLOTHING | The place where it all started in 2000 was at this stand-alone shop on West 4th in Kits. Since then the behemoth of yoga wear has stretched itself into a multibillion-dollar company with locations worldwide and an ever-expanding line of technical athletic apparel. The original store has expanded too, with a multilevel renovation that took over an auto repair shop next door and added a new rooftop deck. The full range of women's and men's technical athletic apparel is available here, and in the men's department, kombucha, and occasionally beer, is on tap. ⊠ *2101 West 4th Ave., Kitsilano* ☎ *604/732-6111* ⊕ *www.lululemon.com.*

FOOD

Chocolate Arts

FOOD/CANDY | Looking for a present for a chocolate lover? Check out the handmade chocolates in First Nations motifs, specially designed by Robert Davidson, one of Canada's premier artists. This delicious shop and café, where you can refuel with a hot chocolate, some bonbons, or some house-made ice-cream, is a short walk from Granville Island. ⊠ *1620 W. 3rd Ave., Kitsilano* ☎ *604/739–0475, 877/739–0475* ⊕ *www.chocolatearts.com* ☾ *Closed Sun.*

★ Les Amis du Fromage

FOOD/CANDY | If you love cheese, don't miss the mind-boggling array of selections from BC, the rest of Canada, and elsewhere at this family-run shop of delicacies. Owner Allison Spurrell and her extremely knowledgeable staff encourage you to taste before you buy. Yum. The fromagerie is located between Granville Island and Kitsilano Beach—useful to keep in mind if you're assembling a seaside picnic. There's a second location at 843 East Hastings Street on Vancouver's East Side. ⊠ *1752 W. 2nd Ave., Kitsilano* ☎ *604/732–4218* ⊕ *www.buycheese.com.*

SHOES AND ACCESSORIES

gravitypope

SHOES/LUGGAGE/LEATHER GOODS | Foot fashionistas make tracks to this Kitsilano shop that's jam-packed with trendy choices, including Camper, Trippen, Common Projects, and other international brands for men and women. Shoppers can complete their outfits with designs by Alexander Wang, Isabelle Marant, and Acne Studios right next door at gravitypope Tailored Goods (*2203 West 4th Avenue*). ⊠ *2205 W. 4th Ave., Kitsilano* ☎ *604/731–7673* ⊕ *www.gravitypope.com.*

🏃 Activities

DIVING

The rugged coastline of southwestern British Columbia offers excellent and varied diving with vistas of below- surface sheer rock walls and thick plots of plumose anemones. From late summer through winter, when water clarity is best and allows visibility of up to 100 feet, the region delivers some of the

Discount Pass 👁

UBC Museums and Gardens Pass:
If you're planning to visit several of the attractions at the University of British Columbia, the UBC Museums and Garden Pass can save you money. The $27 pass includes admission to the Museum of Anthropology, UBC Botanical Garden, Nitobe Memorial Garden, and Beaty Biodiversity Museum. There's also a family version of the pass (C$85) that covers two adults and up to four children under 18. The pass doesn't include the Greenheart Canopy Walkway, but it does give you 10% off walkway tickets. Passes are valid for six months for the museums and 12 months for the gardens, so you don't need to squeeze all your sightseeing into one day. Purchase the pass at any of the participating attractions. ⊕ *botanicalgarden.ubc.ca.*

most spectacular temperate-water (average 4–8°C [39–46°F]) diving in the world, including sightings of the North Pacific Giant Octopus. Dry suits are imperative.

Rowand's Reef Scuba Shop
DIVING/SNORKELING | This PADI-certified scuba and snorkeling business specializes in year-round diving trips to nearby Howe Sound. Courses are also available. ⊠ *1731 W. 4th Ave., Kitsilano* ☎ *604/669-3483* ⊕ *www.rowandsreef.com.*

Point Grey

Some of Vancouver's best gardens, natural sights, and museums, including the renowned Museum of Anthropology on the campus of the University of British Columbia, are southwest of Downtown Vancouver in the Point Grey neighborhood. Established in 1908, UBC is the city's main university campus, with a student population of more than 60,000. The university is also where you'll find the Chan Centre for the Performing Arts, the Botanical Gardens, and Pacific Spirit Regional Park—the latter, although it can't compare with Stanley Park, is where the locals go for meandering forested trails that put you in touch with nature.

👁 Sights

Beaty Biodiversity Museum
MUSEUM | FAMILY | If you can imagine a vast underground library but instead of books, the stacks are filled with bones, fossils, and preserved lizards, then you can begin to imagine this modern museum on the UBC campus that exhibits more than 2 million specimens from the university's natural history collections. The most striking attraction hangs in the entrance atrium: a 25-meter-long (82-foot-long) skeleton of a blue whale—the largest on view in Canada (the blue whale in New York's American Museum of Natural History is 94 feet long). On the lower level, you'll find scads of animal skulls, taxidermied birds, and other creatures displayed through glass windows (many of which are at kids' eye level). In the interactive Discovery Lab, you can play scientist yourself; you might compare the claws of different birds or examine animal poop under a microscope. There's also a family space stocked with books, art supplies, and kid-size furniture. To find the museum from the university bus loop, walk west to the Main Mall and turn left; the museum is just south of University Boulevard. A Museums and Gardens Pass will save you money if you're planning to visit several attractions at UBC. ⊠ *University of British Columbia, 2212*

Main Mall, Point Grey ☎ 604/827–4955 ⊕ www.beatymuseum.ubc.ca ☞ C$14 ⊘ Closed Mon.

Old Hastings Mill Store Museum

MUSEUM | Vancouver's first store and oldest building was built in 1865 at the foot of Dunlevy Street in Gastown and moved to this seaside spot near the Royal Vancouver Yacht Club in 1930. It's a little wooden structure at the corner of Point Grey Road and Alma Street—west of Kitsilano en route to UBC—and is the only building to predate the 1886 Great Fire. The site is now a museum with displays of First Nations artifacts and pioneer household goods. ⊠ 1575 Alma St., Point Grey ☎ 604/734–1212 ⊕ www. hastingsmillmuseum.ca ☞ By donation ⊘ Closed Mon. June to Sept. Off-season closed weekdays and Dec. to Feb.

★ Museum of Anthropology

MUSEUM | Part of the University of British Columbia, the MOA has one of the world's leading collections of Northwest Coast First Nations art. The Great Hall has dramatic cedar poles, bentwood boxes, and canoes adorned with traditional Northwest Coast–painted designs. On clear days, the gallery's 50-foot-tall windows reveal a striking backdrop of mountains and sea. Another highlight is the work of the late Bill Reid, one of Canada's most respected Haida artists. In The Raven and the First Men (1980), carved in yellow cedar, he tells a Haida story of creation. Reid's gold-and-silver jewelry work is also on display, as are exquisite carvings of gold, silver, and argillite (a black shale found on Haida Gwaii, also known as the Queen Charlotte Islands) by other First Nations artists. The museum's visible storage section displays, in drawers and cases, contain thousands of examples of tools, textiles, masks, and other artifacts from around the world. The Koerner Ceramics Gallery contains 600 pieces from 15th- to 19th-century Europe. Behind the museum are two Haida houses, set on the cliff over the water. Free guided tours—given several times daily (call or check the website for times)—are immensely informative. The MOA also has an excellent book and fine-art shop, as well as a café. To reach the museum by transit, take any UBC-bound bus from Granville Street Downtown to the university bus loop, a 15-minute walk, or connect to a shuttle that scoots around the campus and will drop you off opposite the MOA at the Rose Garden. Pay parking is available in the Rose Garden parking lot, across Marine Drive from the museum. A UBC Museums and Gardens Pass will save you money if you're planning to visit several attractions at UBC. ⊠ University of British Columbia, 6393 N.W. Marine Dr., Point Grey ☎ 604/822–5087 ⊕ www.moa.ubc.ca ☞ C$18; Thurs. 5–9 pm C$10 ⊘ Closed Mon. mid-Oct.–mid-May.

Nitobe Memorial Garden

GARDEN | Opened in 1960 in memory of Japanese scholar and diplomat Dr. Inazo Nitobe (1862–1933), this 2½-acre walled garden, which includes a pond, a stream with a small waterfall, and a ceremonial teahouse, is considered one of the most authentic Japanese tea and strolling gardens outside Japan. Designed by Professor Kannosuke Mori of Japan's Chiba University, the garden incorporates many native British Columbia trees and shrubs, pruned and trained Japanese-style, and interplanted with Japanese maples and flowering shrubs. The circular path around the park symbolizes the cycle of life and provides a tranquil view from every direction. Cherry blossoms are the highlight in April and May, and in June the irises are magnificent. Because the garden is so exotic, it's worth renting an audio guide. Japanese tea ceremonies are held the last Saturday of every month, May through September; email krsnyder@shaw.ca for reservations (C$10). A UBC Museums and Gardens Pass will save you money if you're planning to visit several attractions at UBC. ⊠ University of British Columbia, 1895

Did You Know?

The Museum of Anthropology at the University of British Columbia has an excellent collection of Northwest Coast First Nations art, and the building and grounds are spectacular. The museum shop sells unusual art and gift items.

Lower Mall, Point Grey ☎ *604/822–6038* ⊕ *www.botanicalgarden.ubc.ca/nitobe* 🖃 *C$7 Apr.–Oct. 31; by donation Nov.– Mar.* ⊙ *Closed weekends Nov.–Mar.*

Pacific Spirit Regional Park
PARK—SPORTS-OUTDOORS | Close to the University of British Columbia, on Vancouver's West Side, Pacific Spirit Regional Park has 73 km (45 miles) of multiuse walking, hiking, and biking trails within its 763-hectare (1,885-acre) forest. Open dawn to dusk year-round, it also has access to Spanish Banks and Wreck beaches. 🖃 *4915 W. 16th Ave., Point Grey* ☎ *604/224–5739* ⊕ *www.metrovancouver.org.*

University of British Columbia Botanical Garden
GARDEN | FAMILY | Ten thousand trees, shrubs, and rare plants from around the world thrive on this 70-acre research site on the university campus, which edges on Pacific Spirit Park. The complex feels as far away from the city as you can get, with forested walkways through an Asian garden, a garden of medicinal plants, and an alpine garden with some of the world's rarest plants. A Walk in the Woods is a 20-minute loop that takes you through more than 1,000 species of coastal plant life. The garden gift store is one of the best of its kind. One-hour guided tours, free with garden admission, are offered on certain days; call or check the website for schedule. A UBC Museums and Gardens Pass will save you money if you're planning to visit several attractions at UBC.

The 308-meter-long (1,010-foot-long) **Greenheart TreeWalk Canopy Walkway**, a swaying network of suspended bridges weaving a trail between gargantuan cedars and hemlocks, is a thrilling way to explore the garden. Along the way, you stop off on eight platforms in the trees, each more than 15 meters (49 feet) high, while an additional two-story viewing platform tops a freestanding tower more than 22 meters (72 feet) in the air. Visits

to the walkway are at your own pace or by a 45-minute guided tour, where you learn about the forest, local wildlife, environmental issues, and First Nations traditions; call or check the website for seasonal tour schedules. The walkway is a great adventure for kids; just note that small children must either be able to walk on their own or be carried in a child backpack or other carrier (strollers aren't permitted). 🖃 *6804 S.W. Marine Dr., Point Grey* ☎ *604/822–4208* ⊕ *www. botanicalgarden.ubc.ca* 🖃 *C$10; C$26 includes Nitobe Memorial Garden and Greenheart TreeWalk.*

⊙ Beaches

The beaches of Point Grey are a series of wide, sandy swaths stretching along the southern shores of English Bay, starting at Jericho Beach, then Locarno Beach, and Spanish Banks. More laid-back than Kits Beach, these spots are great for picnicking and are popular with families. Farther around the point you'll find the clothing-optional Wreck Beach.

Jericho Beach
BEACH—SIGHT | FAMILY | Home to the Jericho Sailing Centre, this Point Grey beach is popular for windsurfing and kayaking (rentals are available), especially at the western end. Swimmers can use the eastern section, where the expansive sands and a grassy park invite sunbathing. In July, the Vancouver Folk Music Festival brings thousands together over folk, world, and indie bands. **Amenities:** food and drink; lifeguards; parking (fee); toilets; water sports. **Best for:** swimming; walking; windsurfing. 🖃 *1300 Discovery St., Point Grey* ⊕ *www.vancouver.ca/ parks-recreation-culture/jericho-beach. aspx.*

Spanish Banks Beaches
BEACH—SIGHT | FAMILY | The **Spanish Banks** and **Locarno** beaches form a sandy chain, and have huge expanses of sunbathing sand backed by wide lawns full of picnic

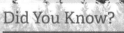

tables. There are also volleyball courts. The shallow water, warmed slightly by sun and sand, is good for swimming. Farther west along the coastline, toward the Spanish Banks Extension, the scene becomes less crowded. Spanish Banks West and Locarno beaches are designated "quiet beaches," which means that amplified music is prohibited. **Amenities:** food and drink; lifeguards; parking (free); toilets; water sports. **Best for:** atmosphere; sunset; swimming; walking; windsurfing. ⊠ *Northwest Marine Dr., at Tolmie St., Point Grey* ⊕ *www.vancouver. ca/parks-recreation-culture/spanish-bank-beach.aspx.*

Wreck Beach

BEACH—SIGHT | Clothing-optional Wreck Beach is in Pacific Spirit Regional Park, accessible via Trail 6—a winding staircase of 483 steps that's near the University of British Columbia campus. On sunny days the beach is busy with locals and visitors, most of whom strip down to their birthday suits and enjoy the clean swimming waters. The welcoming sands also stretch around Point Grey to the north, where beach logs, a foreshore of wildlife, and WWII searchlight towers are some of the many reasons to explore further. **Amenities:** parking (fee); toilets. **Best for:** atmosphere; nudists; sunset; swimming. ⊠ *Trail 6, Foreshore Trail, N.W. Marine Dr. at University Blvd., Point Grey* ⊕ *www. wreckbeach.org.*

🎭 Performing Arts

Chan Centre for the Performing Arts

ARTS CENTERS | This vast arts complex on the campus of the University of British Columbia includes a 1,200-seat concert hall, a theater, and a cinema. ⊠ *University of British Columbia, 6265 Crescent Rd., Point Grey* ☎ *604/822–9197* ⊕ *www. chancentre.com.*

🛍 Shopping

The Point Grey neighborhood has a small shopping district along West 10th Avenue, between Discovery and Tolmie streets, but the main reason shoppers venture this far west is the excellent gift shop at the Museum of Anthropology.

ART AND ANTIQUES

MOA Shop

GIFTS/SOUVENIRS | The Museum of Anthropology gift shop carries an excellent selection of Northwest Coast jewelry, carvings, and prints, as well as books on First Nations history and culture. ⊠ *University of British Columbia, 6393 N.W. Marine Dr., Point Grey* ☎ *604/827–5932* ⊕ *www.moa.ubc.ca.*

🏃 Activities

GOLF

University Golf Club

GOLF | In Point Grey's Pacific Spirit Park, this challenging 18-hole public course has been around since 1929 and includes a restaurant and the British Columbia Golf Museum. The traditional course's narrow fairways, lined with old-growth trees, appeal to golfers of all skill levels. ⊠ *5185 University Blvd., Point Grey* ☎ *604/224–7799* ⊕ *www.universitygolf. com* 🏌 *Green fees C$76 ⅃. 18 holes, 6531 yards, par 72* ☞ *Driving range, putting green, pitching area, golf carts, rental clubs, pro shop, golf academy/lessons, restaurant, bar.*

WINDSURFING

Windsure Windsurfing School

WINDSURFING | Sailboard and wet-suit rentals as well as lessons are available between May and September at Jericho Beach, in Point Grey. Skim boarding (a low-tech activity using a wooden board to skim along wet sand) and stand-up paddling lessons are also offered. ⊠ *1300 Discovery St., Point Grey* ☎ *604/224–0615* ⊕ *www.windsure.com.*

Made in Vancouver

Vancouver doesn't just produce overpriced lattes and undersized condos. The city's creative denizens have designed a range of products from shoes to yoga wear.

Happy Planet Juices: Vancouverites have been supporting this local company's mission to "turn the planet on to 100% organic juices" since the company got its start in 1994.

John Fluevog: Yep, those outrageous shoes took their first steps in Vancouver.

lululemon athletica: The stylized "A" insignia is as recognizable to yoga enthusiasts as the Nike "swoosh" is to sports fans.

Rocky Mountain Bicycles: BC invented the aggressive, stunt-heavy "free-riding" or "north shore" (from the North Shore Mountains) style of riding that's taken over the sport, and Rocky Mountain makes the steeds on which the style was pioneered.

South Granville

The section of Granville Street between 5th and 15th Avenues is the city's traditional "Gallery Row." Although some showrooms have decamped to larger, less expensive quarters on the East Side, a number of high-end galleries remain, alongside furniture stores and upscale clothing boutiques.

Sights

Douglas Reynolds Gallery

ART GALLERIES | In this collection of Northwest Coast First Nations art, which is particularly strong in woodwork and jewelry, some pieces date back to the 1800s, while others are strikingly contemporary. ✉ *2335 Granville St., South Granville* ☎ *604/731–9292* 🌐 *www.douglasreynoldsgallery.com.*

Marion Scott Gallery

ART GALLERIES | Specializing in fine Inuit art from the Canadian North, exhibits here include sculpture, prints, wall hangings, and drawings. ✉ *2423 Granville St., South Granville* ☎ *604/685–1934* 🌐 *www.marionscottgallery.com* 🕒 *Closed Sun. to Tues.*

Restaurants

In this sophisticated district just across the Granville Bridge from Downtown, you'll find equally sophisticated dining rooms.

★ Farmer's Apprentice

$$$ | MODERN CANADIAN | Book ahead to nab one of the 30 or so seats in this cozy bistro, voted one of Canada's 100 Best restaurants, where chef Bardia Ilbeiggi and his team in the open kitchen craft wildly creative "vegetable forward" set menus. It's not a vegetarian restaurant, but fresh local produce plays starring roles both the "omnivore" and "herbivore" (C$65) menus, each featuring six courses that change daily to feature seasonal ingredients like garlic ramps, heirloom tomatoes, and black garlic. **Known for:** six-course menus; seasonal ingredients; great vegetarian dining. [$] *Average main: C$30* ✉ *1535 W. 6th Ave., South Granville* ☎ *604/620–2070* 🌐 *www.farmersapprentice.ca* 🕒 *Closed Mon.*

Vij's Rangoli

$$ | INDIAN | Part of Vikram Vij's growing restaurant empire, this modern bistro serves innovative Indian fare in a relaxed environment. Nab a table in the cozy interior and order grilled chicken marinated in tamarind and yogurt, pulled pork with sautéed greens, or a curry of kale, jackfruit, cauliflower, and potato. **Known for:** modern Indian food; vegetarian-friendly menu; great service. $ *Average main: C$18* ⊠ *1480 W. 11th Ave., South Granville* ☎ *604/736–5711* ⊕ *www.vijs.ca.*

Hotels

Granville House B&B

$$$ | B&B/INN | With its elegant but austere furnishings and individual breakfast tables, this Tudor-revival house feels more like a small hotel than a B&B. **Pros:** top-notch service; hot breakfasts; deluxe amenities. **Cons:** on the neighborhood's main drag; no pets; not Downtown. $ *Rooms from: C$300* ⊠ *5050 Granville St., South Granville* ☎ *866/739–9002* ⊕ *www.granvillebb.com* 🔁 *5 rooms* ❄ *Free breakfast.*

Nightlife

BARS

Grapes and Soda

WINE BARS—NIGHTLIFE | This tiny 25-seater wine bar is contemporary and carefully cultivates an interesting list of organic wines and craft cocktails. It adjoins acclaimed seasonal, farm-to-table eatery Farmer's Apprentice, so the bar nibbles are equally inspired. It gets busy so go early and enjoy a happy hour cocktail of the day and charcuterie board. ⊠ *1541 W. 6th Ave., South Granville* ☎ *604/336–2456* ⊕ *www.grapesandsoda.ca.*

Storm Crow Alehouse

BARS/PUBS | This is the definition of a nerd bar: Star Wars memorabilia, displays of planetary objects, and a wall of board games. It's cozy and friendly, serving a variety of craft beers, two-hander burgers, and sci fi–themed cocktails. ⊠ *1619 W. Broadway, South Granville* ☎ *604/428–9670* ⊕ *www.stormcrow. com.*

Shopping

BOOKS

Indigo

BOOKS/STATIONERY | The Vancouver flagship of this Canadian chain stocks a vast selection of popular books and plenty of giftware, too. Check out the display tables for hot sellers, local authors, and bargain books; the attached Starbucks makes a handy reading nook. Other branches around town include a smaller outlet on Robson Downtown. ⊠ *2505 Granville St., South Granville* ✛ *At Broadway* ☎ *604/731-7822* ⊕ *www.chapters. indigo.ca.*

CLOTHING: MEN'S AND WOMEN'S

Boboli

CLOTHING | Named for the Boboli Gardens, this lavish space, complete with an atrium-like shoe department, focuses on high-end Italian labels for men and women, such as Valentino, Etro, and Giambattista Valli. ⊠ *2776 Granville St., South Granville* ☎ *604/257–2300* ⊕ *www. boboli.ca.*

Turnabout

CLOTHING | The quality of the previously owned clothing here is so good that "used" is almost a misnomer at this long-established luxury resale clothing store. They sell upscale women's wear from labels like Gucci, Missoni, and Prada. Other branches, in Kitsilano and on Main Street, sell more casual clothing as well as men's clothes. ⊠ *3135 Granville St., South Granville* ☎ *604/734-5313* ⊕ *www.turnabout.com.*

Cambie Corridor

Two of Vancouver's top garden attractions are over the Cambie Bridge, south of Downtown: Queen Elizabeth Park (just off Cambie at 33rd Avenue), and the Van-Dusen Botanical Garden, which is at Oak Street at 37th Avenue, west of Cambie. The Cambie Corridor has also become something of a shopping destination, with several big-box stores clustered near the intersection of Broadway and Cambie, and more independent shops in the blocks between 18th and 20th Avenues.

👁 Sights

Queen Elizabeth Park
GARDEN | FAMILY | Lavish sunken gardens (in a former stone quarry), a rose garden, and an abundance of grassy picnicking spots are just a few of the highlights at this 52-hectare (130-acre) park. Poised at the highest point in the city, there are 360-degree views of Downtown. Other park facilities include 18 tennis courts, pitch and putt (an 18-hole putting green), and a restaurant. On summer evenings there's free outdoor dancing on the Plaza—everything from Scottish country dance to salsa, for all ages and levels. In the **Bloedel Conservatory** you can see tropical and desert plants and 100 species of free-flying tropical birds in a glass geodesic dome—the perfect place to be on a rainy day. To reach the park by public transportation, take the Canada Line to King Edward station; from there, it's a six-block walk to the edge of the park (and a hike up the hill to appreciate the views). Cambie Bus 15, which runs south along Cambie Street from the Olympic Village SkyTrain station, will drop you a little closer, at the corner of 33rd and Cambie. Park activities make for a great family excursion, and unlike Stanley Park with its acres of rain forest, Queen Elizabeth Park is all about the flowers. ✉ Cambie St. at 33rd Ave., Cambie ☎ 604/873–7000 ⊕ www.vancouver.ca/parks ✉ Conservatory C$6.75.

VanDusen Botanical Garden
GARDEN | FAMILY | An Elizabethan maze, a formal rose garden, a meditation garden, and a collection of Canadian heritage plants are among the many displays at this 55-acre site. The collections include flora from every continent and many rare and endangered species. The Phyllis Bentall Garden area features hybrid water lilies and carnivorous plants (a hit with kids). From mid-May to early June the Laburnum Walk forms a canopy of gold; in August and September the wildflower meadow is in bloom. The garden is also home to five lakes, a garden shop, a library, and the Truffles Café (serving breakfast, lunch, and afternoon tea) and Shaughnessy Restaurant. Special events throughout the year include the spectacular Christmas-theme Festival of Lights every December. From Downtown, catch the Oak Bus 17 directly to the garden entrance; alternatively, ride the Canada Line to Oakridge/41st Street, then take the UBC Bus 41 to Oak Street, and walk four blocks north to the garden. Queen Elizabeth Park is a 1-km (½-mile) walk away, along West 37th Avenue. Because this was once a golf course, pathways make this garden extremely wheelchair accessible. ✉ 5251 Oak St., at W. 37th Ave., Cambie ☎ 604/257–8335 garden, 604/267–8335 restaurant ⊕ www.vancouver.ca/parks ✉ C$11.25 Apr.–Sept.; C$8 Oct.–Mar.

🍴 Restaurants

★ Seasons in the Park
$$$$ | PACIFIC NORTHWEST | A perennial favorite with locals for special occasions, this restaurant boasts spectacular views overlooking the city and mountains from its perch at the highest point in Queen Elizabeth Park. Service is excellent in the white-tableclothed dining room and the menu showcases regional West Coast cuisine. **Known for:** panoramic views;

special occasions; fine dining. $ *Average main: C$32* ✉ *Queen Elizabeth Park, West 33rd Ave. at Cambie, Cambie* ☎ *604/874-8008* ⊕ *www.vancouverdine. com.*

Peaceful Restaurant

$$ | **CHINESE** | Northern Chinese dishes are the specialty at this friendly storefront restaurant. Particularly good are the hand-pulled noodles that the cooks knead and stretch in the open kitchen; other good choices include the mustard-seed vegetable salad (crisp shredded vegetables fired up with hot mustard), Szechuan green beans, and cumin-scented lamb. **Known for:** authentic Northern Chinese dishes; vegetarian-friendly menu; fast service. $ *Average main: C$16* ✉ *532 W. Broadway, Cambie* ☎ *604/879-9878* ⊕ *www.peacefulrestaurant.com.*

★ Tojo's

$$$$ | **JAPANESE** | Hidekazu Tojo is a sushi-making legend in Vancouver, with thousands of special preparations stored in his creative mind. The first to introduce omakase to Vancouver, he is also the creator of the '"Inside out"' Tojo Roll, now universally known as the "California Roll." In this bright modern, high-ceilinged space, complete with a separate sake lounge, the prime perch is at the sushi bar, a convivial ringside seat for watching the creation of edible art. **Known for:** omakase; top-notch sushi; sake lounge. $ *Average main: C$36* ✉ *1133 W. Broadway, Cambie* ☎ *604/872-8050* ⊕ *www. tojos.com* ⦿ *Closed Sun. No lunch.*

★ Vij's

$$$ | **INDIAN** | Long lauded as Vancouver's most innovative Indian restaurant, and always on the Top Ten lists of restaurants in the country, this dining destination, run by genial proprietor Vikram Vij and his ex-wife Meeru Dhalwala, uses local ingredients to create exciting takes on South Asian cuisine. Mark Bittman said in the *New York Times* it is "easily among the finest Indian restaurants in the

world." Dishes such as lamb "popsicles" in a creamy curry or BC rainbow trout in coconut masala served with a wheat berry pilaf are far from traditional but are beautifully executed. **Known for:** one of the best Indian restaurants in North America; rooftop patio; warm, welcoming service. $ *Average main: C$30* ✉ *3106 Cambie St., Cambie* ☎ *604/736-6664* ⊕ *www.vijs.ca* ⦿ *No lunch.*

🎭 Nightlife

COMEDY CLUBS

Yuk Yuk's

COMEDY CLUBS | This is the place to go Tuesday to Saturday evenings for some of Canada's best professional stand-up comedians and up-and-coming amateurs. ✉ *2837 Cambie St., at 12th Ave., Cambie* ☎ *604/696-9857* ⊕ *www.yukyuks.com.*

🛍 Shopping

GIFTS

Walrus Design

GIFTS/SOUVENIRS | "A pleasant surprise" is the motto of this airy gallerylike shop, where you never quite know what you'll find—perhaps candle holders, jewelry, local crafts, one-of-a-kind T-shirts, or original artwork. They stock a mix of local and international designers and often host small exhibitions. ✉ *3408 Cambie St., Cambie* ☎ *604/874-9770* ⊕ *www. walrushome.com.*

SHOPPING CENTERS

Oakridge Centre

SHOPPING CENTERS/MALLS | If you're intent on browsing, head to the skylighted atrium of Oakridge Centre (perhaps if the weather's bad and you want to be inside). There's a mix of trendy shops, upscale boutiques, and North American chains. It's a quick trip on the Canada Line from Downtown to the Oakridge–41st Avenue stop. ✉ *650 W. 41st Ave., at Cambie St., Cambie* ☎ *604/261-2511* ⊕ *www. oakridgecentre.com.*

Chapter 7

EAST SIDE

MAIN STREET/MT. PLEASANT
AND COMMERCIAL DRIVE

Updated by
Sue Kernaghan

👁 **Sights**   🍴 **Restaurants**   🛏 **Hotels**   👜 **Shopping**   🍸 **Nightlife**

★☆☆☆☆   ★★★☆☆   ★☆☆☆☆   ★★★★☆   ★★★☆☆

NEIGHBORHOOD SNAPSHOT

TOP EXPERIENCES

■ **Ride a Bike Along the Seaside Path:** Rent a bike or pick up a Mobi Bike for a spin along the car-free Seaside Path. The route winds all the way from Coal Harbour to Kitsilano, but the section at the east end of False Creek is one of the least busy.

■ **Browse for Treasures on South Main Street:** A relaxed hipster neighborhood lined with vintage clothing, antiques, and independent shops, South Main Street, or SoMa, is a top spot for one-of-a-kind finds.

■ **Sample the International Flavors of Commercial Drive:** If you're in the mood for Ethiopian, Vietnamese, or Cuban fare; or perhaps Italian coffee, French cheese, or Belgian lager, head to Commercial Drive for some global snacking, generally at bargain prices.

■ **Take a Craft Beer Tour:** There are about a dozen brew pubs and microbreweries in the neighborhood, from the massive Craft Beer Market to the tiny Brassneck Brewery. You can also join a tour with Vancouver Brewery Tours (⊕ *www.vancouverbrewerytours.com*).

GETTING HERE

Vancouver's East Side is well-served by public transport. For Science World and the Olympic Village, hop on a False Creek or Aquabus Ferry from anywhere around False Creek, take the SkyTrain to the Main Street-Science World station (the Olympic Village station is a little farther away), or just walk east along the seaside path from Granville Island. From Downtown or Science World, any bus traveling south on Main Street will take you to Mount Pleasant and South Main. For Commercial Drive, the fastest route is to ride the SkyTrain to the Commercial-Broadway station, and head south on foot from there.

PLANNING YOUR TIME

The East Side is at its most fun during the day, when there's plenty of people-watching to be done. One area to avoid walking after dark is the northern end of Main Street, near the Pacific Central Station.

QUICK BITES

■ **Terra Breads.** The Olympic Village branch of this local chain of bakery-cafés is just steps from the False Creek seaside path. Grab a coffee, a soup, or a panini to fuel you on your way; or just hang out at the outdoor tables and enjoy the people-watching action in Olympic Village Square. ⊠ *1605 Manitoba St. Olympic Village* ⊕ *www.terrabreads.com* Ⓜ *Main Street-Science World or Olympic Village.*

■ **Coco et Olive.** This shabby chic South Main café charms with a subtly Parisian vibe, thanks to the homemade soup, delicate pastries, and clusters of hipsters writing novels at the mismatched tables. ⊠ *3707 Main St., SoMa* Ⓜ *King Edward.*

■ **Cafe Calabria.** Vancouver's oldest Italian coffee bar has been run, and effusively decorated, by the same family since 1976. The espresso, gelato, biscotti, and minestrone are all the real thing; the over-the-top decor (think marble-topped tables, ceiling murals, and full-sized statues) is all part of the fun. ⊠ *1745 Commercial Drive, Commercial Drive* ⊕ *www.cafecalabria.ca* Ⓜ *Commercial-Broadway.*

Vancouver's East Side, from Ontario Street east to the suburb of Burnaby, was originally a working-class district. These days, as real estate prices have continued to climb, many artists and young families have moved east, and this half of the metropolitan area is now a mix of residential communities, galleries, and eclectic restaurants.

The East Side's mix of incoming hipsters and long-established immigrant communities has created several delightful urban villages: Mount Pleasant, South Main, and Commercial Drive, each distinct clusters of offbeat shops, cheap eats (both ethnic and trendy), brewpubs, small performing arts spaces, and pop-up galleries—in essence, the independent, diverse, and charming places that give cities life. A great place to start exploring is the Olympic Village, a pedestrian-friendly district on the southeast shore of False Creek. Originally built to house athletes during the 2010 Winter Olympic Games, it's now a chic waterfront condo development with a public square and a wealth of indoor and outdoor dining and drinking options. Nearby is Science World, a popular hands-on science museum. A little to the south and east, around the junction of Main Street and Broadway, is Mount Pleasant. This rapidly gentrifying area, which extends from Cambie Street to Clark Drive, and from 2nd to 16th Avenues, is home to a changing array of cafés, pubs, and art galleries. A SkyTrain extension, due to start construction in 2020 and begin service in 2025, will bring a new rapid transit station to the neighborhood. Farther south along Main Street, from roughly 20th to 30th Avenues, South Main, or "SoMa" is home to vintage shops, craft breweries, hipster cafés, and cheap eats, all set in a mix of historic and modest newer buildings. The area's diversity and family-friendly vibe make it popular with artists, actors, filmmakers, and young parents; as such, the area can be counted on to launch any new trend going. South of SoMa, around Main and East 49th Avenue, is the Punjabi Market, a long-established "Little India," where jewelry stores, sari shops, and curry houses abound. Another top East Side destination is Commercial Drive, from Broadway south to Venables Street. Originally Vancouver's "Little Italy" and later the heart of the Latin American community, Commercial Drive, or "the Drive", remains one of Vancouver's most ethnically diverse districts. This shows in the food: the Drive is home to a wealth of international snacking and sipping options, from Vietnamese spring rolls to Belgian beer, Cuba libres to Italian pastries, generally in low-key places at bargain prices. Both Commerical and Main streets rely on small independent shops and restaurants, which tend to come and go quickly as Vancouver real estate prices rise. So far, though, East

The Olympic Village features numerous large-scale sculptures including this one depicting a sparrow.

Van's entrepreneurial spirit has kept the vibe alive.

Main Street/Mt. Pleasant

Main Street bisects Vancouver, running from Burrard Inlet and Chinatown south to the Fraser River. The most intriguing sections are Mount Pleasant, around the junction of Main and Broadway (extending west to Cambie), and South Main, or "SoMa", along Main Street roughly between 20th and 30th Avenues. Both areas are home to an eclectic, and frequently changing, mix of independent boutiques, vintage shops, cocktail lounges, and brew pubs, as well as lots of intriguing places to eat.

GETTING HERE AND AROUND

From Downtown, or the Main Street-Science World SkyTrain station, Bus 3 goes down Main Street. Another useful route is the express Bus 99, which travels east–west along Broadway. The Olympic Village SkyTrain station on Cambie accesses the western edge of Mount Pleasant.

◉ Sights

Science World

MUSEUM | FAMILY | Under a gigantic shiny dome on the False Creek waterfront, this hands-on science center encourages children to participate in interactive exhibits and demonstrations about the natural world, the human body, and other science topics. Exhibits change throughout the year, so there's always something new to see; there are special galleries for preschoolers, and an Omnimax theater, too. Adjacent to the museum, and included in the admission, the Ken Spencer Science Park is an outdoor exhibit area focusing on environmental issues. Science World is an easy walk (or miniferry ride) from Yaletown or a short walk from the Olympic Village; the Main Street-Science World SkyTrain station is across the street. Limited paid parking is available. ⊠ *1455 Quebec St., Olympic Village* ☎ *604/443–7440* ⊕ *www.scienceworld.ca* ✉ *C$27.15 Science World, C$33.65 Science World and Omnimax theater* ⊙ *Outdoor exhibits closed late Oct. to early Mar.*

🍴 Restaurants

On trendy but casual Main Street, you'll find a mix of happening neighborhood bistros, interesting ethnic eateries, and some great vegetarian and vegan options.

The Acorn Restaurant

$$$ | VEGETARIAN | Vancouver's first upscale vegetarian dining room, this barely bigger-than-an-acorn restaurant serves imaginative plant-based fare that does its vegetables proud. Look for dishes like beer-battered Halloumi with zucchini and potato pancake; kale Caesar salad with tempeh, olives, and smoked paprika croutons; and red kuri squash with curried hazelnut milk and wild rice. **Known for:** vegan options; gluten-free choices; creative cocktails. $ *Average main: C$22* ✉ *3995 Main St., SoMa* ☎ *604/566–9001* ⊕ *www.theacornrestaurant.ca* ⊗ *Closed Mon. No lunch weekdays.*

Bob Likes Thai Food

$$ | THAI | The staff at this no-frills storefront explains that Bob is just an average guy, and if he likes the authentically prepared Thai fare, then so will you. The menu includes all the classics, from green payaya salad to *laab moo* (minced pork with roasted rice, mint, fish sauce, and lime) to *pad si ew* (fried rice noodles with pork and egg). **Known for:** authentic Thai dishes; tasty curries; lunch specials. $ *Average main: C$16* ✉ *3755 Main St., SoMa* ☎ *604/568–8538* ⊕ *www.boblikesthaifood.com.*

Burdock & Co

$$$ | MODERN CANADIAN | Chef Andrea Carlson previously manned the stoves at locavore destinations Bishop's and Raincity Grill, and she's kept her focus on seasonal local ingredients at her own cheerful storefront bistro. Though she changes the menu regularly, about half of her inventive sharing plates are vegetarian, like the squash cannelloni with chanterelle mushroom cream or the grain "risotto" with potato, miso, and quinoa.

Known for: locavore menu; vegetarian options; fried chicken. $ *Average main: C$23* ✉ *2702 Main St., Mt. Pleasant* ☎ *604/879–0077* ⊕ *www.burdockandco.com* ⊗ *No lunch weekdays.*

Campagnolo

$$$ | ITALIAN | On a dark block near the Main St.–Science World SkyTrain station, just north of Mount Pleasant proper, this relaxed trattoria lights up the neighborhood with its welcoming vibe and casually contemporary Italian fare. Housemade pastas include a simple tagliatelle with pork and beef ragú and basil, and a more unusual ricotta gnudi, made with sweet corn and pancetta succotash and leek ash. **Known for:** house-cured salumi; fresh pasta; trendy bar. $ *Average main: C$22* ✉ *1020 Main St., Mt. Pleasant* ☎ *604/484–6018* ⊕ *www.campagnolorestaurant.ca* ⊗ *No lunch weekends* ☞ *No reservations at Upstairs.*

Chicha

$$$ | PERUVIAN | Ceviches, causas, and other classic Peruvian dishes get a west coast spin at this lively, relaxed bistro just off Main Street. Your ceviche may include local whitefish or BC salmon, while your *causa* (whipped potatoes topped with seafood or vegetables) may feature local tuna with wasabi cream and passion fruit ponzu. **Known for:** Peruvian dishes; tapas; creative cocktails. $ *Average main: C$22* ✉ *136 E. Broadway, Mt. Pleasant* ☎ *604/620–3963* ⊕ *www.chicharestaurant.com* ⊗ *No lunch Mon.–Thurs.*

49th Parallel Café and Lucky's Doughnuts

$ | CAFÉ | Locally run 49th Parallel Coffee Roasters sources and roasts their own coffees, which they feature at their flagship café on Main Street. It's always packed with neighborhood denizens and shoppers enjoying the top-notch brews and the house-made Lucky's Doughnuts, which come in flavors from simple vanilla-glazed to salted caramel to decadent triple chocolate. **Known for:** direct-sourced coffee; exceptional doughnuts;

The East Side

A	B	C	D	E

1

William St.

8

Charles St.
Kitchener St.
Grant St.
Graveley St.
East 1st Ave.
E. 2nd Ave.
E. 3rd Ave.

11

Terminal Ave.

2

W. 3rd Ave.
W. 4th Ave.

MOUNT PLEASANT

W. 7th Ave.

Great Northern Way

1A

Clark Dr.

Woodland Dr.

Commercial Dr.

7

E. 5th
E. 6th Ave.

3

W. 10th Ave.
W. 11th Ave.
W. 12th Ave.
W. 13th Ave.

W. 14th Ave.
W. 16th Ave.

5

3

6

Main Street

East 12th Ave.

9

East Broadway

EAST SIDE

RILEY

East 22nd Ave.

MAIN STREET

Kingsway

4

E. 15th Ave.
E. 16th Ave.

Yukon St.
Columbia St.
Manitoba St.
Ontario St.
Sophia St.
Prince Edward St.
Saint George St.
Carolina St.
Fraser Street
Prince Albert St.
Windsor St.
Glen Dr.
Clark Dr.
Knight Street

2 10

1

W. 22nd Ave.
W. 24th Ave.

East 24th Ave.
East King Edward Ave.

1A

5

CAMBIE CORRIDOR

Main Street

KENSINGTON-CEDAR COTTAGE

6

Queen Elizabeth Park

East 33rd Ave.

7

| 0 | | 1 mi |
| 0 | | 1 km |

KEY

1 *Sights*

1 *Restaurants*

Sights ▼

1 Science World **B2**

Restaurants ▼

1 The Acorn
Restaurant................ **B5**

2 Bob Likes Thai Food **B5**

3 Burdock & Co **B3**

4 Campagnolo............. **B1**

5 Chicha.................... **B3**

6 49th Parallel Café and
Lucky's Doughnuts **B4**

7 Harambe................. **E3**

8 Havana.................... **E2**

9 Osteria Savio Volpe......**C4**

10 Sun Sui Wah **B5**

11 The Ugly Dumpling **E2**

neighborhood hangout. $ *Average main: C$5* ✉ *2902 Main St., Mt. Pleasant* ☎ *604/872–4901* ⊕ *www.49thcoffee. com.*

Osteria Savio Volpe

$$$ | **ITALIAN** | About a 10-minute walk from Main Street and Broadway this bright, high-ceilinged take on a classic osteria fills up with neighborhood families and fashionable young people dining on house-made pasta, inventive vegetable dishes, and rich meats cooked over a wood-fired grill. The menu changes daily to showcase what's in season but always includes staples, like roasted chicken and steaks, along with more unusual items— perhaps meatballs with neck bone gravy, a venison chop, or octopus carpaccio. **Known for:** wood-fired grill; eclectic decor; house-made pasta. $ *Average main: C$30* ✉ *615 Kingsway, Mt. Pleasant* ☎ *604/428–0072* ⊕ *www.saviovolpe.com* ⊗ *No lunch.*

Sun Sui Wah

$$$ | **CHINESE** | **FAMILY** | This bustling Cantonese restaurant is best known for its excellent dim sum (served 10:30 to 3 weekdays and 10 to 3 weekends), which ranges from traditional handmade dumplings to some highly adventurous fare. Dinner specialties include roasted squab marinated in the restaurant's secret spice blend and king crab plucked live from the tanks, then steamed with garlic. **Known for:** dim sum; handmade dumplings; seafood tanks. $ *Average main: C$22* ✉ *3888 Main St., SoMa* ☎ *604/872–8822* ⊕ *www.sunsuiwah.ca.*

Nightlife

Along with a handful of laid-back little cocktail bars, Mount Pleasant is best known for its wealth of brewpubs with, so far, nine microbreweries in less than a square mile. Check out Main Street Brewing Co. (✉ *261 E. 7th Ave.*), 33 Acres Brewing Company (✉ *15 W. 8th*), Big Rock (✉ *310 W. 4th*), Faculty Brewing

(✉ *1830 Ontario*), Red Truck Beer Company (✉ *295 E. 1st. Ave.*), Electric Bicycle Brewing (✉ *20 E. 4th*), R&B Ale and Pizza House (✉ *54 E. 4th*), and Brewhall (✉ *97 E. 2nd Ave.*), along with the Craft Beer Market in the nearby Olympic Village—to create a self-made pub crawl. Or join a ready-made crawl with Vancouver Brewery Tours (⊕ *vancouverbrewerytours.com* ☎ *604/318-2280*).

BARS

Brassneck Brewery

BREWPUBS/BEER GARDENS | Long, lean, and creatively wood-paneled, this is among a fresh crop of Mount Pleasant breweries leading East Vancouver's craft beer resurgence. The brewery operations dictate the layout, and the tasting room's communal tables attract a dedicated after-work crowd for pints, flights, and growler fills. ✉ *2148 Main St., Mt. Pleasant* ☎ *604/259–7686* ⊕ *www.brassneck.ca.*

Cascade Room

BARS/PUBS | Evoking the vibe of a 1950s British cocktail bar, this busy nightspot attracts a loyal crowd with its signature blends, cocktails on tap (try the boozy slushy), and local microbrews. The upscale pub menu riffs on classic Sunday roasts, pot pies, and Scotch eggs, along with charcuterie and veggie snacks. ✉ *2616 Main St., at 10th Ave., Mt. Pleasant* ☎ *604/709–8650* ⊕ *www. thecascade.ca.*

Craft Beer Market

BREWPUBS/BEER GARDENS | The stats at this massive beer hall in the historic Salt Building are impressive: 100 draft beer taps, one of Canada's biggest selections of draft beers, and space for 450 kegs in the keg room (that's up to 26,000 liters or 6,900 gallons). The kitchen does a good job with generous portions of burgers, sandwiches, and other pub standards while the patio on Olympic Village Square makes for great summertime people-watching. ✉ *85 West 1st Ave., Olympic Village* ☎ *604/709–2337* ⊕ *www. craftbeermarket.ca/vancouver.*

Sample local beers at the Craft Beer Market, a massive beer hall housed in a historic building.

The Main

BARS/PUBS | This pub-meets-Greek restaurant is a long-standing neighborhood hangout, with after-work crowds stopping by for microbrews, signature cocktails, big-screen sports, and pub fare that globe-hops from souvlaki to nachos. ✉ *4210 Main St., Mt. Pleasant* ☎ *604/709–8555* ⊕ *www.themainonmain.ca.*

33 Acres Brewing Company

BREWPUBS/BEER GARDENS | This bright tasting room attracts creatives and techies who work in this once industrial, now trendy neighborhood. A crowded layout of communal tables creates a very social feel, and potent house-brewed beers (with happy monikers like 33 Acres of Sunshine) are served up in charming Weck canning jars. The small selection of bready nibbles features local producers, plus there's a rotating selection of food trucks on the doorstep. ✉ *15 W. 8th Ave., Mt. Pleasant* ☎ *604/620–4589* ⊕ *www.33acresbrewing.com.*

Upstairs at Campagnolo

BARS/PUBS | In complement to the cozy Italian restaurant downstairs, this second-floor bar is a welcoming and romantic spot for cocktail lovers and carnivores. A selection of upscale bar meals include the devourable dirty burger, a 45-day dry-aged beef burger. ✉ *1020 Main St., 2nd fl., Mt. Pleasant* ⊕ *www.campagnolorestaurant.ca* ☞ *Reservations not accepted.*

The Whip Restaurant and Gallery

BARS/PUBS | This lofty space with Douglas fir–beamed ceilings, exposed-brick walls, and rotating art exhibits attracts a hip, Main Street crowd. A long list of microbrews meets some interesting cocktails and a well-curated menu of locally sourced comfort food. Try the organic beef burger, the kale Caesar, or the veggie poutine with mushroom gravy. Breakfast and brunch menus appeal to a morning-after crowd. ✉ *209 E. 6th Ave., at Main St., Mt. Pleasant* ☎ *604/874–4687* ⊕ *www.thewhiprestaurant.com.*

MUSIC: ROCK AND BLUES
Biltmore Cabaret

MUSIC CLUBS | A favorite hangout for dance parties and live music, the Biltmore Cabaret hosts a mix of DJs, local bands, international performers, and stand-up comedy. It's a casual spot that comes with a half century of history as a public house. ✉ *2755 Prince Edward St., Mt. Pleasant* ☎ *604/676–0541* ⊕ *www.biltmorecabaret.com.*

🛍 Shopping

South Main Street, or SoMa, between 20th and 30th Avenues, is a funky, ever-changing neighborhood, rich with ethnic restaurants, vintage-fashion shops, and eclectic boutiques that showcase the creations of local designers.

For outdoor gear, check out the stores on Broadway, especially along the area west of Main Street, between Ontario and Cambie streets.

In the Punjabi Market area, Vancouver's "Little India," curry houses, sweets shops, grocery stores, discount jewelers, and silk shops abound. This small community centers on Main Street between 48th and 51st Avenues.

ART AND ANTIQUES
★ Hill's Native Art

ART GALLERIES | This highly respected store has Vancouver's largest selection of First Nations art. The place is crammed with souvenirs, keepsakes, and high-quality pieces, including carvings, masks, and drums. If you think that's impressive, head for one-of-a-kind collector pieces and limited editions. Its recent move from Gastown to East Broadway makes it a 10-minute cab ride from Downtown, but the larger and brighter space makes for easy browsing. ✉ *120 E. Broadway, Mt. Pleasant* ☎ *604/685–4249, 866/685–5422* ⊕ *www.hills.ca.*

CLOTHING
Barefoot Contessa

CLOTHING | This cute shop has a creative take on '40s-style glamour and boho chic. Look for frilly feminine clothing (dresses, dresses, and more dresses), jewelry, and bags—some by local designers—as well as vintage linens and decorative accessories. ✉ *3715 Main St., SoMa* ☎ *604/879–8175* ⊕ *www.thebarefootcontessa.com.*

Eugene Choo

CLOTHING | Local fashionistas swear by this cozy little shop and its well-curated racks of clothing, shoes, and accessories for both men and women. Local and international designers are featured. ✉ *3683 Main St., SoMa* ☎ *604/873-8874* ⊕ *www.eugenechoo.com.*

Front and Company

CLOTHING | Value-conscious fashionistas eagerly browse the consignment and vintage clothing in this smart shop. There's a small section of designer samples and new items, as well as eclectic gifts. ✉ *3772 Main St., SoMa* ☎ *604/879–8431* ⊕ *www.frontandcompany.com.*

HOUSEWARES
Vancouver Special

HOUSEHOLD ITEMS/FURNITURE | This shop carries a stylish selection of household items by local and international designers and stocks an eclectic assortment of books about art, architecture, and design. ✉ *3612 Main St., SoMa* ☎ *604/568-3673* ⊕ *www.vanspecial.com.*

OUTDOOR EQUIPMENT
★ MEC (Mountain Equipment Co-op)

SPORTING GOODS | Vancouver's go-to outdoor store since the 1970s, MEC stocks a good selection of high-performance clothing and equipment for hiking, cycling, climbing, and kayaking, and for just looking good while hanging around outdoors. You can rent sports gear here, too. A one-time C$5 membership is required for purchases or rentals. There are at least six other outdoor gear stores in the surrounding few blocks, so if

Farmers' Markets

Check ⊕ www.eatlocal.org for details about all the weekly markets in town.

Downtown Farmers' Market The Queen Elizabeth Theatre Plaza at Georgia and Hamilton streets is the venue for this lively urban market. Baked treats, artisanal food, crafts, and local beer, wine, and spirits share space with fresh fruit and veggies. The market runs Thursdays 3 pm to 7 pm, from June through October. ⊠ 650 Hamilton St., Downtown ⊕ www.eatlocal.org.

Hastings Park Winter Farmers' Market Christmas wreaths, hot chocolate, food trucks, artisanal cheese and more draw Vancouverites to this winter farmers' market. It runs Sundays 10 am to 2 pm, from early November through to late April at Hastings Park. ⊠ 2901 East Hastings St., East Side ⊕ eatlocal.org.

Kitsilano Farmers' Market More than 60 vendors set up in the Kitsilano Community Centre parking lot every Sunday from 10 am to 2 pm, from mid-May to mid-October. Cheese, chocolate, wine, coffee, baked treats, and food truck snacks are all on offer, along wtih live music and a festive vibe. ⊠ 2690 Larch St., at 10th Ave., East Side ⊕ www.eatlocal.org.

Main Street Station Farmers' Market Local chefs and Downtown foodies do their midweek shop at this busy market in front of Vancouver's VIA Rail Station. Dozens of vendors selling produce and other locally raised fare set up shop here Wednesdays 2 pm to 6 pm, from June to October. The market is close to the Main Street-Science World SkyTrain station. ⊠ 1100 Station St., East Side ⊕ eatlocal.org.

Mount Pleasant Farmers' Market Worth a visit for a photo of the park sign alone, this compact market along Guelph Street borders the delightfully named Dude Chilling Park. It brings a few dozen farmers, bakers, brewers, and food trucks out each Sunday 10 am to 2 pm, from late May until late October. ⊠ Eighth Ave. at Guelph St., East Side ⊕ eatlocal.org.

Riley Park Farmers' Market This lively market between the South Main shopping area and Queen Elizabeth Park runs almost year-round. Dozens of vendors including bakers, farmers, and florists set up shop each Saturday from 10 am to 2 pm. ⊠ Riley Park, Ontario St. at 30th Ave., Vancouver ⊕ eatlocal.org ⊘ Closed April.

Trout Lake Farmers' Market Vancouver's oldest and biggest farmers' market is crowded with East Side denizens on Saturdays from 9 am to 2 pm, mid-May to mid-October. There are prepared foods, baked goods, and often crafts to tempt shoppers, in addition to produce. The market is about a 15-minute walk from the Commercial Drive SkyTrain station. ⊠ John Hendry Park, between Templeton and Lakewood Sts., south of E. 13th Ave., East Side ⊕ www.eatlocal.org.

West End Farmers' Market Hot food and coffee, prepared foods, crafts and local produce fill the stalls at this laid-back market running Saturday 9 am to 2 pm from May to October in Nelson Park. ⊠ Nelson Park, 1100 Comox St., West End ⊕ www.eatlocal.org.

you can't find what you need at MEC, you're bound to find it nearby. ✉ *130 W. Broadway, Mt. Pleasant* ☎ *604/872–7858* 🌐 *www.mec.ca.*

Commercial Drive and Around

East of Main Street, Commercial Drive, or "the Drive" used to be the hub of Vancouver's Italian community. These days, the area is popular for its many cafés, drinking spots, and funky shops.

The SkyTrain runs through the East Side, with a stop at Commercial-Broadway. Plenty of buses travel around this side of town, too. From Downtown, Bus 20 will take you to Commercial Drive.

Beaches

Trout Lake Beach

BEACH—SIGHT | **FAMILY** | The only freshwater lake in the center of Vancouver, Trout Lake, in John Hendry Park, has a sandy beach and a swimming raft. Community festivals and family picnics are popular here, and there's an attractive farmers' market on summer Saturdays. **Amenities:** food and drink; lifeguards; parking (free); toilets. **Best for:** swimming, walking. ✉ *3300 Victoria Dr., between E. 14th and 19th aves., Commercial Drive* ☎ 🌐 *www.vancouver.ca/parks-recreation-culture/trout-lake-beach.aspx.*

Restaurants

Restaurants serving fare from Asia, Africa, and Latin America, as well as local pubs, pizzerias, and coffeehouses line this East Side strip that rumbas to a world beat.

Harambe

$$ | **ETHIOPIAN** | The name means "working together" in Swahili, and the family that owns this welcoming restaurant does just that as it introduces guests to traditional Ethiopian fare. Savory stews are served atop platter-size pancakes of *injera,* a tangy, almost spongy flatbread used to scoop up every morsel. **Known for:** vegetarian-friendly menu; colorful Ethiopian artwork; family-style shared plates. [$] *Average main: C$20* ✉ *2149 Commercial Dr., Commercial Drive* ☎ *604/216–1060* 🌐 *www.harambes.com* 🕘 *No lunch Mon.–Wed.*

Havana

$$ | **CUBAN** | Old Havana meets new Vancouver in this lofty, energetic spot, where the kitchen puts a west coast spin on Cuban classics. Start, for example, with ceviche, patatas bravas, or prawn tacos, then try the Cubano (porchetta, honey ham, and Swiss cheese on a Cuban bun), the squid ink paella, or the grilled octopus. **Known for:** Cuban food; mojitos; theater on-site. [$] *Average main: C$18* ✉ *1212 Commercial Dr., Commercial Drive* ☎ *604/253-9119* 🌐 *havanavancouver.com.*

The Ugly Dumpling

$$ | **ASIAN** | There's nothing ugly about the handmade dumplings, soba noodles, and other pan-Asian fare at this minimalist Commercial Drive spot. Ingredients here skew organic, ethically sourced, and local—some as local as the restaurant's own patio garden. **Known for:** handmade noodles and dumplings; local organic ingredients; sake. [$] *Average main: C$20* ✉ *1590 Commercial Dr., Commercial Drive* ☎ *604/258-0005* 🌐 *uglydumpling.ca* 🕘 *Closed Tues. No lunch.*

Nightlife

BARS

Biercraft

BARS/PUBS | With more than 50 Belgian, craft, and draft beers, the drinks menu here is a lengthy read. There are wine and cocktails, as well as plenty of snacks, from mussels to tacos and burgers as well. A street-side patio is perfect for watching life pass by on eclectic Commercial Drive when the weather's good. More suds are on tap at two other

Biercraft locations, at 3305 Cambie St., and in the Wesbrook Village on the UBC campus. ✉ *1191 Commercial Dr., Commercial Drive* ☎ *604/254–2437* ⊕ *www.biercraft.com.*

Falconetti's East Side Grill

BARS/PUBS | The second-floor patio at Falconetti's has the best neighborhood views, and it's where a diverse crowd of locals-in-the-know take in the laid-back Drive vibe. Downstairs, you're likely to catch an indie folk band or experimental group performing. There are plenty of food options, too; a gourmet sausage from the adjoining butcher shop is a good bet. ✉ *1812 Commercial Dr., Commercial Drive* ☎ *778/957-7773* ⊕ *www.falconettis.com.*

🎭 Performing Arts

The Cultch

DANCE | The Vancouver East Cultural Centre is a multipurpose performance space set in a 1909 church. Usually just called "the Cultch," it hosts concerts, theater productions, dance shows, and more. ✉ *1895 Venables St., Commercial Drive* ☎ *604/251–1363* ⊕ *www.thecultch.com.*

🛍 Shopping

ART AND ANTIQUES
Doctor Vigari Gallery

CRAFTS | In keeping with its offbeat environs on the Drive, this gallery is home to a wildly eclectic assortment of jewelry, crafts, paintings, and household items, most by BC artists. ✉ *1816 Commercial Dr., Commercial Drive* ☎ *604/255–9513* ⊕ *www.doctorvigarigallery.com.*

CLOTHING: MEN'S AND WOMEN'S
Mintage

CLOTHING | Vancouver's biggest vintage shop is a 3,000-square-foot treasure trove of style from decades past. Collections of wedding dresses, cowboy boots, hats, jewelry, menswear, and party frocks galore share space with upcycled designs made from vintage fabrics. A

second location, called Mintage Mall, is at 245 E. Broadway in Mount Pleasant. ✉ *1714 Commercial Dr., Commercial Drive* ☎ *604/646–8243* ⊕ *www.mintagevintage.com.*

SHOES AND ACCESSORIES
Dayton Boot Company

SHOES/LUGGAGE/LEATHER GOODS | These full-grain leather biker boots, handmade on-site since 1948, have a cultlike following because they're durable and hip, too. Originally made for loggers in the British Columbia woods, they're now big with bikers, actors, and rock stars. ✉ *2250 E. Hastings St., Commercial Drive* ☎ *604/253–6671* ⊕ *www.daytonboots.com.*

Kalena's

SHOES/LUGGAGE/LEATHER GOODS | You'll find everything from traditional leather sandals to fanciful purple pumps at this family-run store that's been a fixture on Commercial Drive since the 1960s. Fine Italian shoes are a specialty. ✉ *1526 Commercial Dr., Commercial Drive* ☎ *604/255–3727* ⊕ *www.kalenashoes.com.*

🏃 Activities

Fraserview Golf Course

GOLF | The most celebrated of Vancouver's public courses, the 18-hole Fraserview Golf Course sits on 91 heavily wooded hectares (225 acres) overlooking the Fraser River in Southeast Vancouver. It has a tree-lined fairway, a driving range, and a lovely clubhouse. There's a golf academy staffed with instructors who teach players of all levels. Golf carts are available on a first-come-first-served basis. ✉ *7800 Vivian Dr., South Vancouver* ☎ *604/257-6921* ⊕ *https://vancouver.ca/parks-recreation-culture/fraserview-golf-course.aspx* 💳 *C$62–C$68. Book on teetimes.vancouver.ca* 🏌 *18 holes, 6692 yards, par 72* ⛳ *Driving range, putting green, pitching area, golf carts, rental clubs, pro shop, golf academy/lessons.*

Chapter 8

NORTH SHORE

NORTH VANCOUVER AND WEST VANCOUVER

Updated by
Sue Kernaghan

👁 Sights	🍴 Restaurants	🛏 Hotels	🛍 Shopping	🍸 Nightlife
★★★★★	★★☆☆☆	★★☆☆☆	★★☆☆☆	★☆☆☆☆

NEIGHBORHOOD SNAPSHOT

TOP EXPERIENCES

■ **Explore the Shipyards District:** North Vancouver's historic dry docks are now home to a waterfront public space, complete with a cutting-edge art gallery, a weekend night market, and great views of the Downtown skyline. Concerts, food trucks, and even an outdoor ice rink are all part of the mix.

■ **Ride the Grouse Mountain Skyride:** North America's longest aerial tramway soars a full mile from base to peak at Grouse Mountain. The views are amazing, and there's plenty to do at the mountaintop.

■ **Test Your Mettle on a Suspension Bridge:** The Capilano Suspension Bridge is easy to reach and boasts a wealth of other things to see and do on-site.

GETTING HERE

From Downtown, drive west down Georgia Street to Stanley Park and across the Lions Gate Bridge to North Vancouver.

To get to West Vancouver from Downtown, take the Lions Gate Bridge and bear left for the West Vancouver exit. You'll be on Marine Drive heading west. If you're going to Cypress Mountain, Horseshoe Bay, or Whistler, take the first right onto Taylor Way, go up the hill, then follow the signs for Highway 1 west; it's a left exit.

Cypress Mountain runs a winter-only shuttle bus for skiers and snowboarders. Any time of year, the 250 Horseshoe Bay bus stops along Georgia Street in Downtown Vancouver, then winds its way along Marine Drive in West Vancouver; you can hop off at any of the beaches or parks along the way, including Ambleside Beach and Lighthouse Park. An express bus, 257, goes straight to Horseshoe Bay.

PLANNING YOUR TIME

You need at least a day to see the sights around the North Shore, even more if you want to hike at Grouse Mountain or Capilano River Regional Park or include a meandering drive through West Vancouver.

QUICK BITES

■ **Lonsdale Quay Market.** Just steps from the North Shore SeaBus terminal, this public market has about 20 stalls selling everything from fish-and-chips to Vietnamese food, salmon burgers, and all-day breakfasts. There's water-view seating both inside and out. ⊠ *123 Carrie Cates Court, North Vancouver* ⊕ *lonsdalequay. com* Ⓜ

■ **Honey Doughnuts & Goodies.** Hikers and kayakers flock to this rustic Deep Cove café for big breakfasts and signature housemade doughnuts. ⊠ *4373 Gallant Ave., North Vancouver* ⊕ *honeydoughnuts.com* Ⓜ

■ **Savary Island Pie Company.** Sweet and savory pies (try the pecan brownie) draw locals and tourists alike to this popular bakery in West Vancouver's Ambleside Village. ⊠ *1533 Marine Dr., West Vancouver* ⊕ *savaryisland-piecompany.com* Ⓜ

If a Vancouverite is boasting about skiing and hiking on the same day, chances are they've spent that day on the North Shore. The mountains forming Vancouver's scenic backdrop are where city dwellers go for access to the great outdoors, exploring forest trails, relaxing on a beach, or hitting the slopes.

The North Shore's two communities, the urban North Vancouver to the east and the long-gentrified West Vancouver to the west, also have their share of high-profile attractions. Top sights include the buzzing waterfront Shipyards District, Capilano Suspension Bridge Park, Grouse Mountain and its Skyride, and the seaside hamlets of Deep Cove and Horseshoe Bay. Many of the North Shore's top attractions are easy to reach by public transport. For a great day trip, hop on a SeaBus ferry from Waterfront Station Downtown, and enjoy a 12-minute sailing across busy Burrard Inlet. You'll land at Lonsdale Quay, which is right beside the Shipyards District. This whole waterfront area is alive with cafés, shops, a striking new art gallery, and public spaces, including an indoor market, a summer waterpark, and a winter ice rink. Time it right, and you'll catch a concert, a festival, or a night market. Waterfront walks and great views of the Downtown skyline are on hand any time of day. From Londsdale Quay, Bus 236 up Capilano Road will take you to the Capilano Suspension Bridge and the base of Grouse Mountain.

Alternatively, drive across the Lions Gate or Iron Workers' Memorial Bridge and explore some less-visited corners of the shore: check out the cute villages of Deep Cove or Horseshoe Bay, swing across the Lynn Canyon Suspension Bridge, explore a fjord by boat or kayak, or enjoy any of the miles of hiking and biking trails lacing the mountains. In winter, three ski hills offer a wealth of ways to enjoy the cold weather, from tubing and snowshoeing to cross-country skiing and outdoor ice-skating.

North Vancouver

North Vancouver, or North Van as it is usually called, is the biggest and busiest of the two North Shore communities. A first stop here, especially if you arrive by SeaBus, a foot passenger ferry from Downtown, is Lonsdale Quay, a waterfront public market, and right next door, the Shipyards, historic dry docks reborn as the region's newest public space. The area is abuzz with waterfront cafés, an art gallery and, depending on the time of day and the season, concerts, food trucks, a water park, an outdoor ice rink, and a night market. North Van is also where you'll find the area's most popular tourist destinations, including Grouse Mountain and the Capilano Suspension Bridge, as well as such lesser known

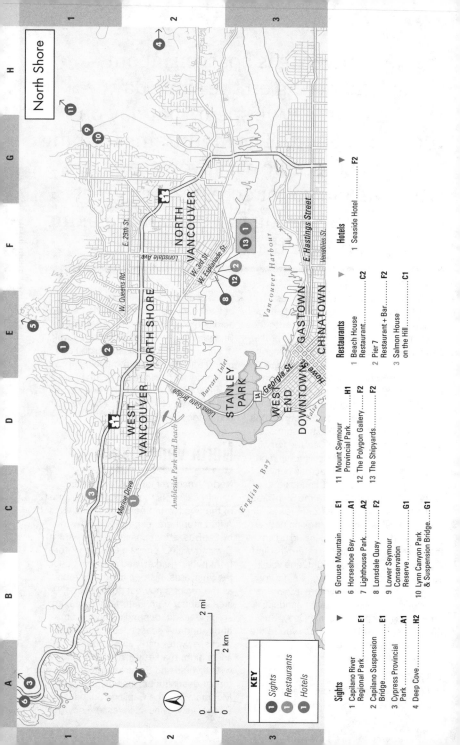

North Shore

KEY

1 Sights
1 Restaurants
1 Hotels

Sights

1 Capilano River
Regional Park..............**E1**

2 Capilano Suspension
Bridge......................**E1**

3 Cypress Provincial
Park.........................**A1**

4 Deep Cove................**H2**

5 Grouse Mountain........**E1**

6 Horseshoe Bay..........**A1**

7 Lighthouse Park.........**A2**

8 Lonsdale Quay...........**F2**

9 Lower Seymour
Conservation
Reserve....................**G1**

10 Lynn Canyon Park
& Suspension Bridge....**G1**

11 Mount Seymour
Provincial Park...........**H1**

12 The Polygon Gallery....**F2**

13 The Shipyards............**F2**

Restaurants ▶

1 Beach House
Restaurant................**C2**

2 Pier 7
Restaurant + Bar........**F2**

3 Salmon House
on the Hill.................**C1**

Hotels ▶

1 Seaside Hotel.............**F2**

gems as Lynn Canyon Park and the seaside village of Deep Cove.

◉ Sights

Capilano River Regional Park
NATIONAL/STATE PARK | This small but spectacular park is where you'll find old-growth Douglas fir trees approaching 61 meters (200 feet). There are 26 km (16 miles) of hiking trails and footbridges over the Capilano River, which cuts through a dramatic gorge. At the park's **Capilano River Hatchery** (*4500 Capilano Park Rd., 604/666–1790*), viewing areas and exhibits illustrate the life cycle of the salmon. The best time to see the salmon run is between July and November. **The Cleveland Dam** (*Capilano Rd., about 1½ km [1 mile] past main park entrance*) is at the north end of the park. Built in 1954, it dams the Capilano River to create the 5½-km-long (3½-mile-long) Capilano Reservoir. A hundred yards from the parking lot, you can walk across the top of the dam to enjoy striking views of the reservoir and mountains behind it. The two sharp peaks to the west are the Lions, for which the Lions Gate Bridge is named. The park is off Capilano Road in North Vancouver, just north of Capilano Suspension Bridge Park. ⊠ *Capilano Park Rd., North Vancouver* ✥ *Off Capilano Rd.* ☏ *604/224–5739* ⊕ *www.metrovancouver.org/services/parks_lscr/regionalparks/pages/capilanoriver.aspx* ⊠ *Free.*

★ Capilano Suspension Bridge
BRIDGE/TUNNEL | **FAMILY** | At Vancouver's oldest tourist attraction (the original bridge was built in 1889), you can get a taste of rain-forest scenery and test your mettle on the swaying, 450-foot cedar-plank suspension bridge that hangs 230 feet above the rushing Capilano River. Across the bridge is the Treetops Adventure, where you can walk along 650 feet of cable bridges suspended among the trees. If you're even braver, you can follow the **Cliffwalk**, a series

of narrow cantilevered bridges and walkways hanging out over the edge of the canyon. Without crossing the bridge, you can enjoy the site's viewing decks, nature trails, and totem park, as well as history and forestry exhibits. There's also a massive gift shop in the original 1911 teahouse, and a restaurant. May through October, guides in 19th-century costumes conduct free tours on themes related to history, nature, or ecology, while fiddle bands, and other entertainers keep things lively. In December, more than 1.5 million lights illuminate the canyon during the Canyon Lights winter celebration. Catch the attraction's free shuttle service from Canada Place; it also stops at hotels along Burrard and Robson streets. ⊠ *3735 Capilano Rd., North Vancouver* ☏ *877/985-7474* ⊕ *www.capbridge.com* ⊠ *C$53.95; Parking: $7.50.*

Deep Cove
TOWN | This charming seaside village, on the shore of a fjord off Burrard Inlet, is just a few minutes' drive from North Vancouver's other sights. You can paddle in the fjord with a guide from the Deep Cove Kayak Centre, or head out on the Quarry Rock Hike. This 4-km (2½-mile) round-trip offers sweeping ocean views, but can get very busy on sunny weekends (choose a weekday, or start early). Honey Doughnuts & Goodies is where locals relax and refuel. ⊠ *Deep Cove Rd., North Vancouver* ✥ *At the end of Deep Cove Road, off Mt.Seymour Parkway* ⊕ *vancouversnorthshore.com/things-to-do/neighbourhoods/deep-cove/.*

Grouse Mountain
VIEWPOINT | **FAMILY** | North America's largest aerial tramway, the **Skyride** is a great way to take in the city, sea, and mountain vistas (be sure to pick a clear day or evening). The Skyride makes the 2-km (1-mile) climb to the peak of Grouse Mountain every 15 minutes. Once at the top, there are plenty of activities included in the ticket price. From spring through

fall, you can catch a lumberjack show, a ranger talk, a documentary video, or a falconry demonstration; go hiking, take a walking tour, ride the chairlift, play disc golf, or visit a pair of grizzly bears in the mountain's wildlife refuge. For an extra fee you can mountain bike with e-bikes, tackle a ropes course, go ziplining (available year-round), take a helicopter flight, or tour the wind turbine that tops the mountain. You can even pay extra to ride on top of the gondola car. Popular family extras include a treetop canopy course and a chance to have breakfast with the bears. In the winter, you can ski, snowshoe, snowboard, sled, ice-skate on a mountaintop pond, take a sleigh ride, or stroll through the Light Walk, an illuminated pathway around a lake. A stone-and-cedar lodge is home to snack shops, a pub-style bistro, and a high-end restaurant, all with expansive city views. The Grouse Grind—a hiking trail up the face of the mountain—is one of the best workouts on the North Shore. Depending on your fitness level, allow between 40 minutes and two hours to complete it (90 minutes is an average time). Then you can take the Skyride down. The BCMC Trail is a less crowded, slightly longer alternative. From late May through September, you can catch a free shuttle to Grouse Mountain from Canada Place. Bus 236 from Lonsdale Quay stops at the base of Grouse Mountain year-round. ⊠ *6400 Nancy Greene Way, North Vancouver* ☎ *604/980–9311* ⊕ *www.grousemountain.com* ⊠ *Skyride and many activities C$59* ⊘ *Closed late October to early November.*

Lonsdale Quay

MARKET | FAMILY | At this two-level indoor market—less frenzied than its Granville Island counterpart—vendors sell prepared foods, just-caught seafood, and fresh produce. You can also shop for crafts, kitchenware, and toys, or sample the beer or kombucha at Green Leaf Brewing on-site. Outside you can wander the quay and enjoy the views of the Downtown skyline across the water. The market is a short ride from Downtown on the SeaBus and just steps from the Polygon Gallery and the Shipyards District. ⊠ *123 Carrie Cates Ct., at foot of Lonsdale Ave., North Vancouver* ☎ *604/985–6261* ⊕ *www.lonsdalequay. com* ⊠ *Free.*

Lower Seymour Conservation Reserve

HIKING/WALKING | Nestled into the precipitous North Shore Mountains, this 5,668-hectare (14,000-acre) reserve includes 100 km (62 miles) of hiking and biking trails—some that are steep and challenging. The meandering **Seymour Valley Trailway** is a 10-km (6-mile) paved pathway, suitable for cyclists, in-line skaters, strollers, and wheelchairs. Popular hikes include the easy 2 km (1 mile) loop around Rice Lake and the steep climb to Lynn Peak. ⊠ *2369 Lillooet Rd., North Vancouver* ☎ *778/452-4583* ⊕ *metrovancouver.org.*

Lynn Canyon Park and Suspension Bridge

BRIDGE/TUNNEL | FAMILY | With a steep canyon landscape, a temperate rain forest complete with waterfalls, and a suspension bridge (circa 1912) 166½ feet above raging Lynn Creek, this 617-acre park provides thrills to go with its scenic views. The park has many hiking trails, including a short walk to a popular swimming hole, and another trail leading to a double waterfall. Longer walks in the park link to trail networks in nearby Lynn Headwaters Regional Park and the Lower Seymour Conservation Reserve. The park's on-site Ecology Centre distributes trail maps, as well as information about the local flora and fauna. There's also a gift shop and a café here. To get to the park, take the Lions Gate Bridge and Capilano Road, go east on Highway 1, take Exit 19, the Lynn Valley Road exit, and turn right on Peters Road. From Downtown Vancouver, you can take the SeaBus to Lonsdale Quay, then Bus 228 or 229 from the quay; both

Did You Know?

The 450-foot-long cedar-plank Capilano Suspension Bridge hangs 230 feet above the rushing Capilano River and makes for an exhilarating walk in the woods.

The hike up Grouse Mountain is no easy feat, but the views from the top, and from Goat Mountain, slightly farther up, are breathtaking. Or you can always take the Skyride gondola.

stop about a 15-minute walk from the park. ■TIP→ **The suspension bridge here is shorter than the Capilano Suspension Bridge (157 feet versus 450 feet at Capilano) so the experience is less thrilling, but also less touristy—and it's free.** ✉ *3663 Park Rd. at end of Peters Rd., North Vancouver* ☎ *604/990–3755 Ecology Centre, 604/739-3663 café* ⊕ *lynncanyonecology-centre.ca* ✉ *Ecology Centre by donation, suspension bridge free.*

Mount Seymour Provincial Park

PARK—SPORTS-OUTDOORS | Just 30 minutes from Downtown Vancouver, this 3,508-hectare (8,668-acre) wilderness park has hiking trails of varying length and difficulty and spectacular views of the Lower Mainland. Warm clothing—and caution—are advised. Popular routes include a scenic 1½-hour trip to Dog Mountain or a more intense four-hour climb to the three peaks of Seymour. You can also hike down to Deep Cove on Indian Arm in less than an hour. In winter, the trails are used for snowshoeing, and you can try tubing and tobogganing,

too. ✉ *Mount Seymour Rd., off Mount Seymour Pkwy., North Vancouver* ⊕ *env. gov.bc.ca.*

The Polygon Gallery

ART GALLERIES—ARTS | Opened in 2017 in a striking purpose-built waterfront facility at the foot of Lonsdale Avenue, this public gallery focuses on photography and media-based art. You can join a tour of the current exhibit, led by an art professional, Saturdays at 2 pm. The on-site shop has an excellent selection of photography books and photo supplies, including Polaroid cameras. ✉ *101 Carrie Cates Court, North Vancouver* ✛ *In the Shipyards District at the foot of Lonsdale Ave.* ☎ *604/986-1351* ⊕ *thepolygon. ca* ✉ *Admission by donation* ☞ *Closed Mon.* Ⓜ *SeaBus.*

The Shipyards

COMMERCIAL CENTER | North Vancouver's historic dry docks have been reimagined as a vibrant waterfront public space, including restaurants, cafés, a hip pub, a boutique hotel, and even a kids' water park reconfigured as an ice rink in winter. Just steps from Lonsdale Quay on the North Vancouver waterfront, the Shipyards are easy to reach by SeaBus. On Friday nights from May through September, more than 120 vendors, a wealth of food trucks, and a beer garden set up shop outdoors for the Shipyards Night Market. The Shipyards are also home to the photo-centric Polygon Gallery. ✉ *Victory Ship Way, North Vancouver* ✥ *South of Esplanade between Lonsdale and St. George's Ave.* 🌐 *theshipyards.net.*

🍴 Restaurants

Pier 7 Restaurant + Bar

$$$ | **PACIFIC NORTHWEST** | This lively Shipyards District eatery juts like a pier into Burrard Inlet, affording 180-degree water, city skyline, and Stanley Park views from tables both inside and out. The covered, heated patio is open year-round, so alfresco dining is pretty much always an option. **Known for:** live music on Thursday nights; handy to the Shipyards Friday Night Market; family-style Cajun seafood boils twice a week. [$] *Average main: C$26* ✉ *25 Wallace Mews, North Vancouver* ✥ *At the foot of Lonsdale Ave.* ☎ *604/929 7437* 🌐 *pierseven.ca.*

🛏 Hotels

Seaside Hotel

$$$$ | **HOTEL** | Floor-to-ceiling windows bring in sweeping ocean and mountain views at this North Vancouver boutique hotel. **Pros:** on-site spa; steps from the cafés and markets of the pedestrian-friendly Shipyards District; handy to North Shore hiking and skiing. **Cons:** a bridge or ferry away from Downtown; no pool; potential construction in the area. [$] *Rooms from: C$379* ✉ *130-125 Victory Ship Way, North Vancouver* ✥ *At the foot of Lonsdale Ave.* ☎ *604/973-1473, 833/256-6276 Toll-free* 🌐 *seasidehotelvancouver.com* 🛏 *70 rooms* 🍽 *No meals.*

🛍 Shopping

North Vancouver is home to the Lonsdale Quay Market (a bustling indoor market filled with snack stalls and boutiques) and the Shipyards Friday Night Market, as well as several unique boutiques in the Lower Lonsdale, or Lolo, district.

FOOD

Lonsdale Quay Market

FOOD/CANDY | At this two-level indoor market—less frenzied than its Granville Island counterpart—vendors sell prepared foods, just-caught seafood, and fresh produce. The Green Leaf Brewing Company on-site makes a range of ales, spirits, and even kombucha. Also look for arts and crafts, toys, kitchenware, and delicious pastries that can be enjoyed on the terrace, which has views of the city skyline. The market is a short ride from Downtown on the SeaBus. ✉ *123 Carrie Cates Ct., North Vancouver* ☎ *604/985-6261* 🌐 *www.lonsdalequay.com.*

🏃 Activities

HIKING

Baden Powell Trail

HIKING/WALKING | This 48-km (30-mile) trail crosses the entire length of the North Shore Mountains, from Horseshoe Bay in the west to Deep Cove in the east. On the way it passes through both Cypress Provincial Park and Mount Seymour Provincial Park, and is best completed in three or four sections. For a quick and scenic taste of the route, make the 4-km (2½-mile) round-trip jaunt up to Quarry Rock in Deep Cove. ✉ *North Shore Mountains, North Vancouver.*

Grouse Grind

PARK—SPORTS-OUTDOORS | Vancouver's most famous, or infamous, hiking route, the Grind, is about a 3-km (about 2-mile) climb straight up 853 meters (2,799 feet) to the top of Grouse Mountain. Thousands do it annually, but climbers are advised to be experienced and in

Did You Know?

The Skyride—North America's largest aerial tramway—makes the 1-mile climb to the peak of Grouse Mountain every 15 minutes.

excellent physical condition. The route is open daily during daylight hours, from spring through autumn (conditions permitting). Hikers can ride the Grouse Mountain Skyride back down for $15 (a round-trip is C$59; hiking down is not permitted). Hiking trails in the adjacent Lynn Headwaters Regional Park are accessible from the gondola, including the **4-hour Goat Mountain Trail**. ✉ *Grouse Mountain, 6400 Nancy Greene Way, North Vancouver* ☎ *604/980–9311* ⊕ *www.grousemountain.com.*

Rockwood Adventures

HIKING/WALKING | This company gives guided walks of rain forest or coastal terrain, in areas including Lighthouse Park, Capilano Canyon, and Bowen Island in Howe Sound. Many of the tours also include a gourmet picnic or box lunch. ✉ *1024 Belvedere Dr., North Vancouver* ☎ *604/913–1621* ⊕ *www.rockwoodadventures.com.*

KAYAKING

Deep Cove Kayak

KAYAKING | Ocean kayak, stand-up paddleboard, and surfski rentals, guided excursions, and lessons for everyone in the family are available between April and October at this company's waterfront base in Deep Cove. Some weekend winter paddling tours are also available. ✉ *2156 Banbury Rd., North Vancouver* ✥ *Foot of Gallant Ave. in Deep Cove* ☎ *604/929–2268* ⊕ *www.deepcovekayak.com.*

MOUNTAIN BIKING

Mountain biking may be a worldwide phenomenon, but its most radical expression, known as free-riding, was born in the 1990s on the steep-and-rugged North Shore Mountains. This extreme type of mountain biking has thrill seekers riding ultra-heavy-duty bikes through gnarly forests, along log-strewn trails, over rocky precipices, and down stony stream beds (not to mention along obstacles like planks and teeter-totters). The **Lower**

Seymour Conservation Reserve has challenging biking trails through alpine meadows, forested slopes, and river flood plains: the Corkscrew and Salvation trails are classified as advanced or extreme. There are also advanced mountain biking trails on the lower slopes of **Mount Fromme** (next to Grouse Mountain) and **Mount Seymour**.

Endless Biking

BICYCLING | Convenient to North Vancouver's challenging trails, this bike shop rents mountain bikes including those with rugged suspension systems. Reservations are recommended. The shop also runs guided tours, which include a shuttle to the trail head. ✉ *101-1467 Crown St., North Vancouver* ☎ *604/985–2519* ⊕ *www.endlessbiking.com.*

SKIING

Grouse Mountain Ski Resort

SKIING/SNOWBOARDING | **FAMILY** | A 25-minute drive from Downtown Vancouver, the Skyride gondola takes skiers up to the ski resort on a slope overlooking the city. The views are fine on a clear day, but at night they're spectacular, and the area is known for its night skiing. Facilities include four quad chairs, 33 skiing and snowboarding runs, and several all-level freestyle-terrain parks. There's a choice of upscale and casual dining in a handsome stone-and-timber lodge. ✉ *6400 Nancy Greene Way, North Vancouver* ☎ *604/980–9311, 604/986–6262 snow report* ⊕ *www.grousemountain.com.*

Mount Seymour Resort

SKIING/SNOWBOARDING | **FAMILY** | A full-service winter activity area, Mount Seymour ski resort sprawls over 81 hectares (200 acres) accessed from eastern North Vancouver. With three chairs for varying abilities; a beginners' lift, equipment rentals, and lessons; as well as toboggan and tubing runs, it's a favorite destination for families. Snowboarding is particularly popular, as is snowshoeing on ski hill trails and provincial park routes. Three

Did You Know?

Cypress Mountain Ski Resort, which has downhill and cross-country skiing in the winter and hiking and biking in the summer, is just 30 minutes from Downtown.

food outlets serve casual fare. During the ski season, the resort runs a shuttle bus from Parkgate Community Centre in North Vancouver and from opposite the Rupert SkyTrain Station in East Vancouver. ✉ *1700 Mt. Seymour Rd., North Vancouver* ☎ *604/986–2261* ⊕ *www. mtseymour.ca.*

West Vancouver

Posh "West Van," as the locals call the North Shore suburb of West Vancouver, has retained its well-heeled character from the time when the Guinness family developed the area in the 1930s. It's a network of winding country roads and multimillion-dollar homes. Cypress Mountain, which hosted the 2010 Winter Olympic freestyle skiing and snowboard competitions, is in West Van. If you have a car, you can drive to the top of Cypress for spectacular vistas of Vancouver and beyond; unlike Grouse Mountain, the views here are free. West Van is also home to the Horseshoe Bay ferry terminal with service to the Sunshine Coast, Bowen Island, and Vancouver Island. Highway 99 through West Vancouver is the start of the Sea-to-Sky Highway, which continues north to Squamish and Whistler.

◉ Sights

★ Cypress Provincial Park
PARK—SPORTS-OUTDOORS | This 3,012-hectare (7,443-acre) park sprawls above Howe Sound, embracing Strachan, Black, and Hollyburn mountains. On a clear day you can see Mt. Baker (in Washington State) and Vancouver Island. Although the park includes a commercial ski area, much of the terrain is a public hiking paradise (bikes are permitted on roadways and some trails). Popular hikes include the route to **Eagle Bluff**, cross-country routes near Hollyburn Lodge and the first

part of the Howe Sound Crest Trail as far as Saint Mark's Summit. This is backcountry, though, and only experienced hikers should attempt the more remote routes, including the multiday Baden Powell and Howe Sound Crest trails. BC Parks runs a bus from Downtown Vancouver to Cypress Provincial Park. ✉ *Cypress Bowl Rd., off Hwy. 1, Exit 8, West Vancouver* ☎ *604/926–5612, 800/928-7101 Park Bus* ⊕ *www.env.gov. bc.ca; www.parkbus.ca.*

Horseshoe Bay
TOWN | This litte town, tucked under the Coast Mountains on the shore of Howe Sound, marks the western edge of West Vancouver. Best known for its BC Ferries terminal, with service to Vancouver Island, Bowen Island, and the Sunshine Coast, Horseshoe Bay also marks the start of the Sea-to-Sky Highway to Whistler. Most people pass through, but it's worth making time for a fish-and-chips lunch at Troll's (operated by the same family since the 1940s) or any of several restaurants with ocean- and mountain-view decks. You can also make a day of it, swimming or scuba diving at Whytecliffe Park or joining an eco-tour with Sewell's Marina. ✉ *Hwy. 1, West Vancouver* ⊹ *At the end of Hwy. 1.*

Lighthouse Park
PARK—SPORTS-OUTDOORS | This 75-hectare (185-acre) wilderness wraps around the historic lighthouse at Point Atkinson, where Howe Sound meets Burrard Inlet in the municipality of West Vancouver. A bank of soaring granite (popular for picnicking) shapes the foreshore, while the interior is an undulating terrain of mostly Douglas fir, arbutus, and rich undergrowth. Fairly short interconnected trails, from easy to challenging, bring you close to the birds and other wildlife. ✉ *Beacon La., off Marine Dr., West Vancouver* ☎ *604/925–7275* ⊕ *westvancouver.ca/ parks-recreation/parks/lighthouse-park.*

Beaches

Ambleside Park and Beach

BEACH—SIGHT | FAMILY | Just off Marine Drive at the foot of 13th Street, this long stretch of sand is West Vancouver's most popular beach. There are tennis courts, volleyball nets, and a water park in the summer, as well as superb views of Stanley Park from all along the Seawall. There's also a pitch and putt course and a huge off-leash area for dogs. Just west of the park, the historic Ferry Building is now a small art gallery. A half-hour walk west along the Seawall path takes you to another beach at Dundarave. West Vancouver's Marine Drive continues west to several quiet litte beaches, including (from east to west) West Bay, Sandy Cove, Caulfeild Park, and Kew Beach. **Amenities**: food and drink; parking; showers; toilets. **Best for:** sunrise; swimming; walking. ⊠ *Argyle Ave. at 13th St., West Vancouver* ⊕ *westvancouver.ca/ parks-recreation/parks/ambleside-park.*

Whytecliff Park

BEACH—SIGHT | This calm cove near Horseshoe Bay is popular for swimming, scuba diving, sunset watching, and, at low tide, hiking out to Whyte Islet just offshore. **Amenities:** food and drink; parking (fee); toilets. **Best for:** swimming; walking. ⊠ *7000 Marine Dr., west of Horseshoe Bay, West Vancouver* ☎ *604/925–7275* ⊕ *www.westvancouver. ca/parks-recreation/parks/whytecliff-park.*

Restaurants

There are some lovely views at the upscale destination restaurants out here, but you'll need a car.

Beach House Restaurant

$$$$ | PACIFIC NORTHWEST | Whether inside the terraced dining room or on the heated beachside patio, almost every table at this 1912 seaside house has views over Burrard Inlet and Stanley Park. The Pacific Northwest menu focuses on unpretentious seafood dishes, such as west coast sablefish or roasted salmon, along with steak, burger, and pasta choices. **Known for:** Pacific Northwest menu; seasonal fish dishes; exceptional views. $ *Average main: C$35* ⊠ *150 25th St., off Marine Dr., West Vancouver* ☎ *604/922–1414* ⊕ *www.thebeachhouserestaurant.ca.*

Salmon House on the Hill

$$$$ | SEAFOOD | Perched halfway up a mountain, this restaurant has stunning water and city views by day and expansive vistas of city lights by night. It's best known for its alder-grilled salmon, though the sablefish is also tempting. **Known for:** local seafood; BC-focused wine list; stunning views. $ *Average main: C$40* ⊠ *2229 Folkestone Way, West Vancouver* ☎ *604/926–3212* ⊕ *www.salmonhouse. com* ⊙ *No lunch Mon.–Sat.*

Activities

SKIING

★ Cypress Mountain Ski Resort

SKIING/SNOWBOARDING | Just 30 minutes from Downtown, the ski facilities at Cypress Mountain include six quad or double chairs, 53 downhill runs, and a vertical drop of 610 meters (2,001 feet). The resort has a snow-tubing area and snowshoe tours. This is also a major cross-country skiing area. Summer activities at Cypress Mountain include hiking, geocaching, wildlife-viewing, and mountain biking. To get there without a car, ride the SeaBus to Lonsdale Quay and catch the privately run Cypress Mountain Express Bus (⊕ *www.cypresscoachlines. com*). ⊠ *Cypress Provincial Park, 6000 Cypress Bowl Rd., West Vancouver* ☎ *604/926–5612* ⊕ *www.cypressmountain.com.*

WILDLIFE TREKS

★ Sewell's Marina

WILDLIFE-WATCHING | This marina in the village of Horseshoe Bay, runs two-hour ecotours of the marine and coastal mountain habitat of Howe Sound. Sightings range from swimming seals to soaring eagles. High-speed rigid hull inflatable boats are used. They also offer guided salmon-fishing charters. ✉ *6409 Bay St., West Vancouver* ☎ *604/921–3474* ⊕ *www.sewellsmarina.com* 🏃 *No tours Nov. 1 to March 31.*

RICHMOND

Updated by
Vanessa Pinniger

👁 **Sights**
★★★★☆

🍴 **Restaurants**
★★★★☆

🛏 **Hotels**
★★★☆☆

🛍 **Shopping**
★★★☆☆

🍸 **Nightlife**
★★☆☆☆

NEIGHBORHOOD SNAPSHOT

TOP EXPERIENCES

■ **Historic Steveston:** This quaint fishing village offers the quintessential Pacific coastal experience.

■ **Olympic Experience:** Take part in simulated Olympic sports at Richmond Olympic Oval, the 2010 Winter Olympics speed-skating venue.

■ **Dumpling Trail:** Grab your chopsticks and hit this trail of 20 dim sum restaurants, voted one of CNN Travel's top-12 food and drink trails in the world.

■ **Whale-Watching:** Cross the Strait of Georgia during migration season (April to October) to catch a glimpse of the gentle giants in their natural habitat.

■ **Richmond Night Market:** Reminiscent of Asia's popular night-time street fairs, vendors at this lively market hawk authentic Asian street food and retail items, weekend evenings from May to October.

■ **Bike the Dike:** Take in scenic mountain and shore-line views from the unpaved pathways along Richmond's windswept dike.

GETTING HERE

The suburban community of Richmond is a 30-minute drive south of Downtown Vancouver and a 30-minute drive north of the Canada/U.S. border. It's easy to get on the Canada Line from either Downtown—about a 20- or 25-minute ride—or from Vancouver International Airport (YVR), which is located here.

PLANNING YOUR TIME

With 800-plus eateries to choose from, a multitude of outdoor activities, lively summer night market, and more than 20 major hotels, Richmond is a welcoming community for visitors anytime. But go during the day if you want to experience some of the best dim sum in North America.

QUICK BITES

■ **Flying Beaver Bar & Grill.** Watch floatplanes take off and land at this buzzy pub on the Fraser River. ⊠ 4760 Inglis Drive, YVR South Terminal ⊕ mjg. ca/flying-beaver Ⓜ South Terminal shuttle from YVR main terminal.

■ **Pajo's on the Wharf.** The original location of this popular fish-and-chips stand draws crowds all summer long. ⊠ On the water at the corner of Bayview and Third Ave., Steveston Ⓜ 406 Steveston bus from Richmond-Brighouse Station.

■ **Peanuts Bubble Tea.** One of Richmond's first bubble tea stalls makes for a refreshing break at the busy public market. ⊠ Richmond Public Market, 8260 Westminster Highway, central Richmond Ⓜ Canada Line, Richmond-Brighouse Station.

This thriving city just south of Vancouver exempfies the melding of Pacific coast cultures, from the fishing village of Steveston to the modern malls and some of the best Asian food outside Asia. It is an outdoor enthusiast's paradise, with miles of walking and biking trails, and a haven for both birders and whale-watchers alike.

◉ Sights

Britannia Shipyards National Historic Site

MUSEUM VILLAGE | FAMILY | Linked to Steveston's historic waterfront, this 8-acre park offers a rare glimpse of life within a once-thriving mix of canneries, boatyards, residences, and stores. Britannia Heritage Shipyard dates back to 1885 and is the oldest remaining shipyard structure on the Fraser River. Weathered to a silver-gray color by a century of exposure, many of the buildings are the last examples of their type on the entire coast. Several buildings have been restored. These include Murakami House, once the three-room home of the 11-member Murakami family; boatworks buildings; shipyard residences; stilt houses; the last surviving Chinese bunkhouse on the west coast; and a board-and-batten First Nations House similar to traditional 19th-century Coast Salish longhouses. Year-round programs include the restoration of wooden boats. ✉ *5180 Westwater Dr., Richmond* ☎ *604/238–8050* ⊕ *www. richmond.ca/culture/sites/britannia* 🎟 *Free.*

★ Gulf of Georgia Cannery National Historic Site

HISTORIC SITE | FAMILY | Located at the mouth of the Fraser River in the historic fishing village of Steveston, this cannery grew from a single salmon canning line in 1894 to BC's biggest salmon cannery—with 2.5 million cans packed annually until the 1930s. Through the years, production was impacted by the landslide at Hells Gate, the onset of the Depression, and World War II, when much of its activities turned to canning herring for wartime consumption by troops and civilians. Designated a Federal Heritage site in 1987, the cannery now operates as a west coast fishing industry museum with ongoing interpretive programs and tours. You can check out the canning line, learn more about BC's fishing industry, and explore the heritage of the various ethnic groups who worked on-site. The Gulf of Georgia Cannery is a 35- to 40-minute drive from Downtown Vancouver; by public transit, take the Canada Line to Brighouse Station, then change to Bus 401, 402, or 407. ✉ *12138 Fourth Ave., Richmond* ☎ *604/664–9009* ⊕ *www. gulfofgeorgiacannery.org* 🎟 *C$11.70.*

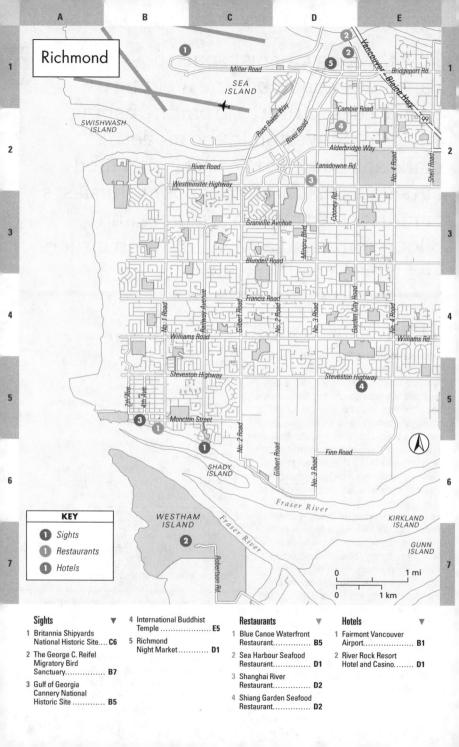

Richmond

KEY

- ① Sights
- ① Restaurants
- ① Hotels

Sights ▼

1 Britannia Shipyards National Historic Site.... **C6**
2 The George C. Reifel Migratory Bird Sanctuary................ **B7**
3 Gulf of Georgia Cannery National Historic Site **B5**
4 International Buddhist Temple **E5**
5 Richmond Night Market **D1**

Restaurants ▼

1 Blue Canoe Waterfront Restaurant............. **B5**
2 Sea Harbour Seafood Restaurant............. **D1**
3 Shanghai River Restaurant............. **D2**
4 Shiang Garden Seafood Restaurant............. **D2**

Hotels ▼

1 Fairmont Vancouver Airport................... **B1**
2 River Rock Resort Hotel and Casino........ **D1**

The International Buddhist Temple holds regular lectures, meditation classes, and tea ceremonies.

International Buddhist Temple

RELIGIOUS SITE | You don't have to be a Buddhist to appreciate the intricate workmanship of traditional Chinese art and culture inside this magnificent Buddhist temple, one of the most exquisite examples of Chinese palatial architecture and second-largest Buddhist temple in North America. Amid the peace and tranquility, the temple holds regular Buddhist ceremonies, lectures, and meditation classes, and conducts tea ceremonies. There is also a renowned bonsai garden, resource library, and museum on the grounds, as well as a cafeteria offering Taste of Zen lunch service on Saturdays and Sundays. Because of the sacred nature of the temple, photography is restricted to outside areas. To reach the temple by public transit, take the Canada Line to Brighouse Station, then catch Bus 403 to the temple. ⊠ *9160 Steveston Hwy. , between No. 3 and No. 4 Rd., Richmond* ☎ *604/274–2822* ⊕ *www.buddhisttemple. ca* ⊠ *Free.*

The George C. Reifel Migratory Bird Sanctuary

NATURE PRESERVE | **FAMILY** | As a major wintering area for more than 260 species of birds, this bird sanctuary is busy year-round with avian activity. Shorebirds start arriving mid-August, followed by northern waterfowl; bird sightings peak in November. Nesting takes place April through June; kids love seeing the goslings and ducklings. Birdseed is 50 cents. Located on Westham Island in Ladner across the Fraser River estuary from Steveston, it takes a bit of a loop route to get there, but, rain or shine, there are always birds to see. ⊠ *5191 Robertson Rd., Delta* ✛ *9.6 km (6 mi) west of Ladner off River Rd., Westham Island* ☎ *604/946–6980* ⊕ *www.reifelbirdsanctuary.com* ⊠ *C$5.*

★ Richmond Night Market

MARKET | **FAMILY** | Now a flagship summertime event and an experience unmatched anywhere else in Canada, the bustling Richmond Night Market has grown to include more than 100 Asian

The Richmond Night Market, held each summer, features retail booths, food stalls, and entertainment.

street food stalls, 250 retail booths, carnival rides, children's amusement area, and family-friendly entertainment. Just steps from the Canada Line's Bridgeport Station beside the River Rock Casino, the market is open nightly Friday to Sunday and holiday Mondays from mid-May to mid-October. For those driving, there are more than 1,000 free parking stalls available on-site. ✉ *8351 River Rd., Richmond* ☎ *604/244–8448* ⊕ *www.richmondnightmarket.com* ✉ *C$4.75.*

🍴 Restaurants

Take the Canada Line to Richmond to sample delicious Chinese food or some of the freshest seafood on the wharf at Steveston.

Blue Canoe Waterfront Restaurant

$$ | SEAFOOD | FAMILY | Located on the pier next to Fisherman's Wharf in Steveston Village, this popular eatery's "canoe-sized" fresh local seafood platters, featuring snow crab legs, smoked salmon, and Salt Spring Island mussels, are designed for sharing. In summer, grab a seat on the deck overlooking the busy boardwalk and watch the marina and river traffic sail by. **Known for:** fresh seafood; waterfront dining; local craft beer and wine. ⓢ *Average main: C$20* ✉ *140-3866 Bayview St., Richmond* ☎ ⊕ *www.bluecanoerestaurant.com.*

Sea Harbour Seafood Restaurant

$$ | CANTONESE | Conveniently located at the entrance to Bridgeport Station on the Canada Line, this upscale Chinese restaurant serves first-rate Hong Kong–style seafood, often plucked live from the tanks and cooked to the specifications of its well-heeled clientele. Ask for whatever fish is freshest, and try the distinctive pork with chayote squash. **Known for:** cooked-to-order seafood; dim sum; upscale dining. ⓢ *Average main: C$20* ✉ *150-8888 River Rd., Richmond* ☎ *604/232–0816* ⊕ *www.seaharbour.com.*

Shanghai River Restaurant
$$$ | **SHANGHAINESE** | **FAMILY** | A brigade of chefs is at work in the open kitchen of this popular restaurant that specializes in Shanghai-style fare, which is richer and slightly sweeter than more delicate Cantonese dishes. They're prepping the handmade dumplings, including the soup-filled *xiao long bao* and the panfried pork buns that are among the specialties here. **Known for:** Shanghai-style dishes; handmade dumplings; hand-pulled noodles. [$] *Average main: C$30* ✉ *7831 Westminster Hwy., Richmond* ☎ *604/233–8885.*

Shiang Garden Seafood Restaurant
$$$ | **CHINESE** | **FAMILY** | Dim sum aficionados make the trek to this upscale Cantonese restaurant for some of the tastiest tidbits in town, served daily for brunch or lunch. Order from the menu (there are no carts circling the dining rooms), or just point at what the other tables are having. **Known for:** dim sum; Cantonese–style seafood; popular with locals. [$] *Average main: C$25* ✉ *4540 No. 3 Rd., Richmond* ☎ *604/273–8858* 🌐 *shiang-garden.com.*

Hotels

Richmond has more than 20 major hotels, ranging from well-known brands to a renowned airport property at YVR. Many offer free guest shuttles to and from YVR and are a quick Canada Line rapid transit ride or short drive from Downtown Vancouver.

★ **Fairmont Vancouver Airport**
$$$$ | **HOTEL** | This hotel is truly a gem in the Fairmont chain's crown. **Pros:** spacious rooms; great spa; convenient in-terminal location. **Cons:** pricey during high season; valet or airport parking only; free Wi-Fi only available for loyalty members (but there is no cost to enroll). [$] *Rooms from: C$529* ✉ *3111 Grant McConachie Way, Vancouver International Airport, Richmond* ☎ *604/207-5200* 🌐 *www.fairmont.com* 🛏 *386 guest rooms and suites* 🍴 *No meals.*

River Rock Resort Hotel and Casino
$$$$ | **RESORT** | **FAMILY** | Located at a 144-berth marina along the Fraser River, this hotel and casino complex features views of the North Shore mountains. **Pros:** spacious suites; huge pool with waterslide; 24-hour casino. **Cons:** can be noisy; parking attached to casino, not hotel; no airport shuttle. [$] *Rooms from: C$390* ✉ *8811 River Rd., Richmond* ☎ *604/247–8900* 🌐 *www.riverrock.com* 🛏 *396 rooms* 🍴 *No meals.*

Shopping

Several large shopping malls—centered around No. 3 Road between Cambie Road and Granville Avenue—mix chain stores with small boutiques and eateries. The Aberdeen Centre, Yaohan Centre, and Parker Place have an Asian focus featuring food courts made for feasting. The Canada Line from Downtown makes several stops in Richmond, convenient for getting to the malls and to the McArthurGlen Designer Outlet which is three mintues on the line from the airport.

SHOPPING CENTERS

★ **Aberdeen Centre**
SHOPPING CENTERS/MALLS | First-rate Asian restaurants, food vendors selling everything from kimchi to cream puffs, clothing stores stocking the latest styles, and Daiso—a Japanese bargain-hunters' paradise —make this swank mall a good introduction to Vancouver's Asian shopping experience. Take the Canada Line south to Aberdeen Station, about 20 minutes from Downtown. ✉ *4151 Hazelbridge Way, Richmond* ☎ *604/273–1234* 🌐 *www.aberdeencentre.com.*

McArthurGlen Designer Outlet
SHOPPING CENTERS/MALLS | Last-minute bargain hunting? This outlet mall, just three minutes on the Canada Line from

Vancouver International Airport and 20 minutes from Downtown, has a wealth of brand outlets, such as Coach, Kate Spade, J.Crew, Nike, Levi's, Hugo Boss, Armani, Michael Kors, and Polo Ralph Lauren, all housed in a European village–style outdoor space. Free parking and storage lockers and free travel on Canada Line between YVR Airport and the outlet. ✉ *7899 Templeton Station Rd., Richmond* ☎ *604/231-5525* ⊕ *www.mcarthurglen. com.*

🏃 Activities

★ Richmond Olympic Oval

ICE SKATING | FAMILY | This speed-skating oval was built alongside the Fraser River for the 2010 Olympics. The state-of-the-art facility, with a gorgeous glass-and-steel design, contains world-class ice rinks and a huge fitness center with a climbing wall. It also houses Canada's only official Olympic museum, the Olympic Experience at the Richmond Olympic Oval. Here you can channel your inner athlete on sports simulators, experiencing what it's like to compete in events such as bobsledding and ski jumping. It's a 15-minute walk from the Canada Line Lansdowne Station. The C94 Community Shuttle runs to the front door of the Oval from the Canada Line Brighouse Station. ✉ *6111 River Rd., Richmond* ☎ *778/296–1400* ⊕ *www.richmondoval.ca* 🖼 *C$20* ☞ *Olympic Experience closed Mon. to Wed.*

WILDLIFE TREKS

Steveston Seabreeze Adventures

WILDLIFE-WATCHING | FAMILY | In April and early May thousands of male California sea lions settle on rocks near the mouth of the Fraser River to feed on the eulachon, a member of the smelt family. Seabreeze's sightseeing boats make the short trip into the estuary from Steveston. Daily whale-watching tours depart April through October, plus there are by-request tours to The George C. Reifel Migratory Bird Sanctuary on Westham Island during the autumn migratory season. They also operate fishing charters as far west as the Gulf Islands. ✉ *12551 No. 1 Rd., Richmond* ☎ *604/272–7200* ⊕ *www.seabreezead-ventures.ca.*

Chapter 10

VICTORIA

WITH THE BUTCHART GARDENS

Updated by
Chris McBeath

British
Columbia

⊙ Sights	🍴 Restaurants	🛏 Hotels	🛍 Shopping	🍸 Nightlife
★★★★★	★★★★★	★★★★☆	★★★☆☆	★★☆☆☆

WELCOME TO VICTORIA

TOP REASONS TO GO

★ **The journey here:** Yup, getting here is one of the best things about Victoria. Whether by ferry meandering past the Gulf or San Juan islands, by floatplane (try to travel at least one leg this way), or on a whale-watching boat, getting to Victoria is a memorable experience.

★ **Spend an afternoon at The Butchart Gardens:** Nearly a million annual visitors can't be wrong—these lavish gardens north of town truly live up to the hype.

★ **Tour the Royal British Columbia Museum:** One of Canada's best regional museums warrants repeat visits just to take in the myriad displays and exhibits.

★ **Embark on a whale-watching cruise:** It's an amazing way to view these magnificent animals in the wild.

★ **Traverse the Inner Harbour via a ferry boat:** The tiny foot-passenger ferries zipping across the Inner Harbour afford passengers a new perspective of the city center.

1 Downtown. Most of Victoria's shopping and sights are around the Inner Harbour and along Government Street.

2 Vic West. Vic West is just across the bridge from Downtown.

3 Fernwood. This charming urban village is northeast of Downtown.

4 Oak Bay. East of Downtown, it's the oldest village in Victoria.

5 Rockland. With B&Bs and Craigdarroch Castle, this neighborhood is also a tourist magnet.

6 Fairfield. This quiet residential area is home to the popular Abkhazi Garden.

7 Saanich. The southernmost town on the Saanich Peninsula is at the base of Mount Douglas.

8 Brentwood Bay. A picturesque community that is also home to The Butchart Gardens.

9 Sidney. This pleasant town is home to the Washington State Ferry Terminal, and minutes from the airport to the west and BC Ferries at Swartz Bay.

10 The West Shore. Wilderness parks and historic sites, including Hatley Castle and Fort Rodd Hill.

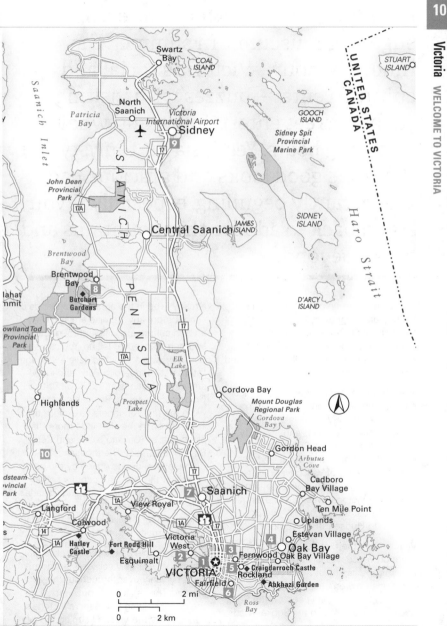

Swartz Bay
COAL ISLAND
STUART ISLAND
UNITED STATES
CANADA
Saanich Inlet
North Saanich
Patricia Bay
Victoria International Airport
Sidney
9
GOOCH ISLAND
Sidney Spit Provincial Marine Park
John Dean Provincial Park
17A
SAANICH
Central Saanich
JAMES ISLAND
SIDNEY ISLAND
Haro Strait
Brentwood Bay
Brentwood Bay
8
Butchart Gardens
lahat nmit
PENINSULA
17
D'ARCY ISLAND
owlland Tod Provincial Park
17A
Elk Lake
Cordova Bay
Mount Douglas Regional Park
Cordova Bay
Highlands
Prospect Lake
10
Gordon Head
Arbutus Cove
dsteam vincial Park
17
Cadboro Bay Village
11
1A
Langford
View Royal
7
Saanich
Ten Mile Point
Uplands
14
Colwood
1A
17
Estevan Village
1A
Hatley Castle
Fort Rodd Hill
Victoria West
4
Oak Bay
2
3
Fernwood Oak Bay Village
Esquimalt
1
5
Craigdarroch Castle
VICTORIA
Rockland
Fairfield
6
Abkhazi Garden
Ross Bay

0   2 mi
0   2 km

Victoria, British Columbia's photogenic capital, is a walkable seaside city of fragrant gardens, waterfront paths, and engaging museums. In summer, the Inner Harbour—Victoria's social and cultural center—buzzes with visiting yachts, street entertainers, and whale-watching boats. Yes, it's a bit touristy, but Victoria's good looks and gracious pace are instantly beguiling, especially if you stand back to admire the mountains and ocean beyond.

At the southern tip of Vancouver Island, Victoria dips slightly below the 49th parallel. That puts it farther south than most of Canada, giving it the mildest climate in the country, with virtually no snow and less than half the rain of Vancouver.

The city's geography, or at least its place names, can cause confusion. Just to clarify: the city of Victoria is on Vancouver Island (not Victoria Island). The city of Vancouver is on the British Columbia mainland, not on Vancouver Island. At any rate, the city of Vancouver didn't even exist in 1843 when Victoria, then called Fort Victoria, was founded as the westernmost trading post of the British-owned Hudson's Bay Company.

Victoria was the first European settlement on Vancouver Island, and in 1868 it became the capital of British Columbia. The British weren't here alone, of course. The local First Nations people—the Songhees, the Saanich, and the Sooke—had

already lived in the area for thousands of years before anyone else arrived. Their art and culture are visible throughout southern Vancouver Island. You can see this in private and public galleries, in the totems at Thunderbird Park, and in the striking collections at the Royal British Columbia Museum. Spanish explorers were the first foreigners to explore the area, although they left little more than place names (Galiano Island and Cordova Bay, for example). The thousands of Chinese immigrants drawn by the gold rushes of the late 19th century had a much greater impact, founding Canada's oldest Chinatown and adding an Asian influence that's still quite pronounced in Victoria's multicultural mix.

Despite its role as the provincial capital, Victoria was largely eclipsed, economically, by Vancouver throughout the 20th century. This, as it turns out, was all to the good, helping to preserve Victoria's historic Downtown and keeping the city largely free of skyscrapers and highways. For much of the 20th century, Victoria was marketed to tourists as "The Most British City in Canada," and it still has more than its share of Anglo-themed pubs, tea shops, and double-decker buses. These days, however, Victorians prefer to celebrate their combined indigenous, Asian, and European heritage, and the city's stunning wilderness backdrop. Locals do often venture out for afternoon tea, but they're just as likely to nosh on dim sum or tapas. Decades-old shops sell imported linens and tweeds, but newer upstarts offer local designs in hemp and organic cotton. And let's not forget that fabric prevalent among locals: Gore-Tex. The outdoors is ever present here. You can hike, bike, kayak, sail, or whale-watch straight from the city center, and forests, beaches, offshore islands, and wilderness parklands lie just minutes away. A little farther afield, there's surfing near Sooke, wine touring in the Cowichan Valley, and kayaking among the Gulf Islands. *For more information, see the Vancouver Island chapter.*

Planning

When to Go

Victoria has the warmest, mildest climate in Canada: snow is rare and flowers bloom in February. Summers are mild, too, rarely topping 75°F. If you're here for dining, shopping, and museums, winter is a perfectly nice time for a visit: it's gray and wet, and some minor attractions are closed, but hotel deals abound. If your focus is the outdoors—biking, hiking, gardens, and whale-watching—you need to come with everyone else, between May and October. That's when the streets come to life with crafts stalls, street entertainers, blooming gardens, and the inevitable tour buses. It's fun and

busy but Victoria never gets unbearably crowded.

Victoria's top festivals take place in summer, when you're also apt to encounter the best weather. For ten nights in late June, international musicians perform during JazzFest International. July brings the weeklong International Buskers Festival, and in early August, during Symphony Splash, the Victoria Symphony plays a free outdoor concert from a barge moored in the middle of Victoria's Inner Harbour. August and September is the time for the Victoria Fringe Theatre Festival, when you can feast from a vast menu of offbeat, original, and intriguing performances around town.

Making the Most of Your Time

You can see most of Victoria's compact core in a day, although there's enough to see at the main museums alone to easily fill two. To save time: prebook tea at the Empress Hotel and buy tickets online for the Royal British Columbia Museum. The Butchart Gardens deserves a half-day or full evening, and if you are driving, take the afternoon to visit nearby Sidney and some of the Saanich Peninsula wineries.

An extra day allows for time on the water, either on a whale-watching trip—a highlight for many visitors—or on a Harbour Ferry, stopping off for a microbrew at Spinnakers Brewpub, or fish-and-chips at Fisherman's Wharf. You can also enjoy the shoreline on foot, following all, or part, of the 7-mile waterfront walkway.

With three days or more, day trips abound. You can explore some of the outlying neighborhoods visiting Craigdarroch Castle, or the delightful Abkhazi Gardens in the Oak Bay and Rockland areas; Hatley Park and Fort Rodd Hill to the west; or farther afield to the wineries of the Cowichan Valley, the beaches past Sooke, or even over to Salt Spring Island (especially on market Saturdays). Be warned, though: many day-trippers become so entranced, they end up staying here for years.

FESTIVALS

Art of the Cocktail Festival

FESTIVAL | It's not only wine drinkers who can enjoy festival fun. Victoria's annual cocktail party includes tastings, workshops, and other sipping and supping events every October. ⊠ *Victoria* ☎ *250/389–0444* ⊕ *www.artofthecocktail. ca.*

Taste: Victoria's Festival of Food and Wine

FESTIVAL | Victoria's annual food and wine fest brings a wealth of local food and wine producers, tastings, and events to town every July. ⊠ *Victoria* ⊕ *www.tour-ismvictoria.com/eat-drink/dine-around.*

Getting Here and Around

It's easy to visit Victoria without a car. Most sights, restaurants, and hotels are in the compact walkable core, with bikes, ferries, horse-drawn carriages, double-decker buses, step-on tour buses, taxis, and pedicabs on hand to fill the gaps. For sights outside the core—The Butchart Gardens, Hatley Castle, Scenic Marine Drive—tour buses are your best bet if you don't have your own vehicle.

Bike paths lace Downtown and run along much of Victoria's waterfront, and long-haul car-free paths run to the ferry terminals and as far west as Sooke. Most buses and ferries carry bikes.

AIR

Air Canada, Pacific Coastal Airlines, and WestJet fly to Victoria from Vancouver International Airport. Alaska Airlines (under its Horizon Air division) flies between Seattle and Victoria.

Victoria International Airport is 25 km (15 miles) north of Downtown Victoria. The flight from Vancouver to Victoria takes

about 25 minutes. To make the 30-minute drive from the airport to Downtown, take Highway 17 south. A taxi is about C$55. The YYJ Airport Shuttle bus service drops off passengers at most major hotels. The one-way fare is C$25. By public transit, take BC Transit Bus 83, 86, or 88 to the McTavish Exchange, where you transfer to Bus 70, which will take you to Downtown Victoria. The one-way fare is C$2.50.

There is floatplane service to Victoria's Inner Harbour in Downtown Victoria with Harbour Air Seaplanes. Harbour Air also flies from Whistler to Downtown Victoria, May–September. Kenmore Air has daily floatplane service from Seattle to Victoria's Inner Harbour. Helijet has helicopter service from Downtown Vancouver and Vancouver International Airport to Downtown Victoria.

CONTACTS YYJ Airport Shuttle.

☎ *778/351–4995, 855/351–4995* ⊕ *www. yyjairportshuttle.com.*

BOAT AND FERRY

PBC Ferries has daily service between Tsawwassen, about an hour south of Vancouver, and Swartz Bay, at the end of Highway 17 (the Patricia Bay Highway), about 30 minutes north of Victoria. Sailing time is about 1½ hours. Fares are C$17.20 per adult passenger and C$57.50 per vehicle each way. Vehicle reservations on Vancouver–Victoria and Nanaimo routes are optional and cost an additional C$17 to C$22. Foot passengers and cyclists don't need reservations.

To reach the Tsawwassen ferry terminal from Downtown Vancouver, take the Canada Line south to Bridgeport Station and change to Bus 620. In Swartz Bay, BC Transit buses 70 (express) and 72 (local) meet the ferries. If you're traveling without a car, however, it's easier to just take either a Pacific Coach (⊕ *www.paci-ficcoach.com*) or a Wilson's Transportation (⊕ *www.bcfconnector.com*) bus between

Downtown Vancouver and Downtown Victoria; the bus travels on the ferry.

BC Ferries also sails from Horseshoe Bay, north of Vancouver, to Nanaimo, about two hours north of Victoria—convenient if you're traveling by car from Whistler or Vancouver Island's north shore to Vancouver Island.

From March to October, V2V Vacations provides passenger ferry service aboard the V2V Empress, from Downtown Vancouver to Downtown Victoria. The trip is 3.5 hours, departing Vancouver early morning and returning from Victoria in the afternoon. One-way fares are from C$200.

The Victoria Harbour Ferry serves the Inner Harbour; stops include the Fairmont Empress, Chinatown, Point Ellice House, the Delta Victoria Ocean Pointe Resort, and Fisherman's Wharf. Fares start at C$7. Boats make the rounds every 15 to 20 minutes. They run 10 to 9 from mid-May through mid-September and 10 to 5 from March through mid-May and mid-September to late October. The ferries don't run from November through February. At 10:45 am on summer Sundays, half a dozen of the little ferries perform a water ballet set to classical music in the Inner Harbour.

CONTACTS Victoria Harbour Ferry. ☎ 250/708–0201 ⊕ www.victoriaharbourferry.com. **V2V Vacations.** ✉ 470 Belleville St.,, Downtown ☎ 855/554-4679 ⊕ www.v2vvacations.com.

BUS
Wilson's Transportation's BC Ferries Connector Service, has frequent daily service between Vancouver and Victoria; the bus travels on the ferry. One-way fares are C$50-C$60 depending on pick up/drop off points, plus the ferry fare (C$17.20), and reservations are required. BC Transit serves Victoria and around, including the Swartz Bay ferry terminal, Victoria International Airport, The Butchart Gardens, Sidney, and Sooke. A one-way

fare is C$2.50 (exact change); an all-day pass is C$5.

CONTACTS Pacific Coach. ✉ Downtown ☎ 800/661-1725 ⊕ www.pacificcoach. com. **Wilson's Transportation.** ☎ 888/788–8840 ⊕ www.bcfconnector.com.

TAXI
In Victoria, call Bluebird, Victoria Taxi, or Yellow Cab. Taxi rates in Victoria begin at C$3.40 at pickup and cost about C$1.97 for each kilometer traveled.

CONTACTS Bluebird Cabs. ☎ 250/382–2222 ⊕ www.taxicab.com. **Victoria Taxi.** ☎ 250/383–7111 ⊕ www.victoriataxi.com. **Yellow Cab.** ☎ 250/381–2222 ⊕ www.yellowcabvictoria.com.

Activities

BIKING
Victoria is a bike-friendly town with more bicycle commuters than any other city in Canada. Bike racks on city buses, bike lanes on Downtown streets, and tolerant drivers all help, as do the city's three long-distance cycling routes, which mix car-free paths and low-traffic scenic routes.

BC Ferries will transport bikes for a nominal fee (just C$2 from Vancouver). You can also rent bikes, bike trailers, and tandem bikes at several Victoria outlets for a few hours, a day, or a week. Helmets are required by law and are supplied with bike rentals.

GOLF
You can golf year-round in Victoria and southern Vancouver Island. Victoria alone has several public golf courses, ranging from rolling sea-view fairways to challenging mountaintop sites.

HIKING AND WALKING
Victoria is one of the most pedestrian-friendly cities in North America. Waterfront pathways make it possible to stroll virtually all around Victoria's waterfront. For some interesting self-guided walks

around the city's historic areas, check out ⊕ *www.victoria.ca/tours* or pick up a free walking-tour map at the city's visitor information center. Though popular with cyclists, the area's long-distance paths are also great for long walks. For views and elevation, check out the trail networks in the area's many provincial and regional parks.

KAYAKING
The Upper Harbour and the Gorge, the waterways just north of the Inner Harbour, are popular kayaking spots.

SCUBA DIVING
The waters off Vancouver Island have some of the best cold-water scuba diving in the world, with clear waters and rich marine life; visibility is best in winter. The Ogden Point Breakwater and Race Rocks Underwater Marine Park are popular spots close to town. In Brentwood Bay on the Saanich Peninsula are the Glass Sponge Gardens, a sea mountain covered with sponges that were thought to be extinct at one point. Off Thetis Island, near Chemainus, divers can explore a sunken 737 jetliner. Dive BC (⊕ *dive.bc.ca/guide/*) has details.

WHALE-WATCHING
With a resident pod of orcas (killer whales) plying the Salish Seas (aka Strait of Georgia), opportunities to watch these impressive mammals are numerous whether by yacht, zodiac kayak, or small cruiser. Prices are more or less the same among the many whale-watching outfitters, primarily based around the Inner Harbour.

Hotels

Victoria has a vast range of accommodations, with what seems like whole neighborhoods dedicated to hotels. Options range from city resorts and full-service business hotels to midpriced tour-group haunts and family-friendly motels, but the city is especially known for its lavish bed-and-breakfasts in beautifully restored Victorian and Edwardian mansions. Outlying areas, such as Sooke and Saanich, pride themselves on destination spa resorts and luxurious country inns, though affordable lodgings can be found there, too.

British Columbia law prohibits smoking inside any public building or within 3 meters (20 feet) of an entrance. As a result, all Victoria hotels are completely smoke-free, including on patios and balconies, and in public areas. Only the larger modern hotels have air-conditioning, but it rarely gets hot enough to need it. Advance reservations are always a good idea, especially in July and August. Watch for discounts of up to 50% in the off-season (roughly November to February), though even then you'll need to book, as many rooms fill with retirees escaping prairie winters. Most Downtown hotels also charge at least C$15 per day for parking. Ask about phone and Internet charges (these can range from free to excessive) and have a look at the hotel breakfast menu; nearby cafés are almost always cheaper.

Downtown hotels are clustered in three main areas. James Bay, on the south side of the Inner Harbour near the Parliament Buildings, is basically a residential and hotel neighborhood. Bordered by the waterfront and Beacon Hill Park, the area is quiet at night and handy for sightseeing by day. It is, however, thin on restaurants and a bit of a hike from the main shopping areas. Hotels in the Downtown core, particularly along Government and Douglas streets, are right in the thick of shopping, dining, and nightlife, but they get more traffic noise. If you're willing to walk a few blocks east of the harbor, several quieter hotels and small inns are clustered amid the condominium towers. Vic West, across the Johnson Street Bridge on the harbor's north shore, is another quiet option, but it's a 15-minute walk or ferry ride to the bulk of shopping, dining, and sightseeing. Even so, you won't need a car to stay in any of these areas, and, given parking charges, you may be better off without one.

Outside Downtown, Rockland and Oak Bay are lush, peaceful, tree-lined residential districts; the mile or so walk into town is pleasant, but you won't want to do it every day. The resorts and inns that we've listed farther afield, in Saanich, the West Shore, and Sooke, are, for the most part, self-contained resorts with restaurants and spas. Each is about 30 minutes from Downtown Victoria, and you'll need a car if you want to make day trips into town.

Hotel reviews have been shortened. For full information, visit Fodors.com.

What It Costs in Canadian dollars

$	$$	$$$	$$$$
HOTELS			
under C$150	C$150–C$225	C$226–C$300	over C$300

Restaurants

Victoria has a tremendous number and variety of restaurants for such a small city; this fact, and the glorious pantry that is Vancouver Island—think local fish, seafood, cheese, and organic fruits and veggies—keeps prices down (at least compared to Vancouver) and standards up. As an island, there's a self-sufficiency and collaborative foodie ethos between chefs, producers, and suppliers that is palpable. It is attracting internationally acclaimed restaurateurs including those who turned Whistler's Araxi restaurant and Vancouver's Blue Water Cafe into internationally acclaimed mega stars.

Restaurants in the region are generally casual. Smoking is banned in all public places, including restaurant patios, in Greater Victoria and on the Southern Gulf

Islands. Victorians tend to dine early—happy hours often start at 3 before restaurants and bars get busy at 6, and many kitchens close by 9. Pubs, lounges, and the few open-late places mentioned here are your best options for an after-hours nosh, some of which re-introduce happy-hour pricing as the evening progresses. Concepts like DoorDash and Skip the Dishes are increasingly popular.

Wild salmon, locally made cheeses, Pacific oysters, organic vegetables, local microbrews, and wines from the island's farm-gate wineries (really small wineries are allowed to sell their wines "at the farm gate") are tastes to watch for. Vegetarians and vegans are well catered to in this health-conscious town, and seafood choices go well beyond traditional fish-and-chips. You may notice an "Ocean Wise" symbol on a growing number of menus: this indicates that the restaurant is committed to serving only sustainably harvested fish and seafood.

There's a quality '"band"' of food trucks and some of the city's best casual (and sometimes not-so-casual) fare is served in pubs—particularly in brewpubs; most have an all-ages restaurant as well as an adults-only bar area.

Afternoon tea is a Victoria tradition, as is good coffee—despite the Starbucks invasion, there are plenty of fun and funky local caffeine purveyors around town.

Restaurant reviews have been shortened. For full information, visit Fodors. com.

What It Costs in Canadian dollars

$	$$	$$$	$$$$
RESTAURANTS			
under C$13	C$13–C$20	C$21–C$30	over C$30

Nightlife

Victoria's nightlife is low-key and casual, with many wonderful pubs, but a limited choice of other nightlife. Pubs offer a casual place for lunch, dinner, or an afternoon pint, often with a view and an excellent selection of beer. The pubs listed here all serve food, and many brew their own beer. Patrons must be 19 or older to enter a bar or pub in British Columbia, but many pubs have a separate restaurant section open to all ages. The city is enjoying a resurgence of cocktail culture, with several of Victoria's trendier restaurants doubling as lounges, offering cocktails and small plates well into the night. Dance clubs attract a young crowd and most close by 2 am. A dress code (no jeans or sneakers) may be enforced, but otherwise, attire is casual. Smoking is not allowed in Victoria's pubs, bars, and nightclubs—this applies both indoors and on patios.

Shopping

In Victoria, as in the rest of British Columbia, the most popular souvenirs are First Nations arts and crafts, which you can pick up at shops, galleries, street markets, and—in some cases—directly from artists' studios. Look for silver jewelry and cedar boxes carved with traditional images and, especially around Duncan (in the Cowichan Valley), the thick hand-knit sweaters made by the Cowichan people. BC wines, from shops in Victoria or directly from the wineries, make good souvenirs, as most are unavailable outside the province. Shopping in Victoria is easy: virtually everything is in the Downtown area on or near Government Street stretching north from the Fairmont Empress hotel.

Tours

AIR TOURS
Harbour Air Seaplanes
AIR EXCURSIONS | In addition to providing air service to the surrounding area, Harbour Air Seaplanes has 20-minute flightseeing tours of Victoria and beyond, starting at C$125. ☎ *250/384–2215, 800/665–0212* ⊕ *www.harbourair.com.*

BOAT TOURS
The best way to see the sights of the Inner and Upper Harbour, and beyond, is by Victoria Harbour Ferry. Pickle Pub Crawls, starting at C$25 for stops at four harborside pubs, are a fun option.

Victoria Harbour Ferry
BOAT TOURS | The best way to see the sights of the Inner and Upper Harbour, and beyond, is by Victoria Harbour Ferry; 45-minute tours cost C$30 and 75-minutes tours are C$40. Pickle Pub Crawls, at C$25 (weekdays) and C$30 (weekends), stop at four harborside pubs and are a fun option. ☎ *250/708–0201* ⊕ *www.victoriaharbourferry.com.*

BUS TOURS
Big Bus Victoria
BUS TOURS | Big Bus has narrated tours on open-top and trolley-style buses between May and October; you can get on and off at any of the 22 stops. One day is C$36; two days is C$46. Or purchase a combo deal (starting at C$48) that includes the entrance fee to selected attractions and you get a second bus day for free. ☎ *250/389–2229, 888/434–2229* ⊕ *www. bigbusvictoria.com.*

CVS Cruise Victoria
BUS TOURS | CVS Cruise Victoria runs a shuttle to The Butchart Gardens, with departures from the Fairmont Empress (there's a ticket office in front of the hotel) and from several other Downtown hotels; the C$75 round-trip fare includes entrance to the gardens. ☎ *877/578–5552* ⊕ *www.cvstours.com.*

Gray Line

BUS TOURS | Gray Line's hop-on, hop-off double-decker bus tours run year-round (except mid-January to mid-February), and make 14 stops around town; tickets are C$38 for one day, C$60 for two. From mid-June through September, Gray Line's Butchart Gardens Express shuttle runs several times a day from the Coho ferry terminal and the Fairmont Empress. Round-trip fare is C$75, including admission to the gardens. ☎ *250/385–6553, 855/385–6553 ⊕ www.sightseeingvictoria.com.*

FOOD AND WINE TOURS

Vancouver Island Wine Tours

SPECIAL-INTEREST | From May through mid-October, Vancouver Island Wine Tours will take you to the Cowichan Valley on a full day tour for C$119, or on a half-day tour for C$100 around the Saanich Peninsula. ☎ *250/661–8844 ⊕ www.vancouverislandwinetours.com.*

WALKING TOURS

Discover the Past Tours

WALKING TOURS | Discover the Past Tours offers year-round historic walking tours, Ghostly Walks, and Chinatown tours. ☎ *250/384–6698 ⊕ www.discoverthe-past.com.*

Victorian Garden Tours

WALKING TOURS | Victorian Garden Tours takes you to private and public gardens. ☎ *250/380–2797 ⊕ www.victoriangardentours.com.*

Visitor Information

CONTACTS Tourism Victoria Visitor Centre. ✉ *812 Wharf St., Victoria* ☎ *250/953–2033, 800/663–3883 ⊕ www.tourismvictoria.com.*

Downtown

Home to the vast majority of Victoria's sights, hotels, and eateries, Downtown *is* Victoria for most visitors. At its heart is the Inner Harbour. Busy with yachts, passenger ferries, whale-watching boats, and floatplanes, and framed by such iconic buildings as the Fairmont Empress hotel, this pedestrian-friendly area is busy with horse-and-carriage rides, street entertainers, tour buses, and, yes, tourists—all summer long. The south shore of the harbor, extending to the Dallas Road waterfront and Beacon Hill Park, is known as James Bay. Two key sites, the Parliament Buildings and the Robert Bateman Centre, are here, but if you stroll just a block south, you'll find a peaceful residential district of modest historic homes, and such interesting historic sites as Emily Carr House. North of the Inner Harbour, a straight shot up Government Street leads to some great shopping and to more historic areas: Bastion Square, Market Square, and Chinatown. Founded in 1858, Victoria's Chinatown, along Fisgard Street between Government and Store streets, is the oldest such district in Canada. At just two square blocks, it's much smaller than Vancouver's but still pleasant to stroll through, particularly as hip boutiques and eateries have moved into the district. If you enter from Government Street, you'll pass under the elaborate Gate of Harmonious Interest, made of Taiwanese ceramic tiles and decorative panels.

GETTING AROUND

Downtown Victoria is safe, clean, and is easy to navigate on foot so unless you have plans to tour farther afield, to the Cowichan Valley for example, park the car (be aware that overnight parking charges at some hotels can run C$10-C$20). Small passenger ferries scoot around the Inner Harbour to get you from point A to point B; several transit options run between Downtown (in front of the

The Inner Harbour area is the heart of Victoria, the capital of British Columbia.

Fairmont Empress hotel) and The Butchart Gardens, as well as tours that take in other star attractions such as Craigdarrach Castle and the wineries in the Saanich Peninsula. Within the Downtown core, there are pedicabs, horse-drawn carriages and small passenger ferries that criss-cross the Inner Harbour, all excellent ways to help you get around. And this being the Bicycle Capital of Canada, bike rentals are plentiful (as are routes all over the city) and several hotels offer complimentary bikes to use.

◉ Sights

Bastion Square
PLAZA | James Douglas, the former colonial governor for whom Douglas Street was named, chose this spot for the original Fort Victoria and Hudson's Bay Company trading post in 1843. In summer the square comes alive with street performers, and crafts vendors (Thursday–Saturday), and on Sunday a weekly farmers' market. The former courthouse, currently closed awaiting

seismic upgrades, creates an historical backdrop to this people-gathering place. ⊠ *Off Wharf St., at View St., Downtown* ☎ *250/885–1387* ⊕ *www.bastionsquare. ca.*

Beacon Hill Park
CITY PARK | **FAMILY** | This 154-acre park links Downtown Victoria to the waterfront. Its rambling lawns overlook the Pacific Ocean, the Olympic Mountains, and the Strait of Juan de Fuca. Kite-fliers, hang gliders, and dog walkers are numerous. Take your photo at the Mile 0 marker of the Trans-Canada Highway, at the foot of Douglas Street. Beacon Hill includes ponds where you can feed ducks, cycling, jogging and walking paths, flowers and gardens, a cricket pitch, and a petting zoo (open daily 10–4). There's live music in the bandshell on summer evenings, and on Saturday nights in August the Victoria Film Festival screens free movies. ⊠ *Bordered by Douglas St., Southgate St., and Cook St., Downtown* ☎ *250/361–0600* ⊕ *www.beaconhillpark. ca* ⊠ *Free.*

Emily Carr House

LOCAL INTEREST | One of Canada's most celebrated artists and a respected writer, Emily Carr (1871–1945) lived in this extremely proper, wooden Victorian house before she abandoned her middle-class life to live in the wilds of British Columbia. Carr's own descriptions, from her autobiography *Book of Small*, were used to restore the house. Art on display includes reproductions of Carr's work—visit the Art Gallery of Greater Victoria or the Vancouver Art Gallery to see the originals. ⊠ *207 Government St., James Bay, Downtown* ☎ *250/383–5843* ⊕ *www.emilycarr.com* ✉ *C$8* ⊗ *Closed Sun.–Mon. May–Sept.; closed Oct.–Apr.*

Fairmont Empress

BUILDING | Opened in 1908 by the Canadian Pacific Railway, the Empress is one of the grand château-style railroad hotels that grace many Canadian cities. Designed by Francis Rattenbury, who also designed the Parliament Buildings across the way, the solid Edwardian grandeur of the Empress has made it a symbol of the city. The elements that made the hotel an attraction for travelers in the past—old-world architecture, ornate decor, and a commanding view of the Inner Harbour—are still here although they exude a fresh, contemporary air. Nonguests can reserve ahead for afternoon tea (the dress code is smart casual) in the chandelier-draped Tea Lobby, meet for Pimm's cocktails or enjoy superb Pacific Northwest cuisine at the Q Lounge and Restaurant, or enjoy a treatment at the hotel's Willow Stream spa. In summer, lunch, snacks, and cocktails are served on the veranda overlooking the Inner Harbour. ⊠ *721 Government St., Downtown* ☎ *250/384–8111, 250/389–2727 tea reservations* ⊕ *www.fairmont.com/empress* ✉ *Free; afternoon tea C$82.*

Fan Tan Alley

PEDESTRIAN MALL | Mah-jongg, fan-tan, and dominoes were games of chance played on Fan Tan Alley, said to be the narrowest street in Canada. Once the gambling and opium center of Chinatown, it's now lined with offbeat shops (few of which sell authentic Chinese goods). Look for the alley on the south side of Fisgard Street between nos. 545½ and 549½. ⊠ *South side of Fisgard St., Chinatown, Victoria.*

Fisherman's Wharf

MARINA | **FAMILY** | This favorite nautical spot is only a 20-minute walk from Downtown, along a waterfront path just west of the Inner Harbour. Or you can get here by hopping aboard one of the many Victoria Harbour Ferries. You can watch fishers unload their catches and admire the various vessels, or picnic in the shoreside park. If you stroll the docks and walk among the colorful houseboats, you'll come across several floating shacks where you can buy ice cream, fish tacos, and live crabs, take kayak tours, or buy tickets for whale-watching cruises. Other booths sell fish to feed the harbor seals who often visit the quay (you can even watch them on the underwater "seal cam"). The busiest vendor is Barb's, an esteemed fish-and-chips spot that is open only in the summer, from May through October. ⊠ *Corner of Dallas Rd. and Erie St., James Bay, Downtown* ⊕ *fishermanswharfvictoria.com.*

Legacy Art Gallery Downtown

MUSEUM | Rotating exhibits from the University of Victoria's vast art collection, as well as contemporary installations, are displayed in this airy Downtown space. Shows in the 3,000-square-foot space focus on mostly Canadian works, including many by First Nations artists, but international painters are represented, too. ⊠ *630 Yates St., Downtown* ☎ *250/721–6562* ⊕ *uvac.uvic.ca* ✉ *Free* ⊗ *Closed Sun.–Tues.*

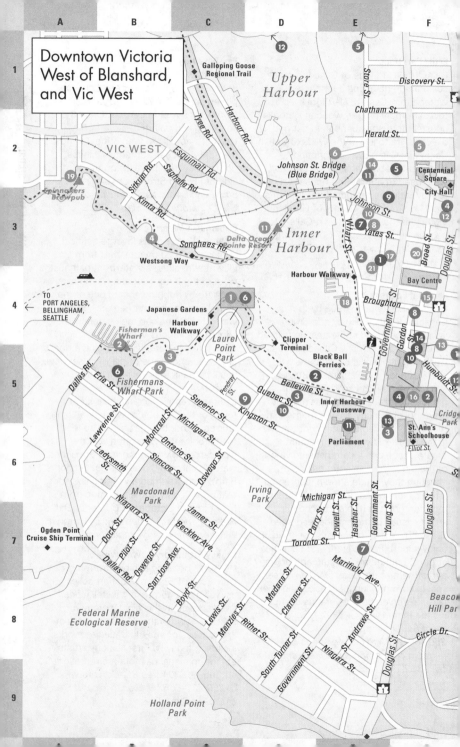

Downtown Victoria West of Blanshard, and Vic West

Grid labels: A B C D E F (columns), 1–9 (rows)

Upper Harbour

Discovery St.

Store St.

Chatham St.

Herald St.

Galloping Goose Regional Trail

Tyee Rd.

Harbour Rd.

VIC WEST

Esquimalt Rd.

Sitkum Rd.

Sagnafre Rd.

Kimta Rd.

⑲
Spinnakers Brewpub

Johnson St. Bridge (Blue Bridge)

Centennial Square

City Hall

⑥

⑭
⑪
⑤

⑨
⑩
⑦ ⑧

④
⑫

Johnson St.

Wharf St.

Yates St.

⑪

Delta Ocean Pointe Resort

Songhees Rd.

④

Inner Harbour

Westsong Way

② ①
㉑
⑰

⑳ Broad St.

Douglas St.

Bay Centre

Harbour Walkway

⑱

Broughton St.

⑮

TO PORT ANGELES, BELLINGHAM, SEATTLE

Fisherman's Wharf

②

③

⑨

Japanese Gardens

Harbour Walkway

① ⑥

Laurel Point Park

Clipper Terminal

Black Ball Ferries

⑧
⑧
⑭
⑧
⑩

Government St.

Gordon St.

⑬
Humboldt St.

Dallas Rd.

Erie St.

⑥ **Fishermans Wharf Park**

②

Lawrence St.

Montreal St.

Michigan St.

Ontario St.

Simcoe St.

Superior St.

Pendrey St.

Kingston St.

Quebec St.

⑨

⑩

③

Belleville St.

②

Inner Harbour Causeway

④ ⑯ ②

Cridge Park

⑬
③

St. Ann's Schoolhouse

Elliot St.

Ogden Point Cruise Ship Terminal

Ladysmith St.

Macdonald Park

James St.

Beckley Ave.

Niagara St.

Dock St.

Pilot St.

Oswego St.

San Jose Ave.

Irving Park

⑪ **Parliament**

Michigan St.

Parry St.

Powell St.

Heather St.

Government St.

Young St.

Douglas St.

Toronto St.

⑦

Marrifield Ave.

③

Beacon Hill Park

Federal Marine Ecological Reserve

Dallas Rd.

Boyd St.

Lewis St.

Menzies St.

Rithet St.

Medana St.

Clarence St.

South Turner St.

Government St.

Niagara St.

St. Andrews St.

Circle Dr.

Holland Point Park

Sights ▼

1 Bastion Square **E4**
2 The Bateman Foundation
  Gallery of Nature **D5**
3 Emily Carr House **E8**
4 Fairmont Empress **F5**
5 Fan Tan Alley **F2**
6 Fisherman's Wharf **B5**
7 Legacy Art Gallery
  Downtown **E3**
8 Maritime Museum of
  British Columbia **F4**
9 Market Square **E3**
10 Miniature World **F5**
11 Parliament Buildings **E6**
12 Point Ellice House **D1**
13 Royal British Columbia
   Museum **F5**
14 Victoria Bug Zoo **F4**
15 Victoria Public Market
   at the Hudson **G2**

Restaurants ▼

1 Aura Waterfront
  Restaurant + Patio **C4**
2 Barb's Fish & Chips **B4**
3 Blue Crab
  Seafood House **B5**
4 Boom + Batten **B3**
5 Brasserie L'École **F2**
6 Canoe Brewpub **E2**
7 E:Ne Raw Food and
  Sake Bar **G3**
8 Ferris' Grill &
  Oyster Bar **E3**
9 Il Covo Trattoria **B5**
10 Il Terrazzo **E3**
11 LURE Restaurant
   & Bar **D3**
12 The Mint **F3**
13 Noodlebox **F4**
14 OLO Restaurant **E2**
15 Pagliacci's **F4**
16 Q at The Empress **F5**
17 Rebar Modern Food **E3**
18 Red Fish Blue Fish **E4**
19 Spinnakers Gastro
   Brewpub **A2**
20 The Tapa Bar **F3**
21 Wind Cries Mary **E4**

Quick Bites ▼

1 Agrius **G3**
2 Farmhouse
  Coffee Shop **E3**
3 Food Trucks behind
  Royal BC Museum **F6**

Hotels ▼

1 Chateau Victoria
  Hotel & Suites **F5**
2 Fairmont Empress **F5**
3 Hotel Grand Pacific **D5**
4 Hotel Rialto **F3**
5 Hotel Zed **E1**
6 Inn at Laurel Point **C4**
7 James Bay Inn **E7**
8 Magnolia Hotel
  & Spa **F4**
9 The Oswego Hotel **C5**
10 Royal Scot
   Hotel & Suites **D5**
11 Swans Hotel **E2**
12 Victoria Marriott
   Inner Harbour **F5**

KEY

① Sights
① Restaurants
① Quick Bites
① Hotels

🛈 Visitor Information Centre
🏞 Trans-Canada Hwy.
⛴ Ferry
---- Pedestrian trail
▲ Harbour Ferries

Did You Know?

More than 3,300 lights outline Victoria's Parliament Buildings; like the Fairmont Empress hotel, the buildings have a prominent position in the Inner Harbour, and were designed by the same architect: Francis Rattenbury.

Maritime Museum of British Columbia

MUSEUM | FAMILY | If you have any interest in the province's seafaring history then this museum is for you. Its current location is a temporary one while its home base in Victoria's original courthouse undergoes seismic upgrades. Although the smaller space means that many of its artifacts are in storage, and displays aren't as interactive as some museums, enthusiasts will still see a selection of model ships, weaponry, ships' wheels, and photographs that chronicle the province's seafaring history, from its early explorers to whale hunters to pirates. ⊠ *634 Humboldt St., Downtown* ☎ *250/385–4222* ⊕ *www.mmbc.bc.ca* ⌖ *C$10* ⊘ *Closed Sun.-Mon. in summer; Sun.-Wed. in winter.*

Market Square

PLAZA | During the late 19th century, this three-level square provided everything a sailor, miner, or lumberjack could want. Restored to its original brick-and-beam architectural character, it's now a pedestrian-only hangout lined with cafés and boutiques. Shops sell gifts, jewelry, and local art while a microbrewery serves its local brews on tap. In the summer, watch for open-air art shows, a flea market, and street entertainers. ⊠ *560 Johnson St., Downtown* ☎ *250/386–2441* ⊕ *www. marketsquare.ca* ⌖ *Free.*

Miniature World

MUSEUM | FAMILY | At this charmingly retro attraction, more than 85 miniature dioramas—including space, castle, and fairy-tale scenes, and one of the world's largest model railways—are housed in kid-height glass cases with recorded narration. The level of detail is impressive in the models, some of which date to the site's 1969 opening. Some of the models are animated, and you can start and stop trains and turn dollhouse lights on and off with push buttons. Most people walk through in 30 minutes, but dollhouse collectors, model-train builders, and preschoolers can be absorbed for hours. ⊠ *Fairmont Empress hotel, 649 Humboldt St., Downtown* ☎ *250/385–9731* ⊕ *www.miniatureworld.com* ⌖ *C$17.*

Parliament Buildings

BUILDING | Officially the British Columbia Provincial Legislative Assembly Buildings, these massive stone structures are more popularly referred to as the Parliament Buildings. Designed by Francis Rattenbury (who also designed the Fairmont Empress hotel) when he was just 25 years old, and completed in 1897, they dominate the Inner Harbour. Atop the central dome is a gilded statue of Captain George Vancouver (1757–98), the first European to sail around Vancouver Island. A statue of Queen Victoria (1819–1901) reigns over the front of the complex. More than 3,300 lights outline the buildings at night. The interior is lavishly done with stained-glass windows, gilt moldings, and historic photographs, and in summer actors play historic figures from British Columbia's past. When the legislature is in session, you can sit in the public gallery and watch British Columbia's democracy at work (custom has the opposing parties sitting 2½ sword lengths apart). Free, informative, 30- to 45-minute tours run every 20 to 30 minutes in summer and several times a day in the off-season (less frequently if school groups or private tours are coming through). Tours are obligatory on summer weekends (mid-May until Labor Day) and optional the rest of the time. Self-guided booklets are available online. ⊠ *501 Belleville St., James Bay, Downtown* ☎ *250/387–3046* ⊕ *www.leg.bc.ca* ⌖ *Free.*

Point Ellice House

HOUSE | The O'Reilly family home, an 1861 Italianate cottage overlooking the Selkirk Waterway, has been restored to its original splendor, with the largest collection of Victorian furnishings in western Canada. You can take a half-hour audio tour of the house (presented from a servant's point of view) and stroll in

Victoria Waterfront on Foot

You can walk most of the way around Victoria's waterfront from Westbay Marina on the Outer Harbour's north shore, to Ross Bay on the Strait of Juan de Fuca. The entire 11-km (7-mile) route takes several hours, but it passes many of the city's sights and great scenery. Waterfront pubs and cafés supply sustenance; ferries and buses offer transport as needed.

Begin with a ride on Harbour Ferries to Westbay Marina, the start of Westsong Way. This 3-km (2-mile) pedestrian path follows the Vic West waterfront past the Victoria International Marina, which opened in 2019 alongside Boom & Batten Restaurant and Cafe, and on to the Johnson Street Bridge. The views across the harbor are rewarding, as is a stop at the waterfront Spinnakers Brewpub. Harbour Ferries stop at Spinnakers and at the Delta Ocean Pointe Resort, so you can choose to start from either point.

Once across the bridge, you can detour to Chinatown and Market Square, turn right and head south on Wharf Street toward the Inner Harbour, or turn right again at Yates (a "Downtown Walk" sign shows the way) and follow the waterfront. The route runs past floatplane docks and whale-watching outfitters to the Inner Harbour Causeway. Snack options en route include fish tacos at Red Fish Blue Fish—a waterfront take-out spot—or burgers and fish-and-chips at The Flying Otter—a café floating at the seaplane dock. Starting from the Visitor Information Centre, this waterfront walkway—busy all summer with street entertainers and

crafts and snack vendors—curves around the Inner Harbour. It's only about a quarter-mile around, but the walk could take a while if you stop to watch all the torch jugglers and caricature artists. The Fairmont Empress, the Royal BC Museum, and the Parliament Buildings are all here—just across the road from the water.

Detour along Belleville Street past the ferry terminals and pick the path up where it enters Laurel Point Park just past the Clipper terminal. From here, the route leads through the pretty waterfront park and past a marina to Fisherman's Wharf, where you can stop for fish-and-chips on the dock or grab a ferry back Downtown. To keep going, follow Dallas Road to the Ogden Point Cruise Ship terminal, where you can walk out on the breakwater for a view of the ships or grab a snack on the ocean-view deck at the Ogden Point Café.

You're now on the shore of Juan de Fuca Strait, where a footpath—the Dallas Road Waterfront Trail—runs another 6.5 km (4 miles) along cliff tops past Beacon Hill Park to the historic cemetery at Ross Bay. Dog walkers, joggers, and kite flyers are usually out in force on the grassy cliff top; stairways lead down to pebbly beaches. A hike north through Beacon Hill Park will get you back Downtown. You can also do this route by bike, though you'll have to follow the streets running parallel to the waterfront, as most of the pathway is pedestrian-only. The ride along Dallas Road and through Beacon Hill Park has the least traffic.

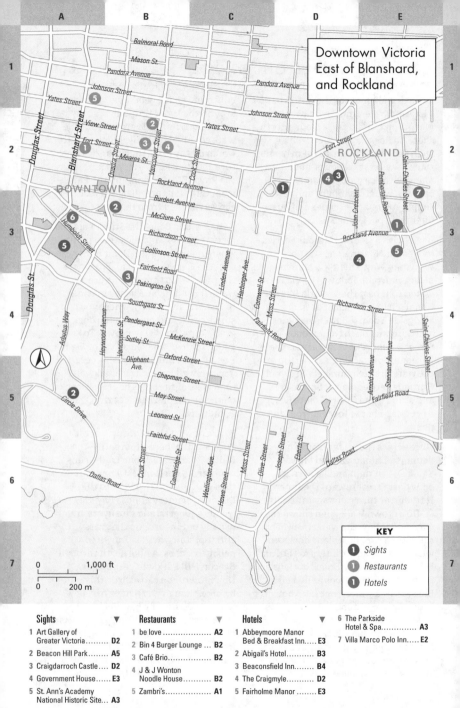

Downtown Victoria
East of Blanshard,
and Rockland

ROCKLAND

DOWNTOWN

0   1,000 ft

0   200 m

KEY

1 Sights

1 Restaurants

1 Hotels

Sights ▼

1 Art Gallery of
  Greater Victoria......... **D2**

2 Beacon Hill Park........ **A5**

3 Craigdarroch Castle.... **D2**

4 Government House...... **E3**

5 St. Ann's Academy
  National Historic Site... **A3**

Restaurants ▼

1 be love **A2**

2 Bin 4 Burger Lounge ... **B2**

3 Café Brio................. **B2**

4 J & J Wonton
  Noodle House........... **B2**

5 Zambri's.................. **A1**

Hotels ▼

1 Abbeymoore Manor
  Bed & Breakfast Inn..... **E3**

2 Abigail's Hotel........... **B3**

3 Beaconsfield Inn........ **B4**

4 The Craigmyle........... **D2**

5 Fairholme Manor **E3**

6 The Parkside
  Hotel & Spa.............. **A3**

7 Villa Marco Polo Inn..... **E2**

the English country garden. Point Ellice House is only a few minutes' drive north of Downtown Victoria, but it's in an industrial area, so it's more fun to come by sea. Victoria Harbour Ferries leave from a dock in front of the Fairmont Empress; the trip lasts about 15 minutes and takes in the sights of the harbor. The house is open only at the weekends, 12 noon–4 pm. ✉ *2616 Pleasant St., Downtown* ☎ *250/380–6506* ⊕ *www.pointellice-house.ca* 🍴 *C$10* 🕑 *Closed weekdays.*

★ **The Bateman Foundation Gallery of Nature**
MUSEUM | This small but impressive gallery displays more than 100 works—from etchings to paintings—spanning seven decades in the career of Canada's best-known wildlife artist. One gallery, where paintings are matched to birdsongs, is especially innovative. The historic waterfront building, Victoria's original steamship terminal, is also home to a waterfront restaurant and a shop selling high-end local art. Proceeds from gallery admissions go to support the Bateman Foundation's conservation work. ✉ *470 Belleville St., James Bay* ☎ *250/940–3630* ⊕ *batemancentre.org* 🍴 *C$10.*

★ **Royal British Columbia Museum**
MUSEUM | **FAMILY** | This excellent museum, one of Victoria's leading attractions, traces several thousand years of British Columbian history. Especially strong is its First Peoples Gallery, home to a genuine Kwakwaka'wakw big house, an intriguing exhibit on First Nations languages, and a dramatically displayed collection of masks and other artifacts. The Natural History Gallery traces British Columbia's landscapes, from prehistory to modern-day climate change, in realistic dioramas. An *Ocean Station* exhibit gets kids involved in running a Jules Verne–style submarine. In the History Gallery, a replica of Captain Vancouver's HMS *Discovery* creaks convincingly, and a re-created frontier town comes to life

with cobbled streets, silent movies, and the rumble of an arriving train. An IMAX theater presents films on a six-story-tall screen. Optional one-hour tours, included in the admission price, run roughly twice a day in summer and less frequently in winter. Most focus on a particular gallery, though the 90-minute Highlights tour touches on all galleries, and the 30-minute Behind the Scenes tour is fascinating. Special exhibits, usually held between mid-May and mid-November, attract crowds despite the higher admission prices. You can skip (sometimes very long) ticket lines by booking online. The museum complex has several more interesting sights, beyond the expected gift shop and café. In front of the museum, at Government and Belleville streets, is the **Netherlands Centennial Carillon.** With 62 bells, it's the largest bell tower in Canada; the Westminster chimes ring out every hour, and free recitals are occasionally held on Sunday afternoon. The Native Plant Garden at the museum's entrance showcases 400 indigenous plant species. Behind the main building, bordering Douglas Street, are the grassy lawns of **Thunderbird Park,** home to 10 totem poles (carved replicas of originals that are preserved in the museum). One of the oldest houses in BC, **Helmcken House** (*open late May–early Sept., daily noon–4*) was built in 1852 for pioneer doctor and statesman John Sebastian Helmcken. Inside are displays of the family's belongings, including the doctor's medical tools. Behind it is **St. Ann's School House,** built in 1858. One of British Columbia's oldest schools, it is thought to be Victoria's oldest building still standing. Both buildings are part of the Royal British Columbia Museum. ✉ *675 Belleville St., Downtown* ☎ *250/356–7226, 888/447–7977 museum, 877/480–4887 IMAX theater* ⊕ *www.royalbcmuseum. bc.ca* 🍴 *C$26.95, IMAX theater C$11.95; combination ticket C$36.90.*

After exploring Downtown Victoria, relax in the 154-acre Beacon Hill Park.

St. Ann's Academy National Historic Site

COLLEGE | This former convent and school, founded in 1858, played a central role in British Columbia's pioneer life. The academy's little chapel—the first Roman Catholic cathedral in Victoria—has been restored to look just as it did in the 1920s. The 6-acre grounds, with their fruit trees and herb and flower gardens, are free to visit. They have also been restored as historic landscapes, and are a delightful, quiet respite from the Downtown bustle. ⊠ *835 Humboldt St., Downtown* ☎ *250/953–8829* ⊕ *www. stannsacademy.com* ✉ *By donation* ⊙ *Closed Mon. in summer; closed Mon.– Wed. in winter.*

Victoria Bug Zoo

ZOO | FAMILY | Local kids clamor to visit this offbeat minizoo, home to the largest collection in North America of live tropical insects. You can even hold many of the 60 or so varieties, which include walking sticks, scorpions, millipedes, and a pharnacia—at 22 inches, the world's longest insect. The staff members know their bug lore and are happy to dispense scientific information and fun entomological anecdotes. ⊠ *631 Courtney St., Downtown* ☎ *250/384–2847* ⊕ *www. victoriabugzoo.com* ✉ *C$14.*

Victoria Public Market at the Hudson

MARKET | Planning a picnic? Stop here first. Bakers and butchers (plant-based no less), pie makers, green grocers, cheesemakers, spice mongers, and other artisanal producers from across Vancouver Island sell their wares in this lofty, century-old indoor space that was once a department store. In summer especially, ready-to-eat treats abound here, from homemade pies and fresh baked bread to tacos, sandwiches, and fish-and-chips. ⊠ *1701 Douglas St., Downtown* ☎ *778/433–2787* ⊕ *www.victoriapublic-market.com* ✉ *Free.*

🍴 Restaurants

★ Aura Waterfront Restaurant + Patio

$ | PACIFIC NORTHWEST | After a 12-month renovation program, the critically acclaimed Aura re-opened November 2019, with inspired west coast-Asian fusion cuisine to rival its drop-dead gorgeous backdrop of the Inner Harbour. Think BBQ sambal skate on banana leaf with XO sauce and jicama slaw and house-made fried spam with crispy rice, aged cheddar, soft-poached egg, and cilantro oil. **Known for:** waterfront patio; imaginative fusion cuisine; stylish dining room. $ *Average main: C$12* ✉ *Inn at Laurel Point, 680 Montreal St., James Bay, Downtown* ☎ *250/414–6739* ⊕ *www.aurarestaurant.ca.*

Barb's Fish & Chips

$$ | SEAFOOD | FAMILY | Funky Barb's, a tin-roofed takeout shack, floats on the quay at Fisherman's Wharf, west of the Inner Harbour off St. Lawrence Street. Halibut, salmon, oysters, mussels, crab, burgers, and chowder are all prepared fresh. **Known for:** fresh seafood; harborside picnic tables; part of Victoria lore. $ *Average main: C$15* ✉ *Fisherman's Wharf, St. Lawrence St., James Bay, Downtown* ☎ *250/384–6515* ⊕ *www.barbsplace.ca* ⊗ *Closed Nov.–early Mar.*

be love

$$$ | VEGETARIAN | An on-trend crowd of locals tucks into plant-based fare: black bean burgers, sweet potato sandwiches, pad Thai, asparagus risotto, and plates piled high with farm-to-fork salads at this chic, bustling Downtown spot. Everything here, from the spring rolls and yam chips to the long list of power juices and smoothies, is free of wheat, gluten, dairy, meat, additives, and processed sugar—but delicious nonetheless. **Known for:** vegetarian menu; gluten-free dining; modern decor. $ *Average main: C$21* ✉ *1019 Blanshard St., Downtown* ☎ *778/433–7181* ⊕ *beloverestaurant.ca.*

Bin 4 Burger Lounge

$$ | BURGER | FAMILY | This slightly out-of-the-way, hip little burger joint elevates the humble patty with local ingredients and naturally raised meats, serving up intriguing burger (and sandwich) combos like beef with chipotle-bourbon barbecue sauce, BC–raised bison with aged cheddar and fried onions, or chicken with bacon, Brie, and balsamic red onion jam. Vegetarians can substitute crispy tofu on any sandwich or opt for the "Mr. Bean," a chickpea, black bean, and goat cheese burger. **Known for:** inventive burgers; house-made dips; lounge-y atmosphere. $ *Average main: C$16* ✉ *911 Yates St., Downtown* ☎ *250/590–4154* ⊕ *www.bin4burgerlounge.com.*

Blue Crab Seafood House

$$$$ | SEAFOOD | Fresh-daily seafood and expansive harbor views make this airy James Bay hotel restaurant a popular lunch and dinner spot. Signature dishes include a crab cake starter, a scallop-and-prawn sauté, cedar plank salmon, and bouillabaisse in coconut green curry, but check the tempting daily specials on the blackboard as well. **Known for:** fresh seafood; harbor views; local wine list. $ *Average main: C$34* ✉ *Coast Harbourside Hotel and Marina, 146 Kingston St., James Bay, Downtown* ☎ *250/480–1999* ⊕ *www.bluecrab.ca.*

★ Brasserie L'École

$$$ | FRENCH | French-country cooking shines at this informal Chinatown bistro, and the historic room—once a schoolhouse for the Chinese community—evokes a timeless brasserie, from the patina-rich fir floors to the chalkboards above the slate bar listing the day's oyster, mussel, and steak options. Owner Sean Brennan, one of the city's better-known chefs, works with local farmers and fishermen to source the best seasonal, local, and organic ingredients. **Known for:** seasonal menus; French-country fare; French wine and Belgian beers.

Victoria: Whale-Watching

The thrill of seeing whales in the wild is, for many, one of the most enduring memories of a trip to Victoria. In summer (roughly April to October), about 85 orca, or "killer whales," reside in the Strait of Georgia between Vancouver and Victoria. They live in pods, and because their movements are fairly predictable, chances are high that you will see a pod on any given trip. Some operators offer guaranteed sightings, meaning that you can repeat the tour free of charge until you spot a whale.

It's not unheard of to see whales from a BC ferry en route to Victoria—but the ferries don't alter their routes to take advantage of whale-watching, so your best bet is to take a dedicated tour. A number of companies leave from Victoria's Inner Harbour, a few are based in Richmond (near Vancouver), and others leave from Sidney and Sooke, outside of Victoria.

Not all tours are alike, and the kind of boat you choose determines the kind of experience you're likely to have—though most companies have naturalists on board as guides, as well as hydrophones that, if you get close enough, allow you to listen to the whales singing and vocalizing.

Motor launches, which carry from 30 to 80 passengers, are comfortable, with restrooms, protection from the elements, and even concessions. Seasickness isn't usually a problem in the sheltered waters near Victoria, but if you're not a good sailor, it's wise to wear a seasickness band or take antinausea medication. Ginger candy often works, too.

Zodiacs are open inflatable boats that carry about 12 passengers. They are smaller and more agile than cruisers and offer both an exciting ride bouncing over the waves and an eye-level view of the whales. Passengers are supplied with warm, waterproof survival suits.

Note that the kind of boat you choose does not affect how close you can get to the whales. For the safety of whales and humans, government and industry regulations require boats to stay at least 100 meters (328 feet) from the pods, though closer encounters are possible if whales approach a boat when its engine is off.

And, although the focus is on whales, you also have a good chance of spotting marine birds, Dall's porpoises, dolphins, seals, and sea lions.

Johnstone Strait, off Telegraph Cove on Vancouver Island's northeast coast, has one of the world's largest populations of orca in summer and is an important center for whale research. Nearby Robson's Bight is a unique ecological reserve, established in 1982 to give sanctuary to killer whales. Tofino and Ucluelet draw whale-watchers every March and April when an estimated 20,000 Pacific gray whales cruise by on their annual migration.

There are dozens of whale-watching operators in the area. The following recommendations are among the more established: Orca Spirit Adventures, Prince of Whales, and Springtide Whale Tours & Charters. *For more information on these companies, see Whale-Watching in Activities.*

$ Average main: C$30 ⊠ 1715 Government St., Downtown ☎ 250/475–6260 ⊕ www.lecole.ca ⊘ Closed Sun. and Mon. No lunch.

★ **Café Brio**

$$$$ | **MODERN CANADIAN** | This intimate yet bustling Italian villa–style room has long been a Victoria favorite, mainly because of its Mediterranean-influenced atmosphere and cuisine, which is prepared primarily with locally raised ingredients. The menu changes almost daily, but you might find local rockfish paired with peperonata (sweet roasted red onion and heirloom tomato syrup), maple-glazed quail, or even an apricot dessert soup. **Known for:** house-made charcuterie; 400-label wine list; seasonal dishes. $ Average main: C$32 ⊠ 944 Fort St., Downtown ☎ 250/383–0009, 866/270–5461 ⊕ www.cafe-brio.com ⊘ No lunch. Closed Sun.–Mon. and two weeks in Jan.

Canoe Brewpub

$$ | **CANADIAN** | The lofty windows of this power station–turned–brewpub open onto one of Victoria's best waterfront patios, overlooking the kayaking and ferry action on the gorge. The casual, locally sourced menu runs from high-end pub snacks such as chickpea fritters, mussels with chorizo, short-rib tacos with dark ale, and crispy duck confit to flatbread pizzas and good old fish-and-chips. **Known for:** waterfront patio; house-brewed beer; local ingredients. $ Average main: C$18 ⊠ 450 Swift St., Downtown ☎ 250/361–1940 ⊕ www.canoebrewpub.com.

Q at The Empress

$$$$ | **CANADIAN** | Candlelight dances beneath a carved mahogany ceiling at the Fairmont Empress hotel's flagship restaurant, where one of the two gracious rooms has expansive harbor views. The classically influenced Pacific Northwest menu changes seasonally but might feature such appetizers as Angus beef tartare or caramelized scallops and pork. **Known for:** finesse in food and service; 800-label wine list; adjoining Q

lounge. $ Average main: C$38 ⊠ Fairmont Empress, 721 Government St., Downtown ☎ 250/389–2727 ⊕ www. QatTheEmpress.com.

E:Ne Raw Food and Sake Bar

$$ | **JAPANESE** | **FAMILY** | Offering a unique take on Japanese specialty dishes, the cuisine here can be paired with the largest sake selection in Canada—so diverse it is curated by two sake sommeliers. In addition to classic temaki, bowls, and charcoal aburi oshi, the big faves are small-portion plates (C$4) paired with sake sangria, and the much grander Omakase Shokado, a showcase of nine different dishes (C$42/person). **Known for:** raw bar; sake selection; creativity in taste and presentation. $ Average main: C$17 ⊠ 737 Pandora St., Downtown ☎ ⊕ nuboene.com ⊘ No lunch.

Ferris' Grill & Oyster Bar

$$$ | **ECLECTIC** | **FAMILY** | The wooden booths at the back of this dim, narrow room belie just how much fun this place can be with its upbeat mood and hop-to-it staff. Most of the arty-looking clientele are here for the oysters (served shucked, smoked, baked, breaded, or as shooters) and large portions of updated comfort food (try the sweet-potato fries; lamb, beef, or halibut burgers; or chicken-penne soup). **Known for:** snappy service; back patio; upstairs oyster bar. $ Average main: C$22 ⊠ 536 Yates St., at street level, Downtown ☎ 250/360–1824 ⊕ www. ferrisoysterbar.com.

Il Covo Trattoria

$$$ | **ITALIAN** | **FAMILY** | The warmth of Italy surrounds you at this family-run trattoria near Fisherman's Wharf. The owner hails from Genoa so much of the menu features cuisine from that region as well as daily specials from other parts of the country. **Known for:** authentic Italian cuisine; welcoming atmosphere; patio garden. $ Average main: C$23 ⊠ 106 Superior St., James Bay ☎ 250/380–0088 ⊕ www.ilcovotrattoria.ca ⊘ No lunch.

Il Terrazzo

$$$ | ITALIAN | A cute redbrick terrace edged with potted greenery, and warmed by fireplaces and overhead heaters, makes Il Terrazzo—tucked away off Waddington Alley near Market Square and not visible from the street—the locals' choice for romantic alfresco dining. Starters might include steamed mussels with sun-dried tomatoes and spicy banana peppers, while mains range from such traditional Northern Italian favorites as breaded scaloppini of pork tenderloin to a more local-leaning halibut with blackberries. **Known for:** romantic terrace; Northern Italian dishes; a local favorite. $ Average main: C$30 ⊠ 555 Johnson St., off Waddington Alley, Downtown ☎ 250/361–0028 ⊕ www.ilterrazzo.com ⊘ No lunch weekends.

J & J Wonton Noodle House

$$ | CHINESE | Fresh house-made noodles and wontons draw local office workers to this long-standing Chinese spot. Szechuan and Cantonese specialties, from shrimp noodle soup to beef with hot-chili bean sauce, dominate the long menu, but Singapore-style noodles and Indonesian chow mein appear, too. **Known for:** house-made noodles; open kitchen; local crowd. $ Average main: C$17 ⊠ 1012 Fort St., Downtown ☎ 250/383–0680 ⊕ www.jjnoodlehouse.ca ⊘ Closed Sun.–Mon.

The Mint

$$ | ASIAN | Ever wondered what a Nepalese nightclub might look like? Well, this subterranean space is as close as it gets, with good, affordable Nepalese and Tibetan dishes, from the traditional—butter chicken curry, spicy lamb curry, and Tibetan dumplings—to the less strictly Himalayan, such as naan pizzas and cheese plates, as well as various appetizer platters to share. **Known for:** DJ sets; late-night menu; mint-based cocktails. $ Average main: C$19 ⊠ 1414 Douglas St., Downtown ☎ 250/386–6468 ⊕ www. themintvictoria.com.

Noodlebox

$$ | ASIAN | Noodles, whether Indonesian-style with peanut sauce, thick Hokkien in teriyaki, or Thai-style chow mein, are scooped straight from the open kitchen's steaming woks into bowls or cardboard take-out boxes. Malaysian-, Singapore-, and Thai-style curries run from mild to scaldingly hot. **Known for:** vegan-friendly menu; gluten-free dining; fast service. $ Average main: C$16 ⊠ 818 Douglas St., Downtown ☎ 250/384–1314 ⊕ www.thenoodlebox. net.

★ OLO Restaurant

$$$ | MODERN CANADIAN | Victoria's foodies rave about this small Chinatown bistro that serves up some of the city's most innovative fare, simply yet superbly. Many items like the smoked salmon and pasta are crafted in-house, and the locally sourced menu changes often, often with a French flair. **Known for:** grass-fed beef; unusual pavlovas; tasting menus. $ Average main: C$30 ⊠ 509 Fisgard St., Downtown ☎ 250/590–8795 ⊕ www. olorestaurant.com ⊘ No lunch.

Pagliacci's

$$$ | ITALIAN | Crowded, frenetic, and buckets of fun, this New York-meets-Victoria trattoria has trumpeted showbiz since it opened in 1979, from the signed photos of owner Howie Siegal's movie-star friends plastering the walls, to the live jazz, swing, blues, or Celtic music playing several nights a week. The tables are so tightly packed that you'll be eyeing your neighbor's food from a menu that runs from the "Mae West" (veal with artichoke hearts) to a number of à la carte fresh, handmade pastas and gluten-free rice bowls to the "Prawns Al Capone" (shell-on butterfly shrimp sautéed in butter and white wine). **Known for:** live music; handmade pasta; upbeat atmosphere. $ Average main: C$25 ⊠ 1011 Broad St., Downtown ☎ 250/386–1662 ⊕ www.pagliaccis.ca.

Afternoon Tea in Victoria 🍴

Maybe it's the city's British heritage, but afternoon tea—a snack of tea, cakes, and sandwiches taken midafternoon and not to be confused with "high tea," a hot meal eaten at dinnertime—lives on in Victoria. Several of Victoria's gardens and historic homes also make atmospheric settings for tea. The most authentic places are near the Inner Harbour and in the very British Oak Bay district, often described as being "behind the tweed curtain."

Fairmont Empress Hotel Tea Lobby Victoria's most elaborate and most expensive afternoon tea is served, as it has been since 1908, in the ornate lobby of the Fairmont Empress hotel. The tea is the hotel's own blend, and the cakes, scones, and crustless sandwiches are prepared by some of Victoria's finest pastry chefs. ✉ *721 Government St., Downtown* ☎ *250/389–2727* 🌐 *www.fairmont.com/empress.*

The Pacific Restaurant For a Pacific Rim twist on the tea tradition, try this window-lined restaurant in the Hotel Grand Pacific. You can choose from an assortment of Asian-style teas, like the cherry haiku or dragon tears (green tea with jasmine), while you nibble on Dungeness crab cakes, tuna tataki, scones with clotted cream, and lemon meringue tarts. ✉ *Hotel Grand Pacific, 463 Belleville St., Downtown* ☎ *250/380–4458.*

The Teahouse at Abkhazi Garden Afternoon teas, with fresh-baked scones and cream, mini-quiches, cucumber sandwiches, and seasonal treats featuring produce from the garden, are served in the sun-drenched living room of the Abkhazi Garden. Teas are C$40-C$55 depending on the grandeur of the food and presentation. ✉ *1964 Fairfield Rd., Fairfield* ☎ *778/265–6466* 🌐 *www.abkhaziteahouse.com* 🕒 *Closed Mon.–Tues. Oct.–Mar.*

Venus Sophia Finding English high tea in Chinatown is unexpected, made all the more so for its many vegetarian options. Tea menus include three-tiers of savories and sweets (C$48) as well as simpler selections of finger sandwiches, scones, and desserts (from C$22). ✉ *540 Fisgard St., Chinatown* 🌐 *www.venussophia.com* 🕒 *Closed Mon.–Tues.*

White Heather Tea Room Everything, including the jam, is homemade for the Scottish-style teas served in the White Heather Tea Room, a lovely place with big windows. Tuesday to Saturday, soup-and-sandwich-style lunch and a much grander afternoon tea (called a Big Muckle or Little Muckle depending on your appetite) are served 10 am to 5 pm. ✉ *1885 Oak Bay Ave., Oak Bay* ☎ *250/595–8020* 🌐 *www.whiteheather-tearoom.com* 🕒 *Closed Sun.–Mon.*

Rebar Modern Food
$$ | VEGETARIAN | FAMILY | Bright and casual, with lime-green walls, hippie nuances, and a splashy Bollywood poster, this kid-friendly café in Bastion Square has long been *the* place for vegetarians in Victoria. But don't worry, the almond burgers, decadent baked goodies, and wild salmon tacos keep omnivores happy, too. **Known for:** vegetarian dining; gluten-free options; weekend brunch. [$] *Average main: C$17* ✉ *50 Bastion Sq., Downtown* ☎ *250/361–9223* 🌐 *www.rebarmodernfood.com* 🕒 *No breakfast weekdays.*

Red Fish Blue Fish

$$ | **SEAFOOD** | If you like your fish both yummy *and* ecologically friendly, look no further than this former shipping container on the pier at the foot of Broughton Street. From the soil-topped roof and biodegradable packaging to the sustainably harvested local seafood, this waterfront takeout shop minimizes its ecological footprint. **Known for:** local wild salmon; barbecued oysters; top-notch fish-and-chips. [$] *Average main: C$13* ✉ *1006 Wharf St., Downtown* ☎ *250/298–6877* 🌐 *www.redfish-bluefish.com* 🕒 *No dinner. Closed Nov.–mid-Feb.*

The Tapa Bar

$$ | **SPANISH** | Chef-owner Danno Lee has re-created the fun and flavors of a Spanish tapas bar in this little pedestrian-only lane off Government Street. Small, flavorful dishes run from simple-but-tasty grilled vegetables to prawns in white wine, spicy mussels, thin-crust pizzas, pastas, and a multitude of vegetarian options. **Known for:** lively room; sunny patio; late-night tapas. [$] *Average main: C$18* ✉ *620 Trounce Alley, Downtown* ☎ *250/383–0013* 🌐 *tapabar.ca.*

Wind Cries Mary

$$$ | **CONTEMPORARY** | The chef is a baker-turned-butcher, so the resulting menu is laden with freshly baked breads like caraway sourdough, house-cranked sausages, and deliciously seasoned tender cuts that all exude the island's "eat local" lore. Selections change weekly. **Known for:** eclectic flavors; central location; cozy atmosphere. [$] *Average main: C$22* ✉ *45 Bastion Square, Downtown* ☎ *250/590-8989* 🌐 *www.windcriesmary.ca* 🕒 *Closed Mon. No lunch.*

Zambri's

$$$ | **ITALIAN** | This lively trattoria, in a glam space with floor-to-ceiling windows and eclectic chandeliers, has a setting to match the top-notch Italian food and service. The kitchen uses local and organic ingredients to turn out contemporary versions of traditional dishes. **Known for:** top-notch pasta; extensive Italian wine list; great service. [$] *Average main: C$28* ✉ *The Atrium Bldg., 820 Yates St., Downtown* ☎ *250/360–1171* 🌐 *www.zambris.ca* 🕒 *Closed Sun.–Mon.*

☕ Coffee and Quick Bites

Agrius

$$ | **CANADIAN** | Half the space is a cozy café with soup, sandwiches, and amazing pastries à la Fol Epi (🌐 *www.folepi.ca*), one of the city's best bakeries; the other half is a tiny restaurant and bar. Either way, food is focused on organic locavorism and both are great to satiate hunger pangs. **Known for:** delicious pastries; food is organic-focused; cozy space. [$] *Average main: C$15* ✉ *732 Yates St., Downtown* ☎ *778/265-6312* 🌐 *www.agriusrestaurant.com* 🕒 *No dinner Sun.–Mon.*

Farmhouse Coffee Shop

$ | **CANADIAN** | You might be tempted to dismiss the Farmhouse, with its busy patio and prime Bastion Square location, as a bit of a tourist trap. True, it's popular, but the service is quick and friendly, and the baked goods, wraps, paninis, and pastas are excellent. **Known for:** central location; friendly service; good sandwiches. [$] *Average main: C$10* ✉ *10 Bastion Sq., Downtown* ☎ *250/555-5555* 🌐 *www.farmhousevictoria.com* 🕒 *No dinner.*

Food Trucks behind Royal BC Museum

$ | **CANADIAN** | **FAMILY** | The small lot behind the Royal BC Museum hosts a variety of food trucks daily and is a quiet getaway from the bustling summer crowds. **Known for:** cheap but good fare; wide variety of cuisines; some trucks have breakfast. [$] *Average main: C$6* ✉ *Behind the Royal BC Museum, 675 Belleville St.,, Downtown.*

Hotels

Abigail's Hotel

$$$$ | **B&B/INN** | A Tudor-style inn built in 1930, this adult-oriented boutique hotel is four blocks from the Inner Harbour. **Pros:** luxurious comforts; free parking and free Wi-Fi; only older kids (over 13) allowed. **Cons:** no pool, pets, or gym; not family-friendly; no elevator. [$] *Rooms from: C$368* ✉ *906 McClure St., Downtown* ☎ *250/388–5363, 800/561–6565* 🌐 *www.abigailshotel.com* 🛏 *23 rooms* 🍴 *Free breakfast.*

Beaconsfield Inn

$$$ | **B&B/INN** | This 1905 building four blocks from the Inner Harbour is one of Victoria's most faithfully restored, antiques-filled mansions. **Pros:** luxurious; free parking; free Wi-Fi. **Cons:** romantic ambience is not suited for kids; several blocks from shopping and dining; a lot of stairs. [$] *Rooms from: C$230* ✉ *998 Humboldt St., Downtown* ☎ *250/384–4044, 888/884–4044* 🌐 *www.beaconsfieldinn.com* 🛏 *9 rooms* 🍴 *Free breakfast.*

Chateau Victoria Hotel & Suites

$$$ | **HOTEL** | **FAMILY** | Far-reaching views from the upper-floor suites are a plus at this good-value, centrally located, independent hotel. **Pros:** indoor pool, gym, and hot tub; free Wi-Fi and local calls in rooms; good rates and location. **Cons:** standard rooms lack views; business oriented midweek; decor a bit dated. [$] *Rooms from: C$249* ✉ *740 Burdett Ave., Downtown* ☎ *250/382–4221, 800/663–5891* 🌐 *www.chateauvictoria.com* 🛏 *117 rooms* 🍴 *No meals.*

★ Fairmont Empress

$$$$ | **HOTEL** | Opened in 1908, this harborside château and city landmark has aged gracefully. **Pros:** central location; professional service; great spa and restaurant. **Cons:** small- to average-size rooms and bathrooms; pricey all round; restaurant and spa get booked up quickly with non-guests. [$] *Rooms from: C$563* ✉ *721 Government St., Downtown* ☎ *250/384–8111, 866/540–4429 central reservations* 🌐 *www.fairmont.com/empress* 🛏 *477 rooms* 🍴 *No meals.*

Hotel Grand Pacific

$$$$ | **HOTEL** | Rooms at the Hotel Grand Pacific are large and surprisingly quiet, with deep soaker tubs, floor-to-ceiling windows, balconies, and a chic monochromatic color scheme. **Pros:** great health club and spa; eight fully accessible rooms; free Wi-Fi. **Cons:** standard hotel decor; limited power/USB outlets in rooms; C$50 pet stay fee. [$] *Rooms from: C$359* ✉ *463 Belleville St., James Bay, Downtown* ☎ *250/386–0450, 800/663–7550* 🌐 *www.hotelgrandpacific.com* 🛏 *304 rooms* 🍴 *No meals.*

Hotel Rialto

$$$ | **HOTEL** | This historic Downtown landmark has been transformed into a 21st-century boutique hotel. **Pros:** central location; free Wi-Fi and local calls; historic ambience. **Cons:** no on-site parking; no pool or fitness room (though patrons can get a pass to a nearby fitness club); at a very busy intersection. [$] *Rooms from: C$264* ✉ *653 Pandora Ave., Downtown* ☎ *250/383–4157, 800/332–9981* 🌐 *www.hotelrialto.ca* 🛏 *51 rooms* 🍴 *Free breakfast.*

Hotel Zed

$$$ | **HOTEL** | **FAMILY** | A self-confessed "rebel against the ordinary," Hotel Zed's megawatt color scheme and retro-chic interior have transformed a former, run-of-the-mill motel into one of Victoria's hippest stays, cocooned in a midcentury vibe with modern elements. **Pros:** lots of free stuff, including Downtown shuttle; übercool vibe; hip, friendly staff. **Cons:** 10 minutes from Downtown core; poolside rooms can be noisy; no elevator. [$] *Rooms from: C$259* ✉ *3110 Douglas St., Victoria* ☎ *250/388–4345* 🌐 *www.hotelzed.com* 🛏 *62 rooms* 🍴 *No meals.*

Inn at Laurel Point

$$$$ | **HOTEL** | With water views from every room, a museum-quality art collection, and public areas designed to feel as if you are on a prow of a ship, this Asian-inspired independent hotel on the Inner Harbour's quiet south shore is a favorite among Victoria regulars. **Pros:** spectacular views; quiet, parklike setting; terrific on-site dining. **Cons:** 10-minute walk from Downtown; Laurel wing rooms need upgrading; room service inconsistent. $ *Rooms from: C$329* ⊠ *680 Montreal St., James Bay, Downtown* ☎ *250/386–8721, 800/663–7667* ⊕ *www.laurelpoint.com* ➔ *200 rooms* ¹⊙¹ *No meals.*

James Bay Inn

$$ | **HOTEL** | **FAMILY** | It's not as fancy as most Downtown hotels in and around the Inner Harbour, but this charming 1911 Edwardian manor offers one of Victoria's best accommodation deals. **Pros:** great value; central location; 15% off on-site pub menu. **Cons:** unsophisticated; no elevator; no parking. $ *Rooms from: C$162* ⊠ *270 Government St., James Bay* ☎ *250/384–7151, 800/836–2649* ⊕ *www.jamesbayinn.bc.ca* ➔ *45 rooms* ¹⊙¹ *No meals.*

★ Magnolia Hotel & Spa

$$$$ | **HOTEL** | From the on-site spa to the soaker tubs, sauna, and herb tea, this locally owned boutique hotel, without actually saying so, caters beautifully to the female traveler—though the attention to detail, hop-to-it staff, and central location won't be lost on men either. **Pros:** great location; friendly and helpful service; welcoming lobby with fireplace, tea, and coffee. **Cons:** no on-site pool or hot tub; some rooms have limited views; valet parking C$30. $ *Rooms from: C$379* ⊠ *623 Courtney St., Downtown* ☎ *250/381–0999, 877/624–6654* ⊕ *www. magnoliahotel.com* ➔ *64 rooms* ¹⊙¹ *Free breakfast.*

The Oswego Hotel

$$$ | **HOTEL** | In quiet-but-handy James Bay, this chic all-suites boutique property has 80 sleek studio, one-, and two-bedroom units. **Pros:** swish design; free local calls and Wi-Fi; pet-friendly. **Cons:** 10-minute walk to town center; no pool; overnight parking C$15. $ *Rooms from: C$289* ⊠ *500 Oswego St., James Bay, Downtown* ☎ *250/294–7500, 877/767–9346* ⊕ *www.oswegohotelvictoria.com* ➔ *80 suites* ¹⊙¹ *No meals.*

The Parkside Hotel & Spa

$$$ | **HOTEL** | From the three-story glass atrium with babbling fountains to the rooftop terrace and on-site spa, this Downtown condo-hotel feels like an escape from the city. **Pros:** spacious accommodations; family-friendly; free Wi-Fi and use of bicycles. **Cons:** no doors on en suite bathrooms creates a lack of privacy; small shower stalls; west-side rooms can be noisy. $ *Rooms from: C$289* ⊠ *810 Humboldt St., Downtown* ☎ *250/940–1200, 855/616–3557* ⊕ *www. parksidevictoria.com* ➔ *126 suites* ¹⊙¹ *No meals.*

Royal Scot Hotel & Suites

$$ | **HOTEL** | **FAMILY** | Large suites, great rates, a handy location, and a friendly staff keep couples, families, and bus tours coming back to this well-run James Bay hotel. **Pros:** great for kids; quiet neighborhood; free Wi-Fi and local calls. **Cons:** lots of kids and tour groups; books up months in advance; no pets. $ *Rooms from: C$220* ⊠ *425 Quebec St., James Bay, Downtown* ☎ *250/388–5463, 800/663–7515* ⊕ *www.royalscot.com* ➔ *176 suites* ¹⊙¹ *No meals.*

Swans Hotel

$$$ | **HOTEL** | **FAMILY** | This 1913 former warehouse in Victoria's old town is one of the city's most enticing small inns and is further enhanced by the all-suites accommodations. **Pros:** handsome suites with kitchens; great for families; handy to shopping and restaurants. **Cons:** only stairs access some suites; pub noise

on the lower floors; parking is off-site. $ *Rooms from: C$245* ⊠ *506 Pandora Ave., Downtown* ☎ *250/361–3310, 800/668–7926* ⊕ *www.swanshotel.com* ⇨ *31 suites* ⦿ *No meals.*

Victoria Marriott Inner Harbour

$$$$ | HOTEL | Film people, business travelers, and tourists like this full-service hotel located two blocks east of the Inner Harbour. **Pros:** great service; work-friendly rooms and free Wi-Fi; indoor pool, hot tub, and large modern gym. **Cons:** patio very near street noise; weekdays can get a lot of business travelers; lobby has impersonal atmosphere. $ *Rooms from: C$323* ⊠ *728 Humboldt St., Downtown* ☎ *250/480–3800, 877/333–8338* ⊕ *www. marriottvictoria.com* ⇨ *236 rooms* ⦿ *No meals.*

🌙 Nightlife

BARS AND LOUNGES

Clive's Classic Lounge

PIANO BARS/LOUNGES | Boasting more than 300 rare and hard-to-find spirits on their racks, the bartenders at this classic lounge in the Chateau Victoria Hotel continue to lead Victoria's cocktail scene. They make their own syrups and bitters and use fresh juices in their traditional and contemporary drinks that are forever evolving into intriguing combinations. Trying is believing—sample one of their liquor flights. ⊠ *Chateau Victoria Hotel, 740 Burdett Ave., Downtown* ☎ *250/361–5684* ⊕ *www.clivesclassiclounge.com.*

Little Jumbo

BARS/PUBS | Well-executed farm-to-fork small plates and possibly the city's longest list of spirits are draws at this welcoming little spot, tucked away off Fort Street. Authenticity and the eco-ethos is serious business here: even the water served with the single malts is imported from the Highlands and cocktails come with glass straws. ⊠ *506 Fort St., Downtown* ✛ *At end of corridor* ☎ *778/433–5535* ⊕ *www.littlejumbo.ca.*

Veneto Tapa Lounge

TAPAS BARS | Signature cocktails (the bartenders get bylines on the menu), tapas, and charcuterie plates makes the Hotel Rialto's hip cocktail lounge a chic after-work gathering venue. In addition to craft beers on tap, drinks include creative custom orders, vintage spirits, spin-the-wheel choices, and a lot of mixology showmanship. ⊠ *Hotel Rialto, 1450 Douglas St., Downtown* ☎ *250/383–7310* ⊕ *www.venetodining.com.*

Vista 18

BARS/PUBS | You can take in lofty views of the city at this lounge on the 18th floor of the Chateau Victoria Hotel. By day, the interior feels a bit bland. By night, the atmosphere is a happening place, with live music on Thursday, Friday, and Saturday. ⊠ *Chateau Victoria Hotel, 740 Burdett Ave., Downtown* ☎ *250/382–9258* ⊕ *www.vista18.com.*

DANCE CLUBS

Distrikt

DANCE CLUBS | This nightclub often hosts live bands, guest DJs, and other special events. Also in the building are a restaurant, a pub, and several bars, including a sports bar and a hillbilly-theme bar—not to mention beach volleyball played on the roof in summer. ⊠ *Strathcona Hotel, 919 Douglas St., Downtown* ☎ *250/383–7137* ⊕ *www.strathconahotel.com.*

Paparazzi

DANCE CLUBS | Victoria's longest-running LGBT night club draws a mixed crowd with resident DJs, fun drag, karaoke, and club nights. ⊠ *642 Johnson St., Downtown* ☎ *250/388–0505* ⊕ *www.paparazzi-inightclub.com.*

MUSIC CLUBS

Hermann's Jazz Club

MUSIC CLUBS | Dinner, dancing, and live jazz, blues, and Dixie are on the menu at this venerable Downtown restaurant and jazz club. ⊠ *753 View St., Downtown* ☎ *250/388–9166* ⊕ *www.hermannsjazz.com.*

Lucky Bar

MUSIC CLUBS | A veteran of Victoria's nightclub scene, Lucky's draws DJs, live bands, and a friendly crowd of locals who make the most of Lucky's great sound system and dance floor. ☒ *517 Yates St., Downtown* ☎ *250/382–5825* ⊕ *www. luckybar.ca.*

PUBS

The Bard and Banker Pub

BARS/PUBS | This sumptuously decorated Scottish pub, which occupies a historic bank building on Victoria's main shopping street, has bangers and mash and shepherd's pie on the menu, as well as a great selection of ales and live music every night. Plus, there's no cover charge. ☒ *1022 Government St., Downtown* ☎ *250/953–9993* ⊕ *www. bardandbanker.com.*

Canoe Brewpub

BARS/PUBS | One of Victoria's biggest and best pub patios overlooks the Gorge, the waterway just north of the Inner Harbour. The interior of the former power station has been stylishly redone with high ceilings, exposed bricks, and wood beams. There's a wide range of in-house brews, top-notch bar snacks, and an all-ages restaurant. Live music from Thursday to Saturday adds to its happening vibe, usually with no cover charge. ☒ *450 Swift St., Downtown* ☎ *250/361–1940* ⊕ *www. canoebrewpub.com.*

Irish Times Pub

BARS/PUBS | Tourists and locals flock here for the stout on tap, live music nightly, the summertime patio, and a menu of traditional (think Irish stew), and modern pub fare. Located inside a former bank building on Victoria's main shopping strip adds grandeur to the fun, and very Irish, setting. ☒ *1200 Government St., Downtown* ☎ *250/383–7775* ⊕ *www. irishtimespub.ca.*

Swans Brewpub

BARS/PUBS | A stunning array of First Nations masks and other artworks hangs from the open rafters in this popular Downtown brewpub, where jazz, blues, and swing bands play nightly. ☒ *506 Pandora Ave., Downtown* ☎ *250/361–3310* ⊕ *www.swanshotel.com.*

🅜 Performing Arts

Victoria isn't the busiest destination after dark. But there are two important local sources to help visitors keep on top of the happenings, whether they're looking for a quiet pint, a music festival, or a night on the town. One is a monthly digest of arts and nightlife; the other is the local tourist office, which also sells tickets.

Monday Magazine

NIGHTLIFE OVERVIEW | For entertainment listings, pick up a free copy of this monthly arts magazine, or check out listings online. ☒ *Victoria* ⊕ *www.mondaymag.com.*

Victoria Visitor Information Centre

TICKETS | Tourism Victoria provides free self-guided walking maps, kid-friendly activity lists, and various event listings. You can also buy tickets for many events at the Victoria Visitor Information Centre. ☒ *812 Wharf St., Victoria* ☎ *250/953– 2033, 800/663–3883* ⊕ *www.tourismvictoria.com.*

MUSIC

Summer in the Square

MUSIC | Free jazz, classical, and folk concerts; cultural events; and more run all summer at Centennial Square, which is next to city hall. Free lunchtime concerts are offered Tuesday to Thursday from noon to 1, from July through September. ☒ *Centennial Sq., Pandora Ave. at Douglas St., Downtown* ☎ *250/361–0500* ⊕ *www.victoria.ca/cityvibe.*

Victoria Jazz Society

MUSIC | Watch for music events hosted by this group, which also organizes the annual TD Victoria International JazzFest in late June and the Vancouver Island

An ornate gate at the entrance of Victoria's Chinatown greets visitors.

Blues Bash in early September. ✉ *Victoria* ☎ *250/388–4423* ⊕ *www.jazzvictoria.ca.*

Victoria Symphony

MUSIC | With everything from solo performances to chamber music concerts to full-scale orchestral works, the Victoria Symphony has something for everyone. Watch for Symphony Splash on the first Sunday in August, when the orchestra plays a free concert, accompanied by fireworks, from a barge in the Inner Harbour. ✉ *Victoria* ☎ *250/385–6515* ⊕ *www. victoriasymphony.ca.*

THEATER

Phoenix Theatre

THEATER | University of Victoria theater students stage productions at this on-campus venue. ✉ *University of Victoria, 3800 Finnerty Rd., University of Victoria Campus* ☎ *250/721–8000* ⊕ *www.phoenixtheatres.ca.*

Theatre SKAM

THEATER | This small and imaginative troupe stages summer shows at offbeat venues such as the Galloping Goose Bike Path (the audience pedals from one performance to the next), a workshop wearing headphones, and on the back of a pickup truck in city parks. ✉ *Victoria* ☎ *250/386–7526* ⊕ *www.skam.ca.*

Victoria Fringe Festival

FESTIVALS | Each August and September, a vast menu of original and intriguing performances takes place at several venues around town. It's part of a circuit of fringe-theater events attracting performers—and fans—from around the world. ✉ *Victoria* ☎ *250/383–2663* ⊕ *www. victoriafringe.com.*

🛍 Shopping

AREAS AND MALLS

Antique Row

SHOPPING NEIGHBORHOODS | Fort Street between Blanshard and Cook streets was once *the* place for antiques, curios, and collectibles. The "Antique Row" street signs are still up but the number of antiques stores there is lean, having given way to outlets selling artisanal food and eco-friendly fashions. ⊠ *Downtown*.

Bay Centre

SHOPPING CENTERS/MALLS | Downtown Victoria's main shopping mall has about 100 boutiques and restaurants. ⊠ *1150 Douglas St., Downtown* ☎ *250/952–5690* ⊕ *www.thebaycentre.ca*.

Chinatown

SHOPPING NEIGHBORHOODS | Exotic fruits and vegetables, children's toys, wicker fans, fabric slippers, and other Chinese imports fill the shops along Fisgard Street. Fan Tan Alley, a narrow lane off Fisgard Street, has more nouveau-hippie goods, with a record store and yoga studio tucked in among its tiny storefronts. ⊠ *Downtown*.

Lower Johnson Street

SHOPPING NEIGHBORHOODS | This row of candy-color Victorian-era shopfronts in LoJo (Lower Johnson) is Victoria's hub for independent fashion boutiques. Storefronts—some closet size—are filled with local designers' wares, funky boutiques, and shops selling ecologically friendly clothes of hemp and organic cotton as well as outlets for BC's now-legal "bud" (marijuana); just *don't* take any purchases across the border. Market Square (⊕ *www.marketsquare.ca*) is especially eclectic, particularly during the summer when the open courtyard fills with local vendors. ⊠ *Johnson St., between Government and Store Sts., Downtown*.

Trounce Alley

SHOPPING CENTERS/MALLS | Art Galleries and high-end fashion outlets line this pedestrian-only lane north of View Street squeezed in between Broad and Government streets. ⊠ *Downtown*.

MARKETS

Victorians seem to relish any excuse to head outdoors, which may explain the boom in outdoor crafts, farmers', and other open-air markets around town.

Bastion Square Public Market

OUTDOOR/FLEA/GREEN MARKETS | Crafts vendors and entertainers congregate in this historic square Thursday, Friday, and Saturday from May through September. On Sunday, area farmers join the mix, selling local produce, homemade baked goods, cheeses, jams, and other goodies. ⊠ *Bastion Square, off Government St., Downtown* ☎ ⊕ *www.facebook/ BastionSquarePublicMarkets/*.

James Bay Community Market

OUTDOOR/FLEA/GREEN MARKETS | Organic food, local produce, creative crafts, and live music draw shoppers to this summer Saturday market south of the Inner Harbour. Look for it behind the Parliament Buildings. ⊠ *Superior St. at Menzies St., James Bay, Downtown* ☎ *250/381–5323* ⊕ *www.jamesbaymarket.com*.

Moss Street Market

OUTDOOR/FLEA/GREEN MARKETS |"Make it, bake it, or grow it" is the rule for vendors at this street market, held 10 to 2 on Saturday from May through October. The market continues November to April at Fairfield Community Centre (⊠ *1335 Thurlow St.*) making it a year-round affair, come rain or shine. ⊠ *Fairfield Rd. at Moss St., Fairfield* ⊕ *www.mossstreet-market.com*.

Ship Point Night Market

OUTDOOR/FLEA/GREEN MARKETS | **FAMILY** | Music, jugglers, local crafts, and food vendors are spotlighted at this night market, held Friday and Saturday evenings in summer on the Inner Harbour. ⊠ *Ship Point Pier, Downtown* ⊹ *Just below Visitor Info Centre on Inner Harbour* ☎ *250/383-8326* ⊕ *www.gvha.ca*.

Sidney Thursday Night Market

OUTDOOR/FLEA/GREEN MARKETS | **FAMILY** | More than 150 vendors of food, arts, crafts, and more take over the main street of this town, a 30-minute drive north of Victoria, each Thursday evening from June through August. It's very much a festive family outing. ✉ *Beacon Ave., Sidney* ⊕ *www.sidneystreetmarket.com.*

RECOMMENDED STORES

Artina's

JEWELRY/ACCESSORIES | Canadian-made jewelry—all handmade, one-of-a-kind pieces—fills the display cases at this unique jewelry shop. ✉ *1002 Government St., Downtown* ☎ *250/386–7000* ⊕ *www.artinas.com.*

Cook Culture

HOUSEHOLD ITEMS/FURNITURE | A hive of foodie activity, this upscale kitchenware store in the Atrium Building is also a cooking school, offering workshops on topics like knife skills and how to make sushi or Indian street food. ✉ *1317 Blanshard St., Downtown* ☎ *250/590–8161* ⊕ *www.cookculture.com.*

Cowichan Trading

CRAFTS | First Nations jewelry, art, moccasins, and Cowichan sweaters are the focus at this long-established outlet. ✉ *1328 Government St., Downtown* ☎ *250/383–0321* ⊕ *www.cowichantrading.com.*

idar

JEWELRY/ACCESSORIES | This tiny Tudor-framed shop on Fort Street (look for the three brass honeybees in the sidewalk) houses the workshop of one of the few goldsmiths in North America still forging gold by hand. All the pieces here, in gold, silver, and platinum, are made entirely by hand in original designs reflecting Northwest, Celtic, Nordic, and other traditions. ✉ *946 Fort St., Downtown* ☎ *250/383–3414* ⊕ *www.idar.com.*

Irish Linen Stores

TEXTILES/SEWING | In business since 1917, this tiny shop has kept Victorians in fine linen, lace, and hand-embroidered items for generations. ✉ *1019 Government St., Downtown* ☎ *250/383–6812* ⊕ *www.irishlinenvictoria.com.*

Munro's Books

BOOKS/STATIONERY | Move over, Chapters-Indigo: this beautifully restored 1909 former bank now houses one of Canada's best-stocked independent bookstores. Deals abound in the remainders bin. ✉ *1108 Government St., Downtown* ☎ *250/382–2464* ⊕ *www.munrobooks.com.*

Murchie's

FOOD/CANDY | You can choose from more than 90 varieties of tea to sip here or take home, plus coffees, tarts, and cakes at Victoria's oldest tea purveyor (the company's been around since 1894). The café is a bright stop for a latte, biscotti, or a cup of tea. ✉ *1110 Government St., Downtown* ☎ *250/383–3112* ⊕ *www.murchies.com.*

Rogers' Chocolates

FOOD/CANDY | The staff at Rogers' has been making chocolates since 1885, and they're getting pretty good at it. Victoria creams, in 19 different flavors, are a local favorite. The richly decorative shop dates to 1903. ✉ *913 Government St., Downtown* ☎ *800/663-2220* ⊕ *www.rogerschocolates.com.*

★ Silk Road Tea Store

FOOD/CANDY | Tea aspires to new heights in this chic emporium at the edge of Chinatown. Shelves are stacked with more than 300 intriguing varieties; some you can enjoy in flights at an impressive tasting bar, and others have been restyled into aromatherapy remedies and spa treatments, including a green tea facial, which you can try out in the tiny spa downstairs. Or check out Silk Road's afternoon teas at HotelGrand Pacific (res: 250/380-4458). ✉ *1624 Government St., Downtown* ☎ *250/382-0006* ⊕ *www.silkroadtea.com.*

⚡ Activities

BIKING

Cycle BC Rentals

BICYCLING | This centrally located shop rents bikes for adults and children, as well as bike trailers, motorcycles, and scooters. ✉ *685 Humboldt St., Downtown* ☎ *250/380–2453, 866/380–2453* ⊕ *www.victoria.cyclebc.ca.*

Seawall Adventure Centre

BICYCLING | Besides renting bikes, this company runs bike tours of Victoria, multiday trips to the Gulf Islands, and vineyard tours of the Saanich Peninsula and the Cowichan Valley. Their self-guided trips include bikes, maps, and a ride to Butchart Gardens or the end of the Galloping Goose or Lochside trail so that you can pedal back. ✉ *950 Wharf St., Downtown* ☎ *250/414-4284* ⊕ *www.seawalladventurecentre.com.*

The Pedaler Bicycle Tours and Rentals

BICYCLING | Pedal and sample your way around Victoria's craft breweries, wineries, culinary sites, and bike-friendly neighborhoods on these behind-the-scenes bike tours; the company rents bikes, too. ✉ *321 Belleville St., Downtown* ☎ *778/265–7433* ⊕ *www.thepedaler.ca.*

Victoria Seaside Touring Route

BICYCLING | This vista-inspired, self-guided cycling tour starts at the corner of Government and Belleville streets on the Inner Harbour. It's a 39-km (24-mile) route along city streets and coastal roads, marked with bright yellow signs, that leads past Fisherman's Wharf and along the Dallas Road waterfront to Beacon Hill Park. It then follows the seashore to Cordova Bay, where it connects with Victoria's other two long-distance routes: the Lochside and Galloping Goose regional trails. ✉ *Government St. at Belleville St., Inner Harbour, Downtown.*

KAYAKING

Victoria Kayak

KAYAKING | Setting out from the Inner Harbour, this company runs 2½-hour and full-day tours to see seals and other marine life around Seal Island at the entrance to the harbor. It's a good tour for beginners. The company runs evening sunset tours and rents kayaks, too. ✉ *1006 Wharf St., Downtown* ☎ *250/216–5646* ⊕ *www.victoriakayak.com.*

SCUBA DIVING

Ogden Point Dive Centre

SCUBA DIVING | Guided dives, weekend charters, PADI courses, and equipment sales and service are all available at this PADI-certified dive center at the Ogden Point Breakwater near Downtown Victoria. Great shore dives start along the breakwater right outside the shop. ✉ *199 Dallas Rd., Downtown* ☎ *250/380–9119* ⊕ *www.divevictoria.com.*

SPAS

Since health, nature, and relaxing seem to be major preoccupations in Victoria, it's not surprising that the city has enjoyed a boom in spas. Aesthetics are important, but natural healing, ancient practices, and the use of local products such as wine and seaweed are more the focus here. Local specialties include seaweed treatments, and vinotherapy (applying the antioxidant properties of wine grapes externally, rather than internally).

Float House Victoria

SPA/BEAUTY | This contemporary spa offers five float tanks, each filled with 1,200 pounds of Epsom salts for a deeply relaxing sensory-free session bar none. There's a second location on the West Shore at 2871 Jacklin Rd. Booking on-line for either location can be faster than calling. ✉ *662 Herald St., Downtown* ☎ *778/433–3166* ⊕ *www.floathousevictoria.com.*

Silk Road Spa

SPA/BEAUTY | Essential oils and organic skin and body products are the draw at this small and serene Chinatown spa, located inside the Silk Road tea shop. The green-tea facial is especially popular. ⊠ *1624 Government St., Downtown* ☎ *250/704–2688* ⊕ *www.silkroadtea. com.*

Spa at Delta Victoria Ocean Pointe Resort

SPA/BEAUTY | Organic skin-care products and harbor-view treatment rooms are among the draws at this popular hotel spa. Patrons have access to the hotel's gym and pool. ⊠ *Delta Victoria Ocean Pointe Resort, 100 Harbour Rd., Downtown* ☎ *250/360–5858, 800/575–8882* ⊕ *www.thespadeltavictoria.com.*

Spa Magnolia

SPA/BEAUTY | Organic products, couples treatments, and a hydrotherapy tub are the hallmark of this top-notch spa at the Hotel Magnolia. ⊠ *Magnolia Hotel & Spa, 625 Courtney St., Downtown* ☎ *250/920–7721* ⊕ *www.spamagnolia.com.*

Willow Stream Spa at the Fairmont Empress Hotel

SPA/BEAUTY | Victoria's most luxurious spa offers a value-added treat if you arrive, as suggested, an hour before your appointment to soak in the Hungarian mineral bath, sauna, and steam room, included with every treatment. ⊠ *Fairmont Empress, 633 Humboldt St., Downtown* ☎ *250/995–4650, 866/854–7444* ⊕ *www. willowstream.com.*

WHALE-WATCHING

Orca Spirit Adventures

WILDLIFE-WATCHING | FAMILY | This company offers year-round tours with both Zodiacs and covered vessels. Boats are equipped with hydrophones and all guides are marine biologists. In summer a three-hour tour starts at C$129. The outfitter offers free hotel pickup/drop-off service. A second location is at the Marina Level outside the Victoria Coast Hotel, 146 Kingston St. ⊠ *950 Wharf St., Victoria* ☎ *250/383–8411, 888/672–6722* ⊕ *www. orcaspirit.com.*

Prince of Whales

WILDLIFE-WATCHING | FAMILY | Victoria's biggest whale-watching company offers a whole range of marine excursions, from three-hour boat or Zodiac tours from Victoria, to five-hour trips that include·a stop at Butchart Gardens, to one-way or round-trip crossings between Vancouver and Victoria; all sailings have naturalists on board. Zodiac trips cost C$130 and leave year-round; covered boat sailings on the *Ocean Magic II* are C$130 and run from April to October; and Victoria to Butchart Gardens trips run from late May to late September (the C$160 fare includes admission to the gardens). The company's Vancouver to Victoria crossings, running from late May to late September on the 94-passenger *Salish Sea Dream,* are a great time-saver, combining a sailing to or from Victoria with a whale-watching trip. A stop at The Butchart Gardens or return flights by floatplane or helicopter are options, too. The most popular trip, billed as The Ultimate Day Trip, includes a whale-watching trip from Vancouver to Victoria, a stop in Downtown Victoria, a bus transfer to Butchart Gardens, and a sunset sailing back to Vancouver. This C$340 trip runs daily from late May to late September. The company's Victoria office is on the Inner Harbour Causeway, below the Visitor Info Centre. ⊠ *812 Wharf St., Lower Causeway Level, Downtown* ☎ *250/383–4884, 888/383–4884* ⊕ *www.princeofwhales. com.*

SpringTide Whale Watching & Eco Tours

WILDLIFE-WATCHING | FAMILY | Using marine biologists as guides, this company runs tours on Zodiacs and on 61-foot motor yachts. Summer tours are three hours long, and the boats are equipped with hydrophones. Rates are C$129. ⊠ *1119 Wharf St., Downtown* ☎ *250/384–4444, 800/470–3474* ⊕ *www.victoriawhale-watching.com.*

Vic West

Victoria West is just across the Johnson Street Bridge from Downtown Victoria.

Close to Downtown lies the residential neighborhood of Victoria West, or Vic West. Bordered by the Outer and Upper harbors, it's home to the Westsong Way seaside walking path, the Galloping Goose Trail (a long-distance hiking and biking path), and a brace of waterfront eateries warranting a trip across the bridge.

GETTING HERE AND AROUND
The main attractions in Vic West are a short stroll across the Johnson Street Bridge, or you could take Bus 6 from the corner of Government and Johnson.

 Restaurants

★ Boom + Batten
$$$ | CANADIAN | Located along the Songhees Westsong Walkway, adjacent to the new Victoria International Marina, the views match the food at this waterfront restaurant. Its bakery-café offers sweet and savory treats for walkers and coffee aficionados, and the restaurant menu is a combination of charcuterie boards and terrines for sharing, wood-fired-oven pizzas, raw options like scallop with pickled beet citrus vinaigrette, marinated octopus and ceviches, as well as pastas and imaginative takes on classics such as duck Bolognese. **Known for:** views of Inner Harbour; sharing plates; hip and happening place. $ *Average main: C$22* ⊠ *2 Paul Kane Pl., Vic West* ☎ ⊕ *www. boomandbatten.com.*

LURE Restaurant & Bar
$$$ | MODERN CANADIAN | A sunny patio, intimate balconies, and a wall of windows take in sweeping views across the Inner Harbour at this seaside spot in the Delta Victoria Ocean Pointe Resort. Casual mains and shared plates, such as local-brew battered halibut, maple bourbon pork ribs, and spiced-grilled Angus beef striploin, along with elaborate desserts (try the ice cream sandwich with whiskey caramel and sweet pickled cherries) are served all day and into the evening. **Known for:** harbor views; creative cocktails; lively bar scene. $ *Average main: C$21* ⊠ *Delta Victoria Ocean Pointe Resort, 100 Harbour Rd., Vic West* ☎ *250/360–5873* ⊕ *www.lurevictoria. com.*

Spinnakers Gastro Brewpub
$$ | CANADIAN | Victoria's longest list of handcrafted beers is just one reason to trek over the Johnson Street Bridge or hop a Harbour Ferry to this Vic West waterfront pub. Canada's oldest licensed brewpub, Spinnakers relies almost exclusively on locally sourced ingredients for its top-notch casual fare. **Known for:** high-end pub fare; brick-oven pizza; takeaway deli. $ *Average main: C$20* ⊠ *308 Catherine St., Vic West* ☎ *250/386–2739, 877/838–2739* ⊕ *www.spinnakers.com.*

▶ Nightlife

PUBS

Boom + Batten
BARS/PUBS | As one of Victoria's hippest hangouts, this waterfront restaurant and bar is a great spot for cocktails, a late-night snack, and a fab nighttime view of the Inner Harbour. ⊠ *2 Paul Kane Pl., West Shore* ☎ *250/940-5850* ⊕ *www. boomandbatten.com.*

Spinnakers Gastro Brewpub
BARS/PUBS | You can hop on an Inner Harbour Ferry to this local favorite on the Inner Harbour's north shore. Canada's first modern-day brewpub, it also has the city's longest menu of traditionally made in-house brews. A covered waterfront deck, a double-sided fireplace, excellent pub grub, and an all-ages in-house restaurant make this a popular hangout. ⊠ *308 Catherine St., Vic West* ☎ *250/386–2739* ⊕ *www.spinnakers.com.*

Activities

Galloping Goose Regional Trail

BICYCLING | Following an old rail bed, this 55-km (35-mile) route officially starts at the Vic West end of Johnson Street Bridge, which connects Downtown Victoria to Vic West. The multiuse trail runs across old rail trestles and through forests west to the town of Sooke, finishing just past Sooke Potholes Provincial Park. Just north of Downtown it links with the Lochside Regional Trail to the BC Ferries terminal at Swartz Bay, creating a nearly continuous 55-mile car-free route. It has earned many accolades, deservedly so. ⊠ *Johnson St. Bridge, Vic West* ☎ *250/478–3344* ⊕ *www.crd.bc.ca/parks* ☜ *Free.*

Fernwood

Fernwood is just east of Victoria.

Fernwood Square, at Gladstone and Fernwood roads, is framed by historic buildings housing independent galleries and cafés, as well as the Belfry Theatre, a contemporary theater housed in an 1891 church. The square lies at the heart of one of Victoria's most charming urban villages, popular with artists and young families.

GETTING HERE AND AROUND

To get here, catch Bus 22 from Fort and Douglas streets Downtown, or enjoy the pleasant 2½-km (1½-mile) walk along Pandora and up Fernwood Road.

Performing Arts

Belfry Theatre

THEATER | Housed in a former church, the Belfry Theatre has a resident company that specializes in contemporary Canadian dramas. ⊠ *1291 Gladstone Ave., Fernwood* ☎ *250/385–6815* ⊕ *www. belfry.bc.ca.*

Theatre Inconnu

THEATER | Victoria's oldest alternative theater company, housed in a venue across the street from the Belfry Theatre, offers a range of performances at affordable ticket prices. ⊠ *1923 Fernwood Rd., Fernwood* ☎ *250/360–0234* ⊕ *www. theatreinconnu.com.*

Oak Bay

3 km (less than 1 mile) east of Victoria.

One of several urban villages around greater Victoria, Oak Bay is probably the oldest and best-known. Described as a place "behind the tweed curtain" for its adherence to Tudor facades, pubs, and tea shops, this historically British area (with its own mayor and municipal hall) is home to the Penny Farthing Pub and White Heather Tea Room as well as sweet shops, bookstores, galleries, and antiques stores. Several more contemporary boutiques and eateries have moved in, too.

GETTING HERE AND AROUND

Oak Bay Village is oriented around Oak Bay Avenue, between Foul Bay Road and Monterey Avenue. A car or a bike is handy, but not essential, for exploring this area. Big Bus, Gray Line, and other tour companies offer Oak Bay and Marine Drive tours.

By public transit, take Bus 2 to Oak Bay Village (or Bus 2A, which continues to Willows Beach) from Johnson and Douglas streets Downtown.

Beaches

Willows Park Beach

BEACH—SIGHT | FAMILY | This sandy beach, with its calm waters, playground, and shady picnic spots, is a summertime favorite among Victorian families. It's just a few miles from Downtown in the very British Oak Bay neighborhood—there's even a teahouse on the beach. **Amenities:**

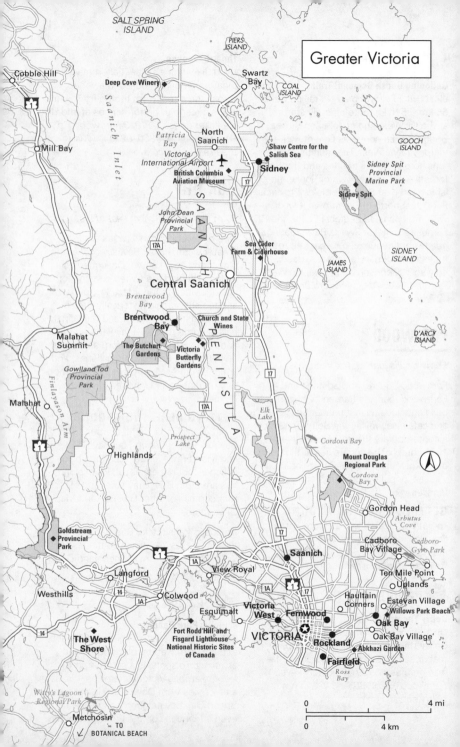

SALT SPRING
ISLAND

PIERS
ISLAND

Cobble Hill

Deep Cove Winery

Swartz
Bay

COAL
ISLAND

Saanich Inlet

Mill Bay

Patricia
Bay

North
Saanich

Victoria
International Airport

British Columbia
Aviation Museum

Shaw Centre for the
Salish Sea

Sidney

GOOCH
ISLAND

Sidney Spit
Provincial
Marine Park

Sidney Spit

John Dean
Provincial
Park

17A

Sea Cider
Farm & Ciderhouse

JAMES
ISLAND

SIDNEY
ISLAND

SAANICH

Central Saanich

Brentwood
Bay

Malahat
Summit

Brentwood
Bay

The Butchart
Gardens

Church and State
Wines

Victoria
Butterfly
Gardens

D'ARCY
ISLAND

PENINSULA

Gowlland Tod
Provincial
Park

17A

Malahat

Finlayson Arm

Prospect
Lake

Elk
Lake

Highlands

Cordova Bay

Mount Douglas
Regional Park

Cordova
Bay

Goldstream
Provincial
Park

Gordon Head

Arbutus
Cove

Cadboro
Bay Village

Cadboro-Gyro Park

Langford

View Royal

Saanich

Ten Mile Point

Westhills

14

Colwood

Esquimalt

1A

Victoria
West

Fernwood

Haultain
Corners

Uplands

Estevan Village

Willows Park Beach

Oak Bay

The West
Shore

Fort Rodd Hill and
Fisgard Lighthouse
National Historic Sites
of Canada

VICTORIA

Rockland

Oak Bay Village

Abkhazi Garden

Fairfield

Ross
Bay

Witty's Lagoon
Regional Park

Metchosin

14

TO
BOTANICAL BEACH

Greater Victoria

0   4 mi

0   4 km

food and drink; parking; toilets. **Best for:** swimming. ⊠ *Dalhousie St., at Beach Dr., Oak Bay* ⊕ *www.oakbay.ca.*

🍴 Restaurants

Marina Restaurant

$$$ | SEAFOOD | This circular room with art deco rosewood booths and a 180-degree view over the sailboats of Oak Bay Marina has a chef with a flair for seafood. As an Ocean Wise advocate, food is all about sustainably sourced seafood including wild salmon and Dungeness crab, all of which are teamed with local organic vegetables. **Known for:** marina view; sustainable seafood; evening sushi bar. $ *Average main: C$26* ⊠ *1327 Beach Dr., Oak Bay* ☎ *250/598–8555* ⊕ *www. marinarestaurant.com.*

Vis à Vis Wine and Charcuterie Bar

$$$ | MODERN CANADIAN | If you think that Oak Bay is all British tweeds and shepherd's pies, pull up a stool at the long, polished-wood bar in this thoroughly modern storefront bistro. The imaginative small-plates menu emphasizes fresh, local ingredients and regional purveyors in a long menu of charcuterie selections as well as updated comfort foods like braised short rib and onion tortiere, Parmesan frites, mouthwatering soups such as Dungeness crab bisque, and salads. **Known for:** local ingredients; BC craft beer; wine pairings. $ *Average main: C$28* ⊠ *2228 Oak Bay Ave., Oak Bay* ☎ *250/590–7424* ⊕ *www.visavisoak-bay.com.*

🛏 Hotels

⭐ **Oak Bay Beach Hotel**

$$$$ | HOTEL | This lavish waterfront hotel, complete with a seaside spa, ocean-view restaurant, and even an on-site theater for live shows and movies nights, offers a resort ambience within a few miles of Downtown Victoria. **Pros:** luxurious surroundings; lavish spa and views; free Wi-Fi, local calls, and use of bicycles.

Cons: not central, but shuttles run the 5 km (3 miles) to Downtown Victoria; can feel a bit remote; pools are adults-only and overall sophisticated vibe not geared to kids. $ *Rooms from: C$410* ⊠ *1175 Beach Dr., Oak Bay* ☎ *250/598–4556, 800/668–7758* ⊕ *www.oakbaybeachho-tel.com* 🛏 *119 rooms* ⦿ *No meals.*

🎭 Performing Arts

The David Foster Foundation Theatre

FILM | Dinner theater performances and film screenings are presented at this lavish venue in the Oak Bay Beach Hotel. ⊠ *The Oak Bay Beach Hotel, 1175 Beach Dr., Oak Bay* ☎ *250/598–4556* ⊕ *www. oakbaybeachhotel.com.*

Rockland

2½ km (1½ miles east of Victoria.

The winding, shady streets of Rockland—roughly bordered by Fort Street, Richmond Avenue, Fairfield Road, and the Strait of Juan de Fuca—are lined with beautifully preserved Victorian and Edwardian homes. These include many stunning old mansions now operating as bed-and-breakfasts, and Victoria's most elaborate folly: Craigdarroch Castle. With mansions come gardens, and several of the city's best are found here.

GETTING HERE AND AROUND

By public transit, take Bus 11 or 14 from the corner of Fort and Douglas streets to Moss Street (for the Art Gallery of Greater Victoria), or to Joan Crescent (for Craigdarroch Castle). Government House is a few blocks south. The walk, about a mile along Fort Street, is also interesting, taking you past a handful of antiques stores and a growing number of intriguing specialty food shops.

Craigdarroch Castle is a mansion-turned-museum complete with turrets and Gothic rooflines.

👁 Sights

Art Gallery of Greater Victoria

MUSEUM | Attached to an 1889 mansion, this modern building houses one of Canada's largest collections of Asian art. The Japanese garden between the buildings is home to the only authentic Shinto shrine in North America. The gallery, a few blocks west of Craigdarroch Castle, displays a permanent exhibition of works by well-known Canadian artist Emily Carr and regularly changing exhibits of Asian and Western art. ⊠ *1040 Moss St., at Fort St., Rockland* ☎ *250/384–4171* ⊕ *www. aggv.ca* 🖾 *C$13.*

★ Craigdarroch Castle

CASTLE/PALACE | This magnificent and somewhat imposing mansion, complete with turrets and Gothic rooflines, was built as the home of one of British Columbia's wealthiest men, coal baron Robert Dunsmuir, who died in 1889, just a few months before the castle's completion. It's now a museum depicting life in the late 1800s. The castle's 39 rooms have ornate Victorian furnishings, stained-glass windows, carved woodwork, and a beautifully restored painted ceiling in the drawing room. A winding staircase climbs four floors to a tower overlooking Victoria. Castles run in the family: son James went on to build the more lavish Hatley Castle west of Victoria. Although the very modern visitor's center is fully accessible, as is the summer-only café, the castle itself is not wheelchair accessible and has no elevators. ⊠ *1050 Joan Crescent, Rockland* ☎ *250/592–5323* ⊕ *www.thecastle.ca* 🖾 *C$14.95.*

Government House

GARDEN | Take a stroll through the walled grounds and 35 acres of formal gardens at Government House, residence of British Columbia's lieutenant governor, the Queen's representative in BC. The 19th-century Cary Castle Mews on-site are home to an interpretive center, a costume museum, and a tearoom. The main house is open for guided tours one Saturday a month. ⊠ *1401 Rockland Ave.,*

Rockland ☎ *250/387–2080* 🌐 *www.ltgov.bc.ca* 🎫 *Free.*

Hotels

★ Abbeymoore Manor Bed & Breakfast Inn
$$$ | **B&B/INN** | This 1912 mansion has the wide verandas, dark wainscoting, and high ceilings of its era, but the attitude is informal and welcoming, from the superhelpful hosts to the free snacks to the coffee on tap all day. **Pros:** good value; friendly hosts; excellent service. **Cons:** a mile from the Inner Harbour; often booked in advance; very quiet neighborhood. [$] *Rooms from: C$279* ✉ *1470 Rockland Ave., Rockland* ☎ *250/370–1470, 888/801–1811* 🌐 *www.abbeymoore.com* 🛏 *7 rooms* 🍴 *Free breakfast.*

The Craigmyle
$$ | **B&B/INN** | **FAMILY** | Affordable and historic, this four-story manor near Craigdarroch Castle has been a guesthouse since 1913. **Pros:** free local calls and Wi-Fi; guest laundry (also free); homey ambiance. **Cons:** no elevator and a lot of stairs; street parking only; no pets. [$] *Rooms from: C$199* ✉ *1037 Craigdarroch Rd., Rockland* ☎ *250/595–5411, 844/595–5411* 🌐 *www.thecraigmyle.com* 🛏 *15 rooms* 🍴 *Free breakfast.*

★ Fairholme Manor
$$ | **B&B/INN** | Original art, Viennese antiques, and dramatic furnishings shine in this lavish 1885 Italianate mansion. **Pros:** beautiful setting; stunning decor; gracious and welcoming host. **Cons:** a mile from Downtown; no elevator; überquiet. [$] *Rooms from: C$209* ✉ *638 Rockland Pl., off Rockland Ave., Rockland* ☎ *250/598–3240, 877/511–3322* 🌐 *www.fairholmemanor.com* 🛏 *6 suites* 🍴 *Free breakfast.*

Villa Marco Polo Inn
$$$ | **B&B/INN** | A classical European garden with a stone terrace, reflecting pool, and fountains is all part of the Tuscan-hideaway feel at this 1923 Italian Renaissance–style manor. **Pros:** lots of comfy common areas; gracious hosts; full concierge services. **Cons:** a mile from Downtown; no elevator; breakfast served only at 8:30 am sharp. [$] *Rooms from: C$269* ✉ *1524 Shasta Pl., off St. Charles St., Rockland* ☎ *250/370–1524, 877/601–1524* 🌐 *www.villamarcopolo.com* 🛏 *4 rooms* 🍴 *Free breakfast.*

Performing Arts

Langham Court Theatre
THEATER | The Victoria Theatre Guild, one of Canada's oldest community theater groups, stages works by internationally known playwrights at this 177-seat venue near the Victoria Art Gallery. ✉ *Langham Court Theatre, 805 Langham Ct., Rockland* ☎ *250/384–2142* 🌐 *www.langhamtheatre.ca.*

Fairfield

1.9 kms (1 mile) southeast of Victoria.

Bordered by Beacon Hill Park to the west and Dallas Road, a winding seaside drive to the south, this quiet residential district is home to heritage homes and seaside walks, bike paths, parkland, and Cook Street Village, a tree-lined stretch of cafés, restaurants, and independent shops on the edge of Beacon Hill Park. Moss Street Market is a popular summer weekend event, and Ross Bay Cemetery, with its deer, tombstones, and tours, is a fount of historic information. A seaside path follows the waterfront from Beacon Hill Park to Clover Point Park, offering views across Juan de Fuca Strait to the Olympic Mountains.

GETTING HERE AND AROUND

A useful route is Bus 7: from Johnson and Douglas Streets, it travels to Ross Bay Cemetery, Abkhazi Garden, and on to Oak Bay Village on the way to the University of Victoria. Seaside-winding Dallas Road also makes a great bike ride.

218

Sights

Abkhazi Garden

GARDEN | Called "the garden that love built," this once-private garden is as fascinating for its history as for its innovative design. The seeds were planted, figuratively, in Paris in the 1920s, when Englishwoman Peggy Pemberton-Carter met exiled Georgian Prince Nicholas Abkhazi. World War II internment camps (his in Germany, hers near Shanghai) interrupted their romance, but they reunited and married in Victoria in 1946. They spent the next 40 years together cultivating their garden. Rescued from developers and now operated by the Land Conservancy of British Columbia, the 1-acre site is recognized as a leading example of west coast horticultural design, resplendent with native Garry Oak trees, Japanese maples, and mature rhododendrons. The teahouse (⊕ *www.abkhaziteahouse.com*), in the parlor of the modernist home, serves lunch and afternoon tea daily until 4 pm, with reduced hours in winter. ✉ *1964 Fairfield Rd., Fairfield* ☎ *778/265–6466* ⊕ *www.conservancy.bc.ca* ✉ *By donation* ☉ *Closed Mon. and Tues. during Oct.–Mar.*

Saanich

4 km (2 miles) north of Victoria.

With its rolling green hills and small family farms, the Saanich Peninsula is also home to the BC and Washington State ferry terminals as well as the Victoria International Airport; its southernmost community is called, simply, Saanich. This is the first part of Vancouver Island that most visitors see. Although it's tempting to head straight for Downtown Victoria, 25 minutes to the south, there are many reasons to linger here, including Mt. Douglas, which offers magnificent views of Victoria and the rest of the peninsula on a clear day.

GETTING HERE AND AROUND
To reach the area by car from Downtown Victoria, follow the signs for the ferries straight up Highway 17, or take the Scenic Marine Drive starting at Dallas Road and following the coast north. It joins Highway 17 at Royal Oak Drive. Victoria transit buses serve the area, though not frequently. Cyclists can take the Lochside Trail, which runs from Victoria to Sidney, detouring, perhaps, to visit some wineries along the way.

Sights

Mount Douglas Regional Park

NATIONAL/STATE PARK | **FAMILY** | A footpath and a road lead to the 213-meter (758-foot) summit of Mt. Douglas, offering a 360-degree view of Victoria and the Saanich Peninsula. On a clear day, you can even see the Gulf and San Juan islands and the Olympic Mountains of Washington. The park, known locally as Mt. Doug, is also home to a long sandy beach, evergreen forests, hiking trails, and wildflower meadows. ✉ *Off Cedar Hill Rd., Saanich* ☎ *250/475–5522* ⊕ *www.saanich.ca* ✉ *Free.*

Sea Cider Farm & Ciderhouse

WINERY/DISTILLERY | Traditional ciders, made with apples grown on-site and nearby, are paired with local cheeses, preserves, and other artisanal delectables at this Saanich Peninsula ciderhouse. It's open year-round for tours and tastings. ✉ *2487 Mt. Saint Michael Rd., off Central Saanich Rd., Saanichton* ☎ *250/544–4824* ⊕ *www.seacider.ca* ✉ *Samples C$7.50.*

Beaches

Cadboro-Gyro Park

BEACH—SIGHT | **FAMILY** | A long, sandy, driftwood-strewn beach backed by a grassy park with plenty of picnic tables and shade trees draws families to this sheltered bay, accessible via the Scenic Marine Drive. Kids enjoy the sea creature structures in the play area (including a replica of the legendary "Cadborosaurus" sea serpent said to live in these waters). Hiking trails, a boat launch, and tennis courts keep adults busy; swimming is safe here, if you don't mind the cold (or the sea creature). Snacks can be had at nearby Cadboro Village. **Amenities:** parking (free); toilets. **Best for:** walking; sunrise. ⊠ *Sinclair Rd., off Cadboro Bay Rd., Saanich* ☎ *250/475–5522* ⊕ *www. saanich.ca.*

Cordova Bay

BEACH—SIGHT | FAMILY | Walkers, swimmers, and sunbathers flock to this long stretch of forest-backed sand, pebble, and driftwood beach, which is just north of Mount Douglas Park. There are several access points along Cordova Bay Road. The Beachhouse Restaurant, perched on the sand about midway along the beach (at 5109 Cordova Bay Road), serves take-out snacks plus casual lunches and dinners. **Amenities:** food and drink; toilets (May 1–October 30). **Best for:** swimming; walking. ⊠ *Cordova Bay Rd., Saanich* ☎ *250/475-5522* ⊕ *www.saanich.ca.*

🏃 Activities

HIKING AND WALKING

Mount Douglas Regional Park

HIKING/WALKING | Trails through the forest to the 260-meter (853-foot) summit of Mt. Douglas reward hikers with a 360-degree view of Victoria, the Saanich Peninsula, and the mountains of Washington State. ⊠ *Off Cedar Hill Rd., Saanich* ☎ *250/475–5522* ⊕ *www.saanich.ca.*

Swan Lake Christmas Hill Nature Sanctuary

HIKING/WALKING | FAMILY | This sanctuary, with its 23-acre lake set in 150 acres of fields and wetlands, is just a few minutes from Downtown Victoria. From the 2.4-km (1½-mile) Lake Loop Trail and floating boardwalk, birders can spot a variety of waterfowl and nesting birds year-round. For great views of Victoria, take the 2.4-km (1½-mile) round-trip hike to the top of Christmas Hill. The sanctuary's Nature

House is open weekdays 8:30–4 and weekends noon–4. ⊠ *3873 Swan Lake Rd., Saanich* ☎ *250/479–0211* ⊕ *www. swanlake.bc.ca* 🎫 *Free.*

SCUBA DIVING

Rockfish Divers

SCUBA DIVING | Based in central Saanich, this internationally accredited PADI dive outfitter offers charters, courses, and equipment rentals. Boats operate out of Brentwood Bay and Canoe Cove. ⊠ *3945 Quadra St., Saanich* ☎ *250/516–3483* ⊕ *www.rockfishdivers.com.*

Brentwood Bay

20 km (12 miles) north of Victoria.

The tiny seaside village of Brentwood Bay is best known as the home of the famous Butchart Gardens. From Brentwood Bay, BC Ferries sail to Mill Bay in the Cowichan Valley, so you don't have to backtrack to Victoria if you're touring the island.

GETTING HERE AND AROUND

If you're not driving, the easiest way to get to Brentwood Bay is on a bus tour. These range from direct shuttles offered by Gray Line and CVS Tours to day trips taking in other Saanich Peninsula sights. Several companies also offer winery tours.

👁 Sights

★ The Butchart Gardens

GARDEN | This stunning 55-acre garden and national historic site has been drawing visitors since it was started in a limestone quarry in 1904. Highlights include the dramatic 70-foot Ross Fountain, the formal Japanese garden, and the intricate Italian garden complete with a gelato stand. Kids will love the old-fashioned carousel and will likely enjoy the 45-minute miniboat tours around Tod Inlet. From mid-June to mid-September the gardens are illuminated at night with hundreds of

The winding stairs in the middle of greenery is a top photo spot in The Butchart Gardens.

hidden lights. In July and August, jazz, blues, and classical musicians play at an outdoor stage each evening, and fireworks draw crowds every Saturday night. The wheelchair- and stroller-accessible site is also home to a seed-and-gift shop, a plant-identification center, two restaurants (one offering traditional afternoon tea), and a coffee shop; you can even call ahead for a picnic basket on fireworks nights. To avoid crowds, come at opening time, in the late afternoon or evening (except ultrabusy fireworks Saturday evenings), or between September and June, when the gardens are still stunning and admission rates are reduced. The grounds are especially magical at Christmas, with themed lighting and an ice rink. The gardens are a 20-minute drive north of Downtown; parking is free but fills up on fireworks Saturdays. You can get here by city Bus 75 from Douglas Street in Downtown Victoria, but service is slow and infrequent. **CVS Tours** (877/578-5552 ⊕ www.cvstours.com) runs shuttles from Downtown Victoria.

✉ 800 Benvenuto Ave., Brentwood Bay ☎ 250/652-5256, 866/652-4422 ⊕ www. butchartgardens.com ✉ C$35 ⌖ Rates are lower between Oct. and mid-June.

Church and State Wines
RESTAURANT—SIGHT | A vineyard-view bistro and tasting bar make this expansive winery a popular stop en route to nearby Butchart Gardens. Pinot Gris and Pinot Noir are grown on-site; several Bordeaux blends from a sister winery in the Okanagan Valley are also worth a try. Wine tastings can be perfectly paired with items from an extensive tasting menu. ✉ 1445 Benvenuto Ave., Brentwood Bay ☎ 250/652-2671 ⊕ churchandstatewines. com ✉ C$9 for tastings.

Victoria Butterfly Gardens
GARDEN | FAMILY | Thousands of butterflies—of up to 70 different species—flutter freely in an indoor tropical garden that's also home to orchids and carnivorous plants, tropical fish, flamingos, tortoises, geckos, poison dart frogs, and 30 kinds of free-flying tropical birds. The

butterflies are sourced from a sustainable farm or bred in-house (displays show the whole life cycle) and all the birds, fish, and animals have been donated or rescued. Be sure to visit the Insectarium, filled with creepy-crawlies from all over the world in a jungle-like setting. The site is a popular stop en route to The Butchart Gardens. Be prepared for tropical temperatures year-round. ✉ *1461 Benvenuto Ave., corner of West Saanich Rd. and Keating Cross Rd., Brentwood Bay* ☎ *250/652–3822, 877/722–0272* 🌐 *www.butterflygardens.com* 🎫 *C$16.50* ☞ *Last admission 1 hr before closing.*

Restaurants

The Arbutus Room
$$$$ | CANADIAN | Locally sourced, west coast cuisine is paired with wines from neighboring vineyards at this lovely ocean-view restaurant in the Brentwood Bay Resort. Start with beet and asparagus salad, then opt for halibut with a touch of ginger or one of the beef, lamb, poultry, and vegetarian dishes. **Known for:** sushi and fresh seafood; heated ocean-view patio; Canadian art collection. [$] *Average main: C$32* ✉ *Brentwood Bay Resort, 849 Verdier Ave., Brentwood Bay* ☎ *250/544–2079* 🌐 *www.brentwoodbayresort.com* 🕒 *No lunch.*

Hotels

★ **Brentwood Bay Resort & Spa**
$$$$ | RESORT | Every room has a private ocean-view patio or balcony at this adult-oriented boutique resort in a tiny seaside village. **Pros:** magnificent setting; close to The Butchart Gardens; free Wi-Fi. **Cons:** pricey rates; 30-minute drive from Downtown; spa service inconsistent. [$] *Rooms from: C$364* ✉ *849 Verdier Ave., Brentwood Bay* ☎ *250/544–2079, 888/544–2079* 🌐 *www.brentwoodbayresort.com* 🛏 *33 rooms, 2 villas* 🍴 *No meals.*

Activities

KAYAKING

Pacifica Paddle Sports
WATER SPORTS | FAMILY | Operating out of Brentwood Bay and Canoe Cove, here's where to find kayak, canoe, and stand-up paddleboard rentals and lessons. Plus, there are five-hour tours, including lunch, that explore the intertidal waters and coves in and around the peninsula. ✉ *Brentwood Bay, 789 Saunders La., Brentwood Bay* ☎ *250/665–7411* 🌐 *www.pacificapaddle.com* 🎫 *Tours C$135.*

Sidney

23 km (14 miles) north of Victoria on Hwy. 17.

Sidney, short for Sidney-by-the-Sea, is an inviting seaside town just 30 minutes north of Victoria. Home to the Washington State Ferry terminal (vessels travel to Anacortes via the San Juan Islands), and just five minutes south of the BC Ferries terminal, it's worth a stop or even a weekend visit. The streets are lined with independent shops, including a wealth of bookstores—so many, in fact, that Sidney has earned a place as Canada's only official Booktown (🌐 *www.sidneybooktown.ca*). Be sure to visit the tiny, pack-to-the-rafters museum (🌐 *www.sidneymuseum.ca*). Sidney's parklike waterfront, which houses a marine ecology center as well as cafés, restaurants, and a wheelchair-accessible waterfront path, is a launching point for kayakers, whale-watchers, and ecotour boats heading out to explore the Gulf Islands National Park Reserve offshore.

GETTING HERE AND AROUND

Bus 72, usually a double-decker, serves Sidney and the Swartz Bay ferry terminal from Downtown Victoria. Sidney itself is easily explored on foot.

◉ Sights

British Columbia Aviation Museum

MUSEUM | **FAMILY** | Volunteers passionate about the history of flight have lovingly restored several dozen historic military and civilian airplanes, and even a 1910-era flying machine, at this museum near Victoria's International Airport. A 1957 Vickers Viscount, one of the world's first commercial turbo-prop airliners, a 1970s kit-built helicopter, and a model of Leonardo da Vinci's Ornithopter are among the many aircraft displayed in the museum's two hangars. Tours take about an hour. ⊠ *1910 Norseman Rd., Sidney* ☎ *250/655–3300* ⊕ *www.bcam. net* 🎫 *C$10.*

Deep Cove Winery

WINERY/DISTILLERY | At the northern tip of the Saanich Peninsula, Deep Cove Winery specializes in estate-grown Ortega and Pinot Gris varieties. There's a year-round tasting bar as well as an area (and a patio in summer) that hosts many special events from jazz evenings, yoga-chocolate-wine sessions, and paint nights. ⊠ *11195 Chalet Rd., North Saanich* ☎ *250/656–2552* ⊕ *www.musewinery.ca* 🎫 *Tastings: C$7.50.*

Sidney Spit

NATIONAL/STATE PARK | **FAMILY** | In summer, a passenger ferry run by Alpine Sidney Spit Ferry (⊕ *www.alpinegroup.ca*), makes the half-hour trip several times a day to this long stretch of beach on Sidney Island, part of the Gulf Islands National Park Reserve. Hiking trails and picnic sites make for a pleasant day on the island. ⊠ *Sidney* ☎ *250/474–5145 ferry information, 250/654–4000 park information* ⊕ *www.pc.gc.ca/gulf* 🎫 *Park: free; ferry: C$19.*

Shaw Centre for the Salish Sea

ZOO | **FAMILY** | A simulated ride underwater in a deep-sea elevator is just the beginning of a visit to this fun and educational marine interpretive center. Devoted entirely to the aquatic life and conservation needs of the Salish Sea—the waters south and east of Vancouver Island—the small but modern center displays local sea life, including luminous jellyfish, bright purple starfish, wolf eels, rockfish, and octopi. Hands-on activities and touch tanks delight kids, who also love the high-tech effects, including a floor projection that ripples when stepped on and a pop-up tank you can poke your head into. ⊠ *9811 Seaport Pl., Sidney* ☎ *250/665–7511* ⊕ *www.salishseacentre.org* 🎫 *C$17.95* ⟳ *Last admission 30 mins before closing.*

🏨 Hotels

Sidney Pier Hotel & Spa

$$$ | **HOTEL** | Stylish and ecologically friendly, this glass-and-stone boutique hotel on the parklike waterfront has helped introduce Sidney to more travelers. **Pros:** lovely views; eco-friendly; free airport and ferry shuttle in summer; pet-friendly. **Cons:** 30 minutes from Downtown; no pool; staff can be a bit nonchalant. 💲 *Rooms from: C$245* ⊠ *9805 Seaport Pl., Sidney* ☎ *250/655–9445, 866/659–9445* ⊕ *www.sidneypier. com* 🛏 *46 rooms, 9 suites* ⦿ *No meals.*

🏃 Activities

Lochside Regional Trail

BICYCLING | This fairly level, mostly car-free route follows an old rail bed for 29 km (18 miles) past farmland, wineries, and beaches from the ferry terminals at Swartz Bay and Sidney to Downtown Victoria. It joins the Seaside Touring Route at Cordova Bay and meets the Galloping Goose Trail just north of Downtown Victoria. ⊠ *Sidney* ☎ *250/360-3000* ⊕ *www. crd.bc.ca/parks.*

The West Shore

View Royal is 6.8 km (4.2 miles) west of Victoria on Hwy. 1A; Metchosin is 22 km (13.6 miles) west of Victoria on Hwy. 1A.

West of Downtown Victoria, along highways 1 and 14, are the rapidly growing communities of View Royal, Colwood, the Highlands, Langford, and Metchosin, collectively known as the West Shore Communities. Although its rural nature is quickly giving way to suburban development, the area is worth a visit for its wilderness parks and national historic sites.

GETTING HERE AND AROUND

The easiest way to reach the West Shore is to take either Highway 1 or Highway 14.

Sights

Fort Rodd Hill and Fisgard Lighthouse National Historic Sites of Canada
MILITARY SITE | FAMILY | The world's best-preserved coastal artillery fort (it dates to 1895) and Canada's oldest west coast lighthouse occupy a parklike backdrop 13 km (8 miles) west of Victoria. You can walk through most of the buildings, including the lighthouse keeper's house, guardhouses, and the delightfully named fortress-plotting room. Interactive exhibits in the lighthouse let you navigate a 19th-century schooner. Wandering deer, forest trails, an interpretive nature trail, and historic military hardware share the rolling seaside site, and the views from the gun emplacements over the entrance to Esquimalt Harbour are fabulous. Between mid-May and mid-October you can stay the night in one of five oTEN-Tiks (a cross between a tent and cabin) on-site. Each sleeps six and must be reserved in advance. To get here, take Highway 1A west to Ocean Boulevard. ⊠ *603 Fort Rodd Hill Rd., off Ocean Blvd., West Shore* ☎ *250/478–5849,*

877/737–3783 cabin reservations ⊕ *www.pc.gc.ca* ⊠ *Fort C$4; tent cabins C$120 per night.*

Goldstream Provincial Park
NATIONAL/STATE PARK | FAMILY | Eagles, bears, and three species of salmon thrive in this 477-hectare (1,180-acre) wilderness park 16 km (10 miles) north of Downtown Victoria. Picnic areas, easy riverside walks, and challenging hikes draw visitors in summer. The latest addition is a skills development trail for mountain-bikers. In winter, a spotting scope is set up in the Goldstream Nature House to watch hundreds of bald eagles gather to feed on salmon. Naturalists provide guidance and interpretive programs at the Nature House, a year-round visitor center that's a 10-minute walk from the parking lot. ⊠ *Hwy. 1, at Finlayson Arm Rd., Langford, West Shore* ☎ *250/474–1336* ⊕ *www.env.gov.bc.ca/bcparks* ⊠ *Donations accepted.*

Beaches

Witty's Lagoon Regional Park
BEACH—SIGHT | FAMILY | About 30 minutes west of Downtown Victoria, this park has a sandy beach, forest trails, marshlands, and a large lagoon—and it's home to 160 species of birds. There's also a nature house (250/474-2454) that presents interpretive programs. **Amenities:** parking; toilets. **Best for:** solitude; walking. ⊠ *Metchosin Rd., between Duke and Witty Beach Rds., West Shore* ☎ *250/360–3000* ⊕ *www.crd.bc.ca/parks.*

🛏 Hotels

The Westin Bear Mountain Golf Resort & Spa, Victoria
$$$$ | RESORT | Two Nicklaus Design golf courses are the draw at this resort about 30 minutes northwest of the city center. **Pros:** challenging golf; great spa and health club; terrific views. **Cons:** a car is essential; C$22 nightly resort fee ;

corridors narrow and a bit tired. $ *Rooms from: C$345* ✉ *1999 Country Club Way, West Shore* ☎ *250/391–7160, 888/533–2327* ⊕ *www.bearmountain.ca* ☉ *Online, advance booking discount available* ⊷ *156 rooms* ⦿ *No meals.*

⚡ Activities

GOLF

Bear Mountain Golf & Country Club

GOLF | Built near the top of a 1,100-foot mountain about 30 minutes north of Victoria, this purpose-built resort is home to Canada's only Nicklaus-designed 36-hole duo. Created by Jack Nicklaus and his son Steve, the rugged Mountain Course is known for its elevation changes and views—especially from the 14th hole, which is built on a cliff ledge with striking views across the city. The more user-friendly Valley Course offers plenty of challenge at a slightly lower elevation. The two courses are the centerpiece of a resort that includes a hotel, a spa, and several restaurants. ✉ *1999 Country Club Way, off Millstream Rd. and Bear Mountain Pkwy., West Shore* ☎ *250/744–2327, 888/533–2327* ⊕ *www.bearmountain.ca* 🏷 *C$199 Valley Course; C$259 Mountain Course* 🏌 *Mountain Course: 18 holes, 6891 yards, par 70. Valley Course: 18 holes, 6807 yards, par 71.*

Golf Vancouver Island

GOLF | This organization has details about the island's courses, golf packages, special deals and the golf trail that takes in 13 courses between Victoria and Campbell River, making up a 250-km golf trail. ✉ *Victoria* ☎ *877/393-6985* ⊕ *www.golfvancouverisland.ca.*

Olympic View Golf Club

GOLF | The distant peaks of the Olympic Mountains are the backdrop to this bucolic par-72 course, home to two waterfalls and 12 lakes. The first BC course played by Tiger Woods, it's about 30 minutes' drive west of Downtown Victoria. ✉ *643 Latoria Rd., off Veterans' Memorial Pkwy., West Shore* ☎ *250/474–3673, 800/446–5322* ⊕ *www.olympicviewgolf.com* 🏷 *C$65; C$79 at weekends; golf packages offered online* 🏌 *18 holes, 6600 yards, par 72.*

HIKING AND WALKING

Goldstream Provincial Park

HIKING/WALKING | This wilderness park, just 16 km (10 miles) north of town, has a vast network of trails, from wheelchair-accessible paths through ancient Douglas fir and cedar forests to challenging hikes to the view-blessed peak of Mt. Finlayson. Trails also lead to the 47-meter-tall (154-foot) Niagara Falls. ✉ *Hwy. 1, at Finlayson Arm Rd., West Shore* ☎ *250/474-1336* ⊕ *www.env.gov.bc.ca/bcparks.*

Chapter 11

VANCOUVER ISLAND

Updated by
Vanessa Pinniger

◉ Sights	🍴 Restaurants	🛏 Hotels	🛍 Shopping	🍸 Nightlife
★★★★★	★★★★★	★★★★★	★★☆☆☆	★☆☆☆☆

WELCOME TO VANCOUVER ISLAND

TOP REASONS TO GO

★ **Storm-Watching in Tofino:** Its beaches and rainforests make Tofino one of BC's most sublime warm-weather environments and one of Canada's top surf spots; come November, the rampant fury of its coastal storms is an even more extraordinary experience.

★ **Enjoying the Rustic Charms of the Gulf Islands:** Whether you choose well-developed Salt Spring Island, pretty Galiano Island, historic Mayne Island, beachy Pender Island, or remote Saturna Island, you'll find a wealth of experiences.

★ **Exploring the Cowichan Valley:** With excellent food, wine, and First Nations culture, the valley makes a great excursion from Victoria for foodies or families.

★ **Traveling to Sooke and Beyond:** Bike or hike along the Galloping Goose Trail to Sooke, or drive scenic Highway 14 to the wilderness beaches and trails of the island's southwest coast.

1 Sooke. The southwest coast of Vancouver Island is heavily forested.

2 Mill Bay. Mill Bay is home to shops and cafés.

3 Cobble Hill. This village is in the heart of the Cowichan Valley.

4 Cowichan Bay. This seaside village teems with maritime charm.

5 Duncan. Located in the Cowichan Valley.

6 Chamainus. This town is known for its huge heritage murals.

7 Tofino. A tiny village on the rugged west coast.

8 Ucluelet. A fishing village with a growing culinary scene.

9 Pacific Rim National Park. Land meets sea along the coastline.

10 Salt Spring Island. The most popular of the Southern Gulf Islands.

11 Galiano Island. Known for its lush forests.

12 Mayne Island. The smallest of the Southern Gulf Islands.

13 Pender Island. These are two islands, North Pender and South Pender.

14 Saturna Island. The most remote of the Southern Gulf Islands.

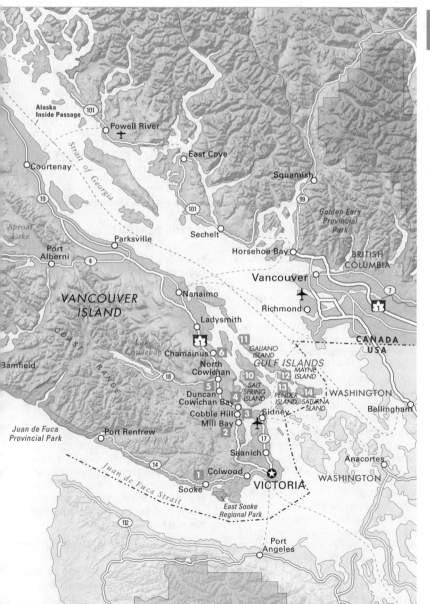

Alaska
Inside Passage

101 Powell River

East Cove

Courtenay

Strait of Georgia

Squamish

19

99

Sproat
Lake

Port
Alberni

4

Parksville

Sechelt

101

Golden Ears
Provincial
Park

Horsehoe Bay

BRITISH
COLUMBIA

Vancouver

VANCOUVER
ISLAND

Nanaimo

Richmond

7

11

COAST

Ladysmith

1

Chamainus 6

11

GALIANO
ISLAND

CANADA
USA

Bamfield

RANGE

18

Lake
Cowichan

North
Cowichan

5

GULF ISLANDS

10

SALT
SPRING
ISLAND

12

MAYNE
ISLAND

Duncan
Cowichan Bay

4

13

PENDER
ISLAND

14

SATURNA
ISLAND

WASHINGTON

Juan de Fuca
Provincial Park

Port Renfrew

Cobble Hill
Mill Bay

3

2

Sidney

Bellingham

17

Saanich

14

Sooke

Colwood

1

VICTORIA

Anacortes

WASHINGTON

Juan de Fuca Strait

East Sooke
Regional Park

112

Port
Angeles

With a few days in the area, you have time to explore farther on Vancouver Island than just Victoria. Sooke and the southwest coast, the Cowichan Valley, or one of the Gulf Islands can make an easy day-trip from Victoria. These three regions can be connected, so you don't have to retrace your steps. More time? Head to Tofino, Ucluelet, and the Pacific Rim National Park Reserve.

How to choose? For wilderness beaches and forested hiking trails, take Highway 14 or cycle the Galloping Goose Trail to Sooke and the southwest coast. For food, wine, and First Nations culture, head north over the stunning Malahat Drive to the Cowichan Valley. Arts, crafts, kayaking, white-shell beaches, and a touch of neo-hippie island culture await those who visit Salt Spring Island, especially on market Saturdays (Salt Spring is also the only side trip easily manageable by public transport). You can truly get away from it all on the islands of Galiano, Mayne, or Pender. For families, the Cowichan Valley, with its interesting nature centers, has the most obvious kid appeal, though all three destinations have beaches, forests, and cute farm animals.

Wherever you go, food will play a big part in your experience. Vancouver Islanders are often credited with starting the "loca-vore" movement. Wild salmon, Pacific oysters, locally made artisanal cheeses, forest-foraged mushrooms, organic vegetables, local microbrews, and wines from the island's many wineries can all be sampled here.

MAJOR REGIONS

Just 45 minutes west of Victoria (and continuing another 48 miles along the coast toward Port Renfrew), **Sooke**, and the rest of the southwest coast of Vancouver Island, is heavily forested and beautiful.

The fertile **Cowichan Valley,** less than an hour north of Victoria, is filled with great restaurants, wineries, and farm stands, and its towns offer a wealth of First Nations culture, making it an excursion suitable for either adults or families. Destinations include Mill Bay, Cobble Hill, Cowichan Bay, Duncan, and Chemainus.

The stretch of open coast along the western edge of Vancouver Island has turned winter storm-watching into an art. And the summers here sparkle. **Tofino** and **Ucluelet** are the tourism-oriented towns at either end of the **Pacific Rim National Park Reserve.**

Of the hundreds of **Gulf Islands** sprinkled across Georgia Strait between Vancouver Island and the mainland, the most popular and accessible are Galiano, Mayne, Pender, Saturna, and Salt Spring. A temperate climate, white-shell beaches, rolling pastures, and forests are common to all, but each island has a unique flavor. Though rustic, they're not undiscovered. Writers, artists, and craftspeople as well as weekend cottagers and retirees from Vancouver and Victoria take full advantage of them. Hotel reservations are a good idea in summer. Only Salt Spring has a town, but food and accommodations are available on all the islands.

Planning

Getting Here and Around

Vancouver Island and the Gulf Islands are located off the southwest coast of mainland British Columbia across the Strait of Georgia, also known as the Salish Sea. The options for getting here and getting around are by air (commercial airlines or floatplanes) or by sea (BC Ferries, water taxi, or chartered boat).

AIR

The major airports on Vancouver Island are Victoria International Airport (YYJ), Nanaimo Airport (YCD), Campbell River Airport (YBL), Comox Valley Airport (YQQ), and Port Hardy Airport (YZT). You can also fly into the tiny Tofino-Ucluelet Airport (YAZ) from Vancouver year-round and from Victoria from May through October.

Floatplanes serve many of the region's islands and coastal areas. For the Gulf Islands, Harbour Air Seaplanes has regular service from Downtown Vancouver to Salt Spring and Pender islands. Seair Seaplanes fly from Vancouver Airport to the Southern Gulf Islands and from the Downtown Vancouver harbor to Nanaimo. Saltspring Air flies from Downtown Vancouver and Vancouver International Airport to the Southern Gulf Islands and to Maple Bay, near Duncan, in the Cowichan Valley. Kenmore Air has summer

floatplane service from Seattle to the Gulf Islands. There is no scheduled floatplane service between Victoria and the Gulf Islands. Charter flights are available on Ocean Air Floatplanes.

Pacific Coastal Airlines operates daily flights (on small 19-passenger planes) into Tofino (YAZ) from Vancouver International Airport's South Terminal (YVR) year-round. Northwest Seaplanes runs charter flights from its terminal at Renton, near Seattle, to Tofino and Ucluelet. Harbour Air Seaplanes runs seaplane charters from Vancouver, Victoria, Nanaimo, and other BC destinations.

BOAT AND FERRY

BC Ferries has frequent, year-round passenger and vehicle service to Vancouver Island: it's a 1½-hour crossing from Tsawwassen, about an hour south of Vancouver, to Swartz Bay, about 30 minutes north of Victoria on the Saanich Peninsula. There are also regular sailings from Horseshoe Bay (a 45-minute drive north of Vancouver) to Departure Bay, 3 km (2 miles) north of Nanaimo, and from Tsawwassen to Duke Point, 15 km (9 miles) south of Nanaimo; these are a good choice if you're en route to Tofino; from Depature Bay it's another two- to three-hour drive, via Port Alberni, to Ucluelet and Tofino. On these routes to and from the mainland, car reservations are highly recommended; for busier sailings, they're required. BC Ferries also sail to the Southern Gulf Islands from Vancouver and Vancouver Island; ferries cross several times a day between Brentwood Bay on the Saanich Peninsula and Mill Bay in the Cowichan Valley.

BC Ferries sail from Swartz Bay to all five of the Gulf Islands, several times a day. Sailings range from half an hour to more than an hour, depending on stops. Bikes, pets, and foot passengers are welcome. Ferries from the BC mainland leave from Tsawwassen, just south of Vancouver. Reservations are recommended for these routes. The ferry journey from Tsawwassen to Salt Spring takes 90 minutes to three hours (depending on the number of intermediate stops) and less for the other islands. Travel between the islands on BC Ferries is possible but generally requires an overnight stay at one of the islands. A fun, low-cost way to cruise the islands is to take one of BC Ferries' Gulf Islands Day Trips—traveling as foot passenger from Swartz Bay, around the islands and back, without disembarking. It's also possible to visit Mayne and Galiano from Salt Spring via water taxi, which doubles as the island school boat.

Lady Rose Marine Services takes passengers on a packet freighter from Port Alberni to various points on Vancouver Island's west coast. The MV *Francis Barkley* sails from Port Alberni to the Broken Group Islands and Ucluelet on Monday, Wednesday, and Friday between early June and mid-September, and to Bamfield and waypoints on Tuesday, Thursday, and Saturday year-round. Sunday stops (in summer) are Bamfield and the Broken Group Islands, where the company operates Sechart Lodge, a floating base for kayakers. Round-trip fares are C$82 to Ucluelet, and C$78 to Bamfield or the Broken Group Islands. ☎ *250/723–8313, 800/663–7192* ⊕ *www.ladyrosemarine. com*

CONTACTS Gulf Islands Water Taxi. ✉ *1206e 115 Fulford-Ganges Rd., Salt Spring Island* ☎ *250/537–2510* ⊕ *www. gulfislandswatertaxi.com.*

BUS

Pacific Coach lines runs several times a day between Downtown Vancouver and Downtown Victoria. Tofino Bus Island Express connects Victoria and Nanaimo to Ucluelet and Tofino. Tofino Bus Island Express also runs Tofino Transit, which offers a summer-only shuttle service in the Tofino area. Greyhound also serves Tofino and most other towns on Vancouver Island. BC Transit provides city bus service in several Vancouver Island communities. BC Transit's Victoria network extends as far as Sooke, Sidney, and Swartz Bay. Cowichan Valley Regional Transit, a separate BC Transit network, offers a limited service in Duncan and the Cowichan Valley. Salt Spring Island has a small BC transit system serving the ferry terminals and the village of Ganges, but it doesn't meet every ferry. The other Gulf Islands don't have transit services. *For information on bus companies, see Bus Travel in Travel Smart.*

CONTACTS BC Transit. ☎ *250/382–6161* ⊕ *www.bctransit.com.* **Greyhound.** ☎ *800/661–8747* ⊕ *www.greyhound.ca.*

When to Go

July and August are, not surprisingly, peak season on Vancouver Island. That's when the weather is fine, and all that hiking, camping, boating, and outdoor fun is at its best. September, with its quieter pace, harvest festivals, and lingering sunshine, may be the perfect time to visit. Increasingly, storm-watchers are flocking to Tofino and Ucluelet in winter to watch dramatic tempests pound the coast. April is also a prime month for the west coast: that's when 20,000 gray whales swim by on their way to Alaska and when the Pacific Rim Whale Festival welcomes visitors.

Making the Most of Your Time

If you're driving (and a car really is essential for exploring the island), pick a circular route to avoid retracing your steps: drive the Pacific Marine Circle Route through Sooke, Port Renfrew and the Cowichan Valley, link the Saanich Peninsula and Cowichan Valley with a ride on BC Ferries' Mill Bay Ferry, or combine a trip to the Saanich Peninsula or Cowichan Valley with a visit to Salt Spring Island. For the Gulf Islands, it's best to pick one or two islands to explore; the ferry schedules are not conducive to island-hopping. In a hurry? Floatplanes serve the Gulf Islands and the Cowichan Valley from Vancouver, and the experience is unforgettable. Another option? Pick a resort or seaside inn, fly in, stay there, and relax.

Tofino, a five-hour drive across the island from Victoria, is a separate trip altogether; but flying in and renting a car in Tofino is always an option. Three full days are about the minimum: once you've made the trek from Vancouver, it takes a day to unwind and adapt to the slower pace here. A quick conversation with your host will help you hit the highlights—the best spots to view wildlife, the top trails (some get washed out in stormy weather), when to browse the galleries (some close Monday), and what musicians are playing (if nightlife is on your list).

Festivals

MARCH
The **Pacific Rim Whale Festival** (⊕ www.pacificrimwhalefestival.com) marks the spring migration of an estimated 20,000 Pacific gray whales between Mexico and the Arctic, with tours, talks, crafts, food, and cultural events for the whole family. You can try everything from building sand sculptures to decorating sea-creature cookies.

MAY
Fishers, diners, and chefs gather to celebrate local fisheries and boat-to-table cuisine at **Feast Tofino** (⊕ www.feasttofino.com), a monthlong culinary event in May. The **Tofino Shorebird Festival** (⊕ www.tourismtofino.com) celebrates the thousands of shorebirds that migrate

north from Central and South America to tundra breeding grounds in the Arctic. The date changes annually, so check with Tourism Tofino.

JULY
The **Pacific Rim Summer Festival** (⊕ www.pacificrimarts.ca) is a celebration of music, dance, and the arts during the first two weeks of July.

AUGUST
Hundreds of imaginatively crafted lanterns make the **Tofino Lantern Festival** (⊕ www.tourismtofino.com) a sight to behold. The same month, the **Vancouver Island Feast of Fields** (⊕ feastoffields.com) celebrates local food in a lavish celebration on an area farm.

NOVEMBER
The humble bivalve is celebrated during the **Clayoquot Oyster Festival** (facebook.com/Clayoquotoysterfestival), a three-day gastronomic adventure.

Restaurants

Rich farmland, plentiful seafood, and a burgeoning wine industry make locavore dining a no-brainer on Vancouver Island, where even take-out places offer wild salmon and organic greens. Global influences, from fish tacos to sushi, have made their mark on the menus, but the ingredients are resolutely local. Must tries? Cowichan Valley wines, cedar plank salmon, and Nanaimo bars—the ubiquitous sweet treats named for the Vancouver Island city. As you move farther from Victoria, prices keep going up, and though food is pricey, it's consistently good—even in the humblest spots. Tofino and, to a lesser extent, Ucluelet, offer a range of eateries, from view-blessed resort dining to funky local hangouts; one thing you won't find in either place is a chain restaurant or fast food outlet. Everything is owner-operated and one-of-a-kind here. Enjoy.

Restaurant reviews have been shortened. For full information, visit Fodors.com.

What It Costs in Canadian dollars			
$	$$	$$$	$$$$
RESTAURANTS			
under C$13	C$13– C$20	C$21– C$30	over C$30
HOTELS			
under C$126	C$126– C$195	C$196– C$300	over C$300

Hotels

Accommodations on Vancouver Island range from cozy farmstays to lavish seaside resorts, from homey country inns to funky beach houses. Typically one-of-a-kind and independently run, hotels here make the most of their stunning forest and seaside settings.

In Tofino and Ucluelet, prices for lodging and dining are relatively high because this is such a remote destination. Rates vary widely through the seasons, winter being the lowest: luxury lodge stays during the winter storm-watching season can cost as little as a third of summer rates.

Hotel reviews have been shortened. For full information, visit Fodors.com.

Visitor Information

Tourism Vancouver Island also offers a good amount of information on Vancouver Island.

CONTACTS Tourism Cowichan. ☏ *888/303–3337* ⊕ *www.tourismcowichan.com.* **Tourism Vancouver Island.** ☏ *250/754–3500* ⊕ *www.tourismvi.ca.*

Sooke

Sooke is 28 km (17 miles) west of Victoria on Hwy. 14.

The village of Sooke, on the shore of Juan de Fuca Strait about a 45-minute drive west of Victoria, is the last stop for gas and supplies before heading out to the beaches and hiking trails of the island's wild and scenic southwest coast.

Watch for the red-and-white lighthouse lamp at the first traffic light as you enter Sooke on Highway 14. It sits in front of the Sooke Visitor Information Centre, which also houses a small museum displaying local First Nations artifacts.

The tiny fishing village of Port Renfrew has national and regional parks in all directions. At the end of Highway 14 you'll find the grueling West Coast Trail and the more accessible but still daunting Juan de Fuca Marine Trail. Salmon fishing is also a big reason for visiting the area. Not to be misssed is spectacular Botanical Beach with its tide pools teeming with marine life at low tide. The town itself has a general store, a pub, restaurants, fishing lodges, B&Bs, a campsite, and a range of rustic and newly renovated cottages. There's no garage in town, but gas is available at the marina, which does not accept credit cards (it's best to play it safe and fill up your tank before leaving Sooke).

GETTING HERE AND AROUND
Sooke is a 45-minute drive, mostly via Highway 14, west from Victoria, or a pleasant three- to four-hour cycle along the car-free Galloping Goose Trail. BC Transit also runs buses from Downtown Victoria as far as the town of Sooke.

From Sooke, the narrow and winding Highway 14 runs 77 km (48 miles) through birch and fir woods, with occasional sea views, to the fishing village of Port Renfrew. From Port Renfrew, a 48-km (30-mile) paved back road leads

Stunning coastal views can be found in Vancouver Island's Juan de Fuca Provincial Park.

inland to Lake Cowichan in the Cowichan Valley.

VISITOR INFORMATION

CONTACTS Sooke Region Museum and Visitor Centre. ⊠ *2070 Phillips Rd., off Hwy. 14, Sooke* ☎ *250/642–6351, 866/888–4748* ⊕ *www.sookeregionmuseum.ca.*

◉ Sights

Botanical Beach

BEACH—SIGHT | FAMILY | This "natural jewel" in Juan de Fuca Provincial Park is known for the abundance of marine life found in its rich tide pools and the geological features carved out along the shoreline. ⊠ *Port Renfrew* ⊹ *A 15-minute walk from the Botanical Beach parking lot located at kilometre 47, the western terminus of the Juan de Fuca Marine Trail.* ⊕ *www.portrenfrew.com/botbeach.*

Carmanah Walbran Provincial Park

NATIONAL/STATE PARK | Logging roads west of Port Renfrew lead to this vast, rugged wilderness park, home to some of the world's largest spruce trees, some more than 800 years old, and ancient cedars over 1,000 years old. Be prepared with supplies, because this is an extremely remote region with no services whatsoever. Watch for logging trucks en route and bears once you're inside the park. ⊠ *Off Hwy. 14, Port Renfrew* ⊹ *Park access is via private logging roads* ⊕ *www.env.gov.bc.ca/bcparks.*

East Sooke Regional Park

NATIONAL/STATE PARK | FAMILY | Hiking trails, tide pools, beaches, and views of the Olympic Mountains draw visitors to this more than 3,500-acre wilderness recreation park 2½ km (1½ miles) east of Sooke on the south side of Sooke Harbour. The park's 10-km (6-mile) coast trail is rated one of the top day hikes in Canada, and the entire area is a birders' paradise, especially during the annual hawk migration from mid-September to late October. ⊠ *East Sooke Rd., Sooke* ⊕ *www.eastsookepark.com.*

Vancouver Island's Grape Escape

Thanks to a Mediterranean-like climate, rich soil, and loads of sunshine southern Vancouver Island is blossoming into one of North America's fastest-growing, if least known, wine regions. Cool-climate varietals—such as Pinot Noir, Ortega, and Pinot Gris—do well here, at a latitude equivalent to northern France, but it's not all about grapes: English-style craft cider, berry wines, and mead are also among the local specialties.

The region centers around the Cowichan Valley, a bucolic area about a 45-minute drive north of Victoria. Dubbed "The New Provence" for its proliferation of organic farms and wineries, the valley is home to more than a dozen wineries. More are on the Saanich Peninsula, about 20 minutes north of Victoria and, increasingly, dotted across the offshore Gulf Islands.

Touring is easy: burgundy-and-white Wine Route signs, as well as maps available in local tourist offices, show the way. BC Ferries' Mill Bay Ferry links the Cowichan Valley to the Saanich Peninsula.

Most of Vancouver Island's wineries are small, family-run, labor-of-love operations. Finding the wineries, hidden down winding country lanes, tucked between farm stands, is part of the fun. Not all of them have enough staff to offer tours, but most offer tastings—it's always a good idea to call ahead. Some of the area's best lunches are served on winery patios.

Cowichan Valley Wineries

There are several notable wineries in the Cowichan Valley.

- Cherry Point Estate Wines in Cobble Hill

- Venturi-Schulze Vineyards in Cobble Hill

- Unsworth Vineyards in Mill Bay

- Enrico Winery in Mill Bay

- Rocky Creek Winery in Cowichan Bay

- Blue Grouse Estate Winery and Vineyard in Duncan

- Averill Creek in Duncan

- Vigneti Zanatta Winery in Duncan

- Emandare Vineyard in Duncan

Saanich Peninsula Wineries

Several wineries and other drink artisans can be found in greater Victoria itself.

- Church & State Wines in Brentwood Bay, Central Saanich

- Deep Cove Winery in North Saanich

- Sea Cider Farm & Ciderhouse in Saanichton

French Beach Provincial Park
NATIONAL/STATE PARK | FAMILY | This provincial park, on the scenic Strait of Juan de Fuca 21 km (13 miles) west of Sooke, comprises a sand-and-pebble beach, a campground, and seaside trails. The shoreline is an excellent spot for whale-watching, as migrating grays and resident killer whales often feed in the area. **Amenities:** toilets; showers; water sports. **Best for:** swimming; walking; windsurfing. ⊠ Hwy. 14, Sooke ☎ 250/474–1336 ⊕ www.env.gov.bc.ca/bcparks.

Juan de Fuca Provincial Park

NATIONAL/STATE PARK | Extending from Jordan River to near Port Renfrew, Juan de Fuca Provincial Park takes in several beaches, including China Beach, with soft, sandy beaches dotted with driftwood; Sombrio Beach, a popular surfing spot; and Botanical Beach, with its amazing tidal pools. The **Juan de Fuca Marine Trail** is a tough 48-km (30-mile) wilderness hiking trail running along the shore from China Beach, west of Jordan River, to Botanical Beach, near Port Renfrew. Several trailheads along the way—at China Beach, Sombrio Beach, Parkinson Creek, and Botanical Beach—allow day hikers to walk small stretches of it. ✉ *Hwy. 14, 35 km (22 miles) west of Sooke and 36 km east of Port Renfrew, Sooke* ☎ *250/474–1336* 🌐 *www.env.gov.bc.ca/bcparks.*

Sooke Potholes Provincial Park

BODY OF WATER | **FAMILY** | Locals and visitors come to cool off at Sooke Potholes Provincial Park, home to a series of natural swimming holes carved out of the bedrock of the Sooke River. The area is a popular destination for swimming and picnicking. ✉ *Sooke River Rd., off Hwy. 14, Sooke* 🌐 *www.env.gov.bc.ca.*

Tugwell Creek Honey Farm and Meadery

FARM/RANCH | **FAMILY** | Ever tried mead? Here's your chance. At this little farm about 10 minutes west of Sooke, beekeeper Bob Liptrot produces traditional honey wine, also known as mead, from a pre-Tudor family recipe. The Solstice Metheglin and Vintage Sac are both award winners. There is also a selection of honey available from the farm's own hives. ✉ *8750 West Coast Rd.* ☎ *250/642–1956* 🌐 *www.tugwellcreekfarm.com* 🎟 *C$2 tasting fee* 🕒 *Closed Mon. and Tues. May to Sept.; closed Mon.–Fri. Oct. to April.*

West Coast Trail

TRAIL | Running along the coast from Bamfield to Port Renfrew, this is an extremely rugged 75-km (47-mile) trail for experienced hikers only. It takes an average of six days to complete and is open from May 1 to September 30. A quota system helps the park manage the number of hikers, and reservations, through Parks Canada, are highly recommended between mid-June and mid-September. Hiking requires payment of a reservation fee, ferry fares, and an overnight-use fee. ✉ *Port Renfrew* ☎ *877/737–3783 trail reservations toll-free in Canada and U.S., 519/826–5391 international* 🌐 *parkscanada.gc.ca* 🎟 *C$127.50 overnight-use fee; C$32 ferry fee; C$24.50 reservation fee.*

Whiffen Spit

BEACH—SIGHT | West of Sooke, you'll reach this mile-long natural breakwater that is great for bird-watching and makes for a leisurely scenic walk past sea grass beds and rocks where harbor seals sprawl in the sun. ✉ *Whiffen Spit Rd., off Hwy. 14, Sooke.*

🍴 Restaurants

Shirley Delicious

$ | **CAFÉ** | **FAMILY** | Heading to the beach? Fuel up with a breakfast burrito, a chai latte, or an organic chocolate brownie at this welcoming café 18 km (11 miles) west of Sooke. **Known for:** favorite with locals; made-from-scratch ingredients; good for breakfast. [$] *Average main: C$10* ✉ *2794 Sheringham Point Rd., Sooke* ☎ *778/528–2888* 🕒 *No dinner.*

🛏 Hotels

Best Western Premier Prestige Oceanfront Resort

$$$ | **HOTEL** | This four-story colonial-style hotel opened in 2011 on Sooke's waterfront as the area's first full-service complex, complete with a spa, indoor pool, fitness center, restaurant, wine bar, and convention center. **Pros:** full-service, including valet parking and 24-hour room service; free Wi-Fi throughout; nice recreational activities like a large pool and spa. **Cons:** can get busy with conventions, weddings, and reunions; hotel doesn't really evoke BC; steep walk to the water. [$] *Rooms from: C$205* ✉ *6929 West Coast Rd., Sooke* ☎ *250/642–0805, 800/780–7234* 🌐 *www.bestwestern.com* 🛏 *122 rooms* 🍴 *No meals.*

Point No Point Resort
$$$ | **HOTEL** | **FAMILY** | About 24 km (15 miles) west of Sooke, this cabin compound sits on a bluff next to a long stretch of private beach, with views of Juan de Fuca Strait and the Olympic Mountains; no wonder the 24 cabins and one four-bedroom house are often booked well ahead by repeat visitors. **Pros:** in-room spa treatments available; self-contained cottages assure privacy; good restaurant. **Cons:** remote; no TV or cell coverage in the cabins; Wi-Fi in lobby only. [$] *Rooms from: C$285* ✉ *10829 West Coast Rd., Shirley* ☎ *250/646–2020* 🌐 *www.pointnopointresort.com* 🕒 *Restaurant closed Mon. and Tues. and all of Jan.* 🛏 *25 cabins* 🍴 *No meals.*

Activities

ZIPLINES

A fast-growing sport, zip-trekking involves whizzing through the forest while attached to a cable or zipline.

Adrena Line Zipline Adventure Tours
ZIP LINING | **FAMILY** | About 40 minutes west of Victoria (behind the 17 Mile Pub on the road to Sooke), this adventure center has two suspension bridges and eight zipline routes ranging in length from 150 feet to 1,000 feet. Open daily March to October, it also offers night zipping on full-moon nights. Between May and September, a shuttle bus runs twice daily from the Inner Harbour. ✉ *5128C Sooke Rd., Sooke* ☎ *250/642–1933, 866/947–9145* 🌐 *www.adrenalinezip.com.*

Ucluelet

295 km (183 miles) northwest of Victoria.

Ucluelet, which in the Nuu-chah-nulth First Nations language means "people with a safe landing place," along with the towns of Bamfield and Tofino, serves the Pacific Rim National Park Reserve. Ucluelet is quieter than Tofino and has a less sophisticated ambience. Despite a growing number of crafts shops, restaurants, and B&Bs, it's still more of a fishing village than an ecotourism retreat, although Black Rock Resort competes with Tofino's upscale dining-and-lodging market.

Whale-watching is an important draw as are the winter storms. Ucluelet is the regional base for fishing and for kayaking in the Broken Group Islands, part of the Pacific Rim National Park Reserve. Various charter companies take boats to greet the 20,000 gray whales that pass close to Ucluelet on their migration to the Bering Sea every March and April.

GETTING HERE AND AROUND

Ucluelet is 295 km (183 miles) from Victoria, about a four- or five-hour drive. If you're coming from Vancouver by ferry (to Nanaimo), head north on the Island Highway (Highway 19) to Highway 4, which crosses the island from Parksville to Port Alberni, Ucluelet, and Tofino. It is approximately a two- to three-hour drive from the Nanaimo ferry terminal.

You can also fly from Victoria or Vancouver into Tofino-Ucluelet Airport (YAZ), a more expensive but much faster option. One international car-rental agency (Budget) and one local agency (Tofino Airport Car Rental) rent vehicles. Reservations are highly recommended.

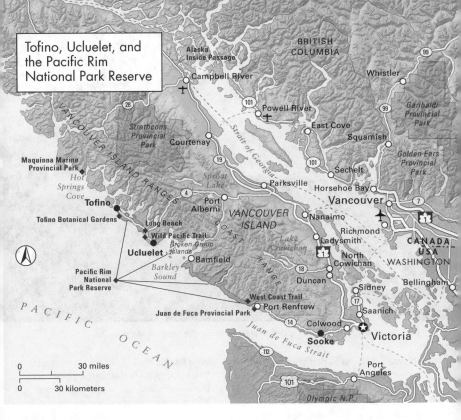

Tofino, Ucluelet, and the Pacific Rim National Park Reserve

Sights

Kwisitis Visitor Centre

INFO CENTER | FAMILY | Perched on a point about a mile off the highway on Wickaninnish Beach, the visitor center offers insights into local culture, flora and fauna, First Nations traditions, local history, and conservation efforts; don't miss the stunning life-size carving of a whaling canoe. Park rangers are on hand to answer questions. The outside deck is perfect for spotting whales, surfers and storms. ⊠ *485 Wick Rd.* ✛ *Off Pacific Rim Hwy. (Hwy. 4) in Pacific Rim National Park* ☎ *250/726–3500* ⊕ *www.pc.gc.ca.*

★ Pacific Rim National Park Reserve

NATIONAL/STATE PARK | This national park has some of Canada's most stunning coastal and rain-forest scenery, abundant wildlife, and a unique marine environment. It comprises three separate units—Long Beach, the Broken Group Islands, and the West Coast Trail—for a combined area of 123,431 acres, and stretches 130 km (81 miles) along Vancouver Island's west coast.

More than 100 islands of the Broken Group Islands archipelago in Barkley Sound can be reached only by boat. The islands and their clear waters are alive with sea lions, seals, and whales, and because the inner waters are much calmer than the surrounding ocean, they provide an excellent environment for kayaking. Guided kayak and charter-boat tours are available from outfitters in Ucluelet, Bamfield, and Port Alberni.

The most popular part of the park, and the only section that can be reached by car, is the Long Beach section. Besides the beach, the Long Beach section of

The still-active Amphitrite Point Lighthouse in Ucluelet is on the scenic Wild Pacific Trail.

the park is home to rich stands of old-growth forest, a wealth of marine and terrestrial wildlife (including black bears, cougars, and sea lions), and a network of coastal and rain-forest hiking paths. A first stop for any first-timer is the visitor center, which doubles as the Ucluelet Visitor Information Office. You can pick up maps and information, and pay park entrance fees here. ☒ *2791 Pacific Rim Hwy.* ☎ *250/726–4600* ⊕ *www.pc.gc.ca* ☞ *Park admission is C$7.80 per person per day.*

Ucluelet Aquarium

ZOO | **FAMILY** | Possibly the world's first catch-and-release aquarium, this intriguing attraction on Ucluelet's waterfront displays local sea life and returns it all to the sea at the end of each season. Touch pools, tanks, and displays reveal the secrets of life right outside the aquarium's doorstep. ☒ *180 Main St.* ☎ *250/726–2782* ⊕ *www.uclueletaquarium.org* ☞ *C$15* ⊙ *Closed Dec.–Mar.*

Wild Pacific Trail

TRAIL | Ucluelet is the starting point for the Wild Pacific Trail, a hiking path that winds along the coast and through the rain forest in two sections: the 2.6-km (1.7-mile) loop starts near Amphitrite lighthouse at the end of Coast Guard road overlooking the Broken Group Islands; the other is 5 km (3 miles) from Big Beach Park to Rocky Bluffs. Take note of the sea-facing trees, bent at right angles in a face-off against the wild and stormy winds. ☒ *Ucluelet* ⊕ *www.wildpacifictrail.com.*

🍴 Restaurants

Heartwood Kitchen Food Outfitter

$$$ | **PACIFIC NORTHWEST** | Located in a historic yellow house, Heartwood serves hearty west coast fare and crowd-pleasing dishes, like chef Ian Riddick's UFC (Ukee fried chicken), buttermilk fried Humboldt squid with pickled bull kelp, and "hipster-style" eggs Benedict. Cooking classes are also offered. **Known for:** west coast feasts; most popular brunch

in town; in the old Matterson House.
[$] *Average main: C$26* ⊠ *1682 Peninsula Rd.* 🕾 ⊕ *www.heartwoodfood.com* ⊙ *No brunch Mon.–Wed.*

Pluvio Restaurant and Rooms

$$$$ | **PACIFIC NORTHWEST** | Former Wickaninnish Inn executive chef Warren Barr and his partner Lily Verney-Downey opened tiny Pluvio to up the culinary scene in Tofino's humble neighboring town. Thoughtfully prepared dishes are made from scratch with local, wild ingredients often foraged by Barr himself. **Known for:** high-end dining in a casual setting; locavore approach; chef forages for ingredients himself. [$] *Average main: C$38* ⊠ *1714 Peninsula Rd.* 🕾 ⊕ *www. pluvio.ca* ⊙ *Closed Jan.–mid-Feb.*

🛏 Hotels

★ Black Rock Oceanfront Resort

$$$$ | **RESORT** | On a rocky ledge at the edge of a shallow inlet, Black Rock Resort is Ucluelet's first upscale, full-service resort. **Pros:** gorgeous views at every turn; chic aesthetic; lovely spa. **Cons:** limited beach access; no pool; fitness room not well equipped. [$] *Rooms from: C$309* ⊠ *596 Marine Dr.* 🕾 *250/726-4800, 877/762-5011* ⊕ *www.blackrock-resort.com* ⇙ *133 suites* ¶◎¶ *No meals.*

A Snug Harbour Inn

$$$$ | **B&B/INN** | On a cliff above the ocean, this couples-oriented B&B has some of the most dramatic views anywhere. **Pros:** friendly vibe; unique location; hot tub. **Cons:** a bit off the beaten track; no on-site dining; no children allowed. [$] *Rooms from: C$429* ⊠ *460 Marine Dr.* 🕾 *250/726-2686, 888/936-5222* ⊕ *www.awesomeview.com* ⇙ *6 rooms* ¶◎¶ *Free breakfast.*

Wya Point Resort

$$$$ | **RENTAL** | **FAMILY** | Choose from ocean-view cedar cottages, rustic yurts, or a family-friendly campground at this resort-style development tucked into 600 acres of coastal rain forest

between Ucluelet and the Pacific Rim National Park Reserve. **Pros:** stunning views; free Wi-Fi; swimmable beach. **Cons:** no restaurant or spa; remote; no pool. [$] *Rooms from: C$676* ⊠ *2695 Tofino-Ucluelet Hwy.* 🕾 *250/726-2625, 844/352-6188* ⊕ *www.wyapoint.com* ⇙ *9 lodges, 15 yurts* ¶◎¶ *No meals.*

🏃 Activities

FISHING
Island West Resort

FISHING | A fleet of 24- to 26-foot boats, knowledgeable guides, and all the gear you need are draws at this full-service fishing resort in Ucluelet. The staff will clean and ice-pack the fish you caught for your departure home. ⊠ *1990 Bay St.* 🕾 *250/726-7515* ⊕ *www.islandwestresort.com.*

KAYAKING
Majestic Ocean Kayaking

KAYAKING | Excursions range from three-hour paddles around the harbor to trips to the Broken Group Islands and Barkley Sound, as well as multiday adventures to Clayoquot Sound and the Deer Group Islands. ⊠ *1167 Helen Rd.* 🕾 *250/726-2868, 800/889-7644* ⊕ *www.oceankayaking.com.*

SURFING

Ucluelet, like Tofino, is a popular year-round surf destination with waters that are equally as cold, so bring your full dry suit summer and winter.

Relic Surf Shop and Surf School

SURFING | These guys are cool dudes, with a shop packed with surfboards and gear. Private and group lessons are offered year-round; they also offer rentals and lessons for stand-up paddleboards. ⊠ *1998 Peninsula Rd.* 🕾 *250/726-4421* ⊕ *www. relicsurfshop.com.*

Wya Point Surf Shop Cafe

SURFING | Just north of the Tofino-Ucluelet Junction, this friendly little surf shop, run by the local Ucluelet First Nation, rents boards and wet suits, sells gear, and offers lessons at all levels. Most of the instructors grew up surfing here and know the local breaks intimately. A food truck parked on-site fuels surfers with homemade breakfasts, elk burgers, and salmon wraps. Heading home? Savvy road-trippers grab a meal here before the long drive to Port Alberni. ⊠ *2201 Pacific Rim Hwy.* ⊹ *Just north of junction between Tofino and Ucluelet* ☎ *250/726–2992* ⊕ *www.wyapointsurfshop.com.*

WHALE-WATCHING

Jamie's Whaling Station

WHALE-WATCHING | If you don't see a whale on your first trip with this well-regarded company, you can take another at no charge. You can book a range of adventures, including kayaking trips and hot-springs tours. The season runs mid-March through October. ⊠ *168 Fraser La.* ☎ *250/726–7444, 877/726–7444* ⊕ *www.jamies.com.*

Subtidal Adventures

WHALE-WATCHING | This company specializes in whale-watching and nature tours to the Broken Group Islands. Choose between trips on an inflatable Zodiac or a 36-foot former coast-guard rescue boat. ⊠ *1950 Peninsula Rd.* ☎ *250/726–7336, 877/444–1134* ⊕ *www.subtidaladventures.com.*

Tofino

42 km (26 miles) northwest of Ucluelet, 337 km (209 miles) northwest of Victoria.

Tofino may be the birthplace of North American storm-watching, but the area's tempestuous winter weather and roiling waves are only two of the many stellar attractions you'll find along British Columbia's wildest coastline. Exquisite tide pooling, expansive wilderness beaches, excellent surfing, and the potential to see some of the continent's largest sea mammals lure thousands of visitors each year.

No one "happens" upon Tofino; it's literally at the end of the road, where Highway 4 meets the mouth of Clayoquot Sound. As Canada's premier surfer village, Tofino has shed much of its 1960s-style counter-culture vibe and transformed itself into a happening tourist destination where fine dining, spa treatments, and eco adventures are par for the course. You can enjoy meandering through old-growth forests, exploring pristine beaches and rocky tidal pools, bathing in natural hot springs, and spotting whales, bears, eagles, and river otters in a natural setting.

While many outdoor activities are confined to spring through fall, surfing continues year-round, regardless of the temperature. November through February is devoted to storm-watching (best enjoyed from a cozy waterfront lodge).

GETTING HERE AND AROUND

Tofino is 314 km (195 miles) from Victoria, about a four- or five-hour drive. If you're coming from Vancouver by ferry (to Victoria or Nanaimo), head north to Parksville via the Trans-Canada Highway (Highway 1) and the Island Highway (Highway 19). From there pick up Highway 4, which crosses the island from Parksville to Port Alberni, Ucluelet, and Tofino. Break up the trip with a lunch or ice-cream break at the Coombs Old Country Market, about 15 km (9 miles) west of Parksville; a good stop for picnic supplies, the store is known for the goats grazing on its sod roof. If you don't want to drive yourself, there's regular bus service from Victoria, but you really need a car to explore the area, so you might have to rent one after arrival.

You can also fly from Victoria or Vancouver, a more expensive but much faster option. One international car-rental agency (Budget) and one local agency (Tofino Airport Car Rental) rent vehicles at Tofino–Long Beach Airport. Reservations are highly recommended.

The seaplane is a common mode of transport in and around the village of Tofino.

Tofino Taxi provides service in Tofino, including airport pickups. Book in advance for night or off-hours service. The Tofino Water Taxi is a boat shuttle to Meares Island, Hot Springs Cove in Maquinna Marine Provincial Park, and other remote offshore sites.

CONTACTS Tofino Airport Car Rental.
☎ 800/311–1512 ⊕ www.tofinoairportcar-rental.com. **Tofino Taxi.** ☎ 250/725–3333 ⊕ www.tourismtofino.com. **Tofino Water Taxi.** ☎ 250/725–8844, 866/794–2537 ⊕ www.tofinowatertaxi.com.

VISITOR INFORMATION

The Pacific Rim Visitor Centre, at the Tofino–Ucluelet junction on Hwy 4, sells park permits and provides free information and maps on the Pacific Rim National Park Reserve and the Tofino-Ucluelet area. The Tofino Vistor Centre, also known as the Cox Bay Visitor Info Centre, is about 10 minutes south of Tofino on Highway 4. Park passes and information are also available at the Kwisitis Visitor Centre, in the Pacific Rim National Park Reserve.

CONTACTS Tofino Visitor Info Centre.
✉ 1426 Pacific Rim Hwy. ☎ 250/725–3414, 888/720–3414 ⊕ www.tourismtofino.com.

Sights

Long Beach
BEACH—SIGHT | FAMILY | The most accessible—and visited—section of the park is the Long Beach Unit, the highlight of which is a 15-km (9-mile) stretch of pristine forest-backed sand just off Highway 4 between Ucluelet and Tofino. Four-hour "beach walk" passes are available at Long Beach Parking Lot only. **Amenities:** parking (fee); toilets. **Best for:** surfing; walking. ✉ Hwy. 4 ✛ 18 km (11 miles) south of Tofino ⊕ www.pc.gc.ca/eng/pn-np/bc/pacificrim/index.aspx ⌦ C$6.20 per adult or C$12.50 per group (4-hr beach walk pass only).

Maquinna Marine Provincial Park
HOT SPRINGS | Geothermal springs tumble down a waterfall and into a series of oceanside rock pools at idyllic Hot

Springs Cove, accessible only by boat or air from Tofino. Here, day trips—which are offered by several Tofino outfitters—usually include a bit of whale-watching en route. Once you arrive at the park, there's a half-hour boardwalk trail through old-growth forest to the site. If you can't bear to leave, or just like the idea of having the springs to yourself in the evening, book a cabin on the *InnChanter* (☎ *250/670–1149* 🌐 *www.innchanter.com*), a historic boat moored near the park. Another popular day trip is to Meares Island, where an easy 20-minute boardwalk trail leads to trees up to 1,600 years old. ✉ *Tofino* 🌐 *www.env.gov.bc.ca/bcparks/explore/parkpgs/maquinna.*

Tofino Botanical Gardens

GARDEN | Trails wind through displays of indigenous plant life, and the occasional whimsical garden sculpture may catch your eye at Tofino Botanical Gardens. The 12-acre waterfront site, about 2 km (1 mile) south of Tofino on the Pacific Rim Highway, is also home to a café and an affordable ecolodge. The admission fee is good for three days. ✉ *1084 Pacific Rim Hwy.* ☎ *250/725–1220* 🌐 *www.tbgf.org* 🎫 *C$12.*

🍴 Restaurants

1909 Kitchen

$$$ | **ECLECTIC** | A new spot on Tofino's ever-expanding culinary scene can be found at the Tofino Resort + Marina, where chef Paul Moran, winner of Top Chef Canada 2019, is working his magic. The avid forager uses locally sourced ingredients on his signature sourdough crust to create artisanal pizzas in an impressive 1000-degree wood-fired Mugnaini oven. **Known for:** Top Chef Canada winner in the kitchen; foraged ingredients; "cook your catch" program. [$] *Average main: C$30* ✉ *634 Campbell St.* ☎ *250/726-6122* 🌐 *www.tofinoresortandmarina.com* 🕒 *No lunch.*

The Common Loaf Bake Shop

$ | **BAKERY** | This red-turreted village-center building has been a bakery and local hangout since the late 1970s. Everything from the panini and muffins to the breakfast pizza is made fresh in-house. **Known for:** cinnamon buns; breakfast pizza; popular with locals. [$] *Average main: C$10* ✉ *180 1st St.* ☎ *250/725–3915* 💳 *No credit cards.*

★ **The Pointe**

$$$$ | **CANADIAN** | With 180-degree views of the crashing surf, the Pointe is *the* top-notch Tofino dining experience. It's renowned for its refined west coast cuisine, which is superbly presented and excellently paired with options from the award-winning wine list—an impressive 11,000-bottle wine cellar is the latest jewel in this grande dame's crown. **Known for:** impeccable service; incredible views; an unforgettable dining experience. [$] *Average main: C$46* ✉ *The Wickaninnish Inn, 500 Osprey La.* ☎ *250/725–3106* 🌐 *thepointerestaurant.ca.*

★ **Schooner Restaurant**

$$$$ | **SEAFOOD** | An institution in downtown Tofino (it's been operating since 1949), the Schooner's main-floor dining room is comfortable and casually upscale. The seafood dishes change frequently, but ask for the signature halibut filet stuffed with Brie, crab, and shrimp in an apple-peppercorn brandy sauce. **Known for:** serving epic seafood and steaks since 1949; great views; stuffed halibut. [$] *Average main: C$38* ✉ *331 Campbell St.* ☎ *250/725–3444* 🌐 *www.schoonerrestaurant.ca* 🕒 *Closed Mon. No lunch.*

Shelter

$$$ | **CANADIAN** | This big, bustling spot on the edge of town draws both locals and visitors for burgers, chowder, and fish-and-chips for lunch, and dinners of shucked oysters, pan-seared salmon, and grilled rib eyes. Chef Matty Kane's handmade fettuccini with freshly caught mussels and side-striped prawns has

Pacific Rim Storm-Watching

No one's really sure when the concept of "bad weather" morphed into "good weather," but on the tourism-friendly Pacific Rim, nasty storms are usually considered quite fine indeed.

November through March is formally storm-watching season, and thousands of people travel from around the world to witness spectacularly violent weather. Veteran storm-watchers are known to keep an eye on the weather channels and pack their bags quickly for Tofino or Ucluelet when storm predictions are particularly, well, grim.

Throughout the winter, but particularly during the "peak season" of December through February, as many as 15 "good storms" arrive per month. Winds from the ocean exceed 50 kph (30 mph) and teeming rain—even hail, sleet, or snow—arrives horizontally. Massive waves thunder onto the beaches and crash over the rocky headlands and islets, sending spray soaring. Towering evergreen trees crackle and lean; logs are tossed helter-skelter, high onto kelp-strewn beaches. Unusual storm clouds, mists, and rainbows add to the beauty. And as if the sights weren't enough, expect to hear the eerie sounds of a screaming wind, pounding surf—even the rattling of double-paned windows—unless you happen to be behind reinforced triple-glazed windows, in which case the whole show unfolds in near silence. And that's even more surreal.

The hotels and B&Bs love the storm season because it fills rooms in what could otherwise be a bleak time of year. And it must be admitted that most storm-watching takes place in considerable comfort—particularly at the luxury hotels along Cox Bay, Chesterman Beach, and MacKenzie Beach. These and other waterfront properties in the Tofino-Ucluelet region have shrewdly developed "storm-watching packages," in which treats abound (and rates tumble). Champagne on arrival, fashionable wet-weather gear, complimentary nature walks, and gourmet dinners are among the offerings. Perhaps most important, expect a cozy room, often with a fireplace and a soaker tub with an ocean outlook, in which you can relax in security, while the outer world rages on.

Serious thrill seekers take to the beaches and lookouts to experience storms firsthand. That said, conditions can be decidedly unfriendly, and visitors should remember that people are injured here every year by rogue waves and rolling logs. Storm-watchers planning on walking the Wild Pacific Trail, for example, should go with a companion, and preferably with an experienced naturalist or guide. Long Beach Nature Tours (⊕ www.longbeachnaturetours.com) is a good choice. Other notable storm-watching venues include Wickaninnish Beach, with the largest swells and greatest concentration of logs and driftwood; Long Beach, famed for its rolling swells, wave-washed islands, and panoramic views; Cox Bay, said to receive the largest and most powerful waves; and Chesterman Beach, beloved for its varied conditions and outlooks.

11

Vancouver Island TOFINO

been on the menu from the start and is his personal fave. **Known for:** the freshest seafood; the tuna stack; two different dining spaces. [$] *Average main: C$30* ✉ *601 Campbell St.* ☎ *250/725–3353* 🌐 *www.shelterrestaurant.com.*

★ Sobo

$$$$ | ECLECTIC | FAMILY | The name, short for "sophisticated bohemian," sums up the style here: a classically trained chef serving casual fare influenced by international street food. The offbeat concept started in a purple truck before finding a permanent home in this light-filled café and bistro. **Known for:** fresh seafood; fish tacos; international street food influence. [$] *Average main: C$31* ✉ *311 Neill St.* ☎ *250/725–2341* 🌐 *www.sobo.ca.*

Tacofino

$ | MEXICAN | Heading to the beach? Follow the surfers to this orange catering truck at Outside Break, a cluster of driftwood- and cedar-sided shops just south of town. **Known for:** fresh, healthy ingredients; Mexican-inspired beach food; original food truck location. [$] *Average main: C$12* ✉ *1180 Pacific Rim Hwy.* ✣ *5 min south of Tofino* ☎ *250/726–8288* 🌐 *tacofino.com* ⏲ *No dinner.*

Wildside Grill

$$ | SEAFOOD | Just steps away from the popular Tacofino truck is another take-out shack, Wildside Grill, where a commercial fisherman and a chef have joined forces to keep Tofitians and visitors supplied with straight-from-the-dock, panko-crusted-fish-and-chips, plus juicy fish and beef burgers. Gather a beach picnic, or enjoy a meal under the shade of Wildside's driftwood gazebo. **Known for:** locally sourced seafood; order by phone; good for picnics. [$] *Average main: C$15* ✉ *1180 Pacific Rim Hwy.* ✣ *5 min south of Tofino* ☎ *250/725–9453* 🌐 *www.wildsidegrill.com* 💳 *No credit cards* ⏲ *No dinner.*

★ The Wolf in the Fog

$$$$ | CANADIAN | Chef Nick Nutting and his crew present a unique west-coast dining experience here that puts an inspired twist on freshly caught seafood and foraged local ingredients; think seaweed combed from the shore and wild forest mushrooms. The big platters of charred octopus and steamed mussels beg to be shared. **Known for:** award winning; innovative hyper-local cuisine; foraged ingredients. [$] *Average main: C$32* ✉ *150 4th St.* ☎ *250/725–9653* 🌐 *www.wolfinthefog.com.*

Hotels

★ Chesterman Beach Bed & Breakfast

$$$$ | B&B/INN | This charming beachside inn, opened as Tofino's first B&B in 1984, is the kind of intimate seaside getaway that brought people to Vancouver Island's west coast in the first place. **Pros:** gracious owners knowledgeable about area; private; scenic. **Cons:** 10-minute drive to restaurants; breakfast not actually included in rates; breakfast not available at the cottage. [$] *Rooms from: C$420* ✉ *1345 Chesterman Beach Rd.* ☎ *250/725–3726* 🌐 *www.tofinoaccommodation.com* 🔑 *2 suites; 1 1-bedroom cottage* 🍴 *No meals.*

★ Clayoquot Wilderness Resort

$$$$ | RESORT | FAMILY | People from around the globe arrive via floatplane or a 30-minute boat ride from Tofino to experience this Relais & Châteaux property, one of the region's top wilderness resorts. **Pros:** escapism at its best, with no phone or other distractions; excellent food; a ton of outdoorsy activities. **Cons:** it's extremely pricey; fairly isolated; requires a long trip to reach the property. [$] *Rooms from: C$6,201* ✉ *1 Clayoquot* ☎ *250/266–0397, 888/333–5405* 🌐 *www.wildretreat.com* ⏲ *Closed Oct.–mid-May* 🔑 *25 tents, 20 with private bath* 🍴 *All-inclusive* ☞ *Actual price is per-person for three nights.*

Inn at Tough City

$$$ | **HOTEL** | Vintage furnishings and First Nations art make this harborside redbrick two-star inn funky, if a bit cluttered. **Pros:** prime Tofino location; loads of character; eclectic furnishings. **Cons:** the lobby is small and noisy; front-desk staffing friendly but inconsistent; a bit cluttered. [$] *Rooms from: C$210* ✉ *350 Main St.* ☎ *250/725–2021, 877/725–2021* 🌐 *www.toughcity.com* ⏲ *Closed Dec.–Feb.* 🛏 *8 rooms* 🍴 *No meals.*

Long Beach Lodge Resort

$$$$ | **HOTEL** | **FAMILY** | With handcrafted furnishings, dramatic pieces of First Nations art, and a tall granite fireplace, the great room at this luxury lodge offers front-row seats to the surf (and surfers) rolling into miles of sandy beach on Cox Bay. Accommodations include comfortable lodge rooms, two-bedroom cottages, and suites leading directly onto the sand with patios to store beach and surf gear. **Pros:** exceptional beachfront location; terrific restaurant; cozy areas within the great room. **Cons:** beach gets busy with guests from neighboring resorts; no swimming pool; ground-floor rooms get a lot of foot traffic. [$] *Rooms from: C$509* ✉ *1441 Pacific Rim Hwy.* ☎ *250/725–2442, 877/844–7873* 🌐 *www.longbeachlodgeresort.com* 🛏 *41 lodge rooms, 20 two-bedroom cottages* 🍴 *No meals.*

Middle Beach Lodge

$$$$ | **RESORT** | On a bluff overlooking a mile of private beach, this rustically elegant lodge is a great choice for a grown-ups' getaway. **Pros:** truly secluded, with an almost exclusive beach; Lodge at the Beach has great rates for the location; complimentary breakfast. **Cons:** limited restaurant hours; kids allowed only in some accommodations; no pool. [$] *Rooms from: C$330* ✉ *400 MacKenzie Beach Rd.* ☎ *250/725–2900, 866/725–2900* 🌐 *www.middlebeach.com* ⏲ *Restaurant closed Sun. and Mon. peak season. No lunch* 🛏 *35 rooms, 10 suites, 20 self-contained cabins* 🍴 *Free breakfast.*

Pacific Sands Beach Resort

$$$$ | **RESORT** | **FAMILY** | On 45 acres of lawn and forest along Cox Bay, Tofino's only all-suite resort underwent a $10-million expansion in 2018 and offers a range of lodge rooms, waterfront suites, and beach villas, all with full kitchens, fireplaces, and private ocean-view decks or patios just steps from the beach, plus the four-bedroom Sunset House at Rosie Bay. The bay is a magnet for surfers (though it's not safe for swimming), and the adjacent forest is a nature lover's paradise. **Pros:** on prime beachfront; good family destination; every room is a suite. **Cons:** no ocean swimming; some suites are on the small side; no pool. [$] *Rooms from: C$439* ✉ *1421 Pacific Rim Hwy.* ☎ *250/725–3322, 800/565–2322* 🌐 *www.pacificsands.com* 🛏 *120 suites, one 4-bedroom house* 🍴 *No meals.*

★ **The Wickaninnish Inn**

$$$$ | **RESORT** | On a rocky promontory with open ocean on three sides and old-growth forest as a backdrop, this cedar-sided inn is exceptional in every sense. **Pros:** at the end of a superb crescent beach; the silence of storms through triple-glazed windows is surreal; excellent staff. **Cons:** no swimming pool; pricey; no hot tub. [$] *Rooms from: C$680* ✉ *500 Osprey La., at Chesterman Beach* ☎ *250/725–3100, 800/333–4604* 🌐 *www.wickinn.com* 🛏 *Pointe Building: 45 rooms. Beach Building: 18 rooms, 12 suites* 🍴 *No meals.*

Tofino Resort + Marina

$$$ | **RESORT** | **FAMILY** | Offering a different side of Tofino, this marina complex is right on the inlet looking across to Meares Island, just a short stroll from town. **Pros:** close to town; good value; can fly right into the resort. **Cons:** not on the beach; rooms need soundproofing; furnishings are sparse. [$] *Rooms from: C$289* ✉ *634 Campbell St.*

Tofino has surfable waves year-round, making it the Surf Capital of Canada.

☎ 844/680–4184 ⊕ www.tofinoresortand-marina.com ⇔ 62 rooms ⦿ No meals.

🏃 Activities

Thinking about some side trips? Then why not hop on a boat or floatplane and explore the surrounding roadless wilderness? The most popular day trip is to Hot Springs Cove in Maquinna Marine Provincial Park, where you can soak in natural rock pools by the sea. Other trips head to Meares Island, where an easy 20-minute boardwalk trail leads to trees up to 1,600 years old. Whale- and bear-watching tours are great options, too; a popular trip combines whale-watching with a visit to Hot Springs Cove, with wildlife-spotting opportunities en route to the thermal springs.

FISHING

Tofino Chinook Fishing Charters

FISHING | At Chinook Charters, Captain Mike Hansen is an independent guide born and raised in the area. His custom-designed 30-foot vessel is well-equipped to land a prized coho. Prices are in line with other Tofino operators at around C$600 per day for up to two people. ✉ 380 Main St. ☎ 250/726–5221 ⊕ www.chinookcharters.com.

Cleanline Sportfishing Charters

FISHING | Experienced anglers appreciate the expertise of this company, a multi-boat operator offering both saltwater and freshwater fishing. Prices are competitive at C$140 per hour in the ocean and about C$1,300 per day on the rivers. For a spectacular day out, you can be flown to a remote mountain lake where you launch a raft and spend the day fishing for trout as you drift along a river back to the coast; the price for this experience, including the flight, is C$1,900 for two people. ✉ 630a Campbell St. ☎ 250/726–3828, 855/726–3828 ⊕ www.cleanline-sportfishing.com.

FLIGHTSEEING

In addition to Atleo River Air Service, Tofino Air, which provides small-plane transportation throughout the region, also operates flightseeing tours over outlying forests and beaches to Hot Springs Cove in Maquinna Marine Provincial Park. Other trips take you to the lakes and glaciers of Strathcona Provincial Park. If you can, soar over Cougar Annie's Garden, a century-old wilderness homestead that was once the home of a legendary local character. *See Air Travel in Travel Smart.*

Atleo River Air Service

FLYING/SKYDIVING/SOARING | This locally owned company offers breathtaking flightseeing tours around Clayoquot and Barkley Sounds, plus fly-in fishing, hot springs tours, and more by both floatplane and helicopter. ⊠ *50 Wingen La.* ☎ *250/725–2205, 866/662–8536* ⊕ *www. atleoair.com.*

HIKING

Long Beach Nature Tours

HIKING/WALKING | FAMILY | Learn about local ecosystems on a beach or forest walk with experienced naturalists. Half- and full-day trips include intertidal and rain-forest exploration, treks to remote beaches and, in winter, a chance to watch storms in action. ⊠ *109 605 Gibsons St.* ☎ *250/725–3320* ⊕ *www. longbeachnaturetours.com.*

KAYAKING

Remote Passages Marine Excursions

KAYAKING | No experience is necessary for these relaxed guided paddles in sheltered waters. Also on offer are whale-watching and bear-watching trips and excursions to Meares Island and Hot Springs Cove in Maquinna Marine Provincial Park. ⊠ *51 Wharf St.* ☎ *250/725–3330, 800/666–9833* ⊕ *www. remotepassages.com.*

Tofino Sea Kayaking

KAYAKING | Tofino Sea Kayaking rents kayaks, runs a kayaking school, and provides day and multiday wilderness kayaking trips. No experience is necessary for the day trips. ⊠ *320 Main St.* ☎ *250/725–4222, 800/863–4664* ⊕ *www. tofinoseakayaking.com.*

SURFING

The coast from Tofino south to Ucluelet is, despite perpetually chilly waters, an increasingly popular surf destination—year-round.

Live to Surf

SURFING | You can rent boards and other gear at Live to Surf. Jean-Paul Froment runs the business (founded by his parents in 1984) with his sister Pascale from the funky Outside Break commercial hub south of Tofino, which is conveniently close to the major surfing spots of Long Beach, Cox Bay, Chesterman Beach, and MacKenzie Beach. The shop also sells boards, wet suits, and accessories, and provides rentals and lessons. ⊠ *1180 Pacific Rim Hwy.* ☎ *250/725–4464* ⊕ *www.livetosurf.com.*

Pacific Surf School

SURFING | This company offers everything from three-hour introductory sessions to multiday camps. ⊠ *441 Campbell St.* ☎ *250/725–2155, 888/777–9961* ⊕ *www. pacificsurfschool.com.*

Storm

SURFING | This hip surf shop in Downtown Tofino carries all the latest gear, including boards, clothing, and wet suits. ⊠ *444 Campbell St.* ☎ *250/725–3344* ⊕ *www. stormcanada.ca.*

Surf Sister

SURFING | This well-respected school has women-only lessons as well as those for everyone. Check out mother-daughter surf packages, teenager surf camps, and progressive sessions. Open year-round. ⊠ *625 Campbell St.* ☎ *250/725–4456, 877/724–7873* ⊕ *www.surfsister.com.*

WHALE-WATCHING

In March and April, up to 22,000 Pacific gray whales migrate along the coast here; resident grays can be seen anytime between March and October. In addition, there are humpback whales, sea otters, sea lions, orcas, black bears, and other wildlife. Most whale-watching operators also lead bear-watching trips by sea

Pacific Rim Surfing

Though the water tends to be nippy—full-length wet suits are worn in summer and winter alike—Tofino has skimmed its way onto the international surfing map for several reasons. Framed by rocky headlands, the curvaceous hard-sand beaches are smack on the open Pacific Ocean, guaranteeing long swells and sizable waves year-round; the area is also a rain forest, providing a genuine wilderness experience. What's more, the Tofino region nurtures an easy-going, even mildly anarchic lifestyle. It's no surprise that a distinctive "free style" of surfing has taken root here as local surfers often eschew competitions in favor of doing their own thing. The culture attracts many warm-climate surfers to test themselves in what's considered a more challenging environment. What they find, along 32 km (20 miles) of rugged shoreline between Ucluelet and Tofino, are at least four spectacular surfing beaches.

The most famous, Long Beach, together with Wickaninnish Beach, is within the Pacific Rim National Park Reserve. The next beach northward is Cox Bay, arguably the most popular—and most challenging—of the surfing beaches located outside the park. This is where the most skilled surfers launch their boards and where competitions, when they're held, take place.

That said, there's space for everyone on this long and lovely stretch of forgiving sand, even for beginners. Several lodges, all suitable for families, are located on Cox Bay. Chesterman Beach, the next major beach as you travel toward Tofino, is similarly picturesque and is considered the best beach for those just starting out in the sport. Finally, MacKenzie Beach is conveniently close to the town of Tofino.

Whichever beach you choose, take note that the waves and rip currents present real danger, and first-time surfers are advised to take lessons. Wave-hazard signs are posted along the highway and updated daily.

The Pacific Rim Highway, running the length of the Tofino peninsula, includes a separate bike path, and almost any day of the year you'll see surfers, with a skate, skim, or long board under one arm, cycling their way to their preferred destination. It's quite common to pick up surfers hitch-hiking from one beach to another. And it's equally normal to see local surfers heading out on stormy days and when it snows. The best surfing is said to take place in spring and fall, when the waves are strong and consistent and the weather more or less cooperates. Lessons and equipment rentals are available year-round.

and excursions along the coast and to the region's outlying islands, including Meares Island and Hot Springs Cove in Maquinna Marine Provincial Park, where you can soak in natural seaside hot springs. Services range from no-frills water-taxi drop-off to tours with experienced guides; prices vary accordingly. Want to stay longer at Hot Springs Cove?

Book a cabin on the *InnChanter* (⊕ *www. innchanter.com*). This historic boat is moored at the cove, and overnights include lavish meals and a chance to have the hot springs to yourself.

Jamie's Whaling Station & Adventure Centre

WHALE-WATCHING | One of the most established whale-watching operators on the coast, Jamie's has motorized inflatable boats as well as more comfortable 65-foot tour boats. You can book a whole range of adventures, including kayaking, bear-watching, and sightseeing trips to Meares Island or Hot Springs Cove from March through October. Jamie's also has a location in Ucluelet. ⊠ *606 Campbell St.* ☎ *250/725–3919, 800/667–9913* ⊕ *www. jamies.com.*

Ocean Outfitters

WHALE-WATCHING | **FAMILY** | Whale- and bear-watching trips, Meares Island trips, and Hot Springs Cove tours are all on the menu at this popular outfitter. ⊠ *368 Main St.* ☎ *250/725–2866, 877/906–2326* ⊕ *www.oceanoutfitters.bc.ca.*

Remote Passages Marine Excursions

WHALE-WATCHING | A well-established operator, Remote Passages offers whale-watching and bear-watching excursions as well as trips to Hot Springs Cove and Meares Island. Tours have an ecological and educational focus. ⊠ *51 Wharf St.* ☎ *250/725–3330, 800/666–9833* ⊕ *www. remotepassages.com.*

West Coast Aquatic Safaris

WHALE-WATCHING | **FAMILY** | If comfort is a priority, check out this company's covered, wheelchair-accessible, all-weather tour boats, with heated cabins and inside seating as well as viewing decks. The company offers whale- and bear-watching trips, Hot Spring Cove trips, and fishing charters. ⊠ *101 4th St.* ☎ *250 /725–9227, 877/594–2537* ⊕ *whalesafaris.com.*

The Whale Centre

WHALE-WATCHING | **FAMILY** | This long-established company has a 40-foot-long gray whale skeleton that you can study while waiting for your boat. It runs whale-watching and bird-watching trips from March to mid-October, and bear-spotting tours between April and October as well as daily, year-round trips to Hot Springs Cove in a 30-foot covered boat. ⊠ *411 Campbell St.* ☎ *250/725–2132, 888/474–2288* ⊕ *www.tofinowhalecentre.com.*

🛍 Shopping

ART GALLERIES

Roy Henry Vickers Gallery

ART GALLERIES | In a traditional longhouse, this magnificent gallery houses a collection of prints, paintings, and carvings by renowned BC artist Roy Henry Vickers. ⊠ *350 Campbell St.* ☎ *250/725–3235, 800/663–0669* ⊕ *www.royhenryvickers. com.*

House of Himwitsa

ART GALLERIES | You'll find a good selection of First Nations crafts, jewelry, and clothing at this Native art gallery. The complex also has a dockside smoked-fish store and four waterfront suites. ⊠ *300 Main St.* ☎ *250/725–2017, 800/899–1947* ⊕ *www.himwitsa.com.*

FLEA MARKETS

Tofino Public Market

OUTDOOR/FLEA/GREEN MARKETS | **FAMILY** | Head to the Village Green on Campbell Street for food, crafts, and entertainment every Saturday from May to mid-October. ⊠ *Tofino Village Green, 2nd St. at Campbell St.* ⊕ *www.tofinomarket.com.*

FOOD

Chocolate Tofino

FOOD/CANDY | Everything from the wild blackberry butter creams and lavender truffles to the sorbets and gelatos are handmade in-house at this tiny chocolate and gelato shop just south of Tofino. You can even watch chocolatiers at work in the open kitchen. ⊠ *Outside Break, 1180A Pacific Rim Hwy.* ✛ *3 km (2 miles) south of Tofino* ☎ *250/725–2526, 855/286–3466* ⊕ *www.chocolatetofino. com.*

Tofino Brewing Co

WINE/SPIRITS | This sustainable, locally focused craft brewery is producing small-batch, handcrafted beer. Enjoy a flight of their west coast-inspired brews with a charcuterie platter picked up from Picnic Charcuterie, located across the street. ✉ *691 Industrial Way* ☎ *250/725-2899* 🌐 *www.tofinobrewingco.com.*

Tofino Craft Distillery

WINE/SPIRITS | Stop in for a mini cocktail in the Tasting Room at Tofino Craft Distillery. This new kid on the craft spirit block opened in 2018 making flagship spirits, including small-batch vodka, West Coast Gin, Old-Growth Cedar Gin (made with western red cedar tips and organic botanicals), Rose Hibiscus Gin, and a Psychedelic Jellyfish Absinthe. Tasting Room infusions change weekly. ✉ *681 Industrial Way* ☎ *250/725-2182* 🌐 *www.tofinocraftdistillery.com.*

Mill Bay

42 km (26 miles) north of Victoria on Trans-Canada Hwy., or Hwy. 1.

From Mill Bay, home to a cluster of shops and cafés at the southern end of the Cowichan Valley, ferries sail across the Saanich Inlet to Brentwood Bay on the Saanich Peninsula. South of Mill Bay, Highway 1 crosses the Malahat, a stunning ocean-view route to Victoria.

GETTING HERE AND AROUND

Follow Highway 1 north from Victoria – it cuts north–south through the valley, while winding side roads lead to studios, wineries, and roadside farm stands. Turn right on Deloume Rd., then right onto Mill Bay Rd. You can also take the Mill Bay Ferry from Brentwood Bay on the Saanich Peninsula.

👁 Sights

Unsworth Vineyards

RESTAURANT—SIGHT | Plan to spend a couple of hours at this family-owned and-operated boutique winery, where tastings of Pinot Gris, Pinot Noir, and port-style dessert wine are on offer. The business has also extended to include vodka production. The picturesque grounds are also home to Unsworth Restaurant, a charming bistro in a restored early-1900s farmhouse serving lunch and dinner Wednesday through Sunday, overlooking the vineyards. In summer months, dine alfresco on the Pizza Patio. ✉ *2915 Cameron Taggart Rd., Mill Bay* ☎ *250/929–2292* 🌐 *www.unsworthvineyards.com* 🎟 *C$5 tasting fee reimbursed with purchase.*

🍴 Restaurants

Bridgemans Bistro

$$$ | PACIFIC NORTHWEST | This bright bistro sits over the water at the Mill Bay Marina and is a lovely spot for lunch or dinner, with breathtaking views from every table through the floor-to-ceiling windows. Part of the Bridgmans Family of Restaurants (other outposts are on Pender Island and in Port Renfrew), the vibe here is west-coast casual. **Known for:** fresh halibut; seafood chowder; views. [$] *Average main: C$21* ✉ *740 Handy Rd., Mill Bay* ☎ *778/356–3568* 🌐 *www.bridgemans.ca.*

Cobble Hill

7½ km (4¾ miles) north of Mill Bay.

Cobble Hill, at the heart of the Cowichan Valley wine district, is centered on a cluster of shops at the junction of Cobble Hill and Hutchinson roads. Wine is the big draw here, but consider stopping for a latte at Olde School Coffee, complete with a drive-through window, in a historic schoolhouse.

GETTING HERE AND AROUND

Follow Highway 1 north. Turn left on Cobble Hill Rd.

Sights

Cherry Point Estate Wines

WINERY/DISTILLERY | This 24-acre family-owned and-operated vineyard, one of the first licensed wineries in the Cowican Valley, is now the second-largest on Vancouver Island. The tasting room is open daily and features varietals including Gewürztraminer, Pinot Noir, Pinot Blanc, Pinot Gris, Ortega, Auxerrois, and Agria. The winery's highly rated bistro serves lunch Wednesday to Sunday from May to October. ✉ *840 Cherry Point Rd., Cobble Hill* ☎ *250/743–1272* 🌐 *www.cherrypointestatewines.com.*

Damali Lavender and Winery

FARM/RANCH | **FAMILY** | Stroll the grounds, have a picnic or take a tour and tasting at this working lavender farm and winery. The original barn has been converted into a winery producing popular wines made from Cowichan Valley fruit. Pick up a bottle to enjoy with your own picnic in the licensed picnic area. ✉ *3500 Telegraph Rd., Cobble Hill* ☎ *250/743–4100* 🌐 *www.damali.ca* 🕒 *Closed weekdays mid-Oct. to late Dec. By appt. Dec. 24 to Apr.*

Merridale Ciderworks

WINERY/DISTILLERY | Cider is made in the traditional English way at this apple orchard, cidery and distillery; in addition to several varieties of cider and fortified wines, they also make spirits, like brandy, vodka, gin, and an apple *eau de vie*. Visitors can tour the cidery, taste the wares, and linger over lunches of local fare served on the orchard-view patio. There's also a shop selling ciders, juices, baked goods, and jams, and you can even spend the night in a glamorous yurt on the property. ✉ *1230 Merridale Rd., Cobble Hill* ☎ *250/743–4293, 800/998–9908* 🌐 *www.merridalecider.com* 🎫 *C$6 for tasting flight, C$15 for Gin & Tonic Mixologist (groups of 4 or more).*

Venturi-Schulze Vineyards

WINERY/DISTILLERY | This small family business prides itself on not using any pesticides or herbicides in its limited-release products. While it started out making wine, Venturi-Schulze is quickly becoming known more for its balsamic vinegars, which are crafted using an ancient process. Regular, maple, and 100-year-old balsamics are available. Enjoy a glass of wine and lunch on the picnic patio. Tastings are available Wednesday to Sunday in their tasting room. Tours are available by appointment. ✉ *4235 Vineyard Rd., Cobble Hill* ☎ *250/743–5630* 🌐 *www.venturischulze.com* 🎫 *Tastings $5* 🕒 *Closed Mon. and Tues. Jan. and Feb. by appt.*

Restaurants

The Eatery at Merridale

$$ | **CONTEMPORARY** | Neighboring farms supply much of the fare at this bistro, tucked down a country lane at Merridale Ciderworks. The bistro, part of the gambrel-roofed cider house, showcases local art on whitewashed walls within, and orchard and forest views from the wide, covered veranda. **Known for:** located within Merridale Ciderworks; ingredients supplied by local farms; local art on the walls. [$] *Average main: C$15* ✉ *1230 Merridale Rd., Cobble Hill* ☎ *250/743–4293, 800/998–9908* 🌐 *www.merridalecider.com.*

Coffee and Quick Bites

Olde School Coffee

$ | **CAFÉ** | A local favorite, stop by this former schoolhouse for a steaming latte, iced mocha, handmade sandwich, or a snack. **Known for:** former schoolhouse; popular with locals; good coffee. [$] *Average main: C$5* ✉ *3515 Cobble Hill Rd., Cobble Hill* ☎ *250/743–6908* 🌐 *oldeschoolcoffee.com.*

Activities

Arbutus Ridge Golf Club

GOLF | Mountain and ocean views from the course and the clubhouse are the draws at this challenging par-70/72 course, 40 minutes north of Victoria in the Cowichan Valley. The back nine climbs a ridge to take advantage of the stunning vistas, including that from the famed par-3 island green on hole 17. ✉ *3515 Telegraph Rd., Cobble Hill* ☎ *250/743–5000* ⊕ *www.arbutusridgegolf.com* ⓢ *C$67* 🏌 *18 holes, 6152 yards, par 70/72.*

Cowichan Bay

8 km (5 miles) north of Cobble Hill.

Often called Cow Bay, this funky little town about 10 minutes south of Duncan (take Cowichan Bay Road off Highway 1) is made up largely of houseboats and houses built on pilings over the water. Seafood restaurants, nautical shops, boatbuilders, kayaking outfitters, and B&Bs line the waterfront.

GETTING HERE AND AROUND
From Victoria, follow Highway 1 north to Cowichan Bay Rd.

Sights

Cowichan Bay Maritime Centre

MARINA | **FAMILY** | The interesting Cowichan Bay Maritime Centre has maritime paraphernalia, including historic vessels and model boats, displayed along a pier, which is also a great place to take in views of the village and boats at harbor. You may also be able to watch boatbuilders at work in the attached studio. ✉ *1761 Cowichan Bay Rd., Cowichan Bay* ☎ *250/746–4955* ⊕ *www.classicboats.org* ⓢ *Free.*

Restaurants

The Masthead Restaurant

$$$ | **CONTEMPORARY** | You know a chef cares about local food when his menu lists how far each ingredient has traveled to reach your plate. At this historic seaside roadhouse in Cowichan Bay, the mussels and clams come from within 5 miles of the restaurant, and the poached Dungeness crab is from the bay outside the door. **Known for:** fresh seafood; "man steak"; sea views. ⓢ *Average main: C$30* ✉ *1705 Cowichan Bay Rd., Cowichan Bay* ☎ *250/748–3714* ⊕ *www.themastheadrestaurant.com* 🕑 *No lunch.*

Shopping

Arthur Vickers Shipyard Gallery

ART GALLERIES | This well-regarded gallery displays the renowned artist's work, with west coast and First Nations themes, in a converted shipyard building dating back to 1926. The gallery has irregular hours in winter. ✉ *1719 Cowichan Bay Rd., Cowichan Bay* ☎ *250/748–7650* ⊕ *www.arthurvickers.com.*

Wild Coast Perfumery

PERFUME/COSMETICS | Artisan perfumer Laurie Arbuthnot uses pure plant-based essential oils and distillations derived from foraged flora, such as red cedar and oak moss, to blend her signature scents on-site. Designed to evoke "scent memories" of BC, the botanical perfumes are inspired by the rain forests, mountains, and Salish Sea, and are named for places along the coast. The tiny shop is open seasonally from May to December. ✉ *1721 Cowichan Bay Rd., Cowichan Bay* ☎ *250/701–2791* ⊕ *www.wildcoastperfumes.com* 🕑 *Closed Mon. and Jan. to Apr.*

Duncan

9.7 km (6 miles) north of Cowichan Bay.

Duncan, the largest town in the valley, is nicknamed the "City of Totems" for the more than 40 totem poles that dot the small community. Between May and September, free walking tours of the totems leave hourly from the south end of the train station building on Canada Avenue (contact the Duncan Business Improvement Area Society, at ☎ 250/715–1700, for more information). On Saturdays year-round, the City Square at the end of Craig Street hosts an outdoor market, where you can browse for local produce, crafts, and specialty foods. Duncan is also home to the world's largest hockey stick—look for it on the outside wall of the Duncan arena on the west side of Highway 1 as you drive through town.

GETTING HERE AND AROUND

From Victoria, follow Hwy. 1 north for 61 km (38 miles). From Nanaimo, follow Hwy. 1 south for 50 km. You can also get to Duncan via a back road from Port Renfrew, west of Sooke, following the Pacific Marine Circle Route.

◉ Sights

Averill Creek Vineyard

WINERY/DISTILLERY | It's all about the Pinot Noir at this estate winery. Even the rosé is 100% Pinot Noir. In the tasting room, take the Pinot glass test to learn why the shape of the glass makes a difference to where you taste the wine on your palate (mid-palate being ideal for the delicate nature of Pinot). Try the Charme de L'ile and Prevost Foch Cab before heading out to the patio overlooking the ocean with your favorite bottle and your own picnic. This is the perfect place to start or end a trip through the Cowichan Valley. ⊠ 6552 North Rd. ☎ 250/709–9986 ⊕ www. averillcreek.ca ⊗ Closed weekdays Jan. and Feb.

Ampersand Distillery

WINERY/DISTILLERY | Father-and-son duo Stephen and Jeremy Schacht built this craft distillery from the ground up, including designing and building their own unique stills. The award-winning gin and vodka they produce here are made with certified organic wheat from the BC mainland and botanicals from around the world, such as Albanian coriander, African grains of paradise, and juniper berries from Bulgaria. They now grow their own wild-harvested botanicals on the five-acre site. Don't miss the *Nocino!*, a seasonal green walnut liqueur which was awarded best nonfruit liqueur in the 2019 Pacific Northwest Sip Awards. ⊠ 4077 Lanchaster Rd. ☎ 250/999–1109 ⊕ www. ampersanddistilling.com ⊗ Tasting room by appt.

Blue Grouse Estate Winery

WINERY/DISTILLERY | One of Vancouver Island's oldest estate vineyards, this family-owned, sustainably farmed winery is a favorite with the locals. Award-winning estate wines include Pinot Gris, Pinot Noir, and Black Muscat, while the Quill label wines are blended with grapes from the Okanagan Valley. Locally made cheese and charcuterie boards, which pair perfectly with the wines, are served daily in the architecturally stunning Tasting Room. Soup Saturdays and monthly Farms Gate Sunday brunches are offered in the off-season. The 65-acre property also boasts the Grouse House, a vineyard "Bed & Bottle" retreat. The beautifully appointed two-bedroom, two-bathroom suite sleeps four. ⊠ 2182 Lakeside Rd. ☎ 250/743–3834 ⊕ www.bluegrouse.ca ☜ C$5 for tasting of five wines (waived with wine purchase) ⊗ Closed Mon. and Tues. Feb. to Apr. and Oct. to Dec. Closed Jan.

British Columbia Forest Discovery Centre

MUSEUM VILLAGE | FAMILY | Kids adore riding the rails at the British Columbia Forest Discovery Centre, a 100-acre outdoor museum just north of Duncan. Pulled by a 1910 steam locomotive, a three-carriage train toots through the woods and over a trestle bridge across a lake, stopping at a picnic site and playground on the way. Forestry-related exhibits around the site include a 1930s-era logging camp, historic logging equipment, and indoor exhibits about the modern science of forestry. Interpretive trails through the forest lead to ancient trees, one dating back more than 500 years. During July and August, the steam train runs daily every half hour. In May, June, and September, the train may be replaced with a gas locomotive. ⊠ *2892 Drinkwater Rd.* ☎ *250/715–1113, 866/715–1113* ⊕ *www. bcforestdiscoverycentre.com* 🖃 *C$16.*

Cowichan Valley Museum & Archives

MUSEUM | FAMILY | This small museum, in a 1912 train station, has exhibits and artifacts about the region's First Nations culture and pioneer history. ⊠ *130 Canada Ave.* ☎ *250/746–6612* ⊕ *www. cowichanvalleymuseum.bc.ca* 🖃 *Donations accepted* ⊘ *Closed Sun. to Tues. during the winter.*

The Raptors Centre

NATURE PRESERVE | FAMILY | At this conservation center about 10 minutes northeast of Duncan, you can see owls, hawks, falcons, and eagles in natural settings. Free-flying bird demonstrations are held daily at 11:30, 1:30, and 3:30; you can also join a trainer on a brief falconry or ecology course. ⊠ *1877 Herd Rd.* ☎ *250/746–0372* ⊕ *www.pnwraptors. com* 🖃 *C$18* ⊘ *Closed Jan. to Mar.*

Westholme Tea Farm

FARM/RANCH | Victor Vesely and Margit Nellemann have proven agriculture officials, who said tea couldn't be grown in Canada, wrong. They planted two terraces of *Camellia sinensis* on about half an acre overlooking an old dairy barn in 2010. The barn has since been converted to a tearoom and their first crop of single-origin spring harvest tea, Swallow Tail Oolong, was released July 1, 2016. Also available are imported artisanal teas

blended with herbs and flowers grown on the farm and popular Chinese zodiac-sign teas, all of which can be paired with such delights as Keemun chocolate torte or Matcha cheese cake. The adjoining gallery features Margit's exquisite ceramic teapots and more. ⊠ *8350 Richards Trail, North Cowichan* ☎ *250/748–3811, 855/748–3811* ⊕ *www.westholmetea. com* ⊘ *Closed Mon. and Tues.*

Vigneti Zanatta Winery

RESTAURANT—SIGHT | A local favorite is Vigneti Zanatta Winery, Vancouver Island's first estate winery which produces lovely Ortega, Pinot Grigio, and Damasco entirely from grapes grown on its own 25 acres. If you can, time your visit for an Italian-style lunch on the veranda at Vinoteca, a restaurant and wine bar in the winery's 1903 farmhouse. ⊠ *5039 Marshall Rd.* ☎ *250/748–2338 winery, 250/709–2279 Vinoteca Restaurant* ⊕ *www.zanatta.ca* ⊘ *Closed Nov. to May.*

Emandare Vineyard

WINERY/DISTILLERY | This small estate vineyard on a south slope overlooking Somenos Lake is a labor of love for husband-and-wife team Mike and Robin Nierychlo. The pair purchased the property, which has some of the oldest Sauvignon Blanc vines on the island, in 2013. Since their first vintage the following year, the Sauv Blanc continually sells out. The property is expanding to offer a 1,000-square-foot, two-bedroom guest house, complete with a six-guest hot tub on the deck overlooking the lake. The tasting room is open three days a week or by appointment. ⊠ *6798 Norcross Rd.* ☎ *250/597–4075* ⊕ *www.emandarevineyard.com* 🖃 *C$5 tasting fee waived with purchase* ⊘ *Closed Sun.–Wed. May to Sept.; Sun.–Fri. Oct. to Apr.*

Red Arrow Brewing Company

WINERY/DISTILLERY | Small-batch beers, handcrafted using local seasonal ingredients are on tap here. Located in a brick building that formerly housed a motorcycle shop along the highway, this popular craft brewery launched in 2015 with signature brews like Sweet Leaf IPA and Piggy Pale Ale. Feature beers, such as a mushroom-infused Lion's Mane Golden Ale and Idle Hands Oaked Orange Ale, change regularly. The Midnite Umber Ale won bronze at the 2019 BC Brewing Awards. A flight of three beers is C$5 and goes perfectly with one of chef Romeo Diaz's tacos, from Jake's on the Road food truck just outside the brewery door. ✉ *5255 Chaster Rd.* ☎ 🌐 *www.redarrowbeer.ca.*

Small Block Brewing Company

WINERY/DISTILLERY | This small brewery, housed in a former garage, is an homage to classic cars and craft brews sourced from local ingredients. In the taproom, local couple Cate and Aaron Scally pour core brews, such as Hornet Blonde Ale and Green Goblin Irish Red, alongside rotating seasonal offerings, Snacks are available from Holy Cow! Indian Eats. In summer, Friday nights feature wood-fired pizza from Vancouver Island Pizza food truck. Across the parking lot at Stillhead Distillery, distiller Brennan Colebank is producing gin, wild blackberry–infused vodka, and whiskey from BC-grown fruits and grains. ✉ *203-5301 Chaster Rd.* ☎ *250/597–0045* 🌐 *www.smallblockbrewery.com* 🎫 *C$7 for flight of 4* 🕒 *Closed Tues.*

🍴 Restaurants

Genoa Bay Café

$$$ | **PACIFIC NORTHWEST** | A winding drive along the water past towering trees brings you to this waterfront eatery. Tucked on the dock at picturesque Genoa Bay, the small bistro offers a Pacific Northwest–inspired menu showcasing the bounty of Vancouver Island. **Known for:** off the beaten path; charming location; west-coast fry bread. [$] *Average main: C$29* ✉ *9-5000 Genoa Bay Rd.* ☎ *250/746–7621, 800/572–6481* 🌐 *www.genoabaycafe.com* 🕒 *Closed Mon. and Tues. No lunch Wed.–Fri.*

Chemainus

20 km (12 miles) north of Duncan.

Chemainus is known for the bold epic murals that decorate its townscape, as well as for its beautifully restored Victorian homes. Once dependent on the lumber industry, the small community began to revitalize itself in the early 1980s when its mill closed down. Since then the town has brought in international artists to paint more than 40 murals depicting local historical events around town. Footprints on the sidewalk lead you on a self-guided tour of the murals. Tours by horse and carriage, replica-train rides, free outdoor concerts, a weekly night market, and plenty of B&Bs, cafés, and crafts shops all help pass the time here. Catch, if you can, a show at the Chemainus Theatre Festival, which offers several professional musical and dramatic productions between March and December. The Chemainus Visitor Information Centre (🌐 *www.chemainus.bc.ca*) has details.

GETTING HERE AND AROUND

Chemainus is located 77 km (48 miles) north of Victoria and 34 km (21 miles) south of Nanaimo along Hwy. 1.

🎫 Performing Arts

Chemainus Theatre

THEATER | The Chemainus Theatre presents popular live musicals and dramas from March to December. ✉ *9737 Chemainus Rd.* ☎ *250/246–9820* 🌐 *www.chemainustheatrefestival.ca.*

🏃 Activities

For those who want to get outdoors, biking and water activities are great around the Lake Cowichan area.

Cowichan Valley Trail

BICYCLING | This 122-km (76-mile) path, part of The Great Trail (formerly known as the Trans-Canada trail), runs from Shawnigan Lake to Lake Cowichan in the Cowichan Valley. A rails-to-trails conversion, the route crosses eight historic bridges, including the 614-foot-long Kinsol Trestle, one of the tallest timber rail trestles in the world. ⊠ *Victoria* ⊕ *www.cvrd.bc.ca* 🖪 *Free.*

Cowichan River Tubing

WATER SPORTS | FAMILY | Lake Cowichan is a freshwater lake that is a playground for houseboating, kayaking, fishing, camping, and "river tubing." From the lake, the Cowichan River flows into the Salish Sea and floating along it, while reclining in a large inner tube, has become a popular summer activity. From the weir in Lake Cowichan it takes three hours to reach Little Beach, approximately 3 kilometers (over a mile) downstream from the starting point. Several companies provide rentals and shuttle back to where you started. Insider tip: rent the larger inner tube and get a paddle. ⊠ *Lake Cowichan, Lake Cowichan* ⊕ *www.tourismcowichan.com.*

Salt Spring Island

5 nautical miles from Swartz Bay, 18 nautical miles from Tsawwassen.

With its wealth of studios, galleries, restaurants, and B&Bs, Salt Spring is the most developed, and most visited, of the Southern Gulf Islands. It's home to the only town in the archipelago (Ganges) and, although it can get busy on summer weekends, has not yet lost its relaxed rural feel. Outside Ganges, the rolling landscape is home to small organic farms, wineries, forested hills, quiet white-shell beaches, and several swimming lakes.

What really sets Salt Spring apart is its status as Canada's '"Island of the Arts."

Island residents include hundreds of artists, writers, craftspeople, and musicians, many of whom open their studios to visitors. To visit more than 35 local artists in their studios, pick up a free Studio Tour map from the tourist information center in Ganges.

Salt Spring's main commercial center is the seaside village of Ganges, about 15 km (9 miles) north of the Fulford Ferry Terminal. It has about a dozen art galleries, as well as the essentials: restaurants, banks, gas stations, grocery stores, and a liquor store. At the south end of Salt Spring Island is the tiny village of Fulford, which has a restaurant, a café, and several offbeat boutiques. On the west side is the small coastal community of Vesuvius, with a restaurant, a tiny grocery store–cum-café, and crafts studios.

GETTING HERE AND AROUND

Salt Spring Island has the most frequent ferry service, as well as service from three terminals. Ferries from Swartz Bay, near Victoria on Vancouver Island, arrive at Fulford Harbour, on the southern tip of the island, 15 km (9 miles) from Ganges, the main town. Ferries from the BC mainland and other Southern Gulf Islands arrive at Long Harbour, on the island's east coast, just east of Ganges. Salt Spring also has BC Ferry service from the Cowichan Valley on Vancouver Island, with sailings every hour or so from Crofton, 20 minutes north of Duncan, to Vesuvius Bay on the west side of Salt Spring.

A BC Transit minibus runs from all three ferry terminals to the town of Ganges, but it doesn't meet every ferry; check online schedules first. For a taxi on Salt Spring, call Silver Shadow Taxi.

Harbour Air Seaplanes operate regularly scheduled flights into Ganges Harbour from Vancouver Harbour and the south terminal at Vancouver International Airport (YVR). Seair Seaplanes fly from the YVR south terminal into Ganges Harbour

To reach Vancouver's nature-rich Gulf Islands, hop aboard a BC ferry.

CONTACTS Silver Shadow Taxi.
☎ 250/537–3030 ⊕ www.saltspringtaxi.
com.

VISITOR INFORMATION

**CONTACTS Salt Spring Island Visitor
Information Centre.** ✉ *121 Lower Ganges
Rd., Salt Spring Island* ☎ *250/537–5252,
866/216–2936* ⊕ *www.saltspringtourism.
com.*

◉ Sights

Every weekend, the Salt Spring Island
Saturday Market is one of the island's
biggest draws. Everyone will be there.
And watching the cheese makers at Salt
Spring Island Cheese is another popular
activity for many visitors.

Burgoyne Bay Provincial Park

NATIONAL/STATE PARK | FAMILY | Easy hikes
and a pretty pebble beach are the draws
at this provincial park, at the end of a
dirt road toward the southern end of the
island. ✉ *Burgoyne Bay Rd., at Fulford-Ganges Rd.* ⊕ *www.env.gov.bc.ca/
bcparks.*

Garry Oaks Winery

WINERY/DISTILLERY | This small winery,
home to valley-view vineyards and a
meditative labyrinth, produces estate-
grown Pinot Gris, Pinot Noir, a Char-
donnay-Gewürztraminer blend, and
an intriguing red made from Zweigelt
grapes. It's open for tastings daily June
through September and on weekends
in April, May, and October (call ahead).
Tours are offered by appointment. ✉ *1880
Fulford-Ganges Rd., Salt Spring Island*
☎ *250/653–4687* ⊕ *www.garryoakswin-
ery.com* 🖾 *C$2 for tasting (fee deducted
from wine purchases)* ☉ *Closed Nov. to
Mar.*

Mount Maxwell Provincial Park

NATIONAL/STATE PARK | FAMILY | Near the
center of Salt Spring Island, Baynes Peak
in Mount Maxwell Provincial Park has
spectacular views of south Salt Spring,
Vancouver Island, and other Gulf Islands.
The last portion of the drive is steep,
winding, and unpaved. ✉ *Mt. Maxwell
Rd., off Fulford–Ganges Rd., Salt Spring
Island* ⊕ *www.env.gov.bc.ca/bcparks.*

Ruckle Provincial Park

FARM/RANCH | **FAMILY** | This provincial park is the site of an 1872 homestead and extensive fields that are still being farmed. Several small sandy beaches and 8 km (5 miles) of trails winding through forests and along the coast make this one of the islands' most appealing parks. A lovely and very popular campground has walk-in tent sites on a grassy slope overlooking the sea as well as a few drive-in sites in the woods. ⊠ *Beaver Point Rd., Salt Spring Island* ☎ *250/539–2115, 877/559–2115* ⊕ *www.env.gov. bc.ca/bcparks.*

Salt Spring Vineyards

WINERY/DISTILLERY | Salt Spring Vineyards produces a dozen wines, including Pinot Gris, Pinot Noir, and blackberry port, almost entirely from island-grown fruit. Be sure to try one of the Evolution series, made with a grape variety developed right on Salt Spring Island, and the Charme de L'Ile bubbly. Tastings are paired with local, seasonal food. Wine by the glass, bread, cheese, smoked fish, and other fixings are available for summer picnics on the vineyard-view patio. Live bands entertain on Friday and Sunday afternoons in summer; events, from food fests to outdoor theater, happen regularly, too. ⊠ *151 Lee Rd., off Fulford-Ganges Rd., Salt Spring Island* ☎ *250/653–9463* ⊕ *www.saltspringvine-yards.com* 🛒 *$4 tasting fee, waived with purchase* ☉ *Closed weekdays Oct. to May. By appt. only in Jan. and Feb.*

 **Restaurants**

Auntie Pesto's

$$$ | **MODERN CANADIAN** | Fresh local ingredients and made-from-scratch fare keep regulars and visitors well fed at this family-run spot on Ganges' waterfront boardwalk. Settle in at lunchtime for a hearty sandwich (try the Grace Point Grill with local chèvre, pesto, and roasted vegetables), homemade soup, or any of almost a dozen pastas. **Known for:** local

ingredients; seasonal fare; waterfront location. 💲 *Average main: C$30* ⊠ *Grace Point Sq., 2104–115 Fulford Ganges Rd., Ganges, Salt Spring Island* ☎ *250/537–4181* ⊕ *www.auntiepestos.com.*

House Piccolo

$$$$ | **EUROPEAN** | Piccolo Lyytikainen, the Finnish-born chef-owner of this tiny restaurant in a quaint village house, serves beautifully prepared and present-ed European cuisine. Creations include Scandinavian-influenced dishes such as BC venison with a juniper-and-lingonberry demi-glace and charbroiled fillet of beef with Gorgonzola sauce. **Known for:** fine dining; Scandinavian-influenced cuisine; wine list. 💲 *Average main: C$36* ⊠ *108 Hereford Ave., Ganges, Salt Spring Island* ☎ *250/537–1844* ⊕ *www.housepiccolo. com* ☉ *Closed Mon. and Tues.*

Rock Salt Restaurant & Café

$$ | **ECLECTIC** | You can watch the ferry coming across the harbor from the sea-view windows of this Fulford Harbour eatery. Wholesome goodies run the gamut from slow-baked ribs to seafood curries to much-loved yam quesadillas. **Known for:** sea views; breakfast; great for take-away. 💲 *Average main: C$20* ⊠ *2920 Fulford Ganges Rd., Fulford, Salt Spring Island* ☎ *250/653–4833* ⊕ *www. rocksaltrestaurant.com.*

The Tree House Café

$$ | **ECLECTIC** | **FAMILY** | Gulf Island charm flourishes at this Ganges outdoor café, where handmade wooden booths are gathered under a spreading plum tree so you can sit and hear live music playing every summer night. Visitors and locals flock here for big wholesome breakfasts (think French toast with real maple syrup) and made-from-scratch burgers, wraps, and quesadillas. **Known for:** live music in summer; hip outdoor café; big breakfasts. 💲 *Average main: C$17* ⊠ *106 Purvis La., Ganges, Salt Spring Island* ☎ *250/537–5379* ⊕ *www.treehousecafe.ca.*

🛏 Hotels

Foxglove Farm

$$ | RENTAL | FAMILY | This 120-acre organic farm and education center on the road to Mount Maxwell has been developed on one of the island's oldest homesteads. **Pros:** beautiful, secluded rural setting; good for kids. **Cons:** far from town; two-or three-night minimum. 🅢 *Rooms from: C$175* ✉ *1200 Mount Maxwell Rd., Salt Spring Island* ☎ *250/537–1989* ⊕ *www. foxglovefarmbc.ca* ⌁ *3 cottages* 🍴 *No meals.*

⭐ Hastings House Country House Hotel

$$$$ | HOTEL | The centerpiece of this 22-acre Relais & Châteaux seaside estate—with its gardens, meadows, and harbor views—is a 1939 country house, built in the style of an 11th-century Sussex manor. **Pros:** wonderful food; top-notch service; historic character. **Cons:** no pool; some rooms overlook a nearby pub; pricey. 🅢 *Rooms from: C$485* ✉ *160 Upper Ganges Rd., Ganges, Salt Spring Island* ☎ *250/537–2362, 800/661–9255* ⊕ *www.hastingshouse.com* ⊗ *Closed Nov.–Feb.* ⌁ *18 suites and cottages* 🍴 *Free breakfast.*

Hedgerow House B and B

$$$ | B&B/INN | A great choice for a car-free vacation, this three-room inn on a quiet Ganges village street is just a five-minute walk to restaurants, cafés, shops, and the popular Saturday Market. **Pros:** close to town; hosts are tourism industry pros; yoga studio and spa. **Cons:** no kids under 12; showers only (no tubs); no ocean views. 🅢 *Rooms from: C$200* ✉ *238 Park Dr., Ganges, Salt Spring Island* ☎ *250/538–1716, 866/773–2838* ⊕ *hedgerowhouse.ca* ⌁ *3 rooms* 🍴 *Free breakfast.*

🛍 Shopping

To visit local artists in their studios, follow the Salt Spring Studio Tour map, listing more than 30 locations. You can either download the map from ⊕ *www. saltspringstudiotour.com* or pick it up at any of the local artist studios, Salt Spring Island Cheese, or at any of the island's hotels.

Salt Spring Island Cheese Company

FOOD/CANDY | FAMILY | Watch the cheese makers at work at this farm and cheese shop north of Fulford Harbour, where tasting is encouraged. Kids can walk through the farmyard to see the animals that provide the milk for the goat's and sheep's milk cheeses. In summer, a café serves baked sandwiches, pizzas, soups, and a goat milk gelato, with seating in the courtyard and garden. ✉ *285 Reynolds Rd., off Beaver Point Rd., Salt Spring Island* ☎ *250/653–2300* ⊕ *www. saltspringcheese.com.*

⭐ Salt Spring Island Saturday Market

OUTDOOR/FLEA/GREEN MARKETS | Locals and visitors alike flock to Ganges for the famous Saturday Market, held in Centennial Park from Easter through October. It's one of the island's most popular attractions. Everything sold at this colorful outdoor bazaar is made or grown on the island; the array and quality of crafts, food, and produce is dazzling. Centennial Park also hosts a farmers' market on summer Tuesdays. ✉ *Centennial Park, Fulford-Ganges Rd., Ganges, Salt Spring Island* ☎ *250/537–4448* ⊕ *www. saltspringmarket.com.*

Galiano Island

14 nautical miles from Swartz Bay, 11 nautical miles from Tsawwassen.

With its 26km-long (16-mile-long) eastern shore and cove-dotted western coast, Galiano is arguably the prettiest of these islands. It's certainly the best for hiking and mountain biking, with miles of trails through the Douglas fir and Garry Oak forest. Mt. Galiano and Bodega Ridge are classic walks, with far-reaching views to the mainland. Most shops and services—including cash machines, gas pumps, galleries, and a bookstore—are clustered near the Sturdies Bay ferry terminal. A visitor information booth is to your right as you leave the ferry.

GETTING HERE AND AROUND

Galiano Island is the gateway to the Southern Gulf Islands. The first stop on the Tsawwassen-Gulf Islands ferry route, it is easily accessible in under an hour from the Tsawwassen terminal or from Swartz Bay terminal on Vancouver Island. Seair Seaplanes flies regularly scheduled flights daily from Downtown Vancouver and the south terminal at Vancouver International Airport into Montague Harbour.

VISITOR INFORMATION

CONTACTS Galiano Island Travel Info Centre. ☎ *250/539–2233* 🌐 *www.galianoisland.com.*

Sights

Montague Harbour Marina
MARINA | You can rent a kayak, boat, or moped at Montague Harbour Marina, or grab a snack at the café on-site. ✉ *3451 Montague Park Rd., Galiano Island* ☎ *250/539–5733* 🌐 *www.montagueharbour.com* 🕐 *Closed Nov. to Apr.*

Montague Harbour Provincial Marine Park
BEACH—SIGHT | **FAMILY** | This provincial park on the island's southwest shore has a long shell beach famed for its sunset views. ✉ *Montague Park Rd., off Montague Rd., Galiano Island* ☎ *250/539–2115* 🌐 *www.env.gov.bc.ca/bcparks.*

Restaurants

Max and Moritz Spicy Island Food Truck
$ | **CANADIAN** | This food truck at the Sturdies Bay Ferry Terminal offers a unique combination of German and Indonesian takeout and all-day breakfast. **Known for:** all-day breakfast; takeaway; quick bite while waiting for the ferry. [$] *Average main: C$8* ✉ *Sturdies Bay Ferry Terminal, Sturdies Bay Rd., Galiano Island* ☎ *250/539–5888* 🕐 *Closed Nov.–Mar.*

★ **pilgrimme**
$$$$ | **CANADIAN** | This small resto in the woods has garnered all sorts of accolades since it first opened in 2014. Here chef Jesse McCleery, who spent a winter in the kitchen at Noma in Copenhagen, focuses on locally sourced food and unusual ingredients presented in the most imaginative ways. **Known for:** one of Canada's best restaurants; homey setting; charming staff. [$] *Average main: C$75* ✉ *2806 Montague Rd., Galiano Island* ☎ *250/539–5392* 🌐 *www.pilgrimme.ca* 🕐 *Closed Mon. to Wed. No lunch* ☞ *7-course fixed-price menu.*

Sturdies Bay Bakery and Cafe
$ | **CAFÉ** | **FAMILY** | Stop into this cheerful local favorite near the ferry terminal for freshly made pastries and sandwiches. The bread is highly praised, and you can often find roasted organic chicken or other cooked food for taking lunch to the beach. **Known for:** great for picnics; comfort food; fresh baked goods. [$] *Average main: C$10* ✉ *44 Madrona Dr., Galiano Island* ☎ *250/539–2004* 🌐 *www.facebook.com/SturdiesBayBakery* 🕐 *No dinner.*

Hotels

★ **Galiano Oceanfront Inn & Spa**
$$$ | **RESORT** | Just a block from the ferry and local shops, this inviting waterfront retreat on Sturdies Bay, which has both a nice restaurant and great spa, is an ideal spot for a car-free vacation. **Pros:** staff pick you up at the ferry; lovely spa; quiet environment. **Cons:** no pool; no hot tub; no fitness center. [$] *Rooms from: C$299* ✉ *134 Madrona Dr., Galiano Island* ☎ *250/539–3388, 877/530–3939* 🌐 *www.galianoinn.com* 🛏 *10 rooms, 10 suites* 🍴 *No meals.*

Bodega Ridge
$$$$ | **RENTAL** | **FAMILY** | Located on 22 acres at the base of Bodega Ridge on the north end of the island, these log cabins and lodge offer a rural escape. **Pros:** good for weddings and large groups; unspoiled scenery; vintage cabins. **Cons:** remote; no grocery stores or restaurants nearby; no TV or Wi-Fi in Ridge cabins. *$ Rooms from: C$350 ⊠ 120 Manastee Rd., Galiano Island ☎ 877/604–2677 ⊕ www.bodegaridge.com ⇨ 7 three-bedroom log cabins; 5 Panabode cabins ⦿ No meals.*

Nightlife

Hummingbird Pub
BARS/PUBS | The Hummingbird Pub is a friendly local hangout, with live music on summer weekends, plus a family-friendly restaurant and a lawn with a play area for kids. Also in summer, the pub runs a free shuttle bus to the Montague Harbour, stopping at both the marina and the campsite. *⊠ 47 Sturdies Bay Rd., Galiano Island ☎ 250/539–5472 ⊕ www.hummingbirdpub.com.*

Mayne Island

11 nautical miles from Swartz Bay, 14 nautical miles from Tsawwassen.

The smallest of the Southern Gulf Islands, Mayne also has the most visible history. The buildings of Miners Bay, the island's tiny commercial center, date to the 1850s, when Mayne was a stopover for prospectors en route to the gold fields. As the quietest and least hilly of the islands, Mayne is a good choice for cycle touring. It's also a popular spot for kayaking.

GETTING HERE AND AROUND
The BC Ferries direct route to Mayne Island takes 60 minutes from the Tsawwassen ferry terminal or 50 minutes from Swartz Bay on Vancouver Island. Ferries arrive at Village Bay on Mayne.

Seair Seaplanes flies regularly scheduled flights into Miners Bay from the south terminal at Vancouver International Airport.

VISITOR INFORMATION
CONTACTS Mayne Island Community Chamber of Commerce. ☎ 250/539–3571 ⊕ www.mayneislandchamber.ca.

Sights

Campbell Point
BEACH—SIGHT | **FAMILY** | Part of the Gulf Islands National Park Reserve, this waterfront area has walking trails and, at Bennett Bay, one of the island's most scenic beaches. *⊠ Bennett Bay ⊕ www.gulfislandsnationalpark.com.*

Georgina Point Heritage Park and Lighthouse
LIGHTHOUSE | **FAMILY** | This waterfront park overlooking Active Pass is part of the Gulf Islands National Park Reserve. It's also home to the Georgina Point Lighthouse; built in 1885, it still signals ships into the busy waterway. The grassy grounds are great for picnicking. *⊠ Georgina Point Rd. ⊕ www.gulfislandsnationalpark.com.*

Japanese Garden
GARDEN | Built entirely by volunteers, this 1-acre garden at Dinner Bay Park honors the island's early Japanese settlers. It's about ½ mile south of the Village Bay ferry terminal. *⊠ Dinner Bay Rd. ⊕ www.mayneisland.com ⊡ Free.*

Mt. Parke
NATIONAL/STATE PARK | A 45-minute hike up this 263-meter (863-foot) peak leads to the island's highest point and a stunning view of the mainland and other Gulf Islands. *⊠ Montrose Rd., off Fernhill Rd. ⊕ www.crd.bc.ca/parks.*

Plumper Pass Lockup
JAIL | Built in 1896, this former jail is now a minuscule museum chronicling Mayne Island's history. *⊠ 433 Fernhill Rd., Miners Bay ☎ 250/539–5286 ⊕ www.mayneisland.com ⊡ Free.*

The Springwater Lodge

HOTEL—SIGHT | You can stop for a meal or a drink on the deck at this lodge, one of the province's oldest continuously operating hotels. It's been around since 1892. ✉ *400 Fernhill Rd., Miners Bay* ☎ *250/539–5521* 🌐 *www.springwater-lodge.com.*

🍴 Restaurants

Sunny Mayne Bakery Café

$ | **BAKERY** | Join the locals for homemade soups, sandwiches, and baked treats at this tiny Miner's Bay spot; it's open for breakfast and lunch daily. **Known for:** baked goods; breakfast; daily pizza. [$] *Average main: C$9* ✉ *472 Village Bay Rd.* ☎ *250/539–2323* 🌐 *www.sunny-maynebakery.com* 🕒 *No dinner.*

🛏 Hotels

Mayne Island Resort

$$$$ | **RESORT** | Overlooking Bennett Bay and just steps from Mayne Island's best-loved beach, this chic modern resort enjoys a prime waterfront location and a wealth of amenities, including an indoor pool, a waterfront restaurant, and a spa. **Pros:** waterfront location; hot tub, steam room, and exercise room; private cottages. **Cons:** drop to the water makes it unsuitable for small children; no air-conditioning; no outdoor pool. [$] *Rooms from: C$329* ✉ *494 Arbutus Dr.* ☎ *250/539–3122,* 🌐 *www.mayneislandresort.com* 🛏 *14 beach homes, 8 waterview rooms* 🍽 *No meals.*

🛍 Shopping

Farmers' Market

OUTDOOR/FLEA/GREEN MARKETS | On Saturdays between mid-May and mid-October, check out the Farmers' Market outside the Miners Bay Agricultural Hall. Open from 10 to 1, it sells produce and crafts while local musicians entertain shoppers. ✉ *430 Fernhill Rd., Miners Bay* ☎ *250/222–0034* 🌐 *www.mayneisland-chamber.ca* 🕒 *Closed mid-Oct. to May.*

🏃 Activities

KAYAKING

Kayaking Gulf Islands

KAYAKING | This outfitter rents kayaks and stand-up paddleboards, and leads kayak day tours from mid-April through mid-October. ✉ *494 Arbutus Dr.* ☎ *250/539–0864* 🌐 *www.kayakinggulfislands.com.*

Pender Island

7.5 nautical miles from Swartz Bay, 18 nautical miles from Tsawwassen.

Just a few miles north of the U.S. border, Pender is actually two islands: North Pender and South Pender, divided by a canal and linked by a one-lane bridge. Most of the population of about 2,250 cluster on North Pender. The Penders are blessed with beaches, boasting more than 30 public beach-access points.

There's no town on either island, but you can find groceries, a bakery, gas, a bank, a pharmacy, a liquor store, and a Visitor Information Centre at North Pender's Driftwood Centre. A farmers' market runs on summer Saturdays at Pender Island Community Hall, and crafts shops, studios, and galleries are open throughout the islands.

GETTING HERE AND AROUND

Pender Island can be reached on BC Ferries in two hours and 15 minutes from Tsawwassen via Galiano and/or Mayne Island depending on the season. In summer there is a direct ferry to Otter Bay on Pender which takes just over an hour. From Swartz Bay on Vancouver Island the sailing takes 40 minutes. Seair Seaplanes flies regularly scheduled flights from the south terminal at Vancouver International Airport.

Once on Pender it's easy to get around the two islands with Pender Island Cab Company.

CONTACTS Pender Island Cab Company. *☎ 250/629–2222 🌐 www.penderisland-cab.com.*

VISITOR INFORMATION

CONTACTS Pender Island Chamber of Commerce. *✉ Driftwood Centre, 4605 Bedwell Harbour Rd. ☎ 250/999-6371 🌐 www.penderislandchamber.com.*

Sights

Gowlland Point Park

BEACH—SIGHT | The small pebble beach at Gowlland Point Park, at the end of Gowlland Point Road on South Pender, is one of the prettiest on the islands, with views across to Washington State. *✉ Gowlland Point Rd. 🌐 www.crd.bc.ca.*

Gulf Islands National Park Reserve

MUSEUM | Both North Pender and South Pender host sections of the Gulf Islands National Park Reserve. On South Pender a steep trail leads to the 800-foot summit of Mt. Norman, with its expansive ocean and island views; in the newer Greenburn Lake section of the park, forest trails circle a pretty freshwater lake. On North Pender, a historic cottage resort called Roesland is now part of the park; one of the circa-1908 cottages houses the Pender Island Museum., An easy 15-minute walk leads to a tiny islet. *✉ Pender Island ☎ 250/654–4000 🌐 www.pc.gc.ca/pn-np/bc/gulf/index.aspx.*

Hope Bay

MARINA | Red Tree Gallery, an artisans' co-op, Pender Chocolates, and views to Saturna and Mayne islands are the draws at Hope Bay, a lovely cove on North Pender's eastern shore. *✉ 4301 Bedwell Harbour Rd., North Pender Island.*

Mortimer Spit

BEACH—SIGHT | The sandy beach at Mortimer Spit is a sheltered spot for swimming and kayaking; it's near the bridge linking the two islands. *✉ Mortimer Spit Rd., off Canal Rd., South Pender Island.*

Pender Islands Museum

MUSEUM | **FAMILY** | In a 1908 farmhouse at Roesland on North Pender, part of the Gulf Islands National Park Reserve, this tiny museum houses local historic artifacts. *✉ 2408 S. Otter Bay Rd., North Pender Island ☎ 250/629–6935 🌐 www.penderislandmuseum.ca 🎫 Donations accepted 🕒 Closed weekdays and Jan. to May.*

Sea Star Estate Farm and Vineyards

WINERY/DISTILLERY | There are actually two vineyards on this lovely 26-acre property—the upper vineyard clings to Mount Menzies while the lower trails down to the sea—both kept trim by a resident flock of small Babydoll Southdown sheep. Vintages from the first two years proved so popular that the vineyard has now increased to maximum production capacity. The award-winning Ortega and Blanc de Noir continue to sell out. Island Time food truck serves appetizers in the licensed picnic area off the Tasting Room. *✉ 6621 Harbour Hill Dr., North Pender Island ☎ 250/629–6960 🌐 www.seastarvineyards.ca 🎫 C$5 tasting fee, waived with purchase 🕒 Tasting room closed Nov. to Apr.*

Restaurants

The Stand

$ | **BURGER** | You can refuel before catching the ferry at the Stand, a rustic take-out shack at the Otter Bay ferry terminal. The burgers—whether beef, salmon, halibut, or veggie—are enormous, messy, and delicious. **Known for:** outdoor seating; good for kids; huge burgers. *[$] Average main: C$11 ✉ Otter Bay Ferry Terminal, 1371 MacKinnon Rd., North Pender Island ☎ 250/629–3292 💳 No credit cards 🕒 No dinner.*

🛏 Hotels

★ Poets Cove Resort & Spa

$$$$ | **RESORT** | One of the Gulf Islands' most well-appointed developments fills a secluded cove on South Pender. **Pros:** great views; family-friendly vibe; beautifully appointed. **Cons:** 20-minute drive from the ferry; spa closes during off-season; restaurant only open in peak season. $ *Rooms from: C$350* ✉ *9801 Spalding Rd., South Pender Island* ☎ *250/629–2100, 888/512–7638* ⊕ *www.poetscove.com* ⛴ *22 lodge rooms, 15 cottages, 9 villas* ⦿ *No meals.*

WOODS on Pender

$$$ | **RESORT** | **FAMILY** | Ever dreamed of sleeping in an Airstream? This unique glamping resort gives you the opportunity to do just that, while offering hassle-free camping with all the extras, including hot tubs, upscale tents, hammocks, propane fire pits, and air-conditioning. **Pros:** hip campground; modern glamping experience; well-appointed Airstream trailers. **Cons:** 2- or 3-night minimum in Airstreams or cabins; no pool; not on the water. $ *Rooms from: C$285* ✉ *4709 Canal Rd.* ☎ *250/629–3353, 800/550–0172* ⊕ *www.woodsonpender.com* ⛴ *8 Airstream trailers, 3 cabins, 9 motel rooms* ⦿ *No meals.*

Saturna Island

16 nautical miles from Swartz Bay, 14 nautical miles from Tsawwassen.

With just 350 residents, remote Saturna Island is taken up largely by a section of the Gulf Islands National Park Reserve and is a prime spot for hiking, kayaking, and beachcombing. The most remote of the Southern Gulf Islands, Saturna usually takes two ferries to reach. It has no bank or pharmacy but it does have an ATM, pub, general store, café, and winery. There's also a full-service restaurant at Saturna Lodge.

GETTING HERE AND AROUND

From the Tsawwassen ferry terminal take BC Ferries to Village Bay on Mayne Island, then connect to Lyall Harbour on Saturna. From Swartz Bay on Vancouver Island there are direct sailings, as well as some with a transfer on Mayne Island. Seair Seaplanes flies three flights daily from the south terminal at Vancouver International Airport.

VISITOR INFORMATION

CONTACTS Saturna Island Tourism Association. ⊕ *www.saturnatourism.com.*

🍴 Restaurants

Saturna Lighthouse Pub

$$ | **PACIFIC NORTHWEST** | This is a great place to grab a bite while waiting for the ferry at Lyall Harbour. Menus are seasonal and offer local, organic ingredients, such as island-grown lamb burger and organic free-range chicken wings. **Known for:** pub grub; great views; fish-and-chips. $ *Average main: C$17* ✉ *100 East Point Rd.* ✛ *Next to the ferry terminal in Lyall Harbour* ☎ *250/539–5725* ⊕ *www.saturnapub.com* ⊘ *Closed Nov. and Dec.*

🛏 Hotels

Saturna Lodge

$$ | **B&B/INN** | **FAMILY** | This cozy five-room inn, surrounded by gardens and overlooking pretty, forested Boot Cove, makes a great base for exploring the island. **Pros:** family- and pet-friendly; free ferry and floatplane shuttle; free Wi-Fi. **Cons:** restaurant closed some evenings; no pool; some rooms are small. $ *Rooms from: C$179* ✉ *130 Payne Rd.* ☎ *250/539–2254, 866/539–2254* ⊕ *www.saturna.ca* ⛴ *5 guest rooms* ⦿ *Free breakfast.*

Chapter 12

WHISTLER

Updated by
Jennifer Foden

British Columbia

◉ Sights	🍴 Restaurants	🛏 Hotels	🛍 Shopping	🍸 Nightlife
★★★☆☆	★★★★☆	★★★★★	★★★★☆	★★★★★

WELCOME TO WHISTLER

TOP REASONS TO GO

★ **Skiing Whistler and Blackcomb:** With more than 8,000 acres of skiing terrain, this is one of North America's premier mountain resorts.

★ **Getting to Whistler:** The incredibly scenic Sea-to-Sky Highway gets you from Vancouver to Whistler in about two hours (longer if you stop off in Squamish to try the awe-inspiring Sea-to-Sky Gondola).

★ **The PEAK 2 PEAK Gondola:** One of Whistler Blackcomb's signature activities, the 11-minute trip is one of the most spectacular rides of its kind in the world.

★ **Zipping Through Whistler's Wilds:** Adrenaline-infused ziplines through stands of hemlock, across canyons, and over raging rivers let you feel Whistler up-close-and-personal.

★ **Catching the Olympic Spirit:** Surge down the bobsleigh and skeleton course, ski with an Olympian, or climb into one of the rings for a digital moment. Visitors can also experience the biathlon and cross-country trails at Whistler Olympic Park.

Whistler is a sophisticated alpine community lying within an easy—and stunningly beautiful—two-hour drive of Vancouver. It is the gateway to year-round, outdoor adventures for every age, ability, and pocketbook. In winter, there are snow activities galore alongside mountaintop fondues. In summer, it's all about mountain biking, picnics on a glacier, fishing, hiking, and rafting. Neighboring Squamish and Pemberton offer pastoral valleys, organic farms, and a gentler pace of life.

1 Whistler Village. The pedestrian-only, compact core of the resort offers a network of paths, trails, and covered walkways lined with shops, eateries, and people-watching opportunities. The bases of Whistler and Blackcomb mountains are at the village edge, so you can even ski to the door of many hotels and condos.

2 Upper Village. The petite Upper Village—Blackcomb Mountain's base and home to the luxurious Four Seasons Resort Whistler and Fairmont Chateau Whistler—provides a quieter option for those who want to be out of the hubbub of the main village. There's also a wonderful footpath and covered bridge that connect the two areas easily.

3 Blackcomb Mountain. At 5,280 feet in elevation, Blackcomb is the resort's original home to snowboarding (but it's equally shared with skiers now) with its main base in the Upper Village.

4 Whistler Mountain. At 5,020 feet, the shorter of the resort's two mountains, Whistler has more skiable terrain and can accommodate 35,500 skiers per hour, with its main base in Whistler Village.

5 Whistler Creekside. Located 10 minutes south of Whistler Village on Highway 99, Creekside is the original village offering renovated shopping and dining developments at the resort.

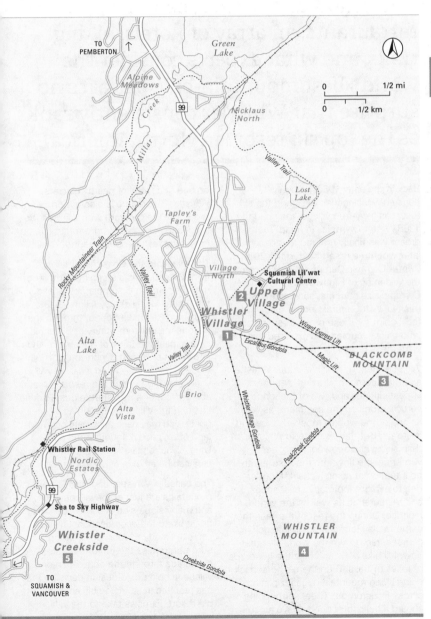

With two breathtaking mountains—Whistler and Blackcomb—enviable skiing, golf courses, shops, and restaurants, an array of hotels, hiking trails, and what experts consider the world's best mountain-bike park, it's no surprise that Whistler consistently ranks as the top ski resort in North America.

Back in the early 1960s, when Whistler's early visionaries designed the ski resort as a car-free village, they had the 1968 Winter Olympics in mind. That dream was finally realized four decades later when the resort hosted the 2010 Winter Olympic Games. With that came the widening of Highway 99 and other Olympic-size benefits, such as the Squamish-Lil'Wat Cultural Centre, a cultural focal point for these proud First Nations who have occupied and explored this wilderness region for millennia.

Whistler Resort, which includes Whistler and Blackcomb mountains, has the largest ski area and two of the longest vertical drops on the continent, as well as one of the world's most advanced lift systems. But there's more to Whistler than skiing and snowboarding; each winter people flow into the resort with no intention of riding a chairlift, preferring to explore the many spas, shops, and restaurants, as well as the varied nightlife. During the rest of the year, they come to play four championship golf courses, race down the world's largest downhill bike park, and hike the hundreds of miles of trails. Then there's horseback riding along mountain ridges, ziplining across Fitzsimmons Creek, or hopping aboard a helicopter ride to have lunch

on one of dozens of nearby glaciers. Whistler Blackcomb is also a member of the Epic Pass program with Vail Resorts, a ski- and perk-pass program that can be used at other top-notch resorts.

The drive into the Coast Mountains from Vancouver is a stunning sampler of mainland British Columbia. You'll follow the Sea-to-Sky Highway (Highway 99) past fjordlike Howe Sound, through the historic mining community of Britannia Beach, past the town of Squamish, and into Whistler Resort. Once you're in Whistler, you don't really need a car; anywhere you want to go within the resort is reachable by foot or a free shuttle bus. Parking lots ring the village, although as a hotel guest, you may have access to coveted (and often pricey) underground parking. Unless you're planning to tour the region, cars can be an expensive hindrance.

The bases of Whistler and Blackcomb mountains are just at the village edge, and many slope-side accommodations boast ski-to-the-door locations. If you can ski directly to your room, though, be sure not to miss the fun of the après-ski parade through the pedestrian-only village, a bold urban-design decision that has resulted in an incredibly accessible resort. Families take to the Village

Stroll in search of Cows Ice Cream and its racks of novelty, bovine-themed T-shirts. Couples shop for engagement rings or the latest Roots sportswear styles. Skiers and snowboarders shuffle through the crowd, leaning their skis and boards against the buildings to dip into the vibrant après-ski scene on a dozen outdoor heated patios. The village warren continues to expand, and Village North (or Marketplace) has all but been absorbed.

Against this backdrop, Whistler has also been building its identity as a progressive, livable, and sustainably green city, with programs for accessible housing and strong schools. Though only 8% of the 161 square km (100 square miles) that comprise Whistler is designated for development, North America's premier four-season resort continues to grow, especially now that the world has visited during the 2010 Winter Games.

Planning

When to Go

Whistler teems with partying Vancouverites, especially during the off-season. Three days provide plenty of time for zipping, skiing, biking, or whatever your alpine adventure may be, but you'll quickly discover that it's a very happening place almost every day, with open-air concerts throughout the summer and weekly shows in winter with the area's best skiers and riders jumping through blazing rings of fire. Spring and fall are also great getaway times—the value, weather and activities still provide an exciting trip.

Festivals

JANUARY–FEBRUARY
During **Whistler Pride and Ski Festival** (⊕ gaywhistler.com), held at the end of January, into the beginning of February, the resort heats up for a week with naughty nightlife, fine dining, fabulous après-ski, and slope-side fun.

APRIL
The raucous **World Ski & Snowboard Festival** (⊕ www.wssf.com) end-of-the-season bash fills 10 days with music, arts, fashion shows, and extreme sports.

JUNE
When the going gets tough, hundreds of die-hard warriors head for the two-day **Tough Mudder** (⊕ www.toughmudder.com), a grueling military-style obstacle course that tests more than physical stamina.

AUGUST
The annual **Crankworx** (⊕ www.crankworx.com) mountain-bike festival showcases the sport's boldest and most talented athletes as they whip down double black-diamond runs; there are also daily concerts and a huge downhill biking scene.

SEPTEMBER
The four-day, suds-filled **Whistler Village Beer Festival** (⊕ wvbf.ca) celebrates everything that makes the craft beer movement one of the world's fastest growing drinking phenomenons.

NOVEMBER
There's a little bit of everything at **Cornucopia** (⊕ www.whistlercornucopia.com), an 11-day annual festival for foodies and oenophiles. The grand gala is a veritable who's who in the Pacific Northwest wine industry. Spirits and craft beer also abound.

DECEMBER
The annual **Whistler Film Festival** (⊕ www.whistlerfilmfestival.com) features world premieres from top directors, industry

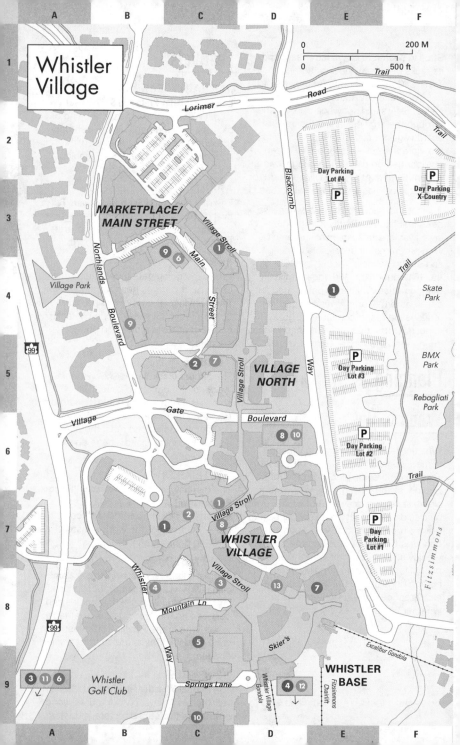

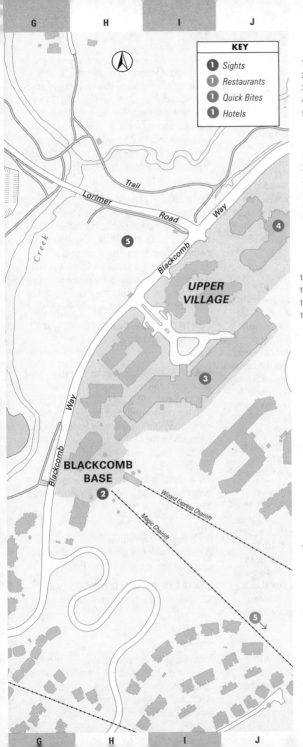

KEY

1 *Sights*

1 *Restaurants*

1 *Quick Bites*

1 *Hotels*

Sights ▼

1 Audain Art Museum **E4**
2 Blackcomb Gondola **H6**
3 Montis Distilling **A9**
4 PEAK 2 PEAK Gondola **D9**
5 Squamish Lil'wat
Cultural Centre **H3**

Restaurants ▼

1 Araxi **C7**
2 Bar Oso **C7**
3 Basalt Wine & Salumeria **C8**
4 Bearfoot Bistro **B8**
5 Christine's on Blackcomb **J8**
6 Elements **C4**
7 Hy's Steakhouse and
Cocktail Bar **C5**
8 La Brasserie **C7**
9 Quattro at Whistler **B4**
10 The Raven Room **D6**
11 Rimrock Café **A9**
12 Steeps Grill and Wine Bar **D9**
13 Sushi Village **D8**

Quick Bites ▼

1 Purebread **C3**

Hotels ▼

1 Adara Hotel **C7**
2 Delta Hotels by Marriott
Whistler Village Suites **C5**
3 Fairmont Château
Whistler Resort **I5**
4 Four Seasons Resort Whistler **J3**
5 Hilton Whistler Resort
and Spa **C8**
6 Nita Lake Lodge **A9**
7 Pan Pacific Whistler
Mountainside **E8**
8 Pan Pacific Whistler
Village Centre **D6**
9 Summit Lodge
Boutique Hotel **C3**
10 The Westin Resort
and Spa, Whistler **C9**

events, and parties, all with a Canadian focus.

Getting Here and Around

Just 120 km (75 miles) north of Vancouver on Highway 99 (Sea-to-Sky Highway), Whistler is easy to get to from Vancouver, depending on your budget. You won't need a car once you're here; even if you choose to stay outside the village, you can get around easily with public shuttle buses or taxis. The closest airport is Vancouver International Airport, about 135 km (84 miles) away.

AIR
If you've got the money, you can travel in style from the airport to the slopes: Blackcomb Helicopters has charter helicopter and airplane service between Whistler and Vancouver International Airport or Vancouver Harbour. Harbour Air connects Victoria and Whistler, from June through September. Its affiliate, Whistler Air, runs two daily flights between Vancouver's Coal Harbour and the Whistler area from mid-May to early October. In the winter, Harbour Air manages many of the online bookings for Westcoast Air and Whistler Air. ⇨ *For more information on these companies, see Air Travel in Travel Smart.*

VIP Whistler runs a private car service from Vancouver International Airport to Whistler starting at C$325 per trip for all size groups. Pearl International Limousine Service has limos, sedans, and 10-passenger vans—all equipped with blankets, pillows, bottled water, and videos so you can enjoy the ride. Rates start at about C$350 from the airport. ⇨ *For more information see Ground Transportation in Travel Smart.*

BUS
YVR Skylynx has daily bus service to Whistler from Vancouver International Airport and from many Vancouver hotels (eight times a day in ski season, five times a day in summer). One-way fares start at C$55; reservations are recommended. Departing from various stops in Vancouver (check the website during the season for stop details), the Snow Bus is a winter-only luxury coach with snacks and movies. Finally, Ridebooker offers service to Whistler from Vancouver Airport. (⇨ *For more information on these bus companies, see Bus Travel in Travel Smart.*)

The Whistler and Valley Express (WAVE) bus system, operated by BC Transit, operates a year-round public-transit system that connects the village, Creekside, and neighborhoods to the north and south. Seasonal, free shuttle services are also available to Lost Lake Park (summer) and Marketplace (winter). ⇨ *See Bus Travel in Travel Smart for more information.*

CONTACTS Snow Bus. ☏ *604/451–1130* ⊕ *www.snowbus.com.*

CAR
Driving from Vancouver to Whistler takes approximately two hours along the scenic Sea-to-Sky Highway (aka Highway 99). It's recommended to check weather conditions during the winter season; in spite of considerable improvements for the Olympics, rockslides still occur and can cause delays. ⇨ *For information on car rentals at the Vancouver airport or in Vancouver itself, see Car Travel in Travel Smart.*

TAXI
For a cab in the Whistler area call Whistler Taxi or Resort Cabs. Service is available around the clock.

CONTACTS Whistler Taxi. ☏ *604/938–3333* ⊕ *www.whistlertaxi.com.*

Hotels

Affordable Whistler is not an oxymoron. Prices may have soared here before the 2010 Vancouver Olympics, but every effort has been made to keep the mountains accessible to as many kinds of pocketbooks as possible. Sure, there are some up-in-the-stratosphere prices to be found, but the range of options among the condos, bed-and-breakfasts, self-service suites, and hotel rooms means that Whistler is as accessible to families and active boomers as it is with the youthful crowd who take advantage of sharing suites with sofa beds, bunk beds, and dorm-style accommodations. The farther away from the village, the cheaper the price. Nevertheless, ski-in ski-out hotels and lodges command premium rates. Unless otherwise noted, hotels offer free Wi-Fi. Contacting Whistler.com (☎ 800/944–7853) is the most efficient way of securing the best accommodations to fit your budget.

Price categories are based on January–April ski-season rates; prices will be higher during Christmas and school breaks, but lower in summer and considerably lower in the shoulder seasons. Minimum stays during all holidays are pretty much the rule. Also, Whistler Village has some serious nightlife: if peace and quiet are important to you, ask for a room away from the main pedestrian thoroughfares, book in the Upper Village, or stay in one of the residential neighborhoods outside the village.

Hotel reviews have been shortened. For full information, visit Fodors.com.

Restaurants

Whistler's restaurant scene is varied enough to please the palates of its more than 12,000 residents and sophisticated enough to cater to the tastes of its thousands of international visitors. You can relax with a cappuccino in an unpretentious back-alley coffee shop; chill out (and people-watch) on a patio with a dish of homemade fusilli, or splurge on award-winning cuisine with magnificent wine pairings. Although some restaurants do close during the shoulder seasons for a brief respite, no one goes

hungry here, especially when you realize that many of Vancouver's celebrity chefs now call Whistler home. Today, some of the top ski-resort restaurants in the world take advantage of the growing locavore or Slow Food movement—as evidenced during four months of Sunday and Wednesday farmers' markets and organic bounty—to provide diners with a surprising array of Northwest cuisine. Foodies will especially enjoy Whistler's Cornucopia Festival, showcasing culinary talents and BC producers (wine, beer, spirits) as well as international producers every November. Then there's the Beer Festival, a sudsy celebration of craft brews from the Pacific Northwest (widely considered the birthplace of North America's craft beer movement) and beyond. And for grazers? Tasting tours will while away an afternoon or evening.

For those on lower dining budgets, there are plenty of sandwich and coffee shops scattered around the village. There are also four full-scale grocery stores should you land a room with a kitchen.

Restaurant reviews have been shortened. For full information, visit Fodors.com.

What It Costs in Canadian dollars

$	$$	$$$	$$$$
RESTAURANTS			
under C$13	C$13–C$20	C$21–C$30	over C$30
HOTELS			
under C$126	C$126–C$195	C$196–C$300	over C$300

Visitor Information

CONTACTS Tourism Whistler. ☎ 800/944–7853 ⊕ www.whistler.com. **Whistler Visitor Centre.** ✉ 4230 Gateway Drive ☎ 604/935–3357 ⊕ www.whistler.com. **Whistler.com.** ☎ 800/944–7853 ⊕ www.whistler.com.

Pedestrian-only Whistler Village is lined with shops, restaurants, and bars.

Sights

Audain Art Museum

MUSEUM | Nestled behind some trees, this museum's architecture is just as striking as the art inside. The collection, donated by Michael Audain and his wife Yoshiko Karasawa, has something for everyone—from over two dozen Emily Carr works to Northwest Coast masks to Vancouver photo-conceptualist works. They also host regular lectures and workshops. ⊠ *4350 Blackcomb Way* ☎ *604/962–0413* ⊕ *www.audainartmuseum.com* 🖾 *C$18* ☞ *Closed Tues.*

★ PEAK 2 PEAK Gondola

VIEWPOINT | FAMILY | The longest and tallest gondola in the world when it opened, the PEAK 2 PEAK delivers jaw-dropping views as it travels 4.3 km (2.7 miles) from Whistler's Roundhouse to Blackcomb's Rendezvous Lodge, which sits at an elevation of 7,000 feet. Two gondolas have a glass-floor viewing area that are worth the extra few minutes' wait; there's a separate lineup for these. A day pass may seem costly until you realize that you can ride PEAK 2 PEAK as many times as you wish, plus travel up and down both Whistler and Blackcomb on a fully enclosed gondola system, a 13.5 km (8.3 miles) loop forming the longest continuous lift system in the world. In summer, the ski runs and the rest of the mountainsides open up to 50 km (31 miles) of incredible hiking. Discounts are offered for multiple days. ⊠ *Roundhouse Lodge, Whistler Mountain* ☎ *800/766–0449* ⊕ *www.whistlerblackcomb.com* 🖾 *C$65* ⊘ *Closed weekdays mid-Sept.– mid-Oct.; closed mid-Oct.–mid-Nov. and mid-Apr.–mid-May.*

Blackcomb Gondola

MOUNTAIN—SIGHT | FAMILY | Opened in December 2018, this 10-person, Doppelmayr lift carries 184 cable cars and transports 4,000 people per hour as it runs from the Upper Village to the Rendezvous Lodge on Blackcomb Mountain. The three consecutive gondola rides—Blackcomb, P2P, and Whistler Village Gondola—form a continuous lift

On-mountain Eating Options 🍴

Like the world's best ski resorts, Whistler has a great variety of on-mountain eating options. You'll find them all listed on the trail/resort map, but these are the key ones to know about.

Both Whistler and Blackcomb have a day lodge, accessible from the gondola, with a cafeteria that serves an array of soup, sandwiches, and hot food options. At the other end of the spectrum, there is fine dining at Christine's on Blackcomb in the Rendezvous lodge and at Steep's Grill & Wine Bar in Whistler's Roundhouse. Should you be moving about on one plank or two, don't miss Whistler's Harmony Hut and Blackcomb's Horstman Hut for chili and other comfort foods to go with spectacular views. Crystal Hut is where to find terrific Belgian waffles and fondues on Blackcomb. In-the-know skiers head to the Glacier Creek Lodge for a shorter lunch line. Raven's Nest on Whistler offers vegetarian and vegan options.

system of 13.5 km (8 miles) and take 43 minutes of ride time to complete. It is the longest continuous lift system in the world. ✉ *Whistler* 🌐 *www.whistlerblackcomb.com/.*

Montis Distilling

WINERY/DISTILLERY | Whistler's first and only craft distillery produces gin and vodka using botanicals from the local natural surroundings. You can book a tour and tasting at their small facility in Function Junction or order a cocktail in Whistler Village at one of the many restaurants and bars that carry their spirits: The Raven Room, Basalt, Bearfoot, and more. ✉ *1062 Millar Creek Rd.* ☎ *778/996-7368* 🌐 *www.montisdistilling.com.*

★ **Squamish Lil'wat Cultural Centre**

NATIVE SITE | **FAMILY** | A collaborative project located on the shared territories of the Squamish Nation and Lil'wat Nation, this cultural center is designed to celebrate these two distinct Salish Nations. The concrete, cedar, and fir structure melds the longhouse concept of the coastal Squamish people with the traditional pit house of the interior Lil'wat people. Inside, carvings adorn the walls and displays of art, artifacts, and tools reveal the similarities and differences of the Nations. Try to catch one of the regularly scheduled guided tours offered on the hour, every hour, 10 am–4 pm. The on-site café, which serves contemporary food with a First Nations twist—think venison chili, bannock tacos, or smoked salmon panini—is worth a visit itself. ✉ *4584 Blackcomb Way* ☎ *866/441–7522* 🌐 *www.slcc.ca* 🎟 *C$18* 🕓 *Closed Mon. in mid-Oct.–mid-Apr.*

🍴 Restaurants

Araxi

$$$$ | **CONTEMPORARY** | Well-chosen antiques and original artwork create a vibrantly chic atmosphere for what has always been one of Whistler's top fine-dining restaurants. Local farmers grow produce exclusively for Araxi's chef, who also makes good use of regional cheeses, game, and fish. **Known for:** semi-private wine room; nightly tasting menus; daily fondue in the winter. [$] *Average main: C$35* ✉ *110–4222 Village Sq.* ☎ *604/932–4540* 🌐 *www.araxi.com* 🕓 *No lunch.*

★ Bar Oso

$$ | TAPAS | This intimate, cozy restaurant serves Spanish-influenced small plates and tapas for lunch and dinner. You can sit right up at the bar and watch (and chat with) the chef as he prepares everything from wild scallops with capers, olives, and oranges to roasted shishito peppers with romesco sauce to their popular charcuterie boards. **Known for:** late-night eats; reservations are not required; seasonal cocktail menu. $ *Average main: C$20* ⊠ *150–4222 Village Sq.* ☎ *604/962–4540* ⊕ *www.baroso.ca.*

Basalt Wine & Salumeria

$$$ | CANADIAN | This trendy spot has an impressive wine list, fun happy hour, and outstanding outdoor patio (which they keep open in the winter with heated lamps). Popular dishes include the Cornish game hen with collard greens, roasted sockeye salmon, and the glazed pork belly with caramelized onion and yam hash. **Known for:** cheese fondue in the fall and winter; in-house made charcuterie; locally sourced menu. $ *Average main: C$29* ⊠ *13–154 Village Green* ☎ *604/962–9011* ⊕ *www.basaltwhistler. com* ⊗ *No lunch in the summer* ⊟ *No credit cards.*

★ Bearfoot Bistro

$$$$ | FRENCH FUSION | As one of Whistler's top destination restaurants, this elegant bistro never fails to impress. The modern Canadian-inspired cuisine means that the menu choices, which change daily depending on the availability of local products, may include anything from a rack of wild caribou with sweet corn to pepper-crusted elk carpaccio to steamed Dungeness crab with garlic herbed butter. **Known for:** 20,000-bottle wine cellar; attached to Ketel One Ice Room, the coldest vodka tasting room in the world; romantic, intimate vibe. $ *Average main: C$45* ⊠ *4121 Village Green* ☎ *604/932–3433* ⊕ *www.bearfootbistro. com* ⊗ *No lunch.*

Christine's on Blackcomb

$$$ | CANADIAN | On-mountain dining is surprisingly accessible to those without skis. On Blackcomb Mountain, there's Christine's, offering classic dishes such as crab risotto or fish curry. **Known for:** located at the eye of Blackcomb Mountain's skiing; open in the summer; seafood-forward menu. $ *Average main: C$28* ⊠ *Rendezvous Lodge, Blackcomb Mountain* ☎ *604/938–7437* ⊕ *www.whis-tlerblackcomb.com* ⊗ *No dinner; closed spring and fall.*

Elements

$$ | CANADIAN | Locals consistently rank Elements, which is found in Summit Lodge, as having the best tapas in the area. It's a hip eatery with everyone from animated thirtysomethings to jet-setting families with young children. **Known for:** gluten-free and vegan menu items; fancy food at affordable prices; extensive Canadian wine list. $ *Average main: C$17* ⊠ *Summit Lodge, 4359 Main St., Whistler Village* ☎ *604/932–5569* ⊕ *www. elementswhistler.com* ⊗ *No dinner Sun.– Tues. in shoulder seasons.*

Hy's Steakhouse and Cocktail Bar

$$$$ | STEAKHOUSE | If beef's your passion, then you don't get much better than Hy's, a hard-core steak house that's famous for the quality of its Alberta Prime fillets, porterhouses, and New York strips. Beef Wellington comes in a handmade flaky crust, and there are steak and lobster combos. **Known for:** irresistible cheese toast; world-class service; extensive wine selection. $ *Average main: C$50* ⊠ *Delta Whistler Village Suites, 4308 Main St., Whistler Village* ☎ *604/905–5555* ⊕ *www. hyssteakhouse.com* ⊗ *No lunch.*

La Brasserie

$$ | EUROPEAN | "The Brass," as it's known, has one of the area's best patios, situated in the square where people-watching is as entertaining as the street performers and free concerts. With this kind of location the food doesn't have to be outstanding, but you can nevertheless get well-priced bistro fare, from burgers to steaks. **Known for:** home-cooked food; amazing patio; reasonably priced. $ *Average main: C$20* ✉ *4232 Village Stroll, Whistler Village* ☎ *604/932–3569* ⊕ *www.orinc.ca.*

Quattro at Whistler

$$$$ | **ITALIAN** | Vancouverites in search of fine Italian fare flock to the Pinnacle Hotel for warming après-ski meals. The dining room exudes a whimsical Venetian style with ornamental ironwork, picturesque tiles, and hand-painted chandeliers. **Known for:** extensive wine list; warm atmosphere; upscale, but not pretentious. $ *Average main: C$33* ✉ *Pinnacle Hotel, 4319 Main St., Whistler Village* ☎ *604/905–4844* ⊕ *www.quattrorestaurants.com* ⊙ *No lunch.*

The Raven Room

$$$ | **PACIFIC NORTHWEST** | Located inside the Pan Pacific Whistler Village Centre, The Raven Room is not your average hotel eatery: it's privately owned by four renowned Whistler restaurateurs. The menu consists of both small plates (tapas) and larger mains and is sure to satisfy everyone, from carnivores to vegans. **Known for:** mountain views; innovative cocktail list; dessert menu. $ *Average main: C$28* ✉ *4299 Blackcomb Way* ☎ *604/962-0311* ⊕ *www.theravenroom.ca* ⊙ *No lunch.*

Rimrock Café

$$$$ | **SEAFOOD** | About 3 km (2 miles) south of the village, this restaurant is a perennial favorite as much for its cozy, unpretentious dining room as for its great seafood. Although seafood takes precedence on the menu—try the raw oysters with champagne—Alberta beef and local game will satisfy carnivores. **Known for:** its sampler dishes; intimate vibe; large, global wine list. $ *Average main: C$42* ✉ *2117 Whistler Rd., Whistler Creekside* ☎ *604/932–5565, 877/932–5589* ⊕ *www.rimrockwhistler.com* ⊙ *No lunch* ⚲ *Closed mid-Oct.–mid-Nov.*

Steeps Grill & Wine Bar

$$$ | **PACIFIC NORTHWEST** | Although it's atop Whistler Mountain, you're likely to see as many nonskiers as skiers in the crowd dining here. That's because Steeps Grill & Wine Bar is located inside the enormous Roundhouse Lodge at the top of Whistler Village Gondola, and lots of the visitors are simply sightseers. **Known for:** incredible views; west coast cuisine; wine flights. $ *Average main: C$22* ✉ *Roundhouse Lodge, Whistler Mountain* ☎ *604/905–2379* ⊕ *www.whistlerblackcomb.com* ▭ *No credit cards* ⊙ *No dinner. Closed in summer and fall.*

Sushi Village

$$ | **JAPANESE** | If you don't equate sushi with social buzz, then you haven't been to this perennial Whistler hot spot, which offers everything from après-ski to latenight dining. The chef's choice sashimi is a favorite, as are the dozen different house special rolls, including one tasty combination of shrimp tempura, avocado, scallops, and salmon. **Known for:** sake selection (and sake margaritas); festive environment; the sashimi is super popular. $ *Average main: C$20* ✉ *4340 Sundial Crescent, Whistler Village* ☎ *604/932–3330* ⊕ *www.sushivillage.com* ⊙ *No lunch Mon.–Thurs.*

☕ Coffee and Quick Bites

Purebread

$ | **BAKERY** | This bustling little bakery is popular with tourists and locals alike. They serve delicious coffee, as well as plenty of sweet and savory goodies, from three-cheese sandwiches and vegan raspberry scones to gourmet banana and chocolate brownies and more. **Known for:** sweet and savory scones; outrageous brownies; huge selection of breads and cakes. $ *Average main: C$8* ✉ *122-4338 Main Street, Whistler Village* ☎ *604/962–1182* ⊕ *www.purebread.ca* ⊙ *No dinner.*

A leisurely hike through Garibaldi Provincial Park.

Hotels

Adara Hotel

$$$ | **HOTEL** | With its designer furniture (think curvy white Verner Panton chairs) and a vibrant color scheme of reds and browns, the Adara provides an urban alternative to the typical ski-lodge experience. **Pros:** free boxed breakfast in winter; hip environment; pet-friendly. **Cons:** no on-site restaurant; no bathtubs, just showers; can get quite noisy. [$] *Rooms from: C$260* ✉ *4122 Village Green, Whistler Village* ☎ *604/905–4009, 866/502–3272* 🌐 *www.adarahotel.com* 🛏 *41 rooms* 🍴 *No meals.*

Delta Hotels by Marriott Whistler Village Suites

$$$ | **HOTEL** | **FAMILY** | Not only is the Southwestern-style decor warm and inviting, the apartment-size studio and one- and two-bedroom suites are great choices for families and were renovated in 2014. **Pros:** central location; nice mountain views; free ski and bike storage. **Cons:** rooms are small; some street noise; high parking fee. [$] *Rooms from: C$295* ✉ *4308 Main St., Whistler Village* ☎ *604/905–3987, 888/299–3987* 🌐 *www.deltahotels.com* 🛏 *207 rooms* 🍴 *No meals.*

★ **Fairmont Chateau Whistler Resort**

$$$$ | **HOTEL** | **FAMILY** | Just steps from the Blackcomb ski lifts, this imposing-looking fortress is a self-contained, ski-in, ski-out resort-within-a-resort with its own shopping arcade, golf course, and impressive spa. **Pros:** ski-in and ski-out option; a terrific spa; shopping and golf on-site. **Cons:** bustling with guests and kids; not particularly intimate; pricey. [$] *Rooms from: C$471* ✉ *4599 Château Blvd.* ☎ *604/938–8000, 800/257–7544* 🌐 *www.fairmont.com* 🛏 *539 rooms* 🍴 *No meals.*

★ **Four Seasons Resort Whistler**

$$$$ | **HOTEL** | **FAMILY** | This plush nine-story hotel gives alpine chic a new twist with warm earth tones and wood interiors, big leather chairs beside the fireplace in the lobby, and amazingly spacious rooms. **Pros:** top-notch spa; great fitness classes; free village shuttles. **Cons:** a

long walk to restaurants and nightlife; expensive parking; busy with kids and families. $ *Rooms from: C$450* ✉ *4591 Blackcomb Way, Whistler Village* ☎ *604/935–3400, 888/935–2460* ⊕ *www.fourseasons.com/whistler* 🛏 *291 rooms* ⏚ *No meals.*

Hilton Whistler Resort and Spa

$$$ | **RESORT** | **FAMILY** | With a wealth of family-friendly facilities, this resort hotel sits at the base of the Whistler and Blackcomb gondolas. **Pros:** steps from the chairlift; huge rooms; pet-friendly. **Cons:** small spa; some unremarkable street views; decor feels a bit ordinary. $ *Rooms from: C$300* ✉ *4050 Whistler Way, Whistler Village* ☎ *604/932–1982, 800/515-4050* ⊕ *www.hiltonwhistler.com* 🛏 *287 rooms* ⏚ *No meals.*

Nita Lake Lodge

$$$$ | **HOTEL** | Within easy reach of the lifts and amenities of Whistler Creekside, this lovely lodge is Whistler's only lakefront hotel, so it feels a world away from the madding crowd. **Pros:** unique lake location; laid-back lounge; on-site spa. **Cons:** shuttle or short walk required to access slopes; away from the village action; some rooms don't have great views. $ *Rooms from: C$375* ✉ *2131 Lake Placid Rd., Whistler Village* ☎ *604/966–5700, 888/755–6482* ⊕ *www.nitalakelodge.com* 🛏 *77 rooms* ⏚ *Free breakfast.*

Pan Pacific Whistler Mountainside

$$$$ | **HOTEL** | With the very lively Dubh Linn Gate Irish Pub on the premises, this hotel tends to attract the active set, most of whom seem to spend their time on the large deck cheering on skiers as they reach the bottom of the slope. **Pros:** about as close to the ski lift as you can get; on-site pub at your door; outdoor pool and hot tubs. **Cons:** gets booked up quickly; common areas can get noisy; pricey parking. $ *Rooms from: C$350* ✉ *4320 Sundial Crescent, Whistler Village* ☎ *604/905–2999, 888/905–9995* ⊕ *www.panpacific.com* ▭ *No credit cards* 🛏 *120 rooms* ⏚ *No meals.*

Pan Pacific Whistler Village Centre

$$$$ | **HOTEL** | Although it bills itself as an all-suite boutique hotel, Pan Pacific Whistler Village Centre feels more like a beautiful apartment building with a fabulous concierge service. **Pros:** extraordinarily friendly staff; free breakfast buffet; central location. **Cons:** loud ground-floor rooms; limited services; parking is pricey. $ *Rooms from: C$350* ✉ *4299 Blackcomb Way, Whistler Village* ☎ *604/966–5500, 888/966–5575* ⊕ *www.panpacific.com* 🛏 *82 rooms* ⏚ *Free breakfast.*

Summit Lodge Boutique Hotel

$$$ | **HOTEL** | Tucked away in a quiet part of the village, this friendly hotel offers gracious service and one of the area's best values in boutique accommodations. **Pros:** quiet rooms; quality spa; free shuttle to the village gondola. **Cons:** small parking spots; lots of pets (and their dander), so it's not recommended for those with allergies; isn't central. $ *Rooms from: C$285* ✉ *4359 Main St., Whistler Village* ☎ *604/932–2778, 888/913–8811* ⊕ *www.summitlodge.com* 🛏 *81 rooms* ⏚ *No meals.*

★ The Westin Resort and Spa, Whistler

$$$$ | **HOTEL** | This recently renovated luxury hotel has not only a prime location on the entrance of the village but also a long list of upscale amenities that will make you want to stay here. **Pros:** quiet, yet central location; excellent spa; outdoor pool and hot tub. **Cons:** the parking is expensive; if you're not a loyalty program member, you must pay for Wi-Fi; pricey. $ *Rooms from: C$450* ✉ *4090 Whistler Way, Whistler Village* ☎ *604/905–5000, 888/634–5577* ⊕ *www.westinwhistler.com* 🛏 *400 rooms* ⏚ *No meals.*

🍸 Nightlife

Whistler has a legendary après-ski scene, and on any given weekend, there may be more nonskiers than skiers filling the local patios, clubs, and saloons. Stag and stagette parties wander the

12

Whistler

An inuksuk—a stone landmark—stands sentry over Whistler and Blackcomb mountains.

pedestrian-only village, and people line up early to get inside Buffalo Bills, Moe Joe's, Garfinkel's, Merlin's, or Dusty's Grill + BBQ, where DJs and bands from Vancouver and beyond come to spin.

The night begins with après, when skiers, bikers, and hikers alike unwind on patios such as the one at the Longhorn Saloon & Grill, Garibaldi Lift Company, or Dubh Linn Gate Irish Pub—think happy hour for the hyped up—and the clubs usually stay open until 2 am except for Sunday and holidays. The minimum age is 19 and smoking is only allowed outside, although even some patios and areas of the village are smoke-free zones. When the bars close, the local constables lead a (usually) well-behaved cattle drive through the village and back to the hotels.

BARS AND PUBS
Black's Pub
BARS/PUBS | You'll find Whistler's largest selection of whiskeys (more than 40 varieties) and 99 beers from around the world at this pleasant pub. The adjoining restaurant is reasonably priced, offering mainly pizzas and pastas. ✉ *7-4340 Sundial Crescent, Whistler Village* ☎ *604/932–6945* ⊕ *www.blackspub.com.*

High Mountain Brewing Company
BREWPUBS/BEER GARDENS | You'll come for the house-crafted ales and lagers and you'll stay to relax in the woodsy atmosphere, complete with fireplaces, a pool table, and a slew of TVs turned to sports channels. The adjacent restaurant and patio are good places for casual meals. ✉ *4355 Blackcomb Way, Whistler Village* ☎ *604/905–2739* ⊕ *www.mjg.ca/brewhouse.*

Dubh Linn Gate Irish Pub
BARS/PUBS | As its name implies, this place is full of the Irish blarney, with an interior that was actually transported all the way from the Emerald Isle. The staff pours a decent pint of Guinness, and the menu includes solid Irish fare like steak and Guinness pie. Celtic music is a highlight most nights. ✉ *Pan Pacific Hotel, 4320 Sundial Crescent, Whistler Village*

☎ 604/905–4047 ⊕ www.dubhlinngate. com.

★ Garibaldi Lift Company

BARS/PUBS | At the base of the Whistler gondola, this popular joint attracts a lively crowd to its iconic après-ski bar that also serves lunch, dinner, and an exciting late-night scene. It's a cozy place to chill out and watch the latest ski and snowboard videos during the day; in the evening, though, things get hopping. Friday night house parties are legendary—the music isn't run-of-the-mill Top 40—and in addition to live bands, it's a venue for top DJ talent from Canada and the U.S. *⊠ 4165 Springs La. ☎ 604/905–2220 ⊕ www. whistlerblackcomb.com/the-village/ dining/glc.*

★ Ketel One Ice Room at Bearfoot Bistro

BARS/PUBS | At -32°C (-26°F), the Ketel One Ice Room is the world's coldest vodka tasting room—and the only permanent subzero vodka room in Canada. The experience (C$48) includes the use of cozy Arctic Expedition, Canada Goose parkas, four shot-glass tasters from a selection of 50 vodka varieties, and one definite "wow" moment to remember. *⊠ 4121 Village Green, Whistler Village ☎ 604/932–3433 ⊕ www.bearfootbistro. com/the-experience.*

Longhorn Saloon & Grill

BARS/PUBS | A veritable institution among Whistler's drinking establishments, the Longhorn has been around since the early 1980s. It still packs them in until the wee hours, with the crowds moving from the saloon to the patio overlooking the base of Whistler. The interior calls to mind Steamboat Springs or Crested Butte, but the variety of local brews makes it clear that you're in BC. The menu is strictly pub food. *⊠ Carleton Lodge, 102-4280 Mountain Square ☎ 604/932–5999 ⊕ www. gibbonshospitality.com/longhorn.*

DANCE CLUBS
Buffalo Bill's Bar & Grill

DANCE CLUBS | This club features 1980s and Top 40; well-known regional bands jam here once or twice a month. There are two dance floors and a pool table. *⊠ 4122 Village Green, Whistler Village ☎ 604/932–6613 ⊕ www.gibbonshospitality.com/buffalobills.*

Garfinkel's

DANCE CLUBS | One of Whistler's most cavernous clubs, Garfinkel's plays rock, hip-hop, and current DJs. It's a hangout for a young crowd, many of whom are weekend partiers from Vancouver. *⊠ 4308 Main St., Suite 1, Whistler Village ☎ 604/932–2323 ⊕ www.garfinkels.ca/.*

Moe Joe's

DANCE CLUBS | Its hot central location makes Moe Joe's a perennial favorite. Theme nights from Ladies' Night Saturdays to Check-in Fridays (via Facebook for free cover) to Glow-in-the-Dark giveaways on Sundays appeal to a diverse crowd. If you're traveling in a group, reserve a party booth or snag a VIP pass to skip the lines. *⊠ 4115 Golfers Approach, Whistler Village ☎ 604/935–1152 ⊕ www. moejoes.com.*

Tommy Africa's

DANCE CLUBS | The club's been around forever, and depending on what's happening on any given night it's definitely worth a look. Guest DJs play alternative and progressive dance music, and with so many youthful patrons drinking the club's trademark shooters (shot glasses of undiluted alcoholic concoctions), it's not long before someone is dancing on the stage. *⊠ 4204 Village Square, Whistler Village ☎ 604/932–6090 ⊕ www.tommys-whistler.com.*

🛍 Shopping

Whistler has more than 200 stores, including chain and designer outlets, gift shops, and outdoor-clothing and ski shops. Most are clustered in the pedestrian-only Whistler Village Centre; more can be found a short stroll away in Village North, Upper Village, and in the shopping concourses of the major hotels.

Where there's skiing, there are spas. Whistler has several outstanding hotel spas—including those at the Four Seasons Resort Whistler and the Westin Resort & Spa—which offer mostly mainstream and European treatments; the Fairmont Chateau Whistler Resort also has a menu of Ayurvedic therapies, while you can get traditional Javanese treatments in the spa at the Summit Lodge & Spa.

CLOTHING
Amos and Andes
CLOTHING | Amid the endless sweater shops, this one stands out. The handmade sweaters and dresses have offbeat designs and fabulous colors. They're really comfortable, especially those made with silky-soft merino wool. ⊠ *4321 Village Gate Blvd., Suite 2, Whistler Village* ☎ *604/932–7202* ⊕ *www.whistlersweatershop.com.*

Helly Hansen
CLOTHING | Here's where to find high-quality Norwegian-made skiing, boarding, and other outdoor wear and equipment. There's a second location at the Westin Resort. ⊠ *4295 Blackcomb Way, Whistler Village* ☎ *604/932–0143* ⊕ *www.hellyhansen.com.*

lululemon athletica
CLOTHING | Best known for its yoga gear, this iconic Canadian retailer carries a wide range of ultracomfortable and flattering athletic wear. ⊠ *Unit 118–4154 Village Green* ☎ *604/938–9642* ⊕ *www.lululemon.com.*

Open Country
CLOTHING | There are several upscale clothing shops in Whistler, but here you'll find many designer labels all under one roof: leisure wear classics for men and women by Jack Lipson, Michael Kors, and more. ⊠ *Fairmont Chateau Whistler Resort, 4599 Chateau Blvd., Whistler Village* ☎ *604/938–9268.*

Roots
CLOTHING | This Canadian-owned enterprise is known for its sweatshirts and cozy casuals, and it's something of a fixture in Whistler. It outfits the Canadian Olympic team, and has clothed many U.S. and U.K. Olympians in the past. ⊠ *4154 Village Green, Unit 100, Whistler Village* ☎ *604/938–0058* ⊕ *www.canada.roots.com.*

JEWELRY
Rocks & Gems
JEWELRY/ACCESSORIES | This interesting shop has an amazing selection of trilobites featuring specimens from around the globe, including rare finds from BC. This is the shop to go to whether you're searching for a one-of-a-kind collector fossil, an exotic stone like ammolite, or a handcrafted necklace or ring. ⊠ *4154 Village Green, Whistler Village* ☎ *604/938–3307* ⊕ *www.rocksandgemscanada.com.*

GALLERIES
Adele Campbell Fine Art Gallery
ART GALLERIES | This gallery has a broad range of paintings and sculptures, many with wildlife and wilderness themes, by both established and up-and-coming BC artists. You'll usually be able to find some affordable pieces. ⊠ *Westin Resort, 109-4090 Whistler Way, Whistler Village* ☎ *888/938–0887* ⊕ *www.adelecampbell.com.*

Art Walk
ART GALLERIES | Organized by Arts Whistler, Art Walk is a self-guided tour in the fall months (September through November) where you can check out the work of the many talented artists who live in the Sea-to-Sky Corridor. Venues include galleries, hotel lobbies, shops, and art studios which display their ceramics, photography, jewelry, and mixed-media art. Guests can explore more than 30 pop-up galleries throughout the village, collect stamps for their Art Walk passport, and

win prizes. There is also a year-round gallery where Arts Whistler host exhibits, workshops, and performances. ✉ *Maury Young Arts Centre, 4335 Blackcomb Way, Whistler Village* ☎ *604/935–8410* ⊕ *www.artswhistler.com.*

Black Tusk Gallery

ART GALLERIES | Specializing in quality regional art, Black Tusk is a showcase for Pacific Northwest Coast Native artists, both from Canada and the United States. Works include limited-edition silk-screen prints and traditional crafts such as masks, paddles, bowls, jewelry, and totem poles. ✉ *Hilton Whistler Resort, 4293 Mountain Sq.* ☎ *604/905–5540* ⊕ *www.blacktusk.ca.*

Plaza Galleries

ART GALLERIES | The range of artists represented at the Plaza Galleries is inspired. Many, such as acclaimed artist Kal Gajoum, hail from British Columbia, though you're just as likely to see the efforts of international names who are just starting to make their mark in North America. ✉ *Whistler Town Plaza, 22–4314 Main St.* ☎ *604/938–6233* ⊕ *www.plazagalleries.com.*

Whistler Contemporary Gallery

ART GALLERIES | With a focus on contemporary painting, sculpture, and glass, this well-established gallery has earned a loyal following from those looking for innovative work by Canadian and international artists. There's a second location at the Four Seasons Resort Whistler (at 4050 Whistler Way). ✉ *Hilton Whistler Resort, 4293 Mountain Sq., Whistler Village* ☎ *604/938–3001* ⊕ *www.whistlerart.com.*

SPAS

★ Scandinave Spa

FITNESS/HEALTH CLUBS | Nudging up to the edge of Lost Lake, a 10-minute drive north of Whistler Village, this place is a find. Following the traditions of Scandinavia, these pools and hydrotherapy baths are intended to soothe sore muscles, relax the body, and improve blood circulation. The circuit involves a eucalyptus steam bath, a Finnish sauna, a soak in the heated outdoor pools—especially wonderful when it's snowing—and then relaxation in a number of lounge areas and solariums. Green Moustache and Blackbird Bakery provide all the food for the on-site café. Day passes start at C$85. ✉ *8010 Mons Rd.* ☎ *604/935–2424* ⊕ *www.scandinave.com/en/whistler.*

The Spa at Four Seasons Resort Whistler

FITNESS/HEALTH CLUBS | Without a doubt, this is the most luxurious and decadent spa in town, featuring 14 treatment rooms, a relaxation lounge, a full-service health club, outdoor pools, whirlpools, steam rooms, and a fitness studio. ✉ *Four Seasons, 4591 Blackcomb Way, Whistler Village* ☎ *604/966–2620* ⊕ *www.fourseasons.com/whistler.*

The Spa at Nita Lake Lodge

FITNESS/HEALTH CLUBS | This tranquil spa, on the southern edge of Nita Lake, offers a range of services: from hot stone massages to body scrubs to their signature Kundalini treatment (a massage that uses chakra and sound healing). Before your treatment, make use of the rooftop hot tubs (with stunning views) or the eucalyptus steam room. The spa works with sustainably sourced, organic products. ✉ *2131 Lake Placid Rd.* ☎ *604/966–5715* ⊕ *www.nitalakelodge.com/spa.*

Taman Sari Royal Heritage Spa

FITNESS/HEALTH CLUBS | True to its name, this spa celebrates the royal wellness traditions and rich stylings of Java and Bali. Exotic-sounding treatments and products include Javanese deep-tissue massage, a sunflower facial, body scrubs, and holistic therapies such as reflexology. ✉ *Summit Lodge & Spa, 4359 Main St., Whistler Village* ☎ *604/938–5982* ⊕ *www.tamansarispa.com.*

284

SPORTING GOODS
Can-Ski
SPORTING GOODS | With more than 40 years in the business, Can-Ski is synonymous with everything having to do with snow. It has a good selection of brand-name ski gear, clothing, and accessories, and does custom boot fitting and repairs. Can-Ski has other locations at Glacier Lodge, Deer Lodge, and Whistler Creekside (winters only). ✉ *Crystal Lodge, 4154 Village Green, Whistler Village* ☎ *604/938–7755* ⊕ *www.whistlerblackcomb.com/stores.*

Fanatyk Co
SPORTING GOODS | In winter you can buy off-the-rack skis and boots, as well as order custom-made boots. In summer the shop specializes in top-of-the-line mountain bikes as well as bike rentals, repairs, and tours. ✉ *6–4433 Sundial Pl., Whistler Village* ☎ *604/938–9455* ⊕ *www.fanatykco.com.*

Showcase Snowboards
SPORTING GOODS | Considered by locals to be the town's best snowboard shop, this place is staffed by guys who live for the board: snow, skate, and surf. The 3,500-square-foot shop showcases all the best gear. ✉ *Sundial Hotel, 4340 Sundial Crescent, Whistler Village* ☎ *604/905–2022* ⊕ *facebook.com/showcaseshop.*

🏃 Activities

Adventurers pour into Whistler during every season and from every corner of the world. In winter, you'll meet Australian and New Zealander skiers and guides who follow the snows around the globe; in summer there are sun-baked guides who chase the warm months to lead white-water rafting or mountain-biking excursions. These globe-trotters demonstrate how Whistler's outdoor sports culture now operates on a global, all-season scale.

The staging of sliding (bobsleigh, luge, skeleton) and alpine and cross-country skiing events in Whistler during the Olympic Games has yielded a host of opportunities for the adventurous, including a world-class cross-country center (and lodge) operated by the Whistler Legacies Society. The sliding center remains a professional training facility (the ice is rumored to be the fastest on the planet), as well as a public venue for those who've always wanted to experience the 100-km-per-hour (62-mile) thrill of a sliding sport. The mountains changed little after the games, other than having some commemorative signage to indicate what happened where.

Hikers and anglers, downhill and touring cyclists, free skiers and ice climbers, kayakers and golfers—there really is something for everyone. Whistler and Blackcomb mountains are the reasons why most people are here, but the immediate environs are equally compelling. Garibaldi Provincial Park, adjacent to the Whistler area, is a 78,000-acre park with dense mountainous forests splashed with hospitable lakes and streams for fishing and kayaking. At Alta Lake, you'll see clusters of windsurfers weaving across the surface, dodging canoeists. At nearby Squamish, the Stawamus Chief, the second largest granite monolith in the world behind Gibraltar, attracts serious rock climbers, although there are milder climbs for novices.

BIKING AND HIKING
The 40-km (25-mile) paved, car-free Valley Trail links the village to lakeside beaches and scenic picnic areas. For more challenging routes, ski lifts whisk hikers and bikers up to the alpine, where marked trails are graded by difficulty. The Peak Chair operates in summer to take hikers to the top of 7,160-foot-high peak of Whistler. Among the most popular routes in the high alpine-trail network is the High Note Trail, an intermediate, 9.5-km (6-mile) route with an elevation change of

1,132 feet and fabulous coastal mountain views. Trails are clearly marked—you take the lift up and choose whichever way you want to come down, just as if you were skiing. The casual stroller can also experience the top of the mountain on the **PEAK 2 PEAK Gondola,** the largest free-span gondola expanse in the world: it crosses Fitzsimmons Valley, connecting Whistler and Blackcomb mountains in just 11 minutes. Free trail maps are available from the Whistler Visitor Information Centre.

Fanatyk Co. Ski and Cycle

BICYCLING | This locally owned outfit rents high-performance bikes, arranges for repairs, and sells gear, too. The staff is passionate and knowledgeable about riding and local trails. It's also a ski shop in the winter. ✉ *6–4433 Sundial Pl., Whistler Village* ☎ *604/938–9455* ⊕ *www.fanatykco.com.*

G1 Rentals

BICYCLING | G1 is where biking enthusiasts, novice or expert, can get rentals. Inside the gondola building and next to the access point for Whistler Mountain Bike Park, here's where to find out about lessons, equipment, safety gear, and park passes. They also rent skis and snowboards in the winter. ✉ *Whistler Gondola Base, Whistler Village* ☎ *604/905–2252* ⊕ *bike.whistlerblackcomb.com.*

★ Garibaldi Provincial Park

PARK—SPORTS-OUTDOORS | A vast wilderness on Whistler's doorstep, Garibaldi Provincial Park is a serious hiker's dream. You can't miss it: the 2,678-meter (8,786-foot) peak of Mount Garibaldi kisses the heavens just north of Squamish. Alpine meadows and wildlife-viewing await you on trails leading to Black Tusk, Diamond Head, Cheakamus Lake, Elfin Lakes, and Singing Pass. Mountain goats, black bears, and bald eagles are found throughout the park. This is truly one of Canada's most spectacular wildernesses, and being easily accessible from Vancouver makes it even more appealing.

A compass is mandatory, as are food and water, rain gear, a flashlight, and a first-aid kit. There are also two medium to advanced mountain bike trails. Take seriously the glacier hazards and avalanche warnings. Snow tires are necessary in winter. Garibaldi Provincial Park is serviced by Parkbus, a seasonal shuttle bus, from Downtown Vancouver (⊕ *www.parkbus.ca* or ☎ *800/928–7101*). ✉ *Hwy. 99, between Squamish and Pemberton* ☎ *800/689–9025 Discover Camping campsite reservations, 800/928–7101 Parkbus* ⊕ *www.env.gov.bc.ca/bcparks/explore/parkpgs/garibaldi.*

Mountain Skills Academy & Adventures

HIKING/WALKING | This year-round outfitter offers everything from avalanche safety courses in winter to mountaineering in summer. Among its signature activities is a hike named Via Ferrata, Italian for "Iron Way," so named because it's straight up a vertical pathway using fixed cables and metal-rung ladders. This thrilling activity is not reserved for seasoned mountain climbers—any reasonably fit hiker can do it. Even older children can tackle it. Besides, it's great for bragging rights. In the winter, these expert mountain guides also offer group tours, instructional clinics, and customized one-on-one trips to get you shredding untouched backcountry powder. Ice climbing, glacier walks, and backcountry overnights add to the roster of activities. ✉ *207B–4368 Main St.* ☎ *604/938–9242* ⊕ *www.mountain-skillsacademy.com.*

★ Whistler Mountain Bike Park

BICYCLING | There's something for riders of every skill level at the Whistler Mountain Bike Park, from gentle rides that satisfy novices to steep rock faces that will challenge the experts. High-season rates range from C$62 for a day to C$180 for a three-day pass. The park is open from mid-May to early October, and rentals are available. The park is accessed from the Whistler Village gondola or Fitzsimmons Express. ✉ *Whistler Mountain*

Mountain Biking

Ski resorts everywhere have latched onto the popularity of downhill biking. Whistler Blackcomb was among the first to realize the potential of converting ski runs to downhill mountain biking, establishing the best downhill-biking center in the world. Fat tire biking trails are available at Whistler Olympic Park. Located on Whistler Mountain, the trails—more than 200 km (124 miles) of them— are marked green through double diamond and groomed with as much care as their winter counterparts.

Riding custom bikes designed specifically for the Whistler terrain, cyclists bomb down the single-track trails, staying high on the steeply banked turns and taking air on the many tables and jumps. Expert riders might add 30-foot rock drops, leaps over streambeds, and 100-foot platform bridges to their brake-free sprints through the forest. Beginners can find plenty of comfortable dirt lanes to follow, though, and you can keep your fingers ready at the hydraulic brake should the speed become uncomfortable. After their first taste of the sport, most novice riders can't wait to sit back on the specially designed chairlift, transition onto the blue terrain, invite a few bumps, and maybe grab some air before the day is through. Downhill biking provides pure, if muddy, adrenaline-fueled bliss.

Whistler Mountain Bike Park, with experienced instructors, is a great place to learn how to downhill bike.

☎ 604/967–8950 ⊕ bike.whistlerblackcomb.com.

BIRDING

Brackendale Eagles Provincial Park

BIRD WATCHING | Between mid-November and mid-February, the world's largest concentration of bald eagles gathers to feed on salmon at Brackendale Eagles Provincial Park, near Squamish, about 40 minutes south of Whistler on the scenic Sea-to-Sky Highway. Eagles Park is on the west shore of the Squamish River, but the most accessible viewing spot is at the Eagle Viewing Shelter just off Government Road in Brackendale. On winter weekends and during Christmas week volunteer interpreters with high-power spotting scopes will be at the shelter. Alternatively, you can spot eagles from a raft on the Squamish River with Canadian Outback Rafting (canadianoutbackrafting. com) or Squamish Rafting (squamish-rafting.com). The Brackendale Art Gallery has a teahouse that's a good place to stop along the way. ⊠ Government Rd., off Hwy. 99, Brackendale ✛ Opposite the BC Easter Seals camp at 41015 Government Rd. in Brackendale ⊕ www. env.gov.bc.ca/bcparks/explore/parkpgs/ brackendale_eagles/.

BOATING

Canoe and kayak rentals are available at Alta Lake at both Lakeside Park and Wayside Park. A perfect place for canoeing is the River of Golden Dreams, which connects Alta Lake with Green Lake, both within a couple of miles of the village.

Wedge Rafting

BOATING | Specializing in whitewater rafting adventures, this company offers two-hour to full-day tours on the Green or Elaho-Squamish rivers. Tours depart from the village and include all equipment and experienced guides. Adventures are suitable for all levels. ⊠ 211–4293 Mountain Sq. ☎ 604/932–7171, 888/932–5899 ⊕ www.wedgerafting.com ☉ Closed. Oct.–Apr.

When the snow melts in Whistler Blackcomb, ski runs are converted to mountain biking trails.

Whistler Jet Boating

BOATING | Owner-operator Eric Pehota runs three daily excursions from May to September, cutting his jet boat through swirling channels and rushing rapids right up to the base of Nairn Falls. Bookings are made directly via cell phone or email. Trips are C$119. ⊠ *The Meadows at Pemberton Golf Course, 1730 Airport Rd., Pemberton* ☎ *604/905–9455,* ⊕ *www. whistlerjetboating.com.*

CROSS-COUNTRY SKIING

Twenty-five kilometers (16 miles) of track-set trails known as the Lost Lake Trails wind around scenic Lost Lake, Chateau Whistler Golf Course, the Nicklaus North Golf Course, and Green Lake, including routes suitable for all levels; 4 km (2½ miles) of trails around Lost Lake are lighted for night skiing from 4 to 10 each evening. Trail maps and rental equipment are available in sports shops throughout the village. There's more than 160 kms (100 miles) of trails for Nordic skiing.

DOWNHILL SKIING AND SNOWBOARDING

When Whistler and Blackcomb Ski Resorts merged in 1997, they created a snow behemoth not seen in these parts since the last sighting of a Sasquatch. Whistler had already garnered top-notch status, but the addition of Blackcomb left the competition buried in the powder. The numbers are staggering: 419 inches of annual snowfall, more than 8,000 skiable acres, 200-plus named runs, 16 alpine bowls, three glaciers, and the world's most advanced lift system. Point yourself downward on Blackcomb, and you can ski or snowboard for a mile from top to bottom. And there are lots of ways to get to the top, either via the Whistler Village, Creekside, or Blackcomb gondolas. According to the locals, many of whom are world-class competitors, picking the day's mountain depends on conditions, time of day, and time of year. While most residents swear by Whistler's bowls and steeps, some prefer the long glade runs and top terrain park of Blackcombs. You can do both in the same day, thanks to

One of the reasons Whistler is so popular is because it's great for skiers.

the PEAK 2 PEAK Gondola, which whisks riders along the 2.7-mile journey in just 11 minutes.

Whistler Blackcomb Hi Performance Rentals

SKIING/SNOWBOARDING | Hi Performance rentals for intermediate to advanced skiers or riders can be found at several outlets in the village, including G1 Rentals. ✉ *Whistler Gondola Base, 4545 Blackcomb Way, Whistler Village* ☎ *604/905–6930* ⊕ *www.whistlerblackcomb.com.*

★ Whistler Blackcomb Ski and Snowboard School

SKIING/SNOWBOARDING | The school offers lessons for skiers and snowboarders of all levels. You can even choose to ski with an Olympian. Whistler Kids remains one of the best children's ski schools anywhere. ✉ *4545 Blackcomb Way, Whistler Village* ☎ *604/967–8950, 800/766–0449* ⊕ *www.whistlerblackcomb.com.*

FISHING

Tourists first discovered this region for the fishing. All five area lakes—Alta, Alpha, Lost, Green, and Nita—are stocked with trout.

Pemberton Fish Finder

FISHING | These experts offer year-round fishing charters in Whistler, Pemberton, Squamish, and beyond. They do everything from fly-fishing and salmon fishing to ice fishing. Packages start at C$149. Note that a valid BC Basic Freshwater Fishing License is required for all tours (anyone 16 years of age or older) and can be purchased online at ⊕ *www.fishing.gov.bc.ca.* ✉ *1380 Birch St., Pemberton* ☎ *877/905–8121* ⊕ *www.pembertonfishfinder.com.*

Whistler Fishing Guides

FISHING | Local guides offer fly and spin fishing excursions throughout the region, including heli-fishing for the more adventurous angler. They look after all transportation, gear, and instruction for all abilities. ✉ ☎ *855/522–3474* ⊕ *www.whistlerfishingguides.ca.*

GOLF

Few visitors associate Whistler with golf, but the four championship courses vie with some of the best in the Pacific Northwest. Golf season in Whistler runs from May through October; greens fees range from C$99 for twilight specials to C$189 for prime-time slots.

Golf Whistler

GOLF | You can arrange advance tee-time bookings through Golf Whistler, an online service that also features last-minute specials and accommodations packages. ☎ 844/955-3263 ⊕ www.golfwhistler. com.

GOLF CLUBS AND COURSES

★ **Big Sky Golf Club**

GOLF | Facing some impressive glaciers, this course follows the Green River. Located 30 minutes north of Whistler, Big Sky sits at the base of 8,000-foot Mt. Currie. It's a favorite with locals, and for good reason. Check out the imaginative metal sculptures along the way. ⊠ 1690 Airport Rd., Pemberton ☎ 604/894–6106, 800/668–7900 ⊕ www.bigskygolf.ca ⌨ C$155 ⅃. 18 holes, 7001 yards, par 72.

Fairmont Chateau Whistler Golf Club

GOLF | Carved from the side of Blackcomb Mountain, this challenging and breathtaking course was designed by prominent golf-course architect Robert Trent Jones Jr. Make sure to carry plenty of balls, though you can reload at the turn. ⊠ 4612 Blackcomb Way ☎ 604/938–2092, 877/938–2092 ⊕ www.whistlermountaingolf.com ⌨ C$189 ⅃. 18 holes, 6635 yards, par 72.

Nicklaus North Golf Course

GOLF | Jack Nicklaus designed this challenging 18-hole track, which finishes beside lovely Green Lake. It's one of the few courses in the world that bears the famous golfer's name. ⊠ 8080 Nicklaus North Blvd. ☎ 604/938–9898, 800/386–9898 ⊕ www.nicklausnorth.com ⌨ C$165 ⅃. 18 holes, 6961 yards, par 71.

Ski Lessons 🏃

For a primer on the ski facilities, Whistler Blackcomb offers a free mountain orientation daily for intermediate and advanced skiers and riders, held at 11:30 am during ski season at the top of Whistler and Blackcomb. First-timers to Whistler, whether beginners or experienced skiers or snowboarders, may want to try private or group lessons. Operated by Whistler Blackcomb Snow School, these single day and three- to four-day programs combine ski or snowboarding lessons and an insider's guide to the mountains.

Whistler Golf Club

GOLF | Often overlooked, this Arnold Palmer–designed course is frequently ranked among the best in the country. It's surprisingly challenging, especially around Bear Island, and it has some spectacular practice facilities. "Five after 5" specials run as little as C$35. ⊠ 4001 Whistler Way ☎ 604/932–3280, 800/376–1777 ⊕ www.whistlergolf.com ⌨ C$169 ⅃. 18 holes, 6722 yards, par 71.

HELI-SKIING AND HELI-HIKING

The Coast Mountains of western Canada have more glaciers than almost anywhere else on the planet. The range is bordered by the Fraser River in the south and the Kelsall River in the north. Helicopter adventures consist of skiing, glacier hikes, and picnics.

Blackcomb Helicopters

FLYING/SKYDIVING/SOARING | Sightseeing tours over Whistler's stunning mountains and glaciers are offered year-round: there are heli-hiking, -biking, -fishing, -picnics, -golfing, and even heli-weddings in summer. The company also operates tours out of Vancouver. ⊠ 9960 Heliport Rd.

☎ 604/938–1700, 800/330–4354 ⊕ www.
blackcombhelicopters.com.

★ **Whistler Heli-Skiing**

SKIING/SNOWBOARDING | Intended for inter-
mediate to expert skiers and snowboarders, Whistler Heli-Skiing offers guided
day trips with three or more glacier
runs. Prices start at C$1,079 per person.
✉ 4545 Blackcomb Way ☎ 888/435–4754
⊕ www.whistlerheliskiing.com.

SNOWMOBILING, SNOWSHOEING, AND SLEIGH RIDES

Blackcomb Snowmobile

SNOW SPORTS | You can book guided
snowmobile trips through the backcountry or learn to mush a dogsled.
Snowmobile trips start at $159 for two
hours; dogsledding trips start at C$229
for two and a half hours; and snowshoeing comes in at C$89 for two hours.
They are open year-round, offering ATV
tours in the summer. ✉ Hilton Whistler
Resort, 4050 Whistler Way, Whistler
Village ☎ 604/932–8484 ⊕ www.black-
combsnowmobile.com.

★ **Canadian Wilderness Adventures**

SNOW SPORTS | Snowmobiles, snowcats,
dogsleds, and snowshoes are just some
of the activity choices here. After a day in
the snow you can reward yourself with a
fondue dinner at the famous Crystal Hut
6,000 feet atop Blackcomb Mountain.
In summer, transport changes to ATVs,
canoes, and more. ✉ Carleton Lodge,
4280 Mountain Sq., Whistler Village
☎ 604/938–1616 ⊕ www.canadianwilder-
ness.com.

TUBING

Coca-Cola Tube Park

SNOW SPORTS | **FAMILY** | Located on
Blackcomb Mountain, this fabulous tube
park is all about family fun. The park has
7,000 feet of lanes rated green, blue, and
black diamond, a magic carpet to get
to the top, a fire pit, a play area, and a
snack station. There are even minitubes
for the little ones. ✉ Blackcomb Excalibur

Summer Skiing 🏃

Whistler is a summer hiking and
outdoors destination, but dedicated
skiers can still get their fix up on
Horstman Glacier. Glacier skiing is
recommended only for intermediate
to advanced skiers. One of the fun
perks is the stares you'll get in the
village as you walk around in your
downhill gear in the summer temps.

Gondola, 4010 Whistler Way, Blackcomb
Mountain ☎ 604/935–3357 ⊕ www.
whistlerblackcomb.com.

ZIPLINING AND CANOPY TOURS

★ **Ziptrek Ecotours**

ZIP LINING | In a rain forest between
Whistler and Blackcomb mountains,
Ziptrek offers tours ranging from Tree Trek
walks along suspension bridges through
the forest to 10-line, five-hour adrena-
line-filled zipline extravaganzas, including
a combo package with the PEAK 2
PEAK Gondola. None of them requires
any experience, although if you're afraid
of heights you should know that the
full course includes a heady zip over a
canyon far, far below you. (The company
claims to have the "longest, highest, and
fastest ziplines in North America.") With
runs ranging from 400 to 7,000 feet in
length, this is a heart-thumping experience worth splurging on for the whole
family. ✉ 4282 Mountain Sq., Whistler
Village ☎ 604/935–0001, 866/935–0001
⊕ www.ziptrek.com.

Chapter 13

THE OKANAGAN VALLEY

Updated by
Jennifer Foden

British
Columbia

👁 Sights	🍴 Restaurants	🛏 Hotels	💼 Shopping	🍸 Nightlife
★★★☆☆	★★★★★	★★★★★	★★★★☆	★★★☆☆

WELCOME TO THE OKANAGAN VALLEY

TOP REASONS TO GO

★ **Okanagan Wines:** Its wineries are producing acclaimed wines and earning top honors in international circles.

★ **Explore Diverse Landscapes:** The region's diverse geography creates an Eden for outdoor activities.

★ **Skiing:** Ski resorts may not have the same caché as Whistler, but for value, quality snow, and family appeal, these mountains are hidden treasures.

★ **The Kettle Valley Railway:** Although a steam locomotive still travels along a preserved section of this historic railway, most of the railbed caters to cyclists and hikers.

★ **World-Class Cuisine:** The Okanagan Valley's climate and landscape are the perfect combination for agricultural growing conditions, so it's no wonder it has some of the country's best cuisine.

Long known as the fruit-growing capital of Canada, the Okanagan has also become a significant wine-producing area that is about a five-hour drive from Vancouver. Within the Okanagan region, the valley stretches about 174 km (108 miles) from the gateway town of Vernon, just north of Kelowna, to Osoyoos, near the U.S. border.

1 Kelowna. As the regional hub of the Okanagan, Kelowna is a vibrant, busy commercial town that manages to juxtapose designer dining with an anything-goes casualness. It's a great base for any style of getaway.

2 Vernon. Vernon is far smaller than Kelowna and surrounded by picturesque communities and rural landscapes that offer some of the region's finest golf, horseback riding trails, and vacation retreats. It is located 50 km (31 miles) north of Kelowna.

3 Peachland. Located 25 km (15 miles) south of Kelowna on the Okanagan Lake stretch of Highway 97 is Peachland, the first main winery stop south of the big city.

4 Summerland. 21 km (13 miles) south of Peachland is Summerland, a small town brimming with wineries.

5 Penticton. Another 17 km (10 miles) south of Summerland is Penticton, the junction point for the Naramata Bench that runs up the east side of the lake.

6 Naramata. If you drive south down the highway along the western edge of Okanagan Lake and then circle back up to drive north on the eastern side, you'll be welcomed into Naramata, about 15 km (9 miles) from Penticton.

7 Oliver. Near the south end of the Okanagan Valley is Oliver, 42 km (26 miles) south of Penticton.

8 Osoyoos. Located just 4 km (2.5 miles) from the Canada/U.S. border, Osoyoos is the southernmost tip of the Okanagan Valley.

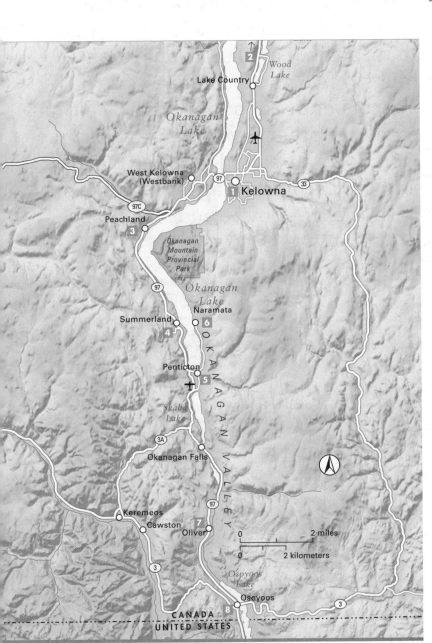

If you think that "wine country" and "British Columbia" have as much in common as "beaches" and "the Arctic," think again. The Okanagan region, roughly five hours northeast of Vancouver by car or one hour by air, has earned another moniker: "Napa of the North," for its award-winning blends and has become a magnet for wine enthusiasts—novice and expert alike.

Its lakeside and scenic vineyards aren't the Okanagan's only draw. Add to that the region's arid summer climate, water activities, numerous golf courses, mountain trails, and abundant snow in winter, and you have a perfect short getaway from Vancouver and the British Columbia coast as well as an ideal setting for a longer stay.

The Okanagan's wineries are concentrated in four general areas: around the city of Kelowna and north toward Vernon, around Summerland, along the Naramata Bench outside the town of Penticton, and in the area between Oliver and Osoyoos, just north of the U.S. border. If you're planning a short trip, you might want to stick to just one of these areas, especially since each one has developed its own wine trail to accommodate visitors with time constraints. That said, with approximately 229 wineries throughout the Okanagan, each area also offers enough to occupy several days of tasting.

As more urbanites, celebrity chefs, and city escapees discover the Okanagan's year-round appeal, the region's restaurants, amenities, and services are growing in sophistication, with wineries taking the lead. Many of them have created unique places to stay, as well as spectacular destination dining on patios, in-house, and even long table events, in the middle of the vineyards themselves.

It may only be about 125 km (75 miles) between Kelowna and Osoyoos, but wine touring, when coupled with unexpected digressions such as visiting a garden in spectacular bloom, an art studio, or a historic site along the way, can turn a two-hour sojourn into a full day of meandering adventure. Just be sure to stop by one of the roadside stalls to pick up a pint of cherries, a box of apricots, apple chutney, peach jam, and honey.

The Okanagan's sandy lake beaches and hot, dry climate have long made it a family-holiday destination for Vancouverites and Albertans, and the region is still the fruit-growing capital of Canada.

Planning

When to Go

The Okanagan hosts wine festivals in spring, fall, and winter; weekends are fun and busy times to visit. High season is from May to October.

The hot, dry summer, especially July and August, is peak season here, and weekends get crowded. May and June are quieter, and most wineries are open, so either month can be a good alternative to the midsummer peak.

Nevertheless, September just might be the best time for an Okanagan wine-tasting trip. Everything is still open, the weather is generally fine, and the vineyards are full of grapes ready to pick. Many wineries release new wines in the fall, so there are more tasting options.

In winter, the Okanagan becomes a popular ski destination, with several first-rate resorts, including Silver Star Mountain Resort, 24 km (15 miles) from Vernon, and Big White, an hour's drive from Kelowna. If your main objective is wine touring, though, many wineries close or reduce their hours from November through April.

Making the Most of Your Time

Three days from Vancouver is barely enough time to enjoy the Okanagan; five days to a week would be optimal.

The best place to start a wine-tasting tour is at the area wine info center in Penticton. You can get an overview of the area's wines, get help in organizing your time, and usually taste a wine or two.

We've included a selection of the best wineries, but our list is only a fraction of the Okanagan's more than 229 wineries.

Because new wineries open every year, ask for recommendations at your hotel, or simply stop in when you see an appealing sign.

FOOD AND WINE FESTIVALS

Festivals are a great way to explore the region's food-and-wine scene. In addition to wine festivals in spring, fall, and winter, many of the smaller communities put on harvest fairs. Penticton's PeachFest began in 1947 and (⊕ www.peachfest.com) celebrates peaches every August with beach fun, square dancing, sand-sculpting competitions, and concerts. In September, Kelowna hosts the Hopscotch Festival (⊕ www.hopscotchfestival.com/kelowna), where Scotch whiskies from around the world vie for tasting attention alongside other spirits and craft beers. Even Oliver and Osoyoos get into the festival scene, with the annual Festival of the Grape (⊕ www.oliverfestivalofthegrape.com) celebrating the area's more than 40 wineries and harvest.

Getting Here and Around

AIR

The main airport for the Okanagan wine country is in Kelowna. There's also a small airport in Penticton.

Air Canada and WestJet both fly into Kelowna from Vancouver. From Vancouver, Air Canada also serves Penticton; flights take about one hour.

Taxis generally meet arriving flights at the Kelowna Airport.

Let's Go! provides shuttle transportation several times daily from the Kelowna Airport to local hotels from C$15 per person, as well as to Big White, Silver Star, Apex, and Crystal ski mountains. Big White Shuttle runs scheduled service between various downtown locations and the resort for C$25 round-trip.

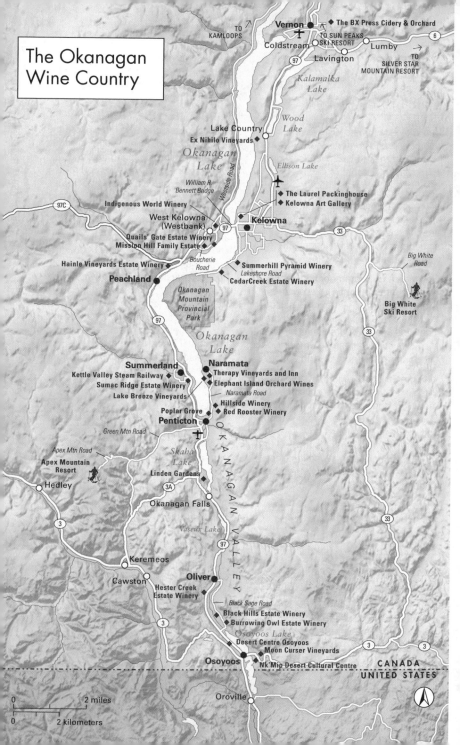

The Okanagan Wine Country

TO KAMLOOPS

Vernon
Coldstream
Lavington
97

◆ The BX Press Cidery & Orchard
TO SUN PEAKS SKI RESORT
Lumby
6
TO SILVER STAR MOUNTAIN RESORT

Kalamalka Lake

Wood Lake

Lake Country
◆ Ex Nihilo Vineyards

Okanagan Lake

Ellison Lake

William R. Bennett Bridge

Westside Road

Indigenous World Winery

West Kelowna (Westbank)
97

◆ The Laurel Packinghouse
◆ Kelowna Art Gallery

Kelowna
33

Quails' Gate Estate Winery
Mission Hill Family Estate ◆

Boucherie Road

Hainle Vineyards Estate Winery ◆

◆ Summerhill Pyramid Winery
Lakeshore Road
CedarCreek Estate Winery

Big White Road

Peachland

Okanagan Mountain Provincial Park

97

Big White Ski Resort

Okanagan Lake

33

Summerland
Kettle Valley Steam Railway ◆
Sumac Ridge Estate Winery
Lake Breeze Vineyards

Naramata
◆ Therapy Vineyards and Inn
◆ Elephant Island Orchard Wines
Naramata Road

Poplar Grove
Penticton

◆ Hillside Winery
◆ Red Rooster Winery

Green Mtn Road

Skaha Lake

Apex Mtn Road

Apex Mountain Resort

◆ Linden Gardens

3A

Hedley

Okanagan Falls

Vaseux Lake

33

3

Keremeos

97

Cawston

Oliver

Hester Creek Estate Winery
Black Sage Road

◆ Black Hills Estate Winery
◆ Burrowing Owl Estate Winery

3

Osoyoos Lake
Desert Centre Osoyoos
◆ Moon Curser Vineyards

Osoyoos

Nk'Mip Desert Cultural Centre

3

3

CANADA
UNITED STATES

Oroville

0   2 miles
0   2 kilometers

AIRPORT TRANSFER CONTACTS Big White Shuttle. ☎ *800/663–2772* ⊕ *www. bigwhite.com.* **Let's Go Transportation.** ☎ *778/821–0101* ⊕ *www.letsgotransportation.ca.*

BUS

The EBus bus system provides services from Vancouver to Kelowna and Vernon and is a viable alternative to driving (⊕ *myebus.ca*). The Kelowna Regional Transit System operates buses in the greater Kelowna area.

CONTACTS Kelowna Regional Transit System. ☎ *250/860–8121* ⊕ *bctransit.com/kelowna.*

CAR

To get to the Okanagan by car from Vancouver, head east on Highway 1 (Trans-Canada Highway). Just east of Hope, several routes diverge. For Oliver or Osoyoos in the South Okanagan, take Highway 3 east through the winding roads of Manning Park. For the Kelowna area, the fastest route is Highway 5 (the magnificent Coquihalla Highway) north to Merritt, then follow Highway 97C (the Okanagan Connector) toward Kelowna. To reach Penticton and Naramata, you can either take the Coquihalla to 97C, then turn *south* on Highway 97, or take Highway 3 to Keremeos, where you pick up Highway 3A north, which merges into 97 *north*. Allow about five hours of driving time from Vancouver to the Okanagan region.

If you're traveling from Whistler, consider the back route. Highway 99 travels through Pemberton to Lillooet. From here, take Highway 12 to Cache Creek, where you'll join Highway 1 traveling east to Kamloops. Take the Highway 97 exit to Vernon, the northernmost town of the Okanagan Valley. This is not a road to drive in winter, and whenever you go remember that gas stations are few and far between. In summer, the 561-km (350-mile) drive can take about seven to eight hours.

Several major agencies, including Avis, Budget, Enterprise, Hertz, and National, have offices in Kelowna.

Hotels

The wine industry has added a quiet sophistication with the development of higher-end lodgings and boutique inns geared to wine-and-food lovers. This means that from July to September you need to reserve early, especially if you're planning on visiting on a weekend. The Kelowna region is more urban, but it has a greater range of accommodations and other services. The Naramata and Oliver/Osoyoos areas are both prettier and more rural.

Hotel reviews have been shortened. For full information, visit Fodors.com.

Restaurants

Like the California wine regions, Okanagan has attracted gourmands, and the restaurants reflect that. They also benefit from the amazing fruit harvest here. From summer to fall, every month reaps a harvest of different fruits, from cherries and plums to nectarines, peaches, and several varieties of apples.

Restaurant reviews have been shortened. For full information, visit Fodors.com.

What It Costs in Canadian dollars			
$	$$	$$$	$$$$
RESTAURANTS			
under C$13	C$13–C$20	C$21–C$30	over C$30
HOTELS			
under C$126	C$126–C$195	C$196–C$300	over C$300

Tours

BUS TOURS

Distinctly Kelowna Tours

Distinctly Kelowna Tours pairs winery visits with walking excursions, ziplining, and other adventures. ☎ 250/979–1211, 866/979–1211 ⊕ www.distinctlykelowna-tours.ca.

Okanagan Wine Country Tours

Okanagan Wine Country Tours offers narrated three-hour, four-hour, and full-day wine-country tours. There's even a floatplane tour over the lush valleys to the Okanagan's Golden Mile near Oliver. ☎ 250/868–9463, 866/689–9463 ⊕ www.okwinetours.com.

PRIVATE TOURS

Okanagan Limousine

With Okanagan Limousine you can tour the wine area in chauffeur-driven style. It offers half-day and full-day tours to wineries in Kelowna, Summerland/Peachland, Naramata, Oliver/Osoyoos, and Okanagan Falls. ☎ 250/717–5466, 866/336–3133 ⊕ www.ok-limo.com.

Visitor Information

The knowledgeable staff at the British Columbia VQA Wine Information Centre will tell you what's new at area wineries and help you plan a self-drive winery tour. The center also stocks more than 900 local wines from 150 wineries and offers complimentary tastings daily. It's a good place to stop and find out about places to stay and eat.

Hello BC has information about the province, including the Okanagan. The Thompson Okanagan Tourism Association is the main tourism contact for the Okanagan. Towns like Osoyoos, Kelowna, and Penticton have visitor information centers, though not all are open year-round. Some, like Discover Naramata, are virtual only.

CONTACTS **British Columbia VQA Wine Information Centre.** ⊠ 553 Vees Dr., Penticton ☎ 250/490–2006 ⊕ www.pentictonwineinfo.com. **Destination Osoyoos.** ☎ 250/495–5070, 888/676–9667 ⊕ www.destinationosoyoos.com. **Discover Naramata.** ⊕ www.discovernaramata.com. **Hello BC.** ☎ 800/435–5622 ⊕ www.hellobc.com. **Penticton & Wine Country Visitor Centre.** ☎ 250/276–2170, 800/663–5052 ⊕ www.visitpenticton.com. **Thompson Okanagan Tourism Association.** ☎ 250/860–5999 ⊕ www.totabc.org. **Tourism Kelowna.** ☎ 250/861–1515, 800/663–4345 ⊕ www.tourismkelowna.com.

Kelowna

390 km (242 miles) northeast of Vancouver, 62 km (39 miles) north of Penticton.

The largest community in the Okanagan Valley, with a regional population of more than 132,000, Kelowna makes a good base for exploring the region's beaches, ski hills, wineries, and numerous golf courses. Although its edges are untidily urban, with strip malls and office parks sprawling everywhere, the town's walkable downtown runs along and up from Okanagan Lake. So even though the city continues to expand, you can still enjoy a stroll in the restful lakeside park.

Okanagan Lake splits Kelowna in two. On the east side of the lake is Kelowna proper, which includes the city's downtown, the cultural district that is the hub of the burgeoning craft brewery scene, and the winery district south of the city center that the locals call the Mission. On the west side of the lake is the community of West Kelowna, which is frequently still known by its former name, Westbank. Several wineries are on the west side, on and off Boucherie Road. The William R. Bennett Bridge connects the two sides of the lake.

GETTING HERE AND AROUND

As the regional hub of the Okanagan Valley, options for getting to Kelowna include air, bus, and car. If traveling from Whistler, a car is your best option to maneuver the back roads and stop along the way to take in the scenery, and such stops are likely to be frequent. Kelowna's transit system runs buses throughout the city and to outlying areas, as well as to Vernon, and shuttle services provide transportation to specific resorts and ski mountains. If you're intent on touring at all, go by car or take a tour.

 Sights

CedarCreek Estate Winery

WINERY/DISTILLERY | South of Kelowna, the award-winning CedarCreek—now a part of the Mission Hill family—is in a lovely spot overlooking the lake. The grand, impressive tasting room is open year-round. The restaurant, Home Block, which serves farm-to-table cuisine, is definitely a must-stop. ⊠ 5445 Lakeshore Rd., Kelowna ☎ 250/738–1020 ⊕ www. cedarcreek.bc.ca ⊠ Tastings complimentary, C$10 or C$22.

Ex Nihilo Vineyards

WINERY/DISTILLERY | Canada is the world's largest producer of ice wine, a specialty of Ex Nihilo Vineyards, a 25-minute drive north of Kelowna. This small but enterprising winery was among the first in the area to court celebrity endorsements, and struck a deal with the Rolling Stones to label its Riesling ice wine "Sympathy for the Devil." The tasting fee is waived if you make a purchase, as is the case at most wineries. There is also a bistro on-site. ⊠ 1525 Camp Rd., Lake Country ☎ 250/766–5522 ⊕ www.exnihilovineyards.com ⊠ Tasting C$7.

Indigenous World Winery

WINERY/DISTILLERY | This is BC's only 100% Indigenous-owned winery, blending traditional Syilx culture with modern style. Their tasting room has spectacular views of Lake Okanagan, their wine bottles are beautifully designed, and the vino is award-winning. There's also a restaurant on-site. ⊠ 218 Horizon Dr., Kelowna ☎ 250/769-2824 ⊕ www.indigenousworldwinery.com/.

Kelowna Art Gallery

MUSEUM | Works by contemporary local, Canadian, and international artists make up the gallery's four exhibition spaces. It's a family-friendly space, too: there is programming and activities for children (worth noting for rainy days). ⊠ 1315 Water St., Kelowna ☎ 250/762–2226 ⊕ www.kelownaartgallery.com ⊠ C$5; free Thurs. ☉ Closed Mon.

The Laurel Packinghouse

MUSEUM | The Laurel Packinghouse are museums depicting the Okanagan's orchard and wine history and have a shop for made-in-Okanagan gifts. ⊠ 1304 Ellis St., Kelowna ☎ 778/478–0325 ⊕ www. kelownamuseums.ca ⊠ By donation ☉ Closed Mon.

Mission Hill Family Estate

WINERY/DISTILLERY | Sitting atop a hill overlooking Okanagan Lake, Mission Hill Family Estate is recognizable for its 12-story bell tower. It was built, as the owner describes it, to resemble "a combination monastery, Tuscan hill village, and French winery." With a vaulted cellar blasted from volcanic rock, the well-established vineyard produces a wide variety of award-winning wines and offers several different winery tours, from a basic 60-minute tour with a tasting of three wines, to a more in-depth visit that includes wine-and-food pairings. An outdoor amphitheater hosts art events, music, and theater. The Terrace Restaurant is one of the Kelowna area's best dining options. ⊠ 1730 Mission Hill Rd., West Kelowna ☎ 250/768–6448, 800/957–9911 ⊕ www.missionhillwinery. com ⊠ Tastings and tours C$10–C$99.

Did You Know?

The Okanagan Valley, with its charming towns and numerous lakeside vineyards, has become a magnet for wine enthusiasts.

Quails' Gate Estate Winery

WINERY/DISTILLERY | Set on 125 acres above the western edge of Okanagan Lake, Quails' Gate Estate Winery runs tours several times daily from June to mid-October (though the exact times vary) and by appointment for the rest of the year. The family-owned winery produces more than a dozen different varieties, although it's best known for its award-winning Chardonnay and Pinot Gris, which were served to the Duke and Duchess of Cambridge during their Canadian visit. Complimentary tastings are offered in the spacious wineshop, and the Old Vines Restaurant is open year-round. The garden patio, open in summer, is a lovely spot for a flight of wine and locally inspired meal. ✉ *3303 Boucherie Rd., Kelowna* ☎ *250/769–4451, 800/420–9463* 🌐 *www.quailsgate.com* 🎫 *Tastings C$5, tours C$15–C$50.*

Summerhill Pyramid Winery

WINERY/DISTILLERY | On the east side of the lake is Summerhill Pyramid Winery, an organic producer best known for its sparkling and ice wines. What startles visitors, though, is the four-story-high replica of the Great Pyramid of Cheops, used to age and store the wine. As a venue for summer concerts, the pyramid's fabulous acoustics are unparalleled. You can tour the pyramid and winery and visit the shop year-round. The Summerhill Sunset Bistro, with a veranda overlooking Okanagan Lake, serves lunch and dinner daily. If the evening is cool, there's plenty of room inside. ✉ *4870 Chute Lake Rd., Kelowna* ☎ *250/764–8000, 800/667–3538* 🌐 *www.summerhill.bc.ca* 🎫 *Tours and tastings are complimentary.*

🍴 Restaurants

Bouchons Bistro

$$$ | **FRENCH** | Lots of windows and crisp white-linen tablecloths make this restaurant as bright as a French café, and the menu offers an array of classics. Signature dishes include a mouthwatering bouillabaisse containing everything from fresh salmon and halibut to scallops, shrimp, and mussels; and a hearty cassoulet that includes duck confit, smoked pork belly, and Toulouse sausage over a navy bean ragout. **Known for:** set-price menu; cozy vibe; extensive wine selection. [$] *Average main: C$29* ✉ *105–1180 Sunset Dr., Kelowna* ☎ *250/763–6595* 🌐 *www.bouchonsbistro.com* 🕓 *No lunch.*

Midtown Bistro

$$ | **MODERN CANADIAN** | This charming little bistro in downtown Vernon serves up delicious local fare admidst beautiful artwork, feel-good music, and warm colors. The pear and goat cheese salad is just divine. **Known for:** rotating paintings from local artists adorn the walls; charcuterie boards; wine list (it is the Okanagan, after all). [$] *Average main: C$16* ✉ *3024 30th Ave., Vernon* ☎ *250/308-7477* 🌐 *www.midtownbistro.ca.*

Pane Vino

$$ | **ITALIAN** | **FAMILY** | This family-owned farm-to-table pizzeria serves authentic Naples 'za in the heart of Lake Country. It's conveniently located next to the electric bike rental shop: following an afternoon of touring the Okanagan Rail Trail or Lake Country wineries on two wheels, you'll be sure to stop in here for some Italian comfort food. **Known for:** outstanding views; vegan desserts; authentic pizza oven all the way from Naples. [$] *Average main: C$17* ✉ *3996 Irvine Rd., Lake Country* ☎ *250/317-1435* 🌐 *www.panevinopizzeria.com/.*

RauDZ Regional Table

$$$ | **CANADIAN** | Rod Butters, one of BC's best-known chefs, created this contemporary eatery to deliver a culinarily interesting yet casual dining experience. The restaurant's interior is simple, with an open kitchen, a 21-foot communal table, and exposed brick and beams revealing the historic building's architectural roots.

A Crash Course in Okanagan Wines 👁

Getting Oriented
A great source of information about Okanagan wines is the British Columbia Wine Institute (🌐 *www.winebc.com*). The website includes a helpful guide to BC wines, as well as detailed itinerary suggestions for Okanagan wine touring. It also includes a calendar of wine-related dinners, tastings, and other events around the province.

A Drop of History
Most wine experts agree that back in the dark ages (aka the 1970s), the wine produced in British Columbia was, to put it charitably, plonk. Okanagan Riesling and sparkling Lambrusco were the best sellers. Beginning in the late 1970s, however, growers began replacing their vines with high-quality Vinifera varieties to start producing more sophisticated wines. In 1984, BC had 13 wineries; today there are more than 380.

What to Drink
In British Columbia overall, the top white varietals are Chardonnay, Pinot Gris, Gewürztraminer, Pinot Blanc, and Sauvignon Blanc. The top reds are Merlot, Pinot Noir, Cabernet Sauvignon, Syrah, and Cabernet Franc. Many Okanagan wineries also produce ice wine, a late-harvest dessert wine made from grapes that have frozen on the vine.

What is VQA?
British Columbia wines that carry a "VQA" (Vintners Quality Alliance) label must meet certain production and quality standards. A professional tasting panel approves each VQA wine. Participation in the VQA program is voluntary, and there are plenty of fine BC wines that have opted not to take part.

To Spit or Not to Spit?
On a daylong wine-tasting excursion, you can taste a good deal of wine. To avoid getting fatigued, or overly inebriated, do as the pros do: sip, swirl, and spit. Most wineries have a bucket on the tasting bar for that purpose, so don't be shy. You'll enjoy your tour more in the long run. And if the sample in your glass is more than you can drink, simply pour it into the bucket.

Transporting Wine
If you're buying bottles at the wineries, be sure you have some way to keep them cool, particularly in summer when soaring temperatures can spoil them quickly. If you must transport wine in your car, put it in a cooler or keep it on ice.

Most wineries will ship wines for you, but *only within Canada;* the majority cannot send wine over the border. If you're traveling back to the United States, have your wine packed for travel and transport it yourself.

Uh-oh: Sold Out?
It's not uncommon for smaller Okanagan wineries to sell out of their wine in a given year. And when there's limited wine left, they generally close or reduce the hours in their tasting rooms. If you have your heart set on visiting a particular winery, check its website or phone in advance to be sure it has wine available.

Known for: historic building; innovative dishes; communal vibe. $ *Average main: C$30* ⊠ *1560 Water St., Kelowna* ☎ *250/868–8805* ⊕ *www.raudz.com* ⊙ *No lunch.*

Summerhill Sunset Organic Bistro

$$$ | **PACIFIC NORTHWEST** | When the sun cooperates, the skies here become a dazzling array of salmon, orange, pink, and turquoise as dusk approaches. The food is impressive enough, though, that you'll be lingering over every mouthful long after the sun goes down. **Known for:** weekly, organic take-home dinners; Robert Bateman wine available to wine club members; extensive organic and biodynamic wine list. $ *Average main: C$30* ⊠ *4870 Chute Lake Rd., Kelowna* ☎ *250/764–8000* ⊕ *www.summerhill. bc.ca.*

The Terrace at Mission Hill

$$$ | **MODERN CANADIAN** | With its panoramic views across the vineyards and the lake, this outdoor eatery at the Mission Hill Family Estate is a winner for alfresco dining for lunch and early dinners to catch the sunset. It's tough to compete with such a classic wine-country locale, but the innovative kitchen here is up to the task. **Known for:** farm-to-table, seasonal food; culinary herb garden and another varietal garden on-site; everything is made on-site, including bread, charcuteries, and condiments;. $ *Average main: C$30* ⊠ *1730 Mission Hill Rd., West Kelowna* ☎ *250/768–6467* ⊕ *www.missionhillwinery.com* ⊙ *Closed early Oct.–Apr.*

Waterfront Wines Restaurant

$$$$ | **PACIFIC NORTHWEST** | The kind of laid-back place every neighborhood should have, this bistro and wine bar concentrates on small—and larger—plates paired with local wines. They make a first-rate, garlicky Caesar salad, and locals rave about the masala-spiced calamari. **Known for:** staff know their wine, heed their suggestions; friendly,

casual vibe; tapas selection. $ *Average main: C$32* ⊠ *104–1180 Sunset Dr., Kelowna* ☎ *250/979–1222* ⊕ *www. waterfrontrestaurant.ca* ⊙ *Closed Sun. No lunch.*

🛏 Hotels

Apple Blossom Bed & Breakfast

$$ | **B&B/INN** | On the western slopes above Okanagan Lake, this cheery B&B offers terrific views and genuine hospitality. **Pros:** warm welcome from owners Jeanette and John Martens; moderate prices; open year-round. **Cons:** if you need high style, look elsewhere; many house rules; not accessible for folks with mobility issues. $ *Rooms from: C$140* ⊠ *3582 Apple Way Blvd., West Kelowna* ☎ *250/768–1163, 888/718–5064* ⊕ *www. applebnb.com* ⊙ *Closed mid-Oct.–mid-Apr.* ⇆ *4 rooms* ⦿| *Free breakfast.*

★ The Cove Lakeside Resort

$$$$ | **RESORT** | **FAMILY** | The guest suites at this resort on the western shore of Okanagan Lake have all the comforts of home and then some: fully equipped kitchens complete with special fridges to chill your wine, 42-inch plasma TVs, washer-dryers, and fireplaces. **Pros:** lakeside location; marina and moorage available for guests; outdoor hot tub. **Cons:** high season gets busy (and noisy) with young families; pricey; far from downtown. $ *Rooms from: C$359* ⊠ *4205 Gellatly Rd., West Kelowna* ☎ *250/707–1800, 877/762–2683* ⊕ *www.covelakeside.com* ⇆ *99 rooms* ⦿| *No meals.*

Delta Hotels by Marriott Grand Okanagan Resort

$$$$ | **RESORT** | On the shore of Okanagan Lake, this resort is a five-minute stroll from downtown Kelowna, though you may never want to leave the grounds because of all the amenities—there's even a casino and show lounge. **Pros:** a full menu of resort activities for kids and adults; within minutes of Kelowna's entertainment and shopping district;

exceptional views. **Cons:** feels like a big convention hotel; pricey; parking is expensive, too. Ⓢ *Rooms from: C$329* ✉ *1310 Water St., Kelowna* ☎ *250/763–4500, 800/465–4651* ⊕ *www.marriott.com/ylwok* ⇨ *324 rooms* ⍭ *No meals.*

Four Points by Sheraton Kelowna Airport

$$ | HOTEL | For jet-lagged travelers on their way to wine country and wishing to bypass Kelowna, a 25-minute drive away, this hotel, which opened in 2013, fits the bill as a resting stop. **Pros:** close proximity to Kelowna International Airport; newer hotel; free breakfast. **Cons:** away from city "action"; typical chain hotel; amenities have odd hours. Ⓢ *Rooms from: C$189* ✉ *5505 Airport Way, Kelowna* ☎ *855/900–5505* ⊕ *www.fourpointskelownaairport.com* ⇨ *120 rooms* ⍭ *Free breakfast.*

Eldorado Resort

$$$ | HOTEL | Eldorado Resort contains both Manteo and Hotel Eldorado—the Hotel Eldorado combines a 1926 building with a modern addition, making this boutiquey lakeside lodging one of Kelowna's more stylish options; the older "heritage" wing features rooms done up with 1930s-style furnishings, vintage radios, and claw-foot tubs. **Pros:** eclectic style; lake views; on-site boat rentals. **Cons:** a short drive from downtown; can get quite noisy; not every room has great views. Ⓢ *Rooms from: C$219* ✉ *3762 Lakeshore Rd., Kelowna* ☎ *250/860–1031, 866/608–7500* ⊕ *www.eldoradoresort.ca* ⇨ *155 rooms* ⍭ *No meals.*

A View of the Lake B&B

$$ | B&B/INN | Owner Steve Marston and his wife Chrissy run this bed-and-breakfast in their contemporary home–he's a former restaurant chef who whips up elaborate breakfasts and offers periodic dinners and cooking demonstrations in his lavish kitchen. **Pros:** lake views; to-die-for kitchen (take a class if you can); impeccably kept home. **Cons:** guest room furnishings are a bit minimalist for some;

limited technology; make sure the owners are in town, as their cooking is the main attraction. Ⓢ *Rooms from: C$185* ✉ *1877 Horizon Dr., West Kelowna* ☎ *250/769–7854* ⊕ *www.aviewofthelake.com* ⇨ *4 rooms* ⍭ *Free breakfast.*

⛉ Shopping

Arlo's Honey Farm

FOOD/CANDY | Bees receive a lot of TLC at this operation. A small demonstration area shows you the bees. Of course, there's a shop filled with honey-related items. ✉ *4329 Bedford La., Kelowna* ☎ *250/764–2883* ⊕ *www.arloshoneyfarm.com.*

Carmelis Goat Cheese

FOOD/CANDY | The drive to Carmelis is up the side of the mountain, so bring your camera to take photos of the stupendous views. Save some shots for the goats—they're responsible for some of the cheeses you can sample (and buy, of course). ✉ *170 Timberline Rd., Kelowna* ☎ *250/764–9033* ⊕ *www.carmelisgoatcheese.com* ⌨ *Tours C$5.*

Okanagan Grocery

FOOD/CANDY | A good place to start if you're assembling a picnic, this first-rate bakery sells a variety of hearty loaves. It also offers a selection of local cheeses and other gourmet items. ✉ *Guisachan Village, 2355 Gordon Dr., Kelowna* ☎ *250/862–2811* ⊕ *www.okanagangrocery.com.*

Okanagan Lavender & Herb Farm

FOOD/CANDY | You can wander through more than 60 varieties at this farm, which like the surrounding wineries, is open to the public. There's a gift shop where you can enjoy a cool lavender lemonade or lavender ice cream to go. They're closed mid-December to April. Arlo's Honey Farm is just around the corner. ✉ *4380 Takla Rd., Kelowna* ☎ *250/764–7795* ⊕ *www.okanaganlavender.com.*

🏃 Activities

BIKING AND HIKING

Kettle Valley Rail Trail

BICYCLING | This former railroad route runs through some of the Okanagan's prettiest and most dramatic countryside. Bikers and hikers can follow the trail in sections, the most popular being from Brodie (along Highway 5) to just east of Midway (on Highway 3). Other sections run between Penticton and Naramata and through the Kelowna area. Pick up trail maps from the visitor center in Kelowna. ⊠ *Kelowna* ⊕ *www.kettlevalleyexpress. com.*

★ Okanagan Rail Trail

HIKING/WALKING | The Okanagan Rail Trail is a new 48.5-km (30-mile) biking and hiking trail that connects Vernon to Kelowna along a discontinued CN rail corridor. The trail runs along the lakefront and has incredible views. It's also low-grade, so it's accessible to people of varying abilities. Pro tip: an excellent way to explore the path is on an electric bicycle (check out Pedego Electric Bikes Oyama). ⊕ *okanaganrailtrail.ca/.*

GOLF

With more than 50 courses in the Okanagan Valley—18 in the Kelowna region alone—golf is a big draw. Several courses have joined forces to create Golf Kelowna (⊕ *www.golfkelowna.com*), a one-stop shop for tee times, accommodations, and visitor information.

Gallagher's Canyon Golf Club

GOLF | Located about 13 km (8 miles) southeast of downtown Kelowna, Gallagher's Canyon is part of a golf community development and has an 18-hole championship course that meanders among ponderosa pines, as well as a shorter nine-hole course. Greens fees include use of a cart. It's a challenging course, and the vistas of the mountains, orchards, and vineyards are a nice bonus. ⊠ *4320 Gallagher's Dr. W, Kelowna*

☎ *250/861–4240, 800/446–5322* ⊕ *www. gallagherscanyon.com* ✉ *C\$125 for 18 holes; C\$29 for 9 holes* 🏌 *18 holes, 6802 yards, par 72.*

Harvest Golf Club

GOLF | Surrounded by lush vineyards and orchards (you can pick peaches, apricots, pears, and five kinds of apples while you play), the 18-hole Harvest Golf Club is aptly named. The championship course has bent-grass fairways and multiple tees so you're always challenged. Greens fees include a cart. Open from mid-March to mid-November, the Harvest Grille serves breakfast and lunch consisting of sandwiches, salads, and other casual fare; more substantial dishes are added to the menu in the evening. ⊠ *2725 KLO Rd., Kelowna* ☎ *250/862–3103, 800/257–8577* ⊕ *www.harvestgolf.com* ✉ *C\$125* 🏌 *18 holes, 7109 yards, par 72.*

Okanagan Golf Club

GOLF | With their Okanagan Valley views, the two courses at the Okanagan Golf Course are a feast for the eyes. The Quail Course is a challenging hillside course with dramatic changes in elevation and tight, tree-lined fairways. The Jack Nicklaus–designed Bear Course is more forgiving. High-season greens fees include a cart. ⊠ *3200 Via Centrale, Kelowna* ☎ *250/765–5955, 800/446–5322* ⊕ *www.okanagangolfclub.com* ✉ *C\$114 walking, C\$135 with cart for 18 holes* 🏌 *Quail course: 18 holes, 6794 yards, par 72. Bear course: 18 holes, 6885 yards, par 72.*

SKIING

★ Big White Ski Resort

SKIING/SNOWBOARDING | With an average annual snowfall of more than 750 cm (24 feet), this family-oriented resort is a hot favorite. The mountain has a vertical drop of 777 meters (2,550 feet) and a good mix of more than 119 runs, served by 16 up-to-date lifts. You can ski or walk anywhere in the compact village, which has more ski-in/ski-out accommodations than any other Canadian resort. There are excellent day-care and children's programs, a ski school, and night skiing five times a week. TELUS Terrain Park, 25 km (16 miles) of cross-country trails, snowmobiling, ice-skating, horse-drawn sleigh rides, dogsledding, a 60-foot ice climbing wall, and Canada's largest snow-tubing park, round out the resort's myriad options. Shuttles run regularly from the Kelowna Airport to the mountain; including weekends and holidays, there's also shuttle service from several Kelowna-area hotels. ⊠ *5315 Big White Rd., off Hwy. 33 about 1 hr southeast of Kelowna, Kelowna* ☎ *250/765–8888, 800/663–2772, 250/765–7669 snow reports* ⊕ *www.bigwhite.com* ⌦ *1-day lift ticket C$109.*

Sun Peaks Resort

SKIING/SNOWBOARDING | With a 2,894-foot vertical drop, 4,270 skiable acres on three mountains, lots of sunshine, powder snow, and a 10-acre terrain park, Sun Peaks Resort can keep most powderhounds happy. Thirteen lifts serve the 137 downhill runs. This family-friendly resort also offers a ski school, day care, more than 37 km (23 miles) of groomed and track set cross-country trails, snowshoeing, dogsledding, snowmobiling, and sleigh rides. The compact Tyrolean-themed village has a number of ski-in, ski-out hotels and places to eat. The mountain is 50 km (31 miles) north of Kamloops, and daily charters are available across the province. Note: In summer, Sun Peaks becomes one of British Columbia's top mountain-bike destinations, and also opens up its 18-hole golf course. ⊠ *1280 Alpine Rd., Sun Peaks* ☎ *250/578–5474, 800/807–3257* ⊕ *www. sunpeaksresort.com* ⌦ *1-day lift ticket C$115; Nordic skiing C$20.*

Vernon

51 km (32 miles) north of Kelowna.

Vernon is at the northernmost point of the Okanagan Valley. Lying in the heart of Lake Country and snuggled against the Monashee Mountains, Vernon is growing in popularity as a year-round vacation destination, most notably because the city's proximity to Kalamalka Lake makes it an ideal summer getaway with sandy beaches and miles of fresh, emerald green water for every kind of water sport. Predator Ridge Golf Resort and Sparkling Hill Resort have put Vernon on the map for international visitors and small, rural communities nearby such as Armstrong (famous for its cheese) and Enderby, on the banks of the Shuswap River, make for exploring a very lush, and quaint part of the Okanagan. And for winter visitors, it's near Silver Star Mountain Resort.

GETTING HERE AND AROUND

Vernon is located 50km (31 miles) north of Kelowna. The city of 40,000 is most easily accessible by car.

⊙ Sights

The BX Press Cidery & Orchard

WINERY/DISTILLERY | Although the Okanagan Valley is known for its wine, there are quite a few cideries popping up as well. One of the best is BX Press Cidery in Vernon. Their tasting room is rustic and intimate; however, call ahead if you have a particular cider you want to try. They're known to sell out. If you can, try the Ginny (cider with gin botanicals) or The Prospector (their driest cider). Open year-round. ⊠ *4667 E. Vernon Rd., Vernon* ☎ *250/503–2163* ⊕ *www.thebxpress. com* ⊗ *Closed Mon. and Tues.*

★ Vernon Boat Rentals

BOATING | For those looking for a change of pace from the usual Okanagan wine circuit, renting a boat in Vernon on the

Okanagan Touring Tips

Okanagan Wineries: Large or Small?

Starting your trip at a larger winery can be a useful orientation. The big ones generally have organized tours, where you can learn about the types of wine they make and the winemaking process, and you can pick up general information about the region as well. They usually have restaurants, too, where you can refuel.

On the other hand, at the smaller producers you may get to talk with the owners themselves and get a more personal feel for their business. Our recommendation is to include a mix of larger and smaller wineries in your itinerary.

Okanagan: North or South?

The Okanagan is a large region. Just remember that the number of wineries dwindles the farther north you travel; however, those en route to Vernon are worth visiting. If your time is limited, consider concentrating on one area:

■ **Go to Osoyoos/Oliver:** if you prefer smaller wineries, a more rural setting, and a dry, desertlike climate.

■ **Visit Penticton/Naramata:** for smaller wineries and if you prefer cycling or other outdoor adventures; there are several biking and hiking options nearby.

■ **Head for Kelowna:** if you're arriving by plane (it has the region's only significant airport), if you prefer a more urban setting, or if you want to check out the largest wineries. Kelowna isn't as appealing, though, so if you're envisioning idyllic wine country, go farther south.

What to Do Besides Wineries?

Before becoming such a hip wine-and-food destination, the Okanagan was a family holiday spot, best known for its "beaches and peaches"—the lakes with their sandy shores and waterfront lodges and campgrounds, as well as the countless farm stands offering fresh produce. The beaches and peaches are still there, and the Okanagan still welcomes families. With its mild, dry climate, the region is also popular with golfers, and there are gardens to visit as well as trails for hiking and biking.

The restaurant scene in the Okanagan is evolving, too, and a growing number of high-end eateries emphasize food-and-wine pairings. Some of the best are at the wineries, especially the Sonora Room at Burrowing Owl in Oliver and the Terrace at Mission Hill in the Kelowna area. For cheap eats, one of your best bets, particularly in the summer and fall, is to stop at one of the many roadside farm stands to pick up fruits, veggies, and picnic fare. Some wineries have "picnic licenses," which means that they're allowed to sell you a glass (or a bottle) of wine that you can enjoy on the grounds, paired with your own picnic supplies or with picnic fare that the winery sells. Check out ⊕ *www.Kelowna-FarmtoTable.com* for food-oriented touring ideas that include markets, honey farms, lavender fields, and herbal gardens. Visit www.okanaganfoodietours.ca for food-oriented touring ideas, or visit the local tourism websites for specific information on each town's markets.

beautiful Okanagan Lake may be just the ticket. Rental rates start at C$685 (depending on the type of boat you rent) for a full day of fun on the water. ☎ *250/308–2088* 🌐 *www.vernonboatrentals.com.*

🍴 Restaurants

Ratio Coffee & Pastry

$ | **CAFÉ** | This laid-back coffee shop is a Vernon gem. They feature a different pastry every day of the week, from eclairs (Tuesday), cakes (Wednesday), and doughnuts (Friday). **Known for:** pizza on Friday nights; order a cocktail or two (yes, they have their liquor license!); the doughnuts. [$] *Average main: C$5* ✉ *3101 29th St., Vernon* ☎ *250/545–9800* 🌐 *www.ratiocoffee.ca* 🕒 *No dinner Sat.-Thurs.* 💳 *No credit cards.*

Phoenix Steak House

$$$$ | **STEAKHOUSE** | Located in downtown Vernon on the main drag, Phoenix Steak House is owned by a husband and wife team, and serves up–you guessed it–steak, alongside plenty of seafood options (the crab cakes are divine), pasta, salads, and more. The vibe is cozy, intimate, and romantic. **Known for:** fine-dining atmosphere; for a steak house, plenty of seafood and vegetarian options; fun cocktails. [$] *Average main: C$34* ✉ *3117 30th Ave., Vernon* ☎ *250/260-1189* 🌐 *phoenixsteakhouseandbar.com* 🕒 *No lunch Sat.–Mon.*

🛏 Hotels

Predator Ridge Golf Resort

$$$ | **RESORT** | Set on two stunning 18-hole golf courses that are part of a vacation-home community, this full-service resort offers a wide range of accommodations, from studio, one-, and two-bedroom units in the modern Craftsman-style lodge to two- and three-bedroom cottages. **Pros:** you can stumble out of bed onto the links; wilderness landscape; proximity to Sparkling Hill Resort. **Cons:** feels understaffed at times; location is rather remote; pricey. [$] *Rooms from: C$249* ✉ *301 Village Centre Pl., Vernon* ☎ *250/542–3436, 888/578–6688* 🌐 *www.predatorridge.com* 🛏 *126 rooms* 🍴 *No meals.*

Prestige Vernon Lodge

$ | **HOTEL** | **FAMILY** | This property is a more affordable hotel option in Vernon. **Pros:** tropical courtyard; pet-friendly; two on-site restaurants. **Cons:** standard rooms; can get loud on busy weekends; views of the highway. [$] *Rooms from: C$125* ✉ *3914 32nd St., Vernon* ☎ *250/545–3385* 🌐 *www.vernonatrium-hotel.ca* 🛏 *124 rooms* 🍴 *No meals* 💳 *No credit cards.*

★ **Sparkling Hill Resort**

$$$$ | **RESORT** | Carved into a granite hillside, this stunning resort has walls made of glass, so views of the Monashee Mountains and the northern shores of Lake Okanagan are always striking, whether from your beautifully furnished room, the excellent restaurant, the state-of-the-art gym, or the heated infinity pool. **Pros:** a mind-boggling spa; unforgettable views; pet-friendly vibe. **Cons:** no in-room coffee; not a central location, especially for wine-touring. [$] *Rooms from: C$420* ✉ *888 Sparkling Pl., Vernon* ☎ *250/275–1556, 877/275–1556* 🌐 *www.sparklinghill.com* 🛏 *149 rooms* 🍴 *Free breakfast.*

🏃 Activities

SKIING

Silver Star Mountain Resort

SKIING/SNOWBOARDING | The friendly Silver Star Mountain Resort, 22 km (14 miles) northeast of Vernon, has six chairlifts, a vertical drop of 2,500 feet, 131 runs on 3,282 skiable acres, and night skiing. The resort also has 60 km (37 miles) of groomed, track-set cross-country trails; a snowcross course; 16 acres of lanes with rails and jumps; snow-tubing, snowmobile, or snowshoe tours; sleigh rides; and skating. The Victorian-style village has several ski-in, ski-out hotels and lodges, restaurants, and a day spa. Although only 65 km (40 miles) from Kelowna International Airport, this smaller mountain is usually quieter than its "big sisters" so lineups are less time-consuming. That holds true in the summer, too, when ski runs convert to mountain-bike trails. ✉ *123 Shortt St., Silver Star Mountain* ☎ *250/542–0224, 800/663–4431 reservations* 🌐 *www.skisilverstar.com* 🎟 *1-day lift ticket C$92.*

Peachland

25 km (15 miles) southwest of Kelowna.

Between Kelowna and Penticton, Highway 97 winds along the west side of Okanagan Lake. Peachland, a small region of 5,000 people is made up of vineyards, orchards, fruit stands, beaches, picnic sites, and some of the region's prettiest lake and hill scenery.

GETTING HERE AND AROUND

BC Transit runs bus services between Kelowna to Osoyoos with a stop at Peachland.

Sights

Hainle Vineyards Estate Winery

WINERY/DISTILLERY | Hainle Vineyards Estate Winery is a hidden gem: British Columbia's first organic winery and the first to make ice wines. It is a small producer open for tastings (though not tours), and its award-winning wines are highly coveted. ✉ *5355 Trepanier Bench Rd., Peachland* ☎ *250/212–5944* 🌐 *www.hainle.com* 🎟 *Tasting C$5* 🕒 *Closed mid-Oct.–mid-Apr.*

Restaurants

Bliss Bakery and Bistro

$ | CAFÉ | Across the street from Okanagan Lake, this café on Peachland's tiny commercial strip epitomizes the small-is-good philosophy. It's the best place in the area for muffins, pastries, and coffee. **Known for:** soups and sandwiches; great location right on the lake; good coffee. [$] *Average main: C$9* ✉ *4200 Beach Ave., Peachland* ☎ *250/767–2711* 🌐 *www.blissbakery.ca* 🕒 *No dinner.*

Summerland

46 km (29 miles) south of Kelowna.

Summerland is 21 km (13 miles) south of Peachland, and there are plenty more wineries and vineyards on the drive south to Penticton, Naramata, Oliver, and Osoyoos.

GETTING HERE AND AROUND

BC Transit runs bus services between Kelowna to Osoyoos with a stop at Summerland.

Sights

Kettle Valley Steam Railway

TOUR—SIGHT | One way to tour the area is aboard the historic Kettle Valley Steam Railway, pulled by a restored 1912 steam locomotive. The 90-minute trip takes you along 16 km (10 miles) of a century-old rail line. Several times a year there's a "Great Train Robbery" reenactment with a barbecue dinner and musical entertainment. Check website for pricing and closures, as it varies. ✉ *18404 Bathville Rd., Summerland* ☎ *877/494–8424* 🌐 *www.kettlevalleyrail.org.*

Sumac Ridge Estate Winery

WINERY/DISTILLERY | The area's first estate winery, Sumac Ridge showcases three unique Okanagan brands that call the winery home—Sumac Ridge, Black Sage

Vineyards, and Steller's Jay. Tastings range from C$5 to C$35. This a great midmorning or midafternoon stop and the shop is open year-round. ✉ *17403 Hwy. 97 N, Summerland* ☎ *250/494–0451* 🌐 *www.sumacridge.com* 🎫 *Tours C$15. Tastings by donation to Food Bank (C$2 suggested).*

Hotels

★ **Summerland Waterfront Resort & Spa**
$$$$ | RESORT | FAMILY | Designed for people who like the feel of a summer cottage but want the amenities of a resort, the condo-style rooms at this modern lakeside hotel are warm and inviting. **Pros:** prime location on the lake; spa; welcomes dogs (a fee applies). **Cons:** not many dining options nearby; gets fairly noisy; small beach area gets very crowded in high season. [$] *Rooms from: C$309* ✉ *13011 Lakeshore Dr. S, Summerland* ☎ *877/494–8111* 🌐 *www.summerlandresorthotel.com* 🛏 *115 rooms* 🍴 *No meals.*

Penticton

16 km (10 miles) south of Summerland, 395 km (245 miles) east of Vancouver.

With its long, sandy beach backed by motels and cruising pickup trucks, Penticton is all about nostalgia-inducing family vacations. There are wineries here, of course (as well as a surprising amount of breweries), but the area is also known for its recreation: boating, fishing, golfing, hiking and biking, rock climbing the bluffs, kayaking, and floating down the river channel that connects Okanagan Lake and Skaha Lake.

GETTING HERE AND AROUND

BC Transit runs bus services between Kelowna to Osoyoos with stops at Penticton; Penticton Transit provides services only within the city, and Okanagan-Similkameen Transit schedules buses to Naramata. Touring is best done with a tour company or independently by car or bicycle.

Sights

Linden Gardens
GARDEN | This former family fruit farm has morphed into a breathtaking 9-acre garden of flowers, trees, ponds, and streams. A path winds through a maze of constantly changing colors, passing over footbridges and beside jungles of wildflowers. Benches are strategically placed beneath weeping willows for shade or beside plants that draw butterflies and hummingbirds. The Frog City Café is an excellent stop for breakfast or a light lunch. ✉ *351 Linden Ave., Kaleden* ☎ *250/497–6600* 🌐 *www.lindengardens.ca* 🎫 *C$5* 🕓 *Closed Oct.–Apr.*

Hillside Winery
WINERY/DISTILLERY | As you drive along the road between Penticton and Naramata, it's hard to miss the 72-foot tower at Hillside Winery & Bistro. Its first commercial release was in 1989, and the old vines Gamay Noir, Cabernet Franc, Syrah, and Pinot Gris are all award winners. It also produces a unique white wine called Muscat Ottonel. ✉ *1350 Naramata Rd., Penticton* ☎ *250/493–6274* 🌐 *www.hillsidewinery.ca* 🎫 *Tastings C$5.*

Restaurants

The Bench Market
$ | CAFÉ | In the morning, the smell of coffee is likely to draw you into this foodie-friendly market and café, where just-from-the-oven pastries or homemade granola will tempt you to stay a while. (There's also a weekend brunch.) You can also assemble your own picnic from the locally made cheeses, charcuterie, and signature sweets. **Known for:** daily features; soups, salad and sandwiches; weekend brunch. [$] *Average main:*

C$12 ✉ 368 Vancouver Ave., Penticton ☎ 250/492–2222 🌐 www.thebenchmarket.com 🕓 No dinner.

The Black Antler

$$ | AMERICAN | This trendy downtown restaurant and cocktail bar serves fantastic comfort food (think chicken wings, calamari, stuffed portobello, and more). They also have an extensive cocktail list and plenty of great vino and suds from the surrounding wineries and breweries. **Known for:** street-side patio; extensive cocktail list; woodsy deer-print, antlers-on-the-wall decor. [$] *Average main: C$17 ✉ 215 Winnipeg St., Penticton ☎ 236/422-4002 🌐 www.blackantlerpenticton.com.*

Hotels

God's Mountain Estate

$$$ | B&B/INN | Filled with intriguing nooks and crannies, this quirky Mediterranean-style villa has a gorgeous whitewashed exterior and sits on 115 rambling acres overlooking Skaha Lake. **Pros:** romantic atmosphere; dinners are extraordinary; beautiful views. **Cons:** the eccentric style is not for everyone; two-night minimum stay; no TVs or Internet. [$] *Rooms from: C$225 ✉ 4898 Lakeside Rd., Penticton ☎ 250/490–4800 🌐 www.godsmountain.com 🛏 13 rooms 🍴 Free breakfast.*

Penticton Lakeside Resort

$$ | HOTEL | This hotel lives up to its name, with its incredible panaromic views of Okanagan Lake. **Pros:** on-site parking; walking distance to plenty of popular downtown eateries; the outstanding views. **Cons:** strange layout in some of the rooms; not all rooms have a bathtub; can be pricey in high season. [$] *Rooms from: C$160 ✉ 21 Lakeshore Dr. West, Penticton ☎ 250/493-8221 🌐 www.pentictonlakesideresort.com/ 🛏 203 rooms 🍴 No meals.*

Activities

Hoodoo Adventures

KAYAKING | FAMILY | This super-friendly outdoor adventure company offers plenty of tours—biking, hiking, climbing, kayaking, snowshoeing, etc.—that explore the region. They even offer kayaking and cycling tours that involve visiting wineries, too. You can also rent equipment. *✉ 131 Ellis St., Penticton ☎ 250/492-3888 🌐 www.hoodooadventures.ca.*

Naramata

15 kim (9 miles) north of Penicton.

Drive through Penticton to the east side of Okanagan Lake and you'll be in the heart of the flourishing Naramata wine country. The route is so peppered with wineries that the seemingly short drive could take all afternoon. Naramata also has a fascinating pioneer history, stop here to experience the idyllic village lifestyle.

GETTING HERE AND AROUND

Naramata is located 15 km (9 miles north of Penticton, an easy drive when exploring the southern Okanagan Valley.

Sights

Elephant Island Orchard Wines

WINERY/DISTILLERY | Although many vintners take advantage of the nearby orchards, this funky winery makes a specialty wine out of fruit. Using recipes that are generations old, it creates some delightful table and dessert wines from pears, cherries, and black currants. They also make grape wine and dry ciders. Best of all, tastings are complimentary. *✉ 2730 Aikins Loop, Naramata ☎ 250/496–5522 🌐 www.elephantislandwine.com 🎟 Free.*

Lake Breeze Vineyards

WINERY/DISTILLERY | On the Naramata Bench above Okanagan Lake, Lake Breeze Vineyards is one of the region's most attractively located small wineries. Its white wines, particularly their Pinot Gris and Pinot Blanc, are well regarded. The tasting room and garden patio make for a lovely setting; the outdoor Patio Restaurant is open for lunch (weather permitting) between May and mid-October. ✉ *930 Sammet Rd., Naramata* ☎ *250/496–5659* 🌐 *www.lakebreeze.ca* 🎟 *Tastings C$3* 🕒 *Closed Mon.–Thurs. in Nov. and Apr.; closed Dec.–Mar.*

Poplar Grove

WINERY/DISTILLERY | Poplar Grove makes respected Merlot, Chardonnay, and Pinot Gris, and the winery's restaurant is a seasonal favorite that really struts its foodie stuff—with pairings—serving organic and local fare in a simple setting overlooking the lake. ✉ *425 Middle Bench Rd. N, Penticton* ☎ *250/493–9463 winery* 🌐 *www.poplargrove.ca* 🎟 *Tastings C$5.*

Red Rooster Winery

WINERY/DISTILLERY | Sampling wine at Red Rooster is a cultural experience. In addition to showcasing the recent vintages, the bright, spacious tasting room sells the work of local artists as well as dining-oriented lifestyle paraphernalia, and the Pecking Room Patio & Grill is a great place to try wine pairings and the farm-to-table menu. If owning a vineyard is your fantasy, Red Rooster's "Adopt A Row" program could be the next best thing. You "own" a row of 50 vines for the season and are guaranteed a case of wine. ✉ *891 Naramata Rd., Penticton* ☎ *250/492–2424* 🌐 *www.redroosterwinery.com* 🎟 *Tastings C$5; private tastings C$10.*

Therapy Vineyards and Inn

WINERY/DISTILLERY | With wines that carry such names as Super Ego, Pink Freud, and Freudian Sip, you may feel like running for the analyst's couch. But never fear, this small vineyard combines its whimsical humor with a number of quality wines, especially its Merlot and Pinot Noir varietals. The winery often hosts special weekends focusing on culinary and yoga programs. But with only a handful of rooms (five modern boutique-style suites), most participants reserve early or stay elsewhere. ✉ *940 Debeck Rd., Naramata* ☎ *250/496–5217* 🌐 *www.therapyvineyards.com* 🎟 *Tastings C$3.*

🍴 Restaurants

The Patio Restaurant at Lake Breeze

$$$ | **MODERN CANADIAN** | A seat at this beautifully landscaped patio is one of the hottest tickets in town, so plan on an early lunch if you hope to get a table. Among the wine-friendly dishes, you might find a salt cod hash with sautéed broccoli, roast chicken with smoked Gouda and focaccia, or a sirloin burger topped with locally made cheese. **Known for:** outdoor dining; wine-friendly dishes; charcuterie plates. [$] *Average main: C$22* ✉ *930 Sammet Rd., Naramata* ☎ *250/496–5659* 🌐 *www.lakebreeze.ca* 🕒 *No dinner. Closed mid-Oct.–May.*

🛏 Hotels

Bench d'or

$$$ | **B&B/INN** | A palatial log cabin with gardens to match the views of Okanagan Lake, this guesthouse makes for a luxurious home base for exploring the Naramata Bench. **Pros:** great wine-tasting home base for Naramata; lovely gardens; amazing views. **Cons:** strict cancellation policies; pricey; can be hard to get a reservation. [$] *Rooms from: C$300* ✉ *2587 Naramata Rd., Naramata* ☎ *250/496–4045* 🌐 *www.benchdor.com* 🕒 *Closed Nov.–Mar.* 🔑 *3 suites* 🍽 *Free breakfast.*

Naramata Heritage Inn & Spa

$$ | **HOTEL** | At this hotel dating back to 1908, many of the Mission-style furnishings, wood floors, and claw-foot tubs are original, but plenty of the amenities—heated bathroom floors, fluffy duvets, central air-conditioning—are au courant. **Pros:** great choices at the wine bar; soothing spa; great location. **Cons:** most guest rooms are small; some spaces feel old and tired vs. vintage and elegant; a stay here can add up. [$] *Rooms from: C$168* ✉ *3625 1st St., Naramata* ☎ *778/514–5444* 🌐 *www.naramatainn.com* ⏲ *Closed Nov.–Apr.* 🛏 *12 rooms* 🍴 *Free breakfast.*

Therapy Vineyards and Inn

$$$ | **B&B/INN** | Independent travelers who want to get away from it all might consider a room at this cozy winery. **Pros:** lake views; private; breakfast delivered to your door. **Cons:** no common space for guests; few amenities; not central. [$] *Rooms from: C$210* ✉ *940 Debeck Rd., Naramata* ☎ *250/496–5217* 🌐 *www.therapyvineyards.com* 🛏 *8 rooms* 🍴 *Free breakfast.*

Activities

SKIING

Apex Mountain Resort

SKIING/SNOWBOARDING | Known for its intimate ambience and soft powder snow, Apex Mountain Resort is a lesser-known ski gem offering snow-bunnies 75 trails, 4 lifts, a vertical drop of 2,000 feet, and a peak elevation of 7,197 feet. Located 33 km (21 miles) west of Penticton, the resort has night skiing, a ski school, three terrain parks, a snow-tube park, an outdoor ice rink, a skating trail through the forest, and snowshoeing tours. Accommodations options near the mountain include a couple of inns, plus condos and town houses. ✉ *Apex Mountain Rd., off Green Mountain Rd., Penticton* ☎ *250/292–8222, 877/777–2739* 🌐 *www.apexresort.com* 🎟 *1-day lift ticket C$87; snow tube park C$15* ☞ *Closed May–Nov.*

Oliver

Oliver is 33km (20 miles) south of Penticton.

South of Penticton, between the southern tip of Lake Okanagan and the U.S. border, Highway 97 passes through the country's only desert and runs along a chain of lakes: Skaha, Vaseux, and Osoyoos. With a hot, dry climate, the lakeshore beaches can be crowded with families in summer; this is also a popular winter destination for snowbirds from the Canadian prairies. The climate makes this a prime wine-producing area, and the roads on both sides of Osoyoos Lake between the towns of Oliver and Osoyoos are lined with vineyards.

Oliver bills itself as "Canada's Wine Capital" and this small town of about 4,900 does have an ever-growing number of wineries and festivals.

GETTING HERE AND AROUND

South of Penticton, between the southern tip of Lake Okanagan and the U.S. border, Highway 97 is the main road through Oliver.

Sights

Black Hills Estate Winery

WINERY/DISTILLERY | On the Black Sage Bench between Osoyoos and Oliver, Black Hills Estate Winery has developed a cult following among Okanagan aficionados and frequently sells out of its much-admired wines. When the wine sells out, however, the tasting room sets some aside for visitors. It's worth calling to check on the status of its Nota Bene (a blend of Cabernet Sauvignon, Merlot, and Cabernet Franc), Alibi (Sauvignon Blanc with a bit of Sémillon), Chardonnay, or whatever the winemaker dreams up next. ✉ *4318 Black Sage Rd., Oliver* ☎ *250/498–0666* 🌐 *www.blackhillswinery.com* 🎟 *Tours C$75* ⏲ *Closed Nov.–Apr.*

Burrowing Owl Estate Winery
WINERY/DISTILLERY | With wines consistently taking home medals in international competitions, Burrowing Owl is one of the area's best-known vineyards. Cellar tours are offered on weekends from May through October, and tastings are available year-round. At the 25-foot tasting bar, the donations asked for tastings go toward the Burrowing Owl Conservation Society. To savor the sweeping views of the vineyards and Osoyoos Lake, enjoy a meal at the terrific Sonora Room Restaurant. ✉ *500 Burrowing Owl Pl., Oliver* ☎ *250/498–0620, 877/498–0620* 🌐 *www.bovwine.ca* 🎟 *Tastings C$3.*

Hester Creek Estate Winery
WINERY/DISTILLERY | Set high on a bluff between Osoyoos and Oliver, Hester Creek has an inviting bistro called Terrafina, a multipurpose tasting venue that includes a main room large enough to host parties, a private dining room for intimate groups, a patio with an outdoor fireplace, and a gourmet demonstration kitchen. There's a grassy picnic area where you can enjoy a snack and a glass of wine—Pinot Blanc, Pinot Gris, Merlot, and Cabernet Franc are all top choices. The best part? Tastings are free. ✉ *877 Road 8, Oliver* ☎ *250/498–4435* 🌐 *www.hestercreek.com* 🎟 *Free.*

🍴 Restaurants

Oliver Eats
$ | **DELI** | **FAMILY** | This charming little delicatessen has strong ties with local farmers and chefs, offering delicious homemade food to-go like frittata, soups and sandwiches, as well as everything you need to create the perfect charcuterie board or picnic. **Known for:** soups and sandwiches; endless supply of pastries; outdoor patio. [$] *Average main: C$10* ✉ *6060 Station St., Oliver* ☎ *778/931-1469* 🌐 *olivereats.com/.*

🛏 Hotels

The Guest House at Burrowing Owl
$$$$ | **B&B/INN** | You could be forgiven for thinking you're in Tuscany while sitting on your balcony sipping a glass of Chardonnay, overlooking the vineyards, at this romantic inn. **Pros:** great views over the vineyards; excellent service; saltwater pool. **Cons:** no resort-style amenities; pricey; design doesn't suit everyone's tastes. [$] *Rooms from: C$350* ✉ *500 Burrowing Owl Pl., Oliver* ☎ *250/498–0620, 877/498–0620* 🌐 *www.bovwine.ca* 🕒 *Closed Jan.; call for availability in Nov. and Dec. and Feb.–Apr.* 🛏 *11 rooms* 🍽 *Free breakfast* ☞ *2-night minimum June–mid-Oct.*

The Villa at Hester Creek
$$$ | **B&B/INN** | All the rooms in this Mediterranean-style B&B overlook rows of vines at the Hester Creek Estate Winery. **Pros:** serene environment; spacious rooms; soaker tubs. **Cons:** no common areas; no swimming pool; two-night minimum. [$] *Rooms from: C$299* ✉ *877 Rd. 8, Oliver* ☎ *250/498–4435, 866/498–4435* 🌐 *www.hestercreek.com* 🛏 *6 rooms* 🍽 *Free breakfast* ☞ *2-night minimum June–mid-Oct.*

Osoyoos

Osoyoos is 63 km (39 miles) south of Penticton, 400 km (250 miles) east of Vancouver.

The southernmost town in the Okanagan region, Osoyoos, has a significant First Nations population among its roughly 5,000 residents. The Osoyoos Indian Band operates North America's first aboriginal-owned winery and also runs an informative desert cultural center that's well worth a visit.

GETTING HERE AND AROUND

BC Transit runs bus services between Kelowna to Osoyoos; stops include Penticton. South Okanagan Transit provides bus transportation in and around Osoyoos.

◉ Sights

Desert Centre Osoyoos

NATURE PRESERVE | The arid, antelope-brush ecosystem is home to flora and fauna found nowhere else in the country. Located at the entrance of the society's 67-acre park, the interpretive center shares displays and more about the unique local ecology. You can also take a one-hour guided tour along a boardwalk leading through the desert. ✉ 14580 146 Ave., Osoyoos ☎ 250/495–2470, 877/899–0897 ⊕ www.desert.org ☑ C$8 ⊘ Closed mid-Oct.–mid-Apr.

Nk'Mip Desert Cultural Centre

MUSEUM | FAMILY | Run by the Osoyoos Indian Band, this well-designed museum—the name is pronounced "in-ka-meep"—has exhibits about the area's aboriginal community, the region's natural setting, and the animals that make their home in this desert environment. Don't miss "Sssnakes Alive!," a daily show featuring live rattlesnakes and other creatures native to the area. You can also walk to a reconstructed village that includes two pit houses, a tepee, and a sweat lodge. (Bring water, since there's little shade along the trails.) The center's exterior is a striking, environmentally friendly earth wall built of a mix of soil, water, a small amount of cement, and pigment. ✉ 1000 Rancher Creek Rd., Osoyoos ☎ 250/495–7901 ⊕ www.nkmipdesert.com ☑ C$12.

Moon Curser Vineyards

WINERY/DISTILLERY | This family-owned, award-winning winery is a bit different than most in the Okanagan. The winery grows grapes not typically seen here, like Tannat, Touriga, and Carménère. They also have more traditional varieties like Cabernet Sauvignon. In addition to the wine, you should come here for the panaromic views and the charming guest house. ✉ 3628 BC-3, Osoyoos ☎ 250/495–5161 ⊕ www.mooncurser.com/win.

🍴 Restaurants

★ The Restaurant at Watermark

$$ | WINE BAR | FAMILY | Part of the swanky Watermark Beach Resort, this restaurant sits on the water and has terrific views. Guests from other resorts head here for a night out, grazing on more than 30 tapas ranging from charcuterie boards to lamb merguez sausage. **Known for:** limited edition wine choices; outdoor dining; extensive tapas menu. $ Average main: C$15 ✉ Watermark Beach Resort, 15 Park Pl., Osoyoos ☎ 250/495–5508 ⊕ www.watermarkbeachresort.com ▭ No credit cards ⊘ No lunch. Closed Sun.–Mon. in low season.

🛏 Hotels

Spirit Ridge Resort by Hyatt

$$$$ | RESORT | FAMILY | At this South-western-style resort, all the accommodations—from the one-, two-, and three-bedroom suites to the one- and two-bedroom villas—have gourmet kitchens, living rooms with fireplaces, and expansive balconies. **Pros:** there's plenty to do; family-friendly environment; great views. **Cons:** lake access is a little awkward; away from the center of town; pricey. $ Rooms from: C$369 ✉ 1200 Rancher Creek Rd., Osoyoos ☎ 250/495–5445, 877/313–9463 ⊕ www.spiritridge.ca ⇆ 226 rooms ⦵ No meals.

Walnut Beach Resort

$$$$ | RESORT | With its own sandy beach on the shores of Okanagan Lake, this lovely resort has an away-from-it-all ambience, helped by the fact that it's at the

end of a road in a quiet residential neighborhood. **Pros:** relaxed atmosphere; great food; friendly staff. **Cons:** popular wedding venue; a bit difficult to find; limited evening entertainment. [$] *Rooms from: C$329* ✉ *4200 Lakeshore Dr., Osoyoos* ☎ *250/495–5400, 877/936–5400* 🌐 *www.walnutbeachresort.com* 🛏 *112 suites* 🍴 *No meals.*

★ **Watermark Beach Resort**

$$$ | **RESORT** | As the name might suggest, this resort, right on the beachfront of Osoyoos Lake offers beautiful views and luxurious suites. **Pros:** waterfront; great restaurant; central location. **Cons:** quite large and can be hard to navigate. [$] *Rooms from: C$249* ✉ *15 Park Pl., Osoyoos* ☎ *250/495–5500* 🌐 *www.watermarkbeachresort.com* 🛏 *153 rooms* 🍴 *No meals.*

Activities

BIKING AND HIKING

International Bicycling and Hiking Trail

BICYCLING | If you want to travel from winery to winery under your own power, follow the International Bicycling and Hiking Trail. This relatively flat trail begins at the north end of Osoyoos Lake and runs north along the Okanagan River for 18 km (11 miles). To get to the south trail parking lot from Osoyoos, follow Highway 97 north for 8 km (5 miles), then head east on Road 22. There are also plenty of shorter trails, around Mt. Kobau as an example. ✉ *Osoyoos* 🌐 *www.destinationosoyoos.com.*

Index

Photo Credits

Front Cover: Peter Pesta Photography [Description: Lions Gate Bridge in Vancouver.]. **Back cover, from left to right:** Cybernesco/iStockphoto, ArkXp/iStockphoto, Wangkun Jia/Shutterstock. **Spine:** BGSmith/ Shutterstock. **Interior, from left to right:** EB Adventure Photography/Shutterstock (1). Oleg Charykov/ iStockphoto (2). **Chapter 1: Experience Vancouver and Victoria:** Dan Breckwoldt/shutterstock (6-7). Courtesy of Tourism Victoria (8). Tourism Vancouver / Coast Mountain Photography (9). Tourism Vancouver / Prince of Whales Whale Watching (9). Tourism Vancouver / Clayton Perry (10). Vancouver Park Board (10). Nicole Lohse, Tourism Tofino (10). Tourism Vancouver / Harbour Air (10). Tourism Vancouver / Coast Mountain Photography (11). Courtesy of Capilano Suspension Bridge Park (11). Denis Kuvaev/Shutterstock (12). Heath Moffatt (12). Fairmont Hotels & Resorts (12). LeonWang/Shutterstock (12). Mike Crane (13). Tourism Vancouver / Hubert Kang (14). Ronnie Chua/Shutterstock (14). Courtesy of Bard on the Beach Shakespeare Festival (14). Heath Moffatt Photography (14). Cory Dawson, courtesy of the Museum of Anthropology at UBC (15). Tourism Vancouver / Devin Manky (15). Ieyang/shutterstock (20). BobNoah/Shutterstock (20). Nong Amory/Shutterstock (20). Elena Shashkina/Shutterstock (21). Mark Yuen (21). Vancouver Candle Co. (22). Alexander Demyanenko/Shutterstock (22). Courtesy of John Fluevog Shoes (22). Jeff Whyte/Dreamstime (23). Sama Jim Canzian / Bill Reid Gallery (23). Jade Stone - All rights reserved (24). Museum of Vancouver (24). The Galley Patio & Grill (24). Courtesy of Rosewood Hotel Georgia (25). Blaine Campbell/Rennie Museum (25). **Chapter 3: Downtown, West End, and Stanley Park:** romakoma/ Shutterstock (49). Marc. Bruxelle/iStockphoto (57). Russ Heinl/Shutterstock (68-69). Jess Harrison/Dreamstime (82). Edgar Bullon/Dreamstime (84). **Chapter 4: Gastown, Chinatown, and Yaletown:** Marc Bruxelle/iStockphoto (87). Dorothy Washbern (92). Wallpaper101/iStockphoto (94). Onepony/Dreamstime (100-101). Josef Hanus/Shutterstock (105). **Chapter 5: Granville Island:** Hpbfotos/Dreamstime (109). Ronnie Chua/Shutterstock (114-115). Ronniechua/Dreamstime (117). **Chapter 6: West Side, Kitsilano, Point Grey, South Granville, Cambie Corridor:** kongxinzhu/iStockphoto (119). Lucas Inacio/Dreamstime (125). Barrett MacKay/agefotostock (130). Bill Perry/Shutterstock (132-133). **Chapter 7: East Side, Main Street/Mt. Pleasant and Commercial Drive:** Dan Breckwoldt/Shutterstock (139). meunierd/ Shutterstock (142). Nico Aguilera/Flickr (146). **Chapter 8: North Shore, North Vancouver and West Vancouver:** ArchonCodex/Shutterstock (151). Songquan Deng/Shutterstock (157). Rich Wheater/ agefotostock (158). Juana Nunez/Shutterstock (160). Marina_Poushkina/iStockphoto (162-163). **Chapter 9: Richmond:** Ronnie Chua/Shutterstock (167). TamasV/Shutterstock (171). Darryl Brooks/Dreamstime (172). **Chapter 10: Victoria with The Butchart Gardens:** poemnist/Shutterstock (175). pr2is/Shutterstock (186). North Light Images/agefotostock (190-191). Bornin54/Dreamstime (196). pr2is/Shutterstock (207). Dendron/iStockphoto (216). Faina Gurevich/iStockphoto (220). **Chapter 11: Vancouver Island:** Menno Schaefer/Shutterstock (225). dirkr/Shutterstock (233). EB Adventure Photography/Shutterstock (238). Elena Elisseeva/Shutterstock (241). fokke baarssen/Shutterstock (246). Spiroview Inc/Shutterstock (257). **Chapter 12: Whistler:** Randy Lincks/agefotostock (265). Volodymyr Kyrylyuk/Shutterstock (274). edb3_16/iStockphoto (278). robcocquyt/Shutterstock (280). Juana Nunez/Shutterstock (287). Randy Lincks/agefotostock (288). **Chapter 13: The Okanagan Valley:** Henry Georgi/agefotostock (291). SMJoness/iStockphoto (300-301). **About Our Writers:** All photos are courtesy of the writers.

Every effort has been made to trace the copyright holders, and we apologize in advance for any accidental errors. We would be happy to apply the corrections in the following edition of this publication.

Notes

Notes

Notes

Notes

Notes

Notes

Notes

Notes

Notes

Notes

Notes